NATIVE AMERICAN RESOURCES SERIES

Advisory Board

1. *Handbook of the American Frontier: Four Centuries of Indian-White Relationships,* by J. Norman Heard
   Volume I: *Southeastern Woodlands.* 1987
   Vollume II: *Northeastern Woodlands.* 1990
   Volume III: *The Great Plains.* 1993

2. *Oliver La Farge and the American Indian,* by Robert A. Hecht. 1991.

3. *Native American Resurgence and Renewal: a reader and a bibliography,* by Robert N. Wells, Jr. 1993.

HANDBOOK OF THE AMERICAN FRONTIER:

Four Centuries of Indian-White Relationships

VOLUME III:
The Great Plains

by

J. NORMAN HEARD

Native American Resources Series, No. 1

The Scarecrow Press, Inc.

Metuchen, N.J., & London

1993

British Library Cataloguing-in-Publication data available

Library of Congress Cataloging-in-Publication Data
(Revised for vol. 3)

Heard, J. Norman (Joseph Norman), 1922-
    Handbook of the American frontier.

    (Native American resources series ; no. 1)
    Includes bibliographical references.
    Contents: v. 1. The southeastern woodlands — v. 2. The northeastern
woodlands — v. 3. The Great Plains.
    1. Indians of North America—History—Encyclopedias. 2. Frontier
and pioneer life—United States—Encyclopedias. 3. United States—
History—Encyclopedias.
E76.2.H43   1987   973'.03'21   86-20326
ISBN 0-8108-1931-7 (v. 1 : alk. paper)
ISBN 0-8108-2324-1 (v. 2 : alk. paper)
ISBN 0-8108-2767-0 (v. 3 : alk. paper)

Dedicated to Dr. Thomas Jefferson Heard, a founder of the Medical Association of Texas, Sam Houston's friend and physician, and a fighter in the Mexican War, the Civil War, and the Texas Indian wars.

EDITOR'S FOREWORD

It is fitting that the first volume in the Native American Resources Series is Norman Heard's *Handbook of the American Frontier.* The *Handbook* brings together reference material on American Indian and non-Indian relationships that can usually only be found after painstaking research in a number of historical, ethnological, and biographical sources. The book contains such topics as American Indian tribes, Indian leaders, frontier settlers, captives, explorers, missionaries, mountain men. The scope is from the time of earliest contact into the twentieth century.

As Professor Heard describes in detail in his preface, the *Handbook* will contain five volumes when completed. Volume I covers the area of the Southeastern Woodlands following the definition of these in John R. Swanton's *The Indians of the Southeastern United States,* Bureau of American Ethnology Bulletin, 137 (1946). Volume II on the area of the Northeast includes materials north of the area covered in Volume I and west to the plains. Volume III is on the Plains, patterned on the delineation of the area of Walter Prescott Webb's *The Great Plains* (1931). It covers the plains from the Canadian border to Texas. Volume IV covers the Southwest and the Pacific Coast. Volume V consists of a comprehensive index, a chronology, and a bibliography.

When completed, the *Handbook of the American Frontier* will contain the widest coverage of the frontier activities of the American Indians and white settlers. The entries are balanced and objective. Professor Heard had eliminated the anti-Indian bias that occurs in almost all of the early accounts of Indian/non-Indian relationships.

Norman Heard has spent his career as a librarian and researcher. Early in his career he contributed twenty articles to Walter Prescott Webb's *Handbook of Texas* (1952), and he has written the article on Indian Captivities for a revised edition of this work now in progress. He is the author of *The Black Frontiersman* (1969) and *White Into Red* (1973), both of which are kept in print by their publishers. With Charles F. Hamsa, he is the author of the ninth edition of *Bookman's Guide to Americana* (1986).

Jack Marken
Brookings, SD

PREFACE

The subject of Indian-white relationships during the exploration and settlement of our nation has been of great interest for centuries to students of history and ethnology, as well as to arm-chair adventurers. Much information on the Indian side of the question is available in the venerable *Handbook of American Indians North of Mexico* (Washington, 1912-13), and a new *Handbook of North American Indians* (twenty volumes projected) is in the process of publication by the Smithsonian Institution. Experiences of prominent white frontiersmen are included in the *Dictionary of American Biography* and the *Dictionary of American History,* as well as in a multitude of historical monographs and articles. Indeed such a mass of material has been published about Indian warfare that it is exceeded by few other topics in American history. Many of the primary source materials are out-of-print and scarce, however, and some secondary works should be used with caution.

A need exists for works of first reference that provide insights into both sides of the Indian-white relationship. It is hoped the *Handbook of the American Frontier* will help to fill this need and that it will guide the reader to reliable sources of additional information. It is the *Handbook*'s objective to provide a series of brief articles in dictionary arrangement about American Indian tribes and leaders, explorers, traders, frontier settlers, soldiers, missionaries, mountain men, captives, battles, massacres, forts, treaties, and other topics of importance or interest in the history of the first forty-eight United States, from the arrival of the earliest seafarers to the end of the Indian wars, four centuries later.

This study will emphasize the frontier aspects of the careers of prominent subjects, and it will present articles on many men and events excluded or mentioned only in passing in general reference sources. As it is intended as ethnohistory, it will exclude frontier topics that are irrelevant to Indian-white relationships. Subjects are gleaned from ethnological studies, tribal histories, state or regional histories, narratives of captivity, compilations of incidents of border warfare, military histories, and other biographical and historical studies readily available only to readers with access to research libraries. The reader may find that the author has devoted a disproportionate amount of attention to the experiences of frontier women, blacks, and captives. These subjects represent lifelong interests which led to a doctoral dissertation and two books, *The Black*

Frontiersmen (New York, 1969), and *White into Red, a Study of the Assimilation of White Persons Captured by Indians* (Metuchen, 1973).

The work will be divided regionally, roughly corresponding to major Indian culture areas. Volume I will compromise the southeastern woodlands, substantially as delineated by John R. Swanton in his monumental study, *The Indians of the Southeastern United States* (Washington, 1946). This area includes the Atlantic coastal states from Chesapeake Bay to the tip of Florida, the Gulf Coast states from Florida to southwestern Louisiana, eastern Texas, most of Arkansas, southeastern Missouri, Kentucky, West Virginia, and Tennessee. It excludes Pennsylvania and most of Maryland. Volume II will be devoted to the Northeast, north of Swanton's line and east of the range of the Plains Indians. Volume III covers the vast region roamed by the Plains tribes from the Canadian border to Texas as depicted in Walter Prescott Webb's enduring study, *The Great PLains* (Boston, 1931). The scope of Volume IV will be the Rocky Mountains, southwestern deserts, and the Pacific Coast. Volume V will provide a general index, chronology, and list of readings.

This geographical arrangement presents difficulties, as a number of Indian nations ranged or resided between Swanton's southeastern tribes and Webb's Great Plains. Coastal tribes of southwestern Louisiana and eastern Texas will be included in Volume I unless they were characterized by Webb as marginal Plains Indians. Southern Texas was raided by Plains Indians but inhabited by peoples with culture traits ranging from the southeastern woodlands to the southwestern deserts, and these tribes will be discussed in Volumes I and IV respectively. At the northern boundary of Swanton's Southeast, the Shawnees, classed by him as a southeastern tribe, lived north of the Ohio River during later frontier times. White men first encountered them in the South, however, and the principal article on the tribe will be included in Volume I. After the Treaty of Greenville in 1795, Shawnee warfare shifted northward, and later leaders and events will be included in Volume II. The Tuscaroras lived in North Carolina and moved to New York after their defeat by the Carolinians in 1713 to become the Sixth Nation of the Iroquois. They are included in Volume I because of their importance in the southern Indian wars and their somewhat subordinate role in Iroquois affairs.

Pennsylvania traders operated both north and south of the Ohio, and some of them were notorious for leading Indian raids into Kentucky and western Virginia. As northerners, they will be included in Volume II, while southern captives held by northern tribes will be assigned to the Southeast. Farther west, explorers and traders transversed the Plains and Rocky Mountains and some, such as Cabeza de Vaca, traveled from coast to coast. Inevitably the author had to choose which volume should contain an article relative to more than one area. Occasionally this problem was resolved by separate articles, such as a division of the Seminole campaigns of Army officers from their later experiences in the West. More often, however, it was decided that a subject's career in one region predominated over that in another, and the volume assignment was made on that basis. The reader should be advised, therefore, that until the general index appears it may be necessary to consult more than one volume to locate the principal article on such a frontier figure as Simon Girty, a "white savage" who led northern and southern Indians in raids both above and below the Ohio River. Like other Pennsylvania "Indian diplomats" he will be found in the volume on the Northeast. His Virginia and Kentucky exploits are described in Volume I, however, in articles on battles, captivities, and forts.

A problem of nomenclature faces a researcher dealing with frontier topics. Names of tribes differ so greatly in primary sources that it sometimes is difficult to identify the Indians described. Even eminent ethnologists differ as to the spelling of tribal names. In this regard it is helpful to consult the synonymy in F. W. Hodge, ed., *Handbook of American Indians North of Mexico,* II, to work one's way through the maze. Name difficulties abound regarding individual Indians as well. A chief may have been known by one Indian name to his own people and by another to other Indians, as well as by a European name to the whites. Settlers' names, too, are spelled so differently in some early chronicles that it is difficult to determine identity. Usually the subject is readily identified, but a question remains as to the spelling to be adopted. The author has attempted to compensate for varying names and spellings by the use of cross-references.

The most formidable problem to be faced by the student of frontier history is credibility of sources. It quickly becomes evident that many frontiersmen and early chroniclers of the Indian wars were prone to exaggeration ("to draw the long bow" as R. W. G. Vail described it in his invaluable *Voice of the Old Frontier,* Philadelphia, 1949). Others, particularly persons claiming to be redeemed captives, published entirely fictitious narratives. Some narratives, while based upon real captivities, deliberately distorted events to increase sales, to foster hatred of Indians, or to promote a religious perspective. (See Richard Van Der Beets, *Held Captive by Indians,* Knoxville, 1973, for an enlightening introduction to this topic.)

It is not surprising that editors who interviewed Indian fighters in later life found that faulty memories led to numerous contradictions. Even nineteenth-century frontier historians who sifted accounts of battles and raids have come to conflicting conclusions, and several of them have taken pains to point out errors in the interpretations of others. Accounts of attacks on Wheeling are a case in point, with reputable scholars in disagreement as to the number of sieges, the names of leaders of war parties, and even the identity of the girl who ran through Indian lines to obtain gun powder for the defenders.

Few studies of racial conflicts reflect the Indian point of view, and the narratives of most white frontiersmen reveal a strong anti-Indian bias. The same tendency is evident in the works of earlier editors who interviewed survivors and published their narratives. It is difficult, therefore, to authenticate details of incidents that took place more than a century ago when confronted by irreconcilable primary sources. Fortunately the studies of twentieth-century scholars are of tremendous assistance in this regard, particularly those of ethnologists and historians who published or edited volumes in the *Bulletins* of the Bureau of American Ethnology, in the University of Oklahoma's "Civilization of the American Indian Series," and in works of other university presses. Even there, however, problems persist: scholarly works disagree in regard to whether or not the Cherokee chief, Bowles, was the son of the white "Creek Emperor," William Augustus Bowles; an eminent ethnologist states in one standard work that the Chowanoc Indians supported the colonists in the Tuscarora War, while asserting in another that they fought on the side of the Tuscaroras. When conflicting accounts could not be otherwise reconciled, final reliance in this study is placed whenever possible on the *Dictionary of American History.*

The *Handbook of the American Frontier* is based upon hundreds of published sources, both primary and secondary. It would have been a more comprehensive study if the author had delved into governmental reports, newspaper files, unpublished letters of frontier people, and other archival materials. Beginning his research at age 60, however, it seemed prudent to embark upon a project of more manageable proportions.

Included in this *Handbook,* therefore, are experiences and events believed to be representative of those of frontier peoples—red, white, and black—some famous, some forgotten. It is hoped that the casual reader will be interested in these incidents and that the student will gain an insight into what life was like when Europeans and their descendants strove for mastery over this magnificent continent and Indian nations fought courageously to preserve their country and culture.

Abbay, George B., Captivity of. George B. Abbay (Abby), a member of Colonel James B. Many's U. S. Mounted Rangers scouting west of Fort Gibson in the spring of 1833, was seized by Indians on June 2, taken across the Red River into Texas, and killed by Comanches. Many sent Captain Nathan Boone's troop on a rescue mission but no trace of the Ranger was found. In 1834, Colonel Henry Dodge, during treaty negotiations with the Wichita Indians, was informed of Abbay's fate.

(Grant Foreman, *Pioneer Days in the Early Southwest*, 1926; Hugh D. Corwin, *Comanche & Kiowa Captives in Oklahoma and Texas*, 1959; Mildred P. Mayhall, *The Kiowas*, 1962.)

Abercrombie, Fort, North Dakota. Fort Abercrombie was established on August 28, 1857, at the head of navigation of the Red River of the North. It was intended to provide protection for Minnesota settlers during times of Sioux hostility. During the uprising of 1862 a large number of settlers took refuge in the fort. Chief Little Crow and his followers attacked the fort on September 26, 1862, but were repulsed. Fort Abercrombie was abandoned on October 23, 1878.

(Robert W. Frazer, *Forts of the West*, 1965; Doane Robinson, *A History of the Dakota or Sioux Indians*, 1974; U.S. National Park Service, *Soldier and Brave*, 1963.)

Abert, James W., Expedition. In August 1845, Lieutenant James W. Abert led a reconnaissance from Bent's Fort on the Arkansas through eastern New Mexico, the Texas Panhandle, across Oklahoma, and to St. Louis. The small force (33 men) encountered bands of Comanches and Kiowas in this little-known territory but managed to avoid hostilities. On one occasion they were surrounded by Kiowas who planned an attack, but when the Indians learned that Abert and his men were not Texans they became friendly and provided guides for the expedition.

"For the first time in history wagons had made the journey from Bent's Fort to the settlements by way of the Canadian, a distance of some six hundred miles, and the feat had been performed without a battle and with no loss." —LeRoy R. Hafen

(LeRoy R. Hafen, *Broken Hand*, 1973; Mildred P. Mayhall, *The Kiowas*, 1962.)

Abraham Lincoln, Fort. Fort Abraham Lincoln was established by General George A. Custer near Bismarck, North Dakota, on June 14, 1872. Intended to protect crews constructing the Northern Pacific Railroad, it was the largest fort Custer had commanded. On October 14, 1872, the fort was attacked by the Sioux, but a sortie drove the hostiles away. Two soldiers and three Indians were killed. The fort, from which Custer departed on the march to his death, was abandoned in 1891.

(Robert W. Frazer, *Forts of the West*, 1965; Elizabeth B. Custer, *Boots and Saddles*, 1961; Doane Robinson, *A History of the Dakota or Sioux Indians*, 1974.)

Absaroka Indians. See Crow Indians

Accault, Michel. See Aco, Michel

Achlin, Christopher B. (Kit). Christopher B. (Kit) Achlin joined the Texas Rangers in 1840. Within five years he had sustained more wounds in Indian fights than any man in the history of that famous organization. He received a severe wound during the Battle of Bandera Pass in 1842. In 1844, while scouting on the Nueces River, he was wounded three times by Comanches, lost his horse, and walked 120 miles to San Antonio, subsisting on mesquite beans and cactus. Later that year he was wounded three more times, and in 1845 he sustained several wounds in fights along the Rio Grande.

During the Mexican War, Achlin served in John Coffee Hays' regiment and, afterward, he accompanied Hays to California.

(John Holland Jenkins, *Recollections of Early Texas*, 1958.)

Aco, Michel. Michel Aco (Accault, Ako), a native of Poitiers, was one of the earliest European captives of the Sioux Indians. A friend and business associate of La Salle, he led an expedition in 1680 to explore the upper Mississippi. Near the Falls of the St. Anthony he, Father Louis Hennepin, and Antoine du Gay Auguel, were seized by the Sioux. After a brief captivity he and his companions were rescued by Duluth.

In 1693, Aco became a partner of Tonti and LaForest. While living at Kaskaskia he married an Indian girl and they had two children.

(Louis Hennepin, *Description of Louisiana*, 1966; Frank H. Severance, *An Old Frontier of France*, 1971.)

Acton, Minnesota, Murders. The Minnesota Sioux uprising, bloodiest in United States history, began at Acton on August 17, 1862, when four young Wahpeton Sioux warriors became involved in an argument. Calling each other cowards, Crawling, Brown Wing, Killing Ghost, and Breaking Up determined to prove their courage by attacking Acton settlers. Within a few hours they murdered Mr. and Mrs. Robinson Jones, Clara Wilson, Viranus Webster, and Howard Baker. When they informed Chiefs Little Six and Little Crow that hostilities had broken out, the Sioux, furious over their treatment by dishonest government agents, seized the opportunity to begin a revolt that resulted in the massacre of some eight hundred settlers.

(C. M. Oehler, *The Great Sioux Uprising*, 1959; Doane Robinson, *A History of the Dakota or Sioux Indians*, 1974.)

Adobe Walls, Battles of. Two of the fiercest Indian fights in the history of the southern plains occurred at Adobe Walls, an abandoned trading post established on the South Canadian River in the Texas Panhandle by William Bent in 1843. The old adobe fort had fallen into crumbling ruins, but it served from time to time as a shelter for buffalo hunters and a camping place for Plains Indians.

The first battle of Adobe Walls was fought on November 26, 1864, between New Mexico Volunteers and the Comanche and Kiowa Indians. Led by Kit Carson, some four hundred Volunteers attacked Indian villages near Adobe Walls. When scouts reported thousands of hostiles converging from all directions, they hastily took refuge among the ruins. Carson had two mountain howitzers and they were employed in breaking up charge after charge, while the soldiers and their Ute and Apache scouts fired at the enemy with deadly accuracy. More than a hundred hostiles were killed or wounded before Carson ordered a retreat the following day. Pursued "by what seemed to be the whole Kiowa and Comanche nations," wrote Fairfax Downey, they fought their way back to Fort Bascom.

> The first Battle of Adobe Walls was claimed by Kit as a victory, mainly because he was able to burn all 150 Kiowa lodges with all of their winter stores. But it was more like a draw; even with the artillery. Carson had two killed and had ten wounded, and probably exaggerated a bit in guessing that his men killed 60 Kiowas and Comanches. —Richard H. Dillon

The second battle of Adobe Walls was fought on June 27, 1874, when 700 Comanches, Kiowas, and Cheyennes attacked 28 buffalo hunters and 1 woman who were using the ruins as their headquarters. The Indians, urged on by the Comanche medicine man (see Ishatai), were led by Quanah Parker and Lone Wolf.

The hunters forted up in the old post store and saloon and fought off the Indians during an attack at dawn. Two whites were killed in the first attack and three others died while repulsing charges that morning.

> Straight up to the door rode the Indians. . . . The fierce warriors hammered on the doors with butts of their rifles trying to break a way in. From the windows the hunters never for a second ceased shooting. Indians dropped fast. The wounded crawled

painfully out of the stockade. Suddenly all were gone as quickly
as they came.—Paul I. Wellman

Having determined that mounted assaults were too costly, the Indians
began exchanging shots with the defenders at long range. But the buffalo
hunters had superior weapons (see Dixon, Billy) and early in the afternoon
the Indians abandoned the fight. Thirteen dead warriors were left near the
walls while many others were carried away.

(*Handbook of Texas, I*, 1952; Paul I. Wellman, *Death on Horseback*, 1947; Fairfax
Downey, *Indian Wars of the U.S. Army*, 1963; Richard H. Dillon, *North American
Indian Wars*, 1983; Mildred P. Mayhall, *Indian Wars of Texas*, 1965; George Bird
Grinnell, *The Fighting Cheyennes*, 1956; W. S. Nye, *Carbine & Lance*, 1969).

Adoeette, Kiowa Chief. See Big Tree, Kiowa Chief

Ako, Michel. See Aco, Michel

Allis, Samuel. Samuel Allis, a Presbyterian clergyman, became a missionary to the Skidi Pawnees in 1830. He accompanied the tribe on
extended buffalo hunts and quickly mastered their language. In 1835, he
brought his bride to his mission at Bellevue, Nebraska. During the
smallpox epidemic of 1837-38 he convinced 2,000 Indians to submit to
vaccination, saving almost all of them.
    In 1842, Allis entered government service as a teacher at a new
Pawnee village on Willow Creek. Four years later he narrowly escaped
death when a Sioux war party attacked the village. In 1857, he accompanied a Pawnee delegation to Washington, and he continued to serve the
tribe for many years.

(George E. Hyde, *The Pawnee Indians*, 1974.)

Amahami Indians. The Amahami Indians, a small Siouan tribe, were
located in North Dakota at the mouth of the Knife River. Lewis and Clark
recognized them as a distinct tribe in 1804, but they were absorbed by the
Hidatsas after the smallpox epidemic of 1837.

(F. W. Hodge, ed., *Handbook of American Indians, I*, 1912.).

American Fur Company, Western Department. In 1822, the Western
Department of John Jacob Astor's American Fur Company was established at St. Louis to control the trade on the Missouri and administer the
lower posts on the Mississippi and Illinois rivers. In 1827, it united with
the Columbia Fur Company and became known as the Upper Missouri
Outfit of the American Fur Company. From then until Astor retired in 1834

it was able to crush competition and to enjoy a virtual monopoly of the western fur trade.

One of the more important roles of the company in Indian-white relations was the destruction of the Indian factory system. Hiram Martin Chittenden, historian of the fur trade, has written that the company "was responsible for the death of that noble experiment, the government trading posts, or factories, as they were called at the time. If the company had not, under Ramsay Crooks' instigations, steered men like Lewis Cass and Thomas Hart Benton into the opposition, the factories, established with high hopes by Washington and Jefferson, might have become decisive in the civilizing of the American Indian."

(Hiram Martin Chittenden, *The American Fur Trade of the Far West,* 1954.)

American Horse (the elder), Oglala Sioux Chief. American Horse, the elder, was one of Crazy Horse's most effective fighters. He claimed to have killed Colonel W. J. Fetterman, and his lodge displayed a guidon that was taken from Custer's regiment during the Battle of the Little Bighorn. He is best known in frontier history for his heroic defense of Oglala women and children during the Battle of Slim Buttes.

When Captain Anson Mills attacked Crazy Horse's village on September 9, 1876, most of the Sioux reached safety on the bluffs. Discovering that 15 women and children had taken refuge in a cave, American Horse and 4 warriors rushed to their defense. The old chief and his followers repulsed two charges, killed two of the attackers, and wounded nine men. The fight had lasted until late in the day when General George Crook arrived and called for American Horse to surrender. "Come in and get us!" retorted the tough old warrior. After a concentration of fire from two hundred rifles, however, the chief agreed to an offer from Crook to send out the women and children.

After two more hours of fighting no return fire came from the cave. Crook again called for surrender and American Horse staggered out, shot through the stomach and biting a chunk of wood to keep from screaming in pain. He greeted the general and surrendered his rifle with one hand while holding his entrails in with the other. Within a few hours he died.

(Paul I. Wellman, *Death on Horseback,* 1947; Joe De Barthe, *Life and Adventures of Frank Grouard,* 1958.)

American Horse (the younger), Oglala Sioux Chief. The second American Horse (Wasechun Tashunka) probably was a nephew of the chief with the same name who died at Slim Buttes. Unlike his uncle, however, he was generally friendly to white people. Born in the Black Hills in 1840, he rose quickly to a position of leadership through his power of speech. He visited Washington several times and, in 1887, he incurred the wrath of his people by favoring a treaty that ceded South Dakota lands. In 1890, he opposed the Ghost Dance religion and led his followers to the Pine Ridge Agency when the dancers threatened his life. He remained there until his death on December 16, 1908.

(Frederick J. Dockstader, *Great North American Indians*, 1977; Robert M. Utley, *The Last Days of the Sioux Nation*, 1963.)

Amidon, Joseph B., Murder of. During the Minnesota Sioux uprising of 1862, Chief White Lodge determined to spread the hostilities into South Dakota. On August 20, his band advanced toward Sioux Falls. Nearby they found Judge Joseph B. Amidon and his son haying and murdered them both. Afterward, fearing that the citizens had been alerted, they withdrew without attacking the town. The Amidon murders so frightened the settlers that Sioux Falls was abandoned. Most of the town subsequently was burned by the Indians.

(Charles S. Bryant, *A History of the Great Massacre by the Sioux Indians in Minnesota*, 1868; Doane Robinson, *A History of the Dakota or Sioux Indians*, 1974.)

Anadarko, Oklahoma, Hostilities. On August 22, 1874, Kiowa and Comanche warriors seized rations at Anadarko, Oklahoma, intended for the Delawares, Wichitas, and Caddos. Soldiers were summoned from Fort Sill to discipline the thieves and a fight broke out following the arrest of Red Food, a Comanche chief. During two days of skirmishing, five civilians were killed before the hostiles fled.

> The Anadarko affair produced an effect which was highly satis-
> factory to the military authorities. The hostile Noconees were
> scattered with a loss of all their property. Lone Wolf's Kiowas,
> most of whom had been friendly in name only, were shown in
> their true colors . . . Furthermore the Indians saw at Anadarko,
> some of them for the first time, that the government was in
> earnest and in a condition to force its will. —W. S. Nye

(W. S. Nye, *Carbine & Lance*, 1969; Mildred P. Mayhall, *The Kiowas*, 1962; William H. Leckie, *The Buffalo Soldiers*, 1967.)

Anderson, Mary, Captivity of. One of the most unfortunate victims of the Minnesota Sioux uprising of 1862 was Mary Anderson, a young woman employed at a government school near the village of Chief Shakopee. While attempting to flee in a wagon she was shot in the stomach. During four days of captivity before she died she underwent terrible torments, rape included.

(C. M. Oehler, *The Great Sioux Uprising*, 1959; Charles S. Bryant, *A History of the Great Massacre by the Sioux Indians in Minnesota*, 1868.)

Antelope Hills, Battle of. The Battle of Antelope Hills was fought on May 12, 1858, between the Comanche Indians and 100 Texas Rangers led by Capt. John S. (Rip) Ford and their allied Kichai, Tonkawa, Shawnee, and Anadarko scouts. Ford's expedition pursued marauding Comanches along the Canadian River until they located a large village near the Antelope Hills in Oklahoma. Ford's Tonkawa scouts led a surprise attack and conquered their enemies quickly, killing most of the men and capturing the women and children. The Comanche chief Iron Jacket (Pohebits Quasho), who believed that his Spanish coat-of-mail made him invincible, was shot to death by the Anadarko warrior Jim Pockmark.

Early in the afternoon another Comanche force, led by Peta Nocona, arrived at Antelope Hills. Five hundred warriors formed a battle line, confronted by Chief Placido's Tonkawas. The traditional enemy tribes faced each other for more than an hour while warriors spurred their horses into individual contests between the lines, "much," wrote Mildred P. Mayhall, "like the ancient days of medieval jousts."

When the Comanche line finally charged, the Rangers joined the fray and several hours of fierce fighting ensued. Finally, after the loss of 75 warriors, the Comanches withdrew. Ford burned their villages before returning to Texas.

(Mildred P. Mayhall, *Indian Wars of Texas*, 1965; Richard H. Dillon, *North American Indian Wars*, 1983; Robert M. Utley and Wilcomb E. Washburn, *The American Heritage History of the Indian Wars*, 1977.)

Anthony, Scott. Major Scott Anthony was an important participant in the Plains Indian War along the Platte River in 1864. He fought a battle with the Cheyennes on the Pawnee Fork, killing a dozen warriors while their chiefs were in Denver attempting to avert war.

On November 2, 1864, Anthony assumed command of Fort Lyon. Convinced that war was inevitable, he instructed Black Kettle's Cheyennes to camp at Sand Creek "in order to have them within reach if he could get a chance to attack them." —George Bird Grinnell

On November 28, when Chivington's Colorado Volunteers arrived at Fort Lyon, Anthony and many of his men joined them in the march to Sand Creek and took part in attacking the unsuspecting Cheyennes. (See Sand Creek Massacre.)

(George Bird Grinnell, *The Fighting Cheyennes*, 1956; John Tebbel and Keith Jennison, *The American Indian Wars*, 1960.)

Arapaho Indians. The Arapaho Indians, an Algonquian tribe, were among the first to leave the northeastern woodlands and emerge on the Great Plains. Eventually they occupied portions of the northern, central, and southern plains simultaneously. During the 19th century, the tribe divided into a northern faction roaming around the headwaters of the Platte and a southern branch located near the Arkansas. Both divisions lived near, and fought beside, their longtime allies, the northern and southern Cheyennes. In 1867, the southern Arapahoes were assigned to a reservation in Oklahoma while the northern division accepted a reservation in Wyoming.

The Arapahoes were more inclined toward peace with the whites than were most Plains tribes. The southern branch, in particular, preferred trade to war. Arapaho close alliance with the Cheyennes involved them in hostilities, however, especially after settlers began seizing lands guaranteed to them by the 1851 Treaty of Laramie. By 1858, they began attacking gold seekers congregated around their heartland near Denver.

> The white men who flooded the Indian country showed a general disregard for the Indians. Besides destroying their only means of subsistence, they cheated them in trade and debauched them with liquor. With starvation their only alternative, the Arapahos showed a surprising amount of restraint when one considers that there was little actual trouble before 1860.—Virginia Cole Trenholm

During the Indian war of 1864, the Arapahoes did not favor hostilities, but the loss of their lands threatened their means of subsistence and they were driven to raid in order to survive. When the Civil War ended they made peace with the United States. In 1868, however, they joined the Cheyennes on the warpath because they doubted that the government would live up to promises made in the Treaty of Medicine Lodge. The tribe's final involvement in warfare occurred during the Ghost Dance unrest of 1890. In 1892, the southern Arapahoes received lands in severalty.

(Virginia Cole Trenholm, *The Arapahoes, Our People*, 1970; W. S. Nye, *Carbine & Lance*, 1969; De B. Randolph Keim, *Sheridan's Troopers on the Borders*, 1870; Margaret Coel, *Chief Left Hand*, 1981.)

Arapoosh, Crow Chief. Arapoosh (Rotten Belly, Sour Belly) was born about 1790. He became a famous war leader with most of his hostilities directed at Indian enemies. In 1825, he refused to sign a treaty with the United States, announcing defiantly that he would not give up his tribe's homeland to live on a reservation. He was killed by the Blackfeet in 1834.

(Frederick J. Dockstader, *Great North American Indians*, 1977; James P. Beckwourth, *The Life and Adventures of James P. Beckwourth*, 1931.)

Arbuckle, Fort. Fort Arbuckle was founded near the present site of Davis, Oklahoma, by Captain R. B. Marcy in April, 1851. The location proved to be too far east to effectively counter Comanche and Kiowa raids, but the post served the purpose of protecting the Chickasaws from the Plains Indians. In May 1861, it was occupied by Confederate troops, and it was abandoned soon afterward.

In 1866, the U. S. Tenth Cavalry rebuilt Fort Arbuckle. During the summer of 1867, a Comanche band visited the post and established trade that resulted in the release of a young white captive. In 1869, the fort was dismantled and the troops transferred to Fort Sill.

(W. S. Nye, *Carbine & Lance*, 1969; Robert W. Frazer, *Forts of the West*, 1965; Grant Foreman, *Advancing the Frontier*, 1933; William H. Leckie, *The Buffalo Soldiers*, 1967.)

Arbuckle, Matthew. Matthew Arbuckle was born in Greenbrier County, West Virginia, in 1776. He joined the Army as an ensign in 1799 and eventually rose to the rank of brigadier general. In 1822, he was assigned to Fort Smith, Arkansas, to prevent warfare between the Cherokees and Osages. For twenty years he played a major role in curtailing hostilities between recently relocated eastern tribes and the Plains Indians while commanding forces at Fort Gibson and Fort Smith. Following his death on June 11, 1851, Fort Arbuckle was named for him.

(John Joseph Mathews, *The Osages*, 1961; Grant Foreman, *Advancing the Frontier*, 1933; Josiah Gregg, *The Commerce of the Prairies*, 1968.)

Arikara Indians. The Arikara Indians, a powerful tribe belonging to the Caddoan linguistic family, moved northward from the southern Caddo homeland together with the Skidi Pawnees. They separated in relatively recent times when the Arikaras adopted a sedentary life on the Missouri River.

The first Europeans to contact the Arikaras were French traders who found them below the Cheyenne River on the Missouri in 1770. At that time the tribe had a population of about 3,000, but many Arikaras had been swept away by the smallpox when Lewis and Clark visited their villages in 1804. They welcomed the earlier white visitors, but as brigades of trappers began invading their territory at the mouth of the Grand River they made

the fatal mistake of assuming a hostile attitude toward the American traders, from whom alone they could hope to obtain a regular supply of arms and ammunition. As the culmination of a series of assaults on Americans, they made a treacherous attack on W. H. Ashley's large brigade of trappers in 1823.—George E. Hyde

When news that Ashley had had 12 men killed and 11 wounded by the Arikaras reached Colonel Henry Leavenworth he determined to punish them. He marched from Fort Atkinson with 220 soldiers, 120 mountain men, and 500 Sioux allies. This powerful force arrived at the two palisaded Arikara villages on August 9, 1823. The first attack was made by the Sioux, but when they failed to dislodge their enemies the soldiers entered the battle. On August 10, they attacked both villages with artillery and, although cannon balls failed to destroy the earth lodges, the defenders appealed for peace. After they agreed to restore property stolen from Ashley, Leavenworth ended this first major battle between U. S. troops and Plains Indians.

On August 12 the Arikaras deserted their villages and lived with the Skidi Pawnees for a brief period. They continued their attacks on trappers until they signed a treaty with the U. S. Government in 1825. In 1832, they settled with the Mandans on the Missouri River and, a few years later, smallpox decimated both tribes. The survivors moved to Fort Berthold in 1862. A reservation was established for them there in 1880, and twenty years later they received land in severalty.

According to Lewis A. Saum, the Arikaras had the worst reputation of all of the western tribes: "While they could halt the traders and exact bribes they did; and long after that tactic was ineffective they continued to harass and commit desultory outrages at every opportunity."

(Lewis O. Saum, *The Fur Trader and the Indian*, 1965; Edwin Thompson Denig, *Five Indian Tribes of the Upper Missouri*, 1961; Ross W. Meyer, *The Village Indians of the Upper Missouri*, 1973; George E. Hyde, *The Pawnee Indians*, 1974; Hiram Martin Chittenden, *The American Fur Trade of the Far West*, 1954; U. S. Park Service, *Soldier and Brave*, 1963.)

Arikara Village, Treaties of. On July 16, 1825, Henry Atkinson and Benjamin O'Fallon negotiated a treaty with the Hunkpapa Sioux at the Arikara village. Two days later the same commissioners negotiated a treaty with the Arikara Indians. The tribes were placed under government protection and traders were promised to them. In return they agreed to avoid trade with citizens of of other nations.

(Charles J. Kappler, ed., *Indian Affairs, Laws and Treaties, II*, 1972.)

Armes, George, Campaigns. George Armes, a captain of the Tenth U. S. Cavalry (Buffalo Soldiers), led a pursuit of Cheyenne raiders who had killed 13 men near Fort Hays in August 1867. On August 2, he and 34

troopers located the hostiles on the Saline River. A battle ensued that lasted several hours, and Armes was wounded before breaking through powerful hostile forces and fighting off the Cheyennes during a 15-mile retreat.

On August 20, Armes again took the field, this time at the head of 130 soldiers. On the Beaver River they were attacked by a large force of Cheyennes. The fight continued for two days before the Indians withdrew. The soldiers killed 50 warriors while losing 3 men and having 16 wounded.

(William H. Leckie, *The Buffalo Soldiers*, 1967.)

Arrow-Going-Home, Osage Chief. See Clermont, Osage Chief

Ash Hollow, Battle of. As a result of hostilities arising from the Grattan massacre, General William S. Harney led six hundred men from Fort Kearny on August 5, 1855, to punish the Sioux. At a place called Ash Hollow on the North Platte, he located the Brulé Sioux village of Chief Little Thunder. On September 3, Harney sent his cavalry around the camp to attack from the northwest while he planned a frontal attack with the infantry. Seeing the village virtually surrounded, Little Thunder rushed forward to parley, but Harney told him to return to his village and prepare for a fight to the death.

The Sioux, fleeing in terror, were overwhelmed by the cavalry. Eighty-five Indians died and 70 women and children were captured. Harney's losses were 5 dead and 7 wounded. "The battle of Ash Hollow was little more than a massacre of the Brulés." —Doane Robinson

(Doane Robinson, *A History of the Dakota or Sioux Indians*, 1974; Richard H. Dillon, *North American Indian Wars*, 1983; Fairfax Downey, *Indian Wars of the U. S. Army*, 1963; Robert M. Utley and Wilcomb E. Washburn, *The American Heritage History of the Indian Wars*, 1977.)

Ashley, William Henry, Arikara Battle. William Henry Ashley, Lieutenant Governor of Missouri, formed a partnership with Andrew Henry in 1822 to enter the far western fur trade. Early in May 1823, he led 90 men up the Missouri River from St. Louis. Arriving at the two fortified Arikara villages on May 31, they anchored their two boats near the shore while Ashley and two companions rowed ashore to trade. The Indians seemed friendly, and Ashley began to trade arms and ammunition for horses on June 1. After acquiring about forty horses, Ashley left a shore party to herd them while he and most of his men returned to the boats. Early on June 2, the Arikaras attacked the herders. Ashley ordered the boats close to shore to assist his men, but the frightened boatmen refused to obey. He managed, however, to send two skiffs to the river bank and some of his men escaped in them. Others managed to swim to the boats. Thirteen trappers died in the attack and eleven survived their wounds. (See Arikara Indians; Leavenworth, Henry.)

(W. J. Ghent, *The Early Far West*, 1936; Roy W. Meyer, *The Village Indians of the Upper Missouri*, 1977.)

Assiniboin Indians. The Assiniboin Indians, a large Siouan tribe, originally were a part of the Yanktonai Sioux. They became a separate tribe prior to 1640 and moved northward to the area of Lake Winnipeg. By 1775 they had spread along the Saskatchewan and Assiniboin rivers, a territory they continued to occupy until confined to reservations.

After the Assiniboins acquired horses (about 1750), they became some of the most skillful buffalo hunters and ranged over a wide area of Canada and the northern United States, fighting many battles with the Blackfeet and Sioux. Edwin Thompson Denig, a fur trader who married into the tribe, observed that they annoyed the whites by stealing horses and killing cattle but seldom fought them on the scale of other Plains tribes. Most of them chose to live in Canada in order to trade at French and British posts. They numbered some 10,000 people until the smallpox began decimating them in 1838. Those who remained in the United States eventually settled at the Fort Belknap and Fort Peck agencies.

(James Larpenteur Long, *The Assiniboines*, 1961; Loretta Fowler, *Shared Symbols, Contested Meanings*,1987; Edwin Thompson Denig, *Five Indian Tribes of the Upper Missouri*, 1961.)

Assiniboine, Fort. Fort Assiniboine was established near the present site of Havre, Montana, on May 18, 1879, to guard against the return of Sitting Bull and his followers from Canada and to prevent hostilities by the Blackfeet. It was abandoned in 1911.

(Robert W. Frazer, *Forts of the West*, 1965.)

Atkinson, Fort, Kansas. Fort Atkinson, Kansas, was established near the present site of Dodge City on August 8, 1850. Named for Colonel Henry Atkinson, it was intended to protect the Santa Fe Trail. The fort was besieged briefly by Comanches and Kiowas and, in 1853, it served as the site of treaty negotiations with those tribes as well as the Kiowa Apaches. Fort Atkinson was abandoned on October 2, 1854, but temporarily reoccupied in 1865 during a campaign against the Indians.

(Robert W. Frazer, *Forts of the West*, 1965.)

Atkinson, Fort, Kansas, Treaty of. On July 27, 1853, Thomas Fitzpatrick negotiated a treaty at Fort Atkinson, Kansas, with the Comanche, Kiowa, and Kiowa-Apache tribes. For an annuity of $18,000, the Indians agreed to keep peace with the whites, the Mexicans, and other Indians and to permit the construction of forts and roads. "The main difficulty in executing the treaty was the unwillingness of the Kiowas to cease raiding in Mexico and to give up their Mexican captives . . . "—Mildred P. Mayhall

(Mildred P. Mayhall, *The Kiowas*, 1962.)

Atkinson, Fort, Nebraska. Fort Atkinson, Nebraska, was established near Council Bluffs on September 29, 1819. Originally called Camp Missouri, it was renamed Fort Atkinson on January 5, 1821. Its primary purpose was to afford protection for traders on the Missouri River. It served in 1823 as the base for Colonel Henry Leavenworth's campaign against the Arikara Indians. It was the site of an important treaty with the Oto and Missouri Indians in 1825. The post was abandoned in 1827.

(Robert W. Frazer, *Forts of the West*, 1965; U. S. National Park Service, *Soldier and Brave*, 1963.)

Atkinson, Fort, Nebraska, Treaties of. On September 26, 1825, Henry Atkinson and Benjamin O'Fallon conducted successful treaty negotiations with the Oto and Missouri Indians at Fort Atkinson, Nebraska. The government agreed to protect the tribes and to provide them with licensed traders. The Indians agreed to stop trading with citizens of other nations. Similar treaties were signed with the Pawnees on September 30 and the Mahas on October 6, 1825.

(Charles J. Kappler, ed., *Indian Affairs: Laws and Treaties, II*, 1972.)

Atsina Indians. The Atsina (Gros Ventre) Indians, a detached Arapaho tribe or band, played a minor role in the history of the northern plains. Located along the upper Missouri and the Milk River in Montana, they became hostile in 1793 because traders had provided firearms to the Crees and Assiniboins. In consequence they attacked British trading posts in Canada. Their numbers were greatly reduced by wars with the Blackfeet, and they agreed to go on the Fort Belknap Reservation after a devastating defeat in 1867.

(John R. Swanton, *Indian Tribes of North America*, 1952; Virginia Cole Trenholm, *The Arapahoes, Our People*, 1970.)

Aubry, Fort, Kansas. Fort Aubry, named for Francis X. Aubry, was established on the Arkansas River in Hamilton County, Kansas, in September, 1865. It was intended to protect the Aubry cutoff and mountain branch of the Santa Fe Trail during a period of Indian warfare and was abandoned on April 15, 1866, after hostilities ceased.

(Robert W. Frazer, *Forts of the West*, 1965.)

- B -

Babb, Theodore Adolphus (Dot), Captivity of. In September 1865, Comanches raided the Babb ranch in Wise County, Texas, killed Mrs. Babb and captured thirteen-year-old T. A. (Dot) Babb and his sister, Louella. Early in his captivity the boy tried to escape. Caught and threatened with death, he was spared because of a brave show of defiance. After a year of captivity he was adopted into the tribe and taken on raids against other Indians. He enjoyed the wild, free life, but he remembered his white family and he managed to send word of his situation to his father.

Through the intercession of Chief Esserhaby, Babb was given the choice of remaining a Comanche or returning to his white relatives. The Indians believed that he was completely assimilated and were surprised and disappointed when he chose to return to his white father. After a year of captivity he was taken to Fort Arbuckle and sold for $210 and $20 worth of clothing. Soon afterward his sister was redeemed for $333.

Babb kept in contact with Comanche friends and visited them on the reservation from time to time. In 1901, both he and Louella applied for land allotments as adopted Comanches, but their appeals were denied. He and his white family lived on the reservation in Oklahoma for a time before returning to Texas.

(T. A. Babb, *In the Bosom of the Comanches,* 1912; W. S. Nye, *Carbine & Lance,* 1937.)

Bacon, John, Campaign. Captain John Bacon of the 9th Cavalry led 198 Buffalo Soldiers and Tonkawa scouts from Fort Concho, Texas, in pursuit of a Kiowa and Comanche war party on October 10, 1869. On October 28, his force was attacked near the headwaters of the Brazos River by 500 hostiles. In a fight so fierce that it reached hand-to-hand combat at times the Indians were defeated and compelled to flee. Bacon and his men located their camp on the following day, charged immediately, and drove the defenders away. Forty warriors were slain and seven women were captured. Eight of Bacon's men were wounded, but all of them recovered.

(William H. Leckie, *The Buffalo Soldiers,* 1967.)

Bad-Tempered Buffalo, Osage Chief. See Mad Buffalo, Osage Chief

Baker, E. M., Massacre. See Marias Massacre

Baldwin, Frank. Frank D. Baldwin was born at Manchester, Michigan, on June 26, 1842. After serving as a Union officer during the Civil War, he became one of the most effective Indian fighters on the Great Plains, serving as a lieutenant in the Fifth Infantry in Kansas and Texas. He rescued the buffalo hunters after the second battle of Adobe Walls and he won the Congressional Medal of Honor for a daring charge on Grey Beard's Cheyenne village at McClellan's Creek, Texas, on November 8, 1874. His small force scattered 300 hostiles and redeemed Julia and Adelaide German from captivity.

Baldwin served throughout the Indian wars and fought in the Philippines during the Spanish-American War. He retired in 1915 and died on April 22, 1923.

(Carl Coke Rister, *Border Captives*, 1940; W. S. Nye, *Carbine & Lance*, 1969.)

Bandera Pass, Battles of. Bandera Pass, separating the valley of the Medina and Guadalupe rivers northwest of San Antonio, Texas, was the scene of two fierce Indian battles, separated by more than a century. The date of the first battle of Bandera Pass is not known with certainty, but historians believe that it occurred about 1720. The Apache Indians used the pass, 500 yards long and 125 feet wide, during frequent forays against the Spanish settlement of San Antonio. Ordered by the King of Spain to punish the hostiles, a force of lancers entered the pass and sustained a furious assault by Apaches on the bluffs. The battle was joined for 72 hours, finally resulting in a Spanish victory. The Apaches withdrew far to the westward.

The second battle of Bandera Pass was fought in 1842 between John Coffee Hays and his Texas Ranger company and a Comanche war party. Hays and his forty men were ambushed in the pass by a hundred warriors. A fierce hand-to-hand battle ensued until Ranger Kit Achlin killed the Comanche chief with a knife. Afterward, both sides withdrew from the pass. Ranger losses were five killed and six wounded.

The final violent act to occur in Bandera Pass was the wounding of Rufus Click in 1866. He was shot in the back with a poisoned arrow, but outran the Indians and finally recovered.

(*The Handbook of Texas, I*, 1952; J. Marvin Hunter, ed., *The Bloody Trail in Texas*, 1931.)

Banta, William. William Banta, a native of Indiana, settled in the Texas hill country in 1843. In 1850 he organized the Burnet County Minute Men to guard the area against Comanche raids. Between 1850 and 1859, Banta and his men fought numerous battles with Indians throughout the area north and west of Austin.

(*Handbook of Texas, I*, 1952.)

Barnard, George. George Barnard was born in Connecticut in 1818 and settled in Texas in 1838. After participating in the Texan Santa Fe Expedition he became an Indian trader associated with the Torrey Trading

Houses until 1848. In 1849, he established a trading post near the present site of Weatherford, Texas, where he supplied horses to the Army and the Texas Rangers. His business improved when he married a Comanche woman.

Barnard's dealings with the Indians brought him both praise and censure. At various times the government employed him to arrange parleys with the tribes ranging over north and central Texas. He was accused, however, of selling guns and liquor to Indians. No agency of government was authorized to supervise the relations of private citizens with the tribes: "The important fact is the revelation of a hopeless tangle which left George Barnard and others as unscrupulous as he sitting high on the Texas border beyond the reach of Indian agents, federal soldiers, and state laws."—Walter Prescott Webb

(Walter Prescott Webb, *The Texas Rangers,* 1965; T. R. Fehrenbach, *Lone Star,* 1983; *Handbook of Texas, I,* 1952; Mildred P. Mayhall, *Indian Wars of Texas,* 1965.)

Barry, James Buckner (Buck). James Buckner (Buck) Barry was born in North Carolina in 1821, moved to Texas in 1845, and served in the Republic of Texas Army. Afterward he settled at Meridian, Texas, and became a famous scout and Indian fighter. In 1864, while serving the Confederacy, he defended the settlers near Fort Belknap against Comanche and Kiowa raids. Afterward he fought the Kickapoos in the battle of Dove Creek and led attacks on several Indian villages.

(*Handbook of Texas, I,* 1952.)

Barton, William. William Barton, born in South Carolina in 1782, moved to Texas soon after fighting in the Creek War of 1816. He settled near Austin in a community now named Barton Springs in his honor. He engaged in so many Indian battles that he was called "the Daniel Boone of Texas." His most famous escapade occurred in 1842 when he was fired upon by Indians. He returned fire with his Kentucky rifle, wounding a warrior, and then fled for his life. With Indians gaining upon him, he stopped at the top of a hill and called upon imaginary companions to open fire, pointing toward his pursuers. The Indians fell for the ruse and retreated, permitting Barton to reach safety in the settlement.

(J. W. Wilbarger, *Indian Depredations in Texas,* 1985; *Handbook of Texas, I,* 1952.)

Bascom, Fort, New Mexico. Fort Bascom, near Tucumcari, New Mexico, was established in 1863 to protect settlers of the southwestern plains from raids by the Comanche, Kiowa, and Cheyenne Indians. It served as Kit Carson's base for his campaign against those tribes at Adobe Walls in the

Texas Panhandle on November 26, 1864, and it was the point of departure for Colonel A. W. Evans when he led an expedition that defeated the Comanches four years later. It was abandoned in 1870.

(Robert W. Frazer, *Forts of the West*, 1965; W. S. Nye, *Carbine & Lance*, 1969.)

Bates Battle. In 1874, the Northern Arapaho Indians were suspected of depredations in the Wind River area of Wyoming. Captain A. E. Bates and his cavalry company took the field to punish them. Led by Shoshoni scouts, the troopers located Chief Black Coal's village on a tributary of Wind River on July 4, 1874, and attacked at dawn. The Indians abandoned the village and fought from neighboring bluffs, killing three soldiers. Arapaho losses were 26 slain and many wounded. Bates withdrew, claiming victory, when his ammunition supplies were depleted. The Indians retained possession of the battlefield and boasted that they had defeated the U. S. Army.

(Virginia Cole Trenholm, *The Arapahoes, Our People*, 1970.)

Battey, Thomas C. Thomas Battey, a Quaker religious leader and teacher, was born in Starksboro, Vermont, on February 19, 1828. Educated in Quaker schools, he acquired a sincere interest in Indian education. In 1871, he received an appointment to teach at the Wichita Agency at Anadarko, Oklahoma, and in May 1872, he felt called to educate the Kiowas, one of the most dangerous tribes in North America.

Battey opened a school in the village of Chief Kicking Bird and the two became firm friends. Not all of the Kiowas wanted their children to attend school, however, and a warrior disrupted the first day of class by threatening the teacher with a tomahawk. Battey convinced the onlookers of his courage by throwing his adversary out the door.

Soon after his arrival among the Kiowas, Battey was called upon to assume diplomatic duties. One of his first assignments was to inform hostile Kiowas that their chiefs, Satanta and Big Tree, must remain in prison in Texas. This announcement so infuriated the tribe that Battey was held as a captive and threatened with death until the Governor of Texas agreed to release the chiefs. The ordeal of captivity imposed such a strain on his health that he never completely recovered.

In 1875 Battey, ignoring his illness, agreed to go far out on the plains to try to prevent the hostile Kiowas from joining in an impending Indian war. His courage in going unarmed into the camps of Satanta and Big Tree gained the tribe's respect and, asserting that "his talk is good," the Kiowas refrained from joining in the northern plains war that led to the Battle of the Little Bighorn.

Battey's school never achieved much success and, after publishing a book about his experiences in 1875, he gave up the attempt and returned to his family in Iowa. He died in 1897.

(Thomas C. Battey, *The Life And Adventures of a Quaker Among the Indians*, 1876; Mildred P. Mayhall, *The Kiowas*, 1962; W. S. Nye, *Carbine & Lance*, 1969.)

Battle Creek Fight. The Battle Creek fight (Surveyor's Fight) occurred on October 8, 1838, in Navarro County, Texas, when 25 surveyors were attacked by an estimated 300 Kickapoo Indians. The battle was fiercely contested for 24 hours. Only seven surveyors survived, four of them wounded, to reach safety at Parker's Fort.

(James T. DeShields, *Border Wars of Texas*, 1976; J. W. Wilbarger, *Indian Depredations in Texas*, 1985.)

Battle Ground. Near the boundary of Oklahoma and Colorado, on the bank of the Cimarron River, is a place known to the early Santa Fe traders as the Battle Ground. There, in 1829, a caravan with an escort of Mexican dragoons was attacked by Gros Ventre Indians. Several Mexicans were slain before the dragoons and American traders drove the hostiles into the hills, killing a considerable number. Two years later, Josiah Gregg's caravan repulsed a Comanche attack near the Battle Ground.

(Josiah Gregg, *The Commerce of the Prairies*, 1968.)

Battle Mountain Fight. In 1841, sixty trappers, led by Henry Fraeb (Frapp), were sent by the Rocky Mountain Fur Company to establish a post on St. Vrain's fork of the Yampah River in southern Wyoming. In August a party of Sioux and Cheyenne warriors attacked the trappers, killing Fraeb and four of his men. Several Indians were slain in the battle, causing the tribes to become increasingly hostile to trappers and explorers.

(Hiram Martin Chittenden, *The American Fur Trade of the Far West*, 1954; Virginia Cole Trenholm, *The Arapahoes, Our People*, 1970.)

Baylor, John R. John R. Baylor was born at Paris, Kentucky, on July 20, 1822. At the age of 17 he moved to Texas and assumed an important role in Indian relations. In 1840, serving under Colonel J. H. Moore, he participated in several campaigns against the Comanches. Strangely this man who developed a deep hatred of Indians was appointed agent to these same Comanches less than fifteen years later. His tenure was brief, however, for he was dismissed soon afterward by Indian Superintendent Robert S. Neighbors for conspiring to have Neighbors removed.

After his dismissal, Baylor bitterly "assumed the role of trouble-maker," wrote Walter Prescott Webb. "He played cruelly on the emotions of Texans who had lost loved ones in Indian raids, until the whites in the vicinity threatened to attack the reservations and massacre every Indian." On May 23, 1859, he led a mob of white men to the Brazos River Reserve, threatening to kill the Caddo, Waco, and Tonkawa Indians and U. S. soldiers as well if they interfered. The Indians showed every intention of defending themselves so the mob killed one woman working in her garden, dragged an old man to his death, and beat a hasty retreat from the reserve. The Indians pursued Baylor to the Merlin Ranch and in a battle that lasted until late afternoon killed five of his men. Afterward Superintendent Neighbors abandoned the reserve and escorted the Indians to Oklahoma.

In June 1860, Baylor learned that Comanche Indians had killed a rancher named Joseph Browning on the Clear Fork of the Brazos River. He recruited a posse, overtook the raiders on Paint Creek, and killed 13 of them. Scalps were taken and Baylor exhibited them in several cities, arousing a hue and cry to exterminate the Indians.

In 1861 Baylor was appointed colonel of the Texas Mounted Rifles. From his base at El Paso he drove out the Federal forces and proclaimed himself Confederate Governor of Arizona. He lost his command, however, when charges were made of lack of wisdom in handling Indian affairs. He was elected to the Confederate Congress in 1863, serving until the end of the war. He died on February 6, 1894.

(A. J. Sowell, *Rangers and Pioneers of Texas,* 1964; J. W. Wilbarger, *Indian Depradations in Texas,* 1985; T. R. Fehrenbach, *Comanches,* 1963; Walter Prescott Webb, *The Texas Rangers,* 1965.)

Beales' Texas Colony. Dr. John Charles Beales, a native of England, received a grant from the Mexican state of Coahuila and Texas in 1832 to establish a colony between the Rio Grande and the Nueces. The first colonists, consisting of British families, Americans, Germans, and Mexicans arrived at Las Moras Creek, near the present site of Del Rio, Texas, in March, 1834. Not realizing that the site lay on a Comanche war trail, they erected cabins and planted crops. But drought discouraged them and Indian raids frightened many into decamping across the Rio Grande.

When the Mexican Army invaded Texas in 1836, the remaining colonists scattered. Many were killed or captured by the Comanches while attempting to reach safety in larger settlements. (See Horn, Mrs. Sarah Ann.)

(James T. De Shields, *Border Wars of Texas,* 1976; Carl Coke Rister, *Border Captives,* 1940.)

Bear Tooth, Arapaho Chief. Bear Tooth, great chief of the Arapahoes and an influential leader of all tribes in the Arkansas River region, was friendly to American explorers. During the Stephen H. Long Expedition of 1820 he assured the soldiers of safety while exploring the area. He addressed them in English, having learned the language from an American escapee from a Mexican prison whom he had protected in his own tepee.

(Virginia Cole Trenholm, *The Araphoes, Our People,* 1970; John R. Bell, *The Journal of Captain John R. Bell,* 1957.)

Bear's Heart, James, Cheyenne Warrior. Born In 1851, Bear's Heart was a prominent raider who fought the U. S. Army, the Mexicans, the Texans, and Indian enemies. He was captured in 1874 and imprisoned at Fort Marion, Florida. There he became an accomplished artist. In 1878, he attended Hampton Institute in Virginia. Three years later he settled on the Cheyenne reservation in Oklahoma, where he died in 1882.

(Frederick J. Dockstader, *Great North American Indians,* 1977.)

Beaver Greek, Minnesota, Massacre. The Beaver Creek settlement, near the Minneseta River, was devastated during the Sioux uprising of 1862. Citizens abandoned the town and fled toward Fort Ridgely, but most of them were intercepted by Chief Cut Nose's war party. More than 80 settlers were slain and a dozen women made captive. At the end of the outbreak, Cut Nose was identified by the captives, tried for murder, and sentenced to death.

(E. M. Oehler, *The Great Sioux Uprising,* 1959; Charles S. Bryant, *A History of the Great Massacre by the Sioux Indians in Minnesota,* 1868.)

Beckwith, Jim. See Beckwourth, James P.

Beckwourth, James P. Jim Beckwourth (Beckwith), one of the most controversial western frontiersmen, was born on April 26, 1798, at Fredericksburg, Virginia. His father was a white planter and his mother a quadroon slave. When he was about eight years old his father took him to St. Louis, where he received some schooling and learned the blacksmith trade. He worked several years as a deckhand on a Mississippi River steamboat before joining William Ashley's trapping brigade in 1822.

Beckwourth's career as a mountain man is legendary, and no historian has been able to separate fact from fiction. It is known that in 1824 he purchased horses from the Pawnees for Ashley's men to use in exploring the Rocky Mountains. In 1824, he trapped in the Yellowstone country. The following year, according to his own account, he was the only trapper courageous enough to live among the Blackfeet. Moreover, he claimed that he married both daughters of an important Blackfoot chief.

In 1828, Beckwourth and Caleb Greenwood, a trapper married to a Crow woman, visited the Crow tribe. Greenwood told the Crows that Beckwourth was an Indian who had been captured as a small boy and raised by the whites. The tribe adopted Beckwourth, and he remained with them six years. He enjoyed the life of an Indian, fought with them against enemy tribes, and gained much influence over them. According to his own account, he became a chief and married ten of the most beautiful women of the tribe.

After leaving the Crows, Beckwourth went to Florida to fight the Seminole Indians. After the Seminole War, he established trading posts in New Mexico and Colorado. He served as a dispatch rider in California during the Mexican War. During the gold rush he discovered a pass through the Sierra Nevada which is still known as Beckwourth Pass, and he settled there for awhile, operating a trading post and hotel. In 1852, he established a ranch near Denver.

In 1864, reluctantly, Beckwourth served as a guide for Colonel J. M. Chivington's Colorado Volunteers in their campaign that resulted in the Sand Creek massacre. In 1866 he accompanied Colonel Henry B. Carrington's army to Montana in an attempt to prevent the Crows from joining the hostiles. He died while visiting his adopted people.

Beckwourth's autobiography, published in 1856, has been branded one of the greatest collections of lies ever printed. But historians have relied upon it while writing about the early fur trade in the Far West.

(James P. Beckwourth, *Life and Adventures of James P. Beckwourth*, 1931; Hiram Martin Chittenden, *The American Fur Trade of the Far West*, 1954; Gordon Speck, *Breeds and Half-Breeds*, 1969; Elinor Wilson, *Jim Beckwourth*, 1972.)

Beecher's Island, Battle of. In September 1865, Major George A. Forsyth led fifty frontiersmen on the trail of a large Cheyenne and Sioux war party under Chiefs Roman Nose, Tall Bull, Pawnee Killer, and others who had participated in the massacre of Lieutenant L. S. Kidder and 11 cavalrymen on the Republican River. Forsyth's men were seasoned Indian fighters and well armed with repeating rifles, but the force was too small to attack the thousand warriors they sought.

On September 16, the Indians turned on their pursuers and Forsyth led his men to a small island covered with plum bushes in the middle of the Arikara Fork of the Republican River, in northeastern Colorado. They hastily dug pits in the sand and crouched behind the bushes while more and more mounted warriors lined the river bottom.

In one of the most famous battles in Great Plains history, the Indians made repeated charges, only to divide and circle the island when met by a continuous fire from the repeaters. Many warriors died, some within a few feet of the island. Finally Roman Nose was mortally wounded leading a charge and the Indians abandoned the attempt to overrun the island. A siege ensued that lasted nine days. On the first night Jack Stillwell and Henry Trudeau slipped through the Indian lines to bring help from Fort

Wallace. When the Indians sighted the relief column they abandoned the siege and withdrew from the battlefield.

Of the 51 defenders, 23 were killed or wounded. Among the mortally wounded was Lieutenant F. W. Beecher, for whom the battle is named. Forsyth believed that his men had killed a hundred warriors.

(Paul I. Wellman, *Death on Horseback,* 1947; George Bird Grinnell, *The Fighting Cheyennes,* 1956; Homer W. Wheeler, *Buffalo Days,* 1925; De B. Randolph Keim, *Sheridan's Troopers on the Border,* 1870; Richard H. Dillon, *North American Indian Wars,* 1983.)

Beeson, Benjamin, Family, Columbus, Texas. Benjamin Beeson (Bessan), one of Stephen F. Austin's earliest colonists, operated a ferry on the Colorado River at Columbus in 1824. His son, Leander, fought in the Battle of San Jacinto. In 1837, Leander and his brother, Collins, pursued some runaway slaves from their plantation near Columbus. Near Gonzales they ran into an Indian ambush while crossing the Guadalupe River. Collins was shot to death. Leander escaped injury, but his horse was killed, and he swam the river with bullets rippling the water all around him. He made his way home on foot, arriving several days later, and recruited ten men to avenge the death of his brother. Near Gonzales they located the Indian camp, put the warriors to flight, and buried Collins.

(James T. De Shields, *Border Wars of Texas,* 1976; *Handbook of Texas, I,* 1952.)

Belknap, Fort, Texas. Fort Belknap was founded in 1851 in Young County, Texas, by General William G. Belknap in order to guard the settlers of the northern part of the state from Indian raids. A link in a chain of forts facing the Comanches and Kiowas north of the Red River, it protected the most dangerous segment of the frontier line. Some of the most devastating Indian attacks in Texas history occurred near Fort Belknap (see Elm Creek Raid), and some of the most destructive retaliatory campaigns originated there (see Rush Springs, Battle of). In addition, the fort played an important role in guarding the tribes on the Brazos Indian Reservation from attacks by white settlers. (See Baylor, John R.)

During the Civil War, Fort Belknap was evacuated by Federal troops, and the Texas Frontier Regiment used it as a base for defending the settlers from Indian raids. After the war it was reoccupied by the U. S. Army, although only token forces remained there until its abandonment in 1876.

(Robert W. Frazer, *Forts of the West,* 1965; Mildred P. Mayhall, *Indian Wars of Texas,* 1965; U. S. National Park Service, *Soldier and Brave,* 1963.)

Bell, William, Murder of. On January 1, 1843, William Bell and Alexander Coleman attended a meeting in Austin, Texas, and were returning to their farms east of town in a buggy when Indians attacked them. The buggy overturned and the two men were captured and lanced. Bell died instantly, but Coleman's back wound was not mortal and the Indians tortured him. Meanwhile two horsemen, Joe Hornsby and James Edmondson, rode into view, observed the Indians tormenting Coleman, and determined to rescue him. Unarmed except for one single-shot pistol, they charged thirty Indians and put them to flight.

John H. Jenkins gave the following account of the aftermath of Bell's death.

> Coleman, although nearly naked, ran back to town and gave the alarm, while Edmondson and Hornsby chased the Indians, putting forth what later became famous as the Rebel Yell and shooting the little pistol as quickly as it could be reloaded. The citizens of Austin soon caught up . . . and fought a little battle with the Indians, killing three and capturing all their accouterments.

(John Holland Jenkins, *Recollections of Early Texas*, 1958; A. J. Sowell, *Rangers and Pioneers of Texas*, 1964.)

Bellevue, Treaty of. The Treaty of Bellevue was negotiated by John Daugherty and Joshua Pilcher on October 15, 1836, at Bellevue, Upper Missouri Territory, with the Missouri, Omaha, Oto, and Santee and Yankton Sioux. The Indians ceded a vast territory "between the State of Missouri and the Missouri River, and south of a line running due west from the northwest corner of the State to the Missouri River" in exchange for gifts valued at $4,500.

(Charles J. Kappler, ed., *Indian Affairs: Laws and Treaties, II*, 1972.)

Bent, Charles (Son of William Bent). Charles Bent, son of William Bent and Owl Woman (daughter of a Cheyenne chief), attended school at Westport (present Kansas City, Missouri) and lied about his age in order to enlist in the Confederate Army. He was captured in October 1862, and released because of his youth. Soon afterward he went to live with the Cheyennes, abandoned the white way of life, and became a warrior. During the Sand Creek massacre, he was captured by Chivington's soldiers and sent to Fort Lyon, but he rejoined the Cheyennes at the first opportunity.

Young Bent's experience at Sand Creek made him such a sanguinary enemy of white people that his father disowned him and a price was put on his head. On one occasion he led a band of Dog Soldiers against Downer's stage station on the Smoky Hill road. By offering safe passage he lured eight men outside, then attacked them without warning. One man was killed and two captured, one of whom died under unspeakable torture.

"It was the beginning of a terrible career of betrayal, cruelty, and ravishment which would make Charles Bent, namesake of William's beloved brother, the worst desperado the plains have ever known."—David Lavender

In 1868, soon after making an unsuccessful attempt to kill his father, Charles was severely wounded in a battle with Pawnee Indians and died in a Cheyenne village.

(David Lavender, *Bent's Fort,* 1954; Walter O'Meara, *Daughters of the Country,* 1968.)

Bent, George (Son of William Bent). George Bent, son of William Bent and Owl Woman, was sent to school at Westport (present Kansas City, Missouri) and St. Louis, leaving at the beginning of the Civil War to join the Confederate Army. He was captured at Cornith in October 1862, and released when he agreed to rejoin his prominent father. A short time later he joined the Cheyennes, became a warrior, and participated in many Indian battles.

George was severely wounded during the Sand Creek massacre but managed to escape to rejoin the Cheyennes. He participated with his brother, Charles, in raids along the Platte River, but became aghast over his brother's cruelty and turned his attention to peace making. In 1867, he persuaded the Cheyennes to attend the Medicine Lodge Treaty negotiations. He lived the rest of his life with his mother's people and provided valuable information about the Cheyennes to ethnologists and historians.

(George Bird Grinnell, *The Fighting Cheyennes,* 1956; David Lavender, *Bent's Fort,* 1954; George E. Hyde, *Life of George Bent,* 1968.)

Bent, Robert. Robert Bent, youngest brother of the famous Indian traders Charles and William Bent, was born about 1816. He helped manage his brothers' freighting business until October 1841, when he left a wagon train on the Arkansas River to go buffalo hunting. He had not gone far when a Comanche war party killed and scalped him.

(David Lavender, *Bent's Fort,* 1954.)

Bent, William. William Bent was born in St. Louis on May 23, 1809. He was the son of Silas Bent, a native of Massachusetts who moved to St. Louis in 1804 and became a government surveyor and clerk. His brother and partner, Charles Bent, served as Governor of New Mexico.

William and Charles Bent met most of the famous frontiersmen and trappers in St. Louis and decided as youths to seek their fortunes in the fur trade. To succeed in this highly competitive and dangerous business, William learned many Plains Indian languages before going with trappers to the upper Missouri at age 15. In 1835, he married Owl Woman, daughter of the important Cheyenne chief, Gray Thunder. They had several sons and daughters who played prominent roles during the Indian wars of the 1860s.

The Bent brothers, unable to compete successfully in the Missouri River trade, shifted their operations southward. In 1833 they established a post on the Arkansas. (See Bent's Fort.) There, along the Santa Fe Trail, they traded extensively with the Cheyennes and to a lesser degree with the Comanches, Kiowas, and Apaches. In 1843, William built a post in the Texas Panhandle, but it was soon abandoned because of Indian hostility. (See Adobe Walls.) In 1846, he guided Kearney's column to Santa Fe.

When Owl Woman died in 1847, William married Yellow Woman, another daughter of Gray Thunder. He obtained a land grant from Mexico in the Arkansas Valley and founded a colony there, but it failed because of Indian hostility. He moved his headquarters in 1849 and again in 1859 while developing a successful freighting business and a ranch south of the Arkansas.

William Bent strove for many years to serve as guardian of the rights of the Cheyenne Indians. In 1858, convinced that the Cheyennes would be deprived of their entire homeland, he applied to the government to "clearly define the Indians' rights" by treaty negotiation. As a result, in 1859, he was appointed Indian agent. He urged the Cheyennes to avoid warfare with the whites and to consider agriculture as a means of survival.

In 1864, when a major Indian war erupted, Bent attempted to stop the fighting, but the Sand Creek massacre ended all hope of success. Two of his sons were with the Cheyennes at Sand Creek, and they became such fierce warriors that one of them threatened to kill him. (See Bent, Charles; Bent, George.) In 1865, Yellow Woman was killed by Pawnee Scouts. Two years later, Bent married Adalina Harvey, daughter of a trapper and a Blackfoot woman. He freighted government goods to army posts until his death of pneumonia on May 19, 1869.

(David Lavender, *Bent's Fort*, 1954; George Bird Grinnell, *The Fighting Cheyennes*, 1956; Frank McNitt, *The Indian Traders*, 1962.)

Benteen, Frederick. Frederick Benteen was born in Baltimore but moved with his family to St. Louis in 1849. He fought for the Union during the Civil War and became a captain of the Seventh Cavalry during the Indian wars that followed, participating in the Battles of the Washita, the Little Bighorn, and others. He was a brave soldier, but he frequently found himself in trouble for becoming drunk and disorderly. He disliked his superior officers in the Seventh, George A. Custer and Marcus Reno.

Just before the Battle of the Little Bighorn, Custer ordered Benteen and 125 troopers to explore the valleys and ridges west of the Indian villages. Benteen considered this division of forces to be a blunder, and after riding several miles without encountering Indians he turned back to follow Custer's trail. When reaching the bluffs he saw Reno's detachment fighting desperately and immediately went to their assistance, disregarding Custer's order to bring ammunition packs. Reno appeared to be incapable of effective command and Benteen provided the leadership that enabled most of the men with him to survive.

During the battle on the bluffs, wrote Bruce A. Rosenberg, Benteen walked "cooly up and down their lines, encouraging them, cautioning them to save ammunition, directing their fire." At one point he led a charge that startled the Indians nearest the bluff into a hasty retreat.

While Benteen probably saved Reno's men he may have doomed Custer by disobeying orders to deliver ammunition packs. But, as Evan S. Connell has contended, "if he had tried to carry out the order it is possible his three troops would have been hacked to pieces en route. Then Reno's weakened battalion surely would have collapsed, and when General Terry arrived he would count every single man of the Seventh Cavalry dead." Immediately after the massacre Benteen was blamed, but in time the wrath of the public shifted toward Reno.

(Evan S. Connell, *Son of the Morning Star,* 1984; Bruce A. Rosenberg, *Custer and the Epic of Defeat,* 1974; Frederic F. Van de Water, *Glory Hunter,* 1963.)

Benton, Fort, Montana. Fort Benton, originally established by the American Fur Company in 1846 at the present site of Fort Benton, Montana, was the scene of several Indian fights and treaty negotiations. On September 21, 1853, Governor Isaac Stevens met a delegation of Blackfoot chiefs at Fort Benton and gave them $600 worth of presents in exchange for their promise to make peace with the Nez Percé and Flathead Indians.

During the spring of 1865 some Blood warriors stole a part of the horse herd at Fort Benton. A few weeks later the traders retaliated by murdering three Bloods visiting the fort. These crimes were avenged two days later when Chief Calf Shirt and his warriors massacred ten woodcutters near the fort.

In 1865, United States commissioners negotiated a peace treaty between the Blackfeet and Gros Ventres at Fort Benton. The fort was leased by the government in 1869 and abandoned in 1881.

(John S. Ewers, *The Blackfeet,* 1961; George Bird Grinnell, *Beyond the Old Frontier,* 1976; Robert W. Frazer, *Forts of the West,* 1965.)

Bent's Fort. Bent's Fort, also known as Fort William, was established in 1833 near the present site of La Junta, Colorado, by Charles and Willian Bent and Ceran St. Vrain. William Bent supervised construction of the huge adobe fortress while his brother, Charles, and their partner, St. Vrain, managed enterprises in New Mexico. After the death of Charles and the retirement of St. Vrain, William became the sole owner of this most important trading post on the Great Plains.

Bent's Fort, described by Hiram Martin Chittenden as the "great cross roads station of the southwest," was a stopping place for travelers bound for the Rocky Mountains or along the Santa Fe Trail. In addition, it was a gathering place for thousands of Indians—Cheyennes, Kiowas, Comanches, Apaches—many of whom obtained their initial introduction to white civilization there and traded furs for goods that transformed their own cultures.

After the Mexican War, Bent's old fort lost its importance as the vanguard of the frontier, and Bent destroyed it in 1849 after failing to sell it to the United States Government. He built a new post forty miles down river in 1853 and leased it to the government in 1859. It became Fort Wise as a military installation.

(David Lavender, *Bent's Fort*, 1954; Hiram Martin Chittenden, *The American Fur Trade of the Far West*, 1954; George Bird Grinnell, *Beyond the Old Frontier*, 1976; George Frederick Ruxton, *Life in the Far West*, 1951.)

Berger, Joseph, Expedition. Joseph Berger was one of the earliest and most courageous trappers on the Great Plains and in the Rocky Mountains. He began his adventures among the Blackfoot Indians as an employee of the Hudson's Bay Company.

After twenty years on the Canadian side of the boundary he was recruited by Kenneth McKenzie to persuade the Blackfeet to visit Fort Union (North Dakota) to establish trade with the American Fur company.

In 1830, carrying an American flag, Berger led a small party of frontiersmen into the country of the hostile Blackfeet. When they encountered a Piegan war party Berger prevented his men from fleeing, displayed the flag, and addressed the Indians in their own language. He persuaded some one hundred Piegans to visit Fort Union, where McKenzie showered them with presents and arranged to establish a trading post in their country.

After Berger opened the Blackfoot trade to the Americans, he served as an American Fur Company interpreter. Business prospered until Alexander Harvey at Fort McKenzie fired a cannon that killed several visiting Blackfeet. As a result of this and other incidents detrimental to Indian relations, Berger and others attempted to murder Harvey in 1845. They succeeded only in driving him from the post.

(John C. Ewers, *The Blackfeet*, 1961; Hiram Martin Chittenden, *The American Fur Trade of the Far West*, 1954; Ray Allen Billington, *The Far Western Frontier*, 1956.)

Berthold, Fort, North Dakota. Fort Berthold was established by James Kipp in 1845 on the Missouri River near the mouth of the Little Missouri. Located near the Mandan villages, it was abandoned a few years later. In

1858, a new trading post named Fort Atkinson was established there. It was bought by the American Fur Company in 1862 and renamed Fort Berthold.

In 1864, troops occupied the fort to protect it against raids by the Sioux. In 1867, with the establishment of Fort Stevenson nearby, the military abandoned Fort Berthold, but the trading post continued to operate until 1874. In 1868, the fort became the agency for a large reservation occupied by the Mandan, Hidatsa, and Arikara Indians.

(Roy W. Meyer, *The Village Indians of the Upper Missouri*, 1977; Robert W. Frazer, *Forts of the West*, 1965.)

Big Bow, Kiowa Chief. Big Bow (Zipkiyah) was born about 1830 and lived until 1900. One of the most feared Kiowa raiders, he was accused of killing more Texas, Oklahoma, and Kansas settlers than any Indian of his time. He was a leader in the Warren wagon train massacre and in an attack on a government wagon train at the Howard Wells waystation in 1872.

In 1875, the progressive Kiowa chief, Kicking Bird, persuaded Big Bow to surrender, assuring him of amnesty in exchange for his agreement to serve as sergeant of Indian scouts. Kicking Bird sent him far out on the plains to contact the rest of the hostiles led by Lone Wolf, and he persuaded them to return to the reservation.

(Frederick J. Dockstader, *Great North American Indians*, 1977; Mildred P. Mayhall, *The Kiowas*, 1962; W. S. Nye, *Carbine & Lance*, 1969.)

Big Foot, Comanche Chief. Big Foot, a large and powerful Comanche raider, is remembered particularly for the events leading to his death. In 1842, Captain Shapley P. Ross and five companions trailed Big Foot and his warriors, who had stolen a horse herd in eastern Texas. They caught up with them near the present city of Temple and, because rain prevented the use of firearms, engaged them in hand-to-hand combat. After most of the Indians fled, Big Foot charged Ross on horseback. When both of their rifles failed to fire, they dismounted and fought with knives. Big Foot slipped in the wet grass and his thrust missed. Before he could rise, Ross seized him by the hair and drove his knife into his heart.

(James T. DeShields, *Border Wars of Texas*, 1976.)

Big Foot, Miniconjou Sioux Chief. Big Foot (Spotted Elk) is important in frontier history because of his death during the last large Indian engagement in the United States—the Wounded Knee Massacre in South Dakota. A war chief throughout the 1870s, he became a progressive and a diplomat soon afterward and strove to establish schools for Sioux children.

In 1890, Big Foot and many members of his band accepted the Ghost Dance religion and armed themselves to prepare for an attack by the U. S. Cavalry. He hoped to avoid war, but he could not control the ardor of his young braves when the medicine man, Yellow Bird, inflamed them to fight.

General Nelson A. Miles ordered Big Foot's arrest at the Cheyenne River Agency in mid-December, but the chief evaded the attempt and led his band toward the Pine Ridge Agency. On the way he became seriously ill with pneumonia and had to ride in a wagon. On December 27, scouts warned him that troops were waiting to arrest him at Wounded Knee Creek, but he was too ill to try to avoid them. The soldiers escorted the band to a camping place and sent a surgeon to examine the chief.

On December 29, the soldiers searched the camp for weapons and Yellow Bird persuaded warriors to resist. Hearing gunfire, Big Foot sat up to look over the side of the wagon and a soldier shot him to death. (See Wounded Knee Massacre.)

(Frederick J. Dockstader, *Great North American Indians*, 1977; Robert M. Utley, *The Last Days of the Sioux Nation*, 1963.)

Big Mound, Battle of. The Battle of Big Mound, North Dakota, was fought on July 24, 1863, when General H. H. Sibley encountered some 3,000 Sioux Indians hunting buffalo in the present Kidder County, North Dakota. Most of the Indians were friendly Sissetons, but they had been joined by Inkpaduta's murderous outlaws. Sibley sought to parley with the Sioux, but fighting erupted when one of Inkpaduta's warriors shot an Army surgeon to death. A running battle ensued and 13 Indians lost their lives.

(U. S. National Park Service, *Soldier and Brave*, 1963; Doane Robinson, *A History of the Dakota or Sioux Indians*, 1974.)

Big Mouth, Arapaho Chief. Big Mouth was an important Arapaho chief who signed the Treaty of Fort Wise on February 18, 1861. Unfortunately he became addicted to alcohol and in August he attacked a wagon train to obtain a supply. He was an active raider along the Santa Fe Trail until 1865 when he signed a peace treaty and promised to mend his ways. Three years later, when his people were attacked by General George A. Custer at the battle of the Washita, he took part in the destruction of Major Joel H. Elliott's 15-man detachment.

By 1871 Big Mouth became a progressive leader, a Christian, and a farmer on the Darlington Reservation. As a reward for persuading hostiles to surrender, he became a medal chief, and the largest house on the reservation was given to him.

(Virginia Cole Trenholm, *The Araphoes, Our People*, 1977.)

Big Mouth, Brulé Sioux Chief. Born about 1830, Big Mouth became an important Sioux chief and an opponent of Spotted Tail's policy of appeasing the whites. In 1873 or 1874, Spotted Tail determined to remove this threat to his authority and shot Big Mouth to death.

(Frederick J. Dockstader, *Great North American Indians,* 1977.)

Big Neck, Iowa Chief. Big Neck (Great Walker) was one of the most hostile Iowa chiefs during the early eighteenth century. In 1824, he signed a land cessation treaty, but he refused to leave the area. He and his band camped away from the agency and, in 1830, they killed three white men. He was arrested on murder charges, but the judge acquitted him because of evidence that the settlers had fired first. In 1831, he lost his life in a battle with the Sioux.

(Martha Royce Blaine, *The Ioway Indians,* 1979.)

Big Sandy Creek, Battle of. The Battle of Big Sandy Creek was fought in Kansas in September 1868, when Captain G. W. Graham led 36 Tenth Cavalry troopers along the stream in search of Cheyennes. The black cavalrymen (Buffalo Soldiers) were ambushed and badly outnumbered, and this was their first Indian fight, but they gave a good account of themselves, killing 11 Cheyennes and wounding 14.

(William H. Leckie, *The Buffalo Soldiers,* 1967.)

Big Snake, Ponca Chief. Big Snake was the brother of the famous Ponca chief, Standing Bear. Considering Big Snake to be a dangerous trouble maker, the tribal agent ordered him arrested on October 31, 1879. The chief resisted attempts by soldiers to handcuff him and they shot him to death. Humanitarians who supported Standing Bear's efforts to obtain justice for the Poncas charged that the United States Government plotted the death of Big Snake.

(Francis Paul Prucha, *American Indian Policy in Crisis,* 1976.)

Big Spotted Horse, Pawnee Chief. Big Spotted Horse (Asawuki Ladaho) became a prominent warrior by the age of 16 when he killed the fearsome Cheyenne, Alights-on-the-Clouds. In 1867, he was arrested by the Pawnee agent for horse theft but regained his freedom after six months when prosecutors failed to find a law prohibiting Indians from stealing horses from other Indians. In 1870, he served the Army as a member of the Pawnee Scouts. Three years later he was shot to death by Texas cowboys while trying to steal horses.

(George S. Hyde, *The Pawnee Indians,* 1974.)

Big Tree, Kiowa Chief. Big Tree (Adoeette), born about 1847, was one of the most daring raiders on the southern plains. In 1870, he led 80 warriors in an attempt to run off Fort Sill's entire horse herd, but the plan was thwarted when his men attacked a woodcutter's camp and alerted the soldiers. In 1871, he, along with Satanta and Satank, led the attack on the Warren wagon train, in which seven teamsters were slain. Convicted of murder and imprisoned in Texas, he spent his time studying white civilization. When pardoned in 1873, he became a Christian and a deacon of the Rainy Mountain Mission. He died on November 13, 1929.

(Mildred P. Mayhall, *The Kiowas,* 1962; Benjamin Capps, *The Warren Wagontrain Raid,* 1974; W. S. Nye, *Carbine & Lance,* 1969.)

Big White, Mandan Chief. Big White (Shahaka), chief of the larger of the two Mandan villages, accompanied Lewis and Clark to Washington during their return from the Pacific coast in 1806. He received an assurance of safe escort back to his village. Ensign Nathaniel Pryor and 11 soldiers and 42 trappers accompanied him on his way back up the Missouri in May 1807. They were not far from the Mandan villages when, on September 9, a large Arikara and Sioux war party attacked their boat, killing six men. Pryor ordered a return to St. Louis.

Big White remained in St. Louis until the spring of 1809; then, Jean Pierre Chouteau recruited 125 men as an escort for the chief. This force was too strong for the Arikaras, and Big White finally rejoined his people. He told them such amazing stories about what he had seen that many refused to believe him. He is said to have wished to return to white civilization.

(Hiram Martin Chittenden, *The American Fur Trade of the Far West,* 1954; Roy W. Meyer, *The Village Indians of the Upper Missouri,* 1977; F. W. Hodge, *ed., Handbook of American Indians, II,* 1912.)

Birch Coulee, Battle of. The Battle of Birch Coulee, one of the fiercest engagements of the Sioux uprising of 1862, was fought on September 2-3 near the present site of Morton, Minnesota. Historians differ as to the officer in command of the 170 volunteer soldiers, Major Joseph R. Brown or Captain Hiram Grant. C. M. Oehler asserts that Grant was in command and that Brown merely accompanied the force to search for missing relatives. Brown, a former Indian agent and an experienced Indian fighter, believed that Grant failed to choose a suitable camp site on September 1, but he refrained from expressing that opinion to the inexperienced Grant.

Chief Little Crow recognized that the terrain was perfect for a surprise attack while the soldiers slept. The Sioux surrounded the camp in the dark and rushed before dawn. An alert sentry fired, waking the soldiers, but several died before they could take refuge behind overturned wagons. "The Sioux," wrote Oehler, "poured into the camp such a storm of bullets that nearly every horse was killed or disabled, and annihilation threatened the whole command." Fortunately, General H. H. Sibley heard the sound of battle and dispatched reinforcements to the scene. The Indians withdrew 31 hours after the attack began.

The volunteers had 13 men killed and 47 wounded. Sioux casualties were two killed and five or six wounded.

(C.M. Oehler, *The Great Sioux Uprising,* 1959; Paul I. Wellman, *Death on Horseback,* 1947; U. S. National Park Service, *Soldier & Brave,* 1963.)

Bird, Blackfoot Chief. Bird was described by Hiram Martin Chittenden as "a half Indian and treacherous, very dangerous man." A former employee of the Hudson's Bay Company and the American Fur Company, he had been captured by the Blackfeet, joined them as a warrior, and rose to the position of a chief of that powerful tribe. About 1835, he led a party of Blackfeet to the Snake River opposite Fort Hall, persuaded Antoine Godin to cross the river to parley, ordered a warrior to shoot him in the back, and scalped him while still alive. The deed was in revenge for the death of a Blackfoot chief at the hands of Godin under a flag of truce as a preliminary to the Battle of Pierre's Hole.

(Hiram Martin Chittenden, *The American Fur Trade of the Far West,* 1954.)

Bird, John. John Bird was born in Tennessee and fought under Andrew Jackson in the War of 1812. An a member of Stephen F. Austin's colony he brought his family to the present Burleson County, Texas, in 1831. Serving as militia captain he proved to be an able Indian fighter when he led a successful campaign against the Comanches on the Brazos River in 1832.

After fighting in the Texas Revolution, Bird became a Ranger captain. In 1839, settlers of central Texas lived in such constant fear of Indian attack that Bird and 50 Rangers were ordered to provide protection. On May 26, they encountered 240 Comanche warriors near the present location of Belton and took refuge in a ravine. The Indians, led by Buffalo Hump, charged the ravine repeatedly but were driven back with heavy losses. Both Bird and Buffalo Hump were among the slain, and six Rangers were killed or wounded. The Comanches could have slain them all, but only at a cost that their leaders would not accept. After sunset they withdrew from the battlefield.

"This battle, often spoken of as 'Bird's Victory,' was Pyrrhic, and further served to set the Indians in commotion for more depredations on the frontier."—Walter Prescott Webb

(Walter Prescott Webb, *The Texas Rangers,* 1965; James T. DeShields, *Border Wars of Texas,* 1976; T. R. Fehrenbach, *The Comanches,* 1983; John Holland Jenkins, *Recollections of Early Texas,* 1958.)

Bird's Fort, Texas. During the winter of 1840-41, Jonathan Bird established a fort near the present site of Arlington, Texas, on the main fork of the Trinity River. It served as a Ranger headquarters offering protection from Indians to families settling in the vicinity. On September 29, 1843, chiefs of nine tribes negotiated treaties at Bird's Fort with commissioners Edward H. Tarrant and George H. Terrell.

(James T. DeShields, *Border Wars of Texas*, 1976; *Handbook of Texas, I*, 1952.)

Black Bear, Arapaho Chief. Black Bear (Wattoma) was a prominent war chief in Wyoming during the Indian conflicts of the 1860s, including the Battle of Tongue River on August 29, 1865. Afterward he signed several Arapaho-United States peace treaties.

In 1870, Black Bear was murdered by miners who invaded his peaceful Arapaho camp. His wife and child were taken captive.

(Virginia Cole Trenholm, *The Arapahoes, Our People*, 1970; George Bird Grinnell, *The Fighting Cheyennes*, 1956; Ruby E. Wilson, *Frank J. North*, 1984.)

Black Beaver, Delaware Scout. Black Beaver, a member of the Delaware Nation, was born in 1806 at Belleville, Illinois. Most of his life was spent as a hunter and guide on the Great Plains and in the Rocky Mountains. He spoke English, French, and Spanish as well as eight Indian languages. In 1834, he guided Colonel Henry Dodge and his dragoons to visit the tribes on the Red River. During the gold rush he guided seven parties of miners to California. When Federal troops were compelled to abandon forts in the Indian Territory in 1861, he guided them to safety.

Black Beaver became a close friend of the Plains Indians and advised them in their dealings with the military. He died at Anadarko on May 8, 1880.

> Black Beaver became a legend in his own time, due largely to the tremendous area of the continent which he had covered, his wide experience with both races, and his own personality as a skilled negotiator, scout, and guide—all of which demanded bravery.—Frederick J. Dockstader

(Frederick J. Dockstader, *Great North American Indians*, 1977; Grant Foreman, *Advancing the Frontier*, 1933.)

Black Buffalo, Minneconjou Sioux Chief. Black Buffalo (Tatonka Sapa), a capricious Minneconjou chief, accompanied the Lewis and Clark Expedition during a portion of their journey to the Pacific. As a reward for his services as guide he received a medal, a flag, and a military uniform.

After Lewis and Clark returned from the Pacific they took a Mandan chief, Big White, to visit Washington, D. C. While escorting him up the

Missouri on his voyage home to his village, Ensign Nathaniel Pryor's boat was attacked by Black Buffalo and an Arikara and Sioux war party and compelled to return down river. In May 1811, Black Buffalo attempted to prevent traders from reaching the Arikara village. He was persuaded by Manuel Lisa to support the United States during the War of 1812 and, after the war, Lisa brought him to Portage des Sioux, where he died.

(Doane Robinson, *A History of the Dakota or Sioux Indians,* 1974; Bernard De Voto, ed., *The Journals of Lewis and Clark,* 1953.)

Black Cat, Mandan Chief. Black Cat (Posecopsahe) was chief of the northern Mandan villages when Lewis and Clark wintered there in 1804-05. The explorers were so favorably impressed that Meriwether Lewis reported "this man possesses more integrity, firmness, intelligence . . . than, any Indian I have met within this quarter."

(Roy W. Meyer, *The Village Indians of the Upper Missouri,* 1977; Bernard De Voto, ed., *The Journals of Lewis and Clark,* 1953.)

Black Elk, Oglala Sioux Medicine Man. Black Elk (Ekhaka Sapa) was born in 1863 and died on August 17, 1950. During his long and incongruous career, he was a warrior with Crazy Horse and Sitting Bull, a performer in Buffalo Bill Cody's Wild West Show, and an advocate of the Ghost Dance religion. Above all, asserted Frederick J. Dockstader, "Black Elk had an uncanny ability to predict certain aspects of the future, and it is said that many times he saved his people from tragedy by timely warning."

(Frederick J. Dockstader, *Great North American Indians,* 1977.)

Black Hills Expedition, 1874. In 1874, General George A. Custer led a military expedition into the Black Hills in violation of the Treaty of Fort Laramie. General Philip Sheridan wanted a fort established in the area in order to deprive the Sioux of sanctuary after their attacks on Nebraska settlers. The settlers considered the expedition an attempt to find gold, and they waited only for the discovery before flocking into the forbidden territory.

On July 24, Custer's forces surrounded a small Sioux camp and invited five warriors to visit the column. After accepting gifts the Sioux became frightened and the soldiers opened fire when they fled. One warrior was shot and another seized to serve as a guide. In spite of this provocation the Sioux refrained from reprisal.

After a rather uneventful reconnaissance, Custer returned to his base at Fort Abraham Lincoln at the end of August. He confirmed the presence of gold and miners began invading the Black Hills.

(Donald Jackson, *Custer's Gold,* 1966; Evan S. Connell, *Son of the Morning Star,*
1984; Frederic F. Van de Water, *Glory Hunter,* 1963.)

Black Horse, Comanche Chief. Black Horse (Tu-ukumah), a subchief
of Quanah Parker's Kwahadi Comanches, was the leader of the last Indian
raids in Texas. In 1875, after Quanah's surrender, Black Horse was
imprisoned in Fort Marion, Florida. He returned to his people in Oklahoma within two years, however, for in February 1877, he and his
followers began attacking buffalo hunters' camps in the Texas Panhandle.
On February 22, they killed Marshall Soule. His friends retaliated by
attacking the Comanche camp in Thompson Canyon on March 18. After
these hostilities, called the Hunters' War, Black Horse retreated to the
reservation at Fort Sill.

In June 1879, Black Horse led 25 warriors on the last Comanche raid
into Texas. The buffalo had been exterminated around the reservation and
the hungry Comanches wanted to kill game rather than settlers. Near the
present site of Big Spring, they shot several ranch horses and were eating
them when suddenly attacked by seven Texas Rangers. One Ranger was
killed and another wounded before they withdrew, leaving the Indians in
control of the field.

Black Horse died at Cache, Oklahoma, about 1900.

(*Handbook of Texas, I,* 1952; W. S. Nye, *Carbine & Lance,* 1969; Paul I. Wellman,
Death on Horseback, 1947; Mildred P. Mayhall, *Indian Wars of Texas,* 1965.)

Black Kettle, Cheyenne Chief. Black Kettle, one of the most unfortunate
chiefs in the history of the Indian wars of the West, was born in 1803. His
Indian name was Moketavato. During his youth he was a noted warrior
against both enemy Indians and whites, but he signed the Fort Wise Treaty
in 1861, and, afterward, he attempted to maintain peaceful relations with
white settlers and soldiers.

During the Sand Creek massacre of 1864, Black Kettle and his wife
advanced toward Chivington's Colorado Volunteers, frantically waving
an American flag. He remained out in front of the village when the battle
began, but, finally abandoning the attempt to prevent the slaughter, he ran
for his life. Both he and his wife survived the massacre, but she was
wounded nine times.

In spite of this murderous attack, Black Kettle continued to believe
that Indians and white people could live peacefully in the same territory.
In 1865, he led his followers to the Arkansas River to avoid hostilities
when other Cheyenne bands raided the Platte River region. In 1867, he
signed the Treaty of Medicine Lodge and moved his people to a reservation at Fort Larned, Kansas.

In 1868, Black Kettle and his followers joined a large Indian encampment in the Washita Valley. There, on November 27, they were attacked

by General George A. Custer. Once more Black Kettle attempted to prevent the slaughter by waving an American flag, but he and his wife were among the first to be shot down. He was 65 years old at the time of his death.

"Black Kettle was a striking example of a consistently friendly Indian, who, because he was friendly and so because his whereabouts was usually known, was punished for the acts of people whom it was supposed he could control."—George Bird Grinnell

(George Bird Grinnell, *The Fighting Cheyennes*, 1956; Stan Hoig, *Peace Chiefs of the Cheyennes*, 1980; Evan S. Connell, *Son of the Morning Star*, 1984; John Tebbel and Keith Jennison, *The American Indian Wars*, 1960.)

Blackbird, Omaha Chief. For thirty years, beginning about 1770, Blackbird was the bane of French traders on the Missouri, compelling them to unload their boats and demanding that they sell their goods on his terms. He got along well, however, with Spanish officials at St. Louis, who gave him the largest medal every presented to a chief on the Missouri when he haughtily refused the regular size.

In 1775, Blackbird obtained British goods and firearms from the Sac and Fox Indians. He traded a portion of these to the Pawnees for horses. Until his death about 1800 he was the dominant figure of Nebraska Indian-white relations.

(George E. Hyde, *The Pawnee Indians*, 1974.)

Blackfoot Indians. The Blackfoot (Siksika) Indians, a large and powerful Algonquian confederacy, consisted of three politically independent but socially and linguistically common tribes, the Blackfoot proper (or Siksika), the Bloods (or Kainah), and the Piegans. During the period of early white contact, they occupied an immense area from the Missouri River headwaters in Montana to the North Saskatchewan River in Canada, and from the base of the Rocky Mountains to a longitude of 105 degrees west. In 1780, they numbered about 15,000, but the smallpox epidemics of the late eighteenth and early nineteenth centuries reduced their population by half.

The life-style of the Blackfeet changed rapidly with the introduction of firearms acquired from the Crees, Assiniboins, and other tribes that traded with the French at Montreal or the English on Hudson Bay. In the 1730s, the French established posts near the Blackfoot country, and in 1781 the British built Buckingham House to facilitate trade. When they acquired large numbers of horses from tribes nearer Mexico, the Blackfeet became some of the most skillful buffalo hunters on the plains.

The first contact between the Blackfeet and Americans led to lasting hostility. In 1806, they had a brief encounter with the Lewis and Clark Expedition. Lewis and a few of his men camped with a small Blackfoot band, and during the night the Indians tried to steal their rifles. One of the explorers stabbed a Blackfoot to death, and when the Indians attempted to run off his horses, Lewis shot a warrior with his pistol. Afterward the Blackfeet traded extensively with the British, but they resisted attempts of American trappers to enter their territory. During the 1820s, they killed 40 to 50 Americans annually. Finally, in 1830, a British trader, Joseph Berger, was employed by the American Fur Company to break the Blackfoot barrier. (See McKenzie, Kenneth.) The attempt succeeded, and Fort Piegan was established at the mouth of the Marias in 1831. It was replaced by Fort McKenzie in 1832, and trade was profitable until 1843, when some traders fired a cannon at visiting Blackfeet. (See Chardon, François; Harvey, Alexander.) A year later, Alexander Culbertson and his Blackfoot wife managed to restore peace and resume trade relations with the tribe.

During the 1850s and 1860s, the Blackfeet were stricken by several severe smallpox epidemics. With population greatly reduced, their raiding proclivities were held in check. By 1870, however, sporadic attacks on miners and ranchers resumed. These raids led General Alfred Sully to launch a campaign against them that resulted in the deaths of 173 Piegans and the capture of 140 women and children. (See Marias Massacre.) As a result the Blackfeet begged for peace and never again waged war against the United States Army. Their descendants live on reservations in Canada and the United States.

(John C. Ewers, *The Blackfeet,* 1961; Hiram Martin Chittenden, *The American Fur Trade of the Far West,* 1954; William Thomas Hamilton, *My Sixty Years on the Plains,* 1905; Hugh A. Dempsey, *Red Crow,* 1980; Adolf Hungry Wolf, *The Blood People,* 1977; Oscar Lewis, *The Effects of White Contact Upon Blackfoot Culture,* 1966; Richard Lancaster, *Piegan,* 1966.)

Blinn, Clara. See Blynn, Clara

Blood Indians. See Blackfoot Indians

Bloody Knife, Arikara Scout. Bloody Knife, whose father was a Sioux and mother an Arikara, became one of the most effective scouts for the Army on the Great Plains. As chief of Indian scouts at Fort Abraham Lincoln, he was Custer's favorite warrior, guiding his expedition to the Black Hills in 1874 and to the Little Bighorn in 1876.

Before the Battle of the Little Bighorn, Bloody Knife warned Custer that there were too many Indians for the cavalry to conquer. The general laughed at his fears and sent him with Major Marcus Reno to open the attack. He was riding at Reno's side when a Sioux marksman shot him in the head, spattering his brains in Reno's face and greatly unnerving that officer.

(Evan S. Connell, *Son of the Morning Star,* 1984; W. A. Graham, *The Story of the Little Big Horn,* 1941; F. W. Hodge, ed., *Handbook of American Indians, I,* 1912; Frederic F. Van de Water, *Glory Hunter,* 1963.)

Bluewater, Battle of. See Ash Hollow, Battle of

Blynn, Clara, Captivity of. Mrs. Clara Blynn (Blinn) was captured with her two-year-old son, Willie, near Fort Lyon when Arapaho and Cheyenne Indians attacked a wagon train in October, 1868. General W. B. Hazen, Indian agent, attempted to redeem them and had almost completed negotiations when Custer's campaign on the Washita led to their deaths.

At the instigation of Jenny Griffinstein, wife of the Fort Cobb trader, a friendly Indian visited the Cheyennes to see if Mrs. Blynn could be helped. She took the opportunity to send a message containing the following plea:

Saturday, November 7, 1868

Kind Friend:—Whoever you may be, I thank you for your kindness to me and my child. . . . If you could only buy us of the Indians with ponies, or anything, and let me come stay with you until I could get word to my friends . . . I am afraid that they will sell us into slavery in Mexico. If you can do nothing write W. T. Harrington, Ottawa, Franklin County Kansas, my father, below Fort Lyon. I cannot tell whether they killed my husband or not.

This was the captive's last contact with those who sought to redeem her. On November 27, Custer attacked the Indian camp on the Washita. Her captors shot her twice in the head, and Willie died with a crushed skull.

(W. S. Nye, *Carbine & Lance,* 1964; Carl Coke Rister, *Border Captives,* 1940; Evan S. Connell, *Son of the Morning Star,* 1984.)

Boone, Nathan. Colonel Nathan Boone, youngest son of Daniel Boone, was born in Kentucky in 1780 and moved to Missouri during his youth. He fought in the War of 1812 and the Blackhawk War, entering the regular army as a captain of rangers during the latter conflict. For the next twenty years he served on the Southwestern plains, principally as a guardian of the Santa Fe Trail and as a diplomat in arranging conferences with Indian tribes. He retired in 1853 and died in 1857.

(Grant Foreman, *Indians & Pioneers,* 1936.)

Botalye, Kiowa Warrior. Botalye gained unprecedented renown among the Kiowas because of an exploit he performed as a 17-year-old apprentice warrior. On September 9, 1874, Kiowas attacked an army wagon train transporting supplies to Colonel Nelson A. Miles. In a siege that lasted three days, Botalye charged the train on horseback four times while every defender tried to bring him down. Bullets bounced off of his saddle horn and knocked feathers from his head, but he remained unhurt. Each time he returned to the Indian line, the chiefs attempted to restrain him, but he insisted on making more charges than any Kiowa had ever attempted. When he returned safely from the fourth charge, Chief Satanta admitted that even he could not have done what the youthful Botalye (who was half Mexican) had accomplished. Reinforcements rescued the wagon train on September 14.

Afterward, Botalye became a medicine man. In 1881, he convinced Kiowas that he could bring the sun down from the sky, and his reputation suffered severely when it remained in its place.

(W. S. Nye, *Carbine & Lance*, 1969; Mildred P. Mayhall, *The Kiowas*, 1962.)

Bourgmont, Étienne Veniard de. Bourgmont, son of a physician, was born in France about 1680 and sailed to Canada at an early age. He became an ensign in the French Army and commanded Fort Detroit in 1705. He deserted in 1707 and lived with the Osages on the Missouri River for ten years. He fathered several Osage children before marrying the daughter of a Missouri Indian chief. During this interval he became a trader to the Pawnees and neighboring tribes. He explored the Platte River region, and his reports about routes to the New Mexico mines led to the extension of French influence among the southwestern tribes.

In 1723 Bourgmont established Fort Orleans among the Missouri Indians, near the mouth of the Grand River. During the following year he restored peaceful relations between the Kansa and Padouca Indians. His efforts to open trade with the Spanish failed, but he paved the way for French commerce with the Indians of the southwest. In 1725, he conveyed chiefs of several tribes to France, and he never returned to America.

(John Joseph Mathews, *The Osages*, 1961; George E. Hyde, *The Pawnee Indians*, 1974.)

Bouyer, Mitch. Mitch Bouyer, son of a French father and a Santee Sioux mother, was one of the most prominent Army scouts in the West. A protégé of Jim Bridger, he knew the Sioux country like the back of his hand. The Indians hated him, calling him Two Bodies because he chose to live with the whites, and they tried to kill him many times.

Bouyer served as Custer's scout during his march to the Little Bighorn. He warned the general to no avail that there were too many

Indians for the Seventh Cavalry to conquer. Custer sent him with Reno's column, and he was mortally wounded during the initial attack. After the battle the Sioux found him alive. His back broken, he begged the Indians to finish him, and they shot him to death.

(Evan S. Connell, *Son of the Morning Star,* 1984; Frederic F. Van de Water, *Glory Hunter,* 1963.)

Box Elder Creek Raid. In the spring of 1864, a Cheyenne and Sioux war party attacked ranches along Box Elder Creek, near Denver, killing four members of the Hungate family. The mutilated bodies were displayed in Denver, causing the citizens to call for the annihilation of all Indians.

(George Bird Grinnell, *The Fighting Cheyenne,* 1956; John Tebbel and Keith Jennison, *The American Indian Wars,* 1960.)

Box, James, Family of. In September 1866, James Box, a Texas rancher, was killed by Kiowa Indians and his wife and four daughters were captured. The Indians brained the youngest child when she refused to stop crying. Shortly thereafter, Satanta surrendered Mrs. Box and her daughters Margaret (17), Josephine (13), and Ida (7), for a ransom of $2,000. After their release a reporter for *Harper's Weekly* interviewed Mrs. Box and described their experiences as follows:

> The mother and two eldest daughters were subjected to the most unheard of cruelties and outrages by their brutal captors, while the youngest, owing to her youth, although she shared a fate less horrible, was, nevertheless, most barbarously used. The child, unable to understand the commands of her fiendish taskmaster, was placed with her feet on live coals until they were literally roasted. This was the pastime of the squaws.

(Carl Coke Rister, *Border Captives,* 1940; Mildred P. Mayhall, *The Kiowas,* 1962.)

Bozeman Trail. John Bozeman blazed the trail named for him between 1863 and 1865 to provide the best route to the Montana gold mines. It led from Julesburg, Colorado, to the eastern base of the Bighorn Mountains, crossed the Oregon Trail near the present site of Casper, Wyoming, and extended to the Yellowstone River before ending at Virginia City. The trail transversed the heart of the Sioux hunting grounds and aroused the resistance of Chief Red Cloud. In 1866, the Sioux and Cheyennes virtually closed the trail, only heavily guarded wagon trains being able to fight their way to deliver supplies to Forts Phil Kearny, Reno, and C. F. Smith. (See Fetterman Massacre; Hayfield Fight; Wagon Box Fight.) The forts were destroyed and the trail abandoned upon Red Cloud's demand during the negotiation of the Treaty of Fort Laramie in 1868.

(U. S. National Park Service, *Soldier and Brave*, 1963.)

Bradford, William, Major, U. S. Army. Major William Bradford, a distinguished veteran of the War of 1812, founded Fort Smith, Arkansas, in 1817. Among his most difficult duties was the assignment to stop the brutal warfare between the Southern Indians, recently removed from their homelands, and Plains tribes. In 1818, he managed to halt a war by guaranteeing that the Cherokees would release captive Osages.

Bradford's second objective was to remove white squatters from Indian lands. He made a sincere effort, but some of the worst offenders evaded him. He was transferred to Natchitoches, Louisiana, in 1822 and died in 1826 of wounds he received at Fort Meigs.

(Grant Foreman, *Indians & Pioneers*, 1936; John Joseph Mathews, *The Osages*, 1961.)

Bright Eyes, Omaha Indian Rights Activist. See La Flesche, Susette

Brown, Frederick H. Captain Frederick Brown, a native of Ohio, was stationed at Fort Phil Kearney in December 1866, during the siege of that post by the Sioux chief Red Cloud. Margaret Carrington, wife of the fort's commanding officer, asserted that Brown became so obsessed with determination to kill Red Cloud that he disobeyed orders by accompanying Colonel Fetterman's force without authorization. (See Fetterman Massacre.) It is believed that he and Fetterman deliberately shot each other to death when the battle was lost in order to avoid the torture awaiting them as Indian captives.

(Margaret Carrington, *Ab-Sa-Ra-Ka, Home of the Crows*, 1868; Paul I. Wellman, *Death on Horseback*, 1947; Richard H. Dillon, *North American Indian Wars*, 1983.)

Brown, John Henry. John Henry Brown was born in Missouri on October 20, 1820. Like his father, Henry Stevenson Brown, he was an early Texas settler and prominent Indian fighter. During the Battle of Plum Creek in 1840 he killed the Comanche chief who was second in command in hand-to-hand combat. He served in John Coffee Hays' Texas Ranger Company west of San Antonio in 1842, participating in several Indian engagements. Afterwards he became a public official, a military officer, and a newspaper editor, publishing many accounts of the Texas Indian wars. He died in 1895.

(J. W. Wilbarger, *Indian Depredations in Texas*, 1985; *Handbook of Texas, I*, 1952.)

Brown, Joseph R. Major Joseph R. Brown, married to a Sioux and father of her nine children, was Indian agent to that tribe during the Spirit Lake massacre of 1857 and sent a guide to help in pursuit of Inkpaduta's outlaws. He was replaced as agent in 1861 and became a prosperous trader. Away from home at the onset of the Minnesota Sioux uprising of 1862, he was unaware for some time that the lives of his wife and children had been spared by Chief Little Crow.

When Captain Hiram Grant's detachment was sent in search of the hostiles, Brown accompanied them in an attempt to ascertain the fate of his family. He was wounded when Grant's force was attacked. (See Birch Coulee, Battle of.) After the defeat of the Sioux, Brown was designated to identify the warriors who were condemned to death by order of President Lincoln.

(C. M. Oehler, *The Great Sioux Uprising,* 1959; Doane Robinson, *A History of the Dakota or Sioux Indians,* 1974.)

Brulé Sioux Indians. The Brulés were a subtribe of the Teton Sioux. During the nineteenth century, they roamed over the vast area drained by the upper Missouri, Teton, White, and Niobara rivers. They were generally friendly to white people because of the influence of chiefs Makatozaza and Swift Bear until Lieutenant John Grattan attacked them in 1854. Afterward they participated in battles from Beecher's Island to Wounded Knee.

In 1868, they agreed to live at the Spotted Tail agency. (See Spotted Tail, Brulé Sioux chief.)

(F. W. Hodge, ed., *Handbook of American Indians, I,* 1912; Robert M. Utley, *The Last Days of the Sioux Nation,* 1963.)

Bucheur, Maria, Captivity of. Maria Bucheur was born on the Frio River in Texas (then part of Mexico) of French parents who had established a trading post among the Comanches. At the age of seven she and her ten-year-old brother, Louis, were captured by the Comanches and compelled to watch while their parents were burned at the stake in retribution for the massacre of Indians by Mexicans on the Rio Grande. The children were adopted by families of different bands and never saw each other again.

Maria grew up among the Comanches and became greatly assimilated. During a visit to a trading post on the Red River, she attracted the attention of an influential Delaware Indian chief named Kistalwa. He purchased her from the Comanches and married her. They had two sons, Black Wolf and Light-Foot. The latter became a convert to Christianity and eventually a Jesuit priest.

(P. J. De Smet, *Western Missions and Missionaries,* 1859.)

Buell, George, Campaigns. In February 1874, Lieutenant Colonel George Buell, commanding officer of Fort Griffin, Texas, led an expedition against the Comanche Indians on the Double Mountain Fork of the Brazos River. Members of his Eleventh Infantry column killed 11 warriors. As a result, the hostiles redoubled their raids.

Buell took the field against the Kiowas in September 1874. In October he destroyed several Kiowa villages on the Salt Fork of the Brazos. Only 11 warriors were killed, but he burned almost 600 lodges and destroyed all of their winter food stores. "The grim, relentless pursuit broke . . . the will to resist of hundreds of Kiowas, Commanches, and Cheyennes."— William H. Leckie

(William H. Leckie, *The Buffalo Soldiers*, 1967; Carl Coke Rister, *Fort Griffin on the Texas Frontier*, 1956.)

Buffalo Hump, Comanche Chiefs. There were at least two prominent Comanche chiefs named Buffalo Hump who participated in the Texas Indian wars during the first half of the nineteenth century. It has been difficult for historians to distinguish between them. (See *Handbook of Texas, I.*)

A chief Buffalo Hump annoyed Stephen F. Austin's colonists on Barton's Creek in 1829 by forcing them to feed his warriors while they were fighting the Tonkawa Indians. He probably was the same chief slain by Ranger leader James Robinett in Bird's battle with the Comanches on May 26, 1839. (See Bird, John.)

Another Chief Buffalo Hump led the destructive raids on Victoria and Linnville, Texas, in August 1840, and fought the Battle of Plum Creek during their retreat. (See Linnville, Texas; Plum Creek, Battle of.) He may have been the Comanche chief who signed a peace treaty with John O. Meusebach on the San Saba River, March 2, 1847.

In 1848 a chief Buffalo Hump refused a demand by Indian Agent Robert S. Neighbors to stop leading war parties into Mexico. He declared that a Mexican officer had seized his daughter and refused to restore her to the tribe. This chief probably was the same Buffalo Hump who guided Neighbors during his explorations of western Texas in 1849. He participated in the Battle of Rush Spring in 1858.

(John Salmon Ford, *Rip Ford's Texas*, 1963; Mildred P. Mayhall, *Indian Wars of Texas*, 1965; James T. De Shields, *Border Wars of Texas*, 1976.)

Buffalo Hunters' War. See Black Horse, Comanche Chief

Buffalo Lake, Battle of. On July 26, 1863, General H. H. Sibley fought the Battle of Buffalo Lake against the Sisseton and Teton Sioux near the Missouri River in Central North Dakota. The Indians charged the soldiers on horseback, but they were driven back by howitzer fire. Three Indians were killed and several wounded before they withdrew from the field.

(Doane Robinson, *A History of the Dakota or Sioux Indians*, 1974; U. S. National Park Service, *Soldier and Brave*, 1963.)

Buffalo Wallow Fight. In September, 1874, Billy Dixon, the hero of Adobe Walls, with another scout and four soldiers were carrying dispatches for General Nelson A. Miles from McClellan Creek, Texas, to Camp Supply, Oklahoma, when attacked by a hundred Comanches and Kiowas. Four of them were wounded in the first fire, but they managed to dig a hole for partial protection and stood off the Indians during the entire day. After dark, Dixon slipped through the Indian lines and located a detachment of soldiers under Major William Price, who came to their rescue. Price reported as follows: "The suffering of these men was extreme and their condition fearful. In a hole six feet square and a half deep were one corpse and three badly wounded men, the hole half full of water and blood, and they had to keep bailing it out . . ."

(W. S. Nye, *Carbine & Lance*, 1969.)

Bull Bear, Cheyenne Chief. Bull Bear was the leader of the Cheyenne Dog Soldiers, a military society that became famous during the wars of the 1860s for the bravery of its leadership. He was less warlike than many of his followers, and in 1867 he saved the life of General W. S. Hancock when Roman Nose intended to shoot him down at the head of his troops. He was determined, however, to preserve the Indian way of life, responding to government agents who urged the tribe to live like white men that the Cheyennes had not yet sunk that low.

(George Bird Grinnell, *The Fighting Cheyennes*, 1956; Virginia Cole Trenholm, *The Arapahoes, Our People*, 1970.)

Bull Bear, Comanche Chief. See Parraocoom, Comanche Chief

Burleson, Edward, Jr., Fight on the Nueces. See Lyons, Warren

Burnet, David G., Indian Experiences. David G. Burnet, a native of New Jersey who eventually became President of the Republic of Texas, established a trading post at Natchitoches, Louisiana, in 1813. There he developed tuberculosis, and his business became bankrupt. Ill and distraught, he rode westward into the Texas wilderness in 1817, finally falling from his horse on the bank of the Colorado River. Comanche Indians found him, nursed him back to health, and treated him kindly until he left them in 1819.

In 1839, while serving as Vice-President of the Republic of Texas, Burnet was appointed by President Lamar to serve on a commission to seek the voluntary removal of the Cherokee Indians from Texas. The result was a battle on July 15, 1839, in which Burnet was wounded during the defeat of the Indians.

(*Handbook of Texas, I*, 1952; James T. De Shields, *Border Wars of Texas*, 1976.)

Caldwell, Mathew. Mathew (Old Paint) Caldwell was born in Kentucky about 1798 and settled in Texas in 1831. He signed the Texas Declaration of Independence and fought in the revolution against Mexico. After Texas gained her independence, he was appointed captain of a company of Rangers and became one of her foremost Indian fighters.

Caldwell was wounded by the Comanche Indians during a fight in the courthouse at San Antonio in March, 1840. (See Council House Fight.) He was unarmed when confronted by an Indian with a bow and arrow in the street. He picked up a rock and struck the Indian in the face, stunning him slightly. He continued to pelt him with stones until John C. Morris appeared on the scene and killed the Comanche with a pistol. On August 12, 1840, he played an important part in the Battle of Plum Creek, one of the major events in the history of Indian warfare. He was captured during the Texan Sante Fe Expedition and spent some time in a Mexican prison. After his release he defeated a Mexican army at the Battle of the Salado.

He died in 1842.

(Walter Prescott Webb, *The Texas Rangers,* 1965; *Handbook of Texas I,* 1952; James T. De Shields, *Border Wars of Texas,* 1976.)

Calf Shirt, Blackfoot Chief. Calf Shirt, chief of the Blood division of the Blackfoot nation, signed a peace treaty with government negotiators in 1855. He kept the peace for ten years, but in 1865, when white traders murdered three members of the tribe at Fort Benton, he exacted revenge by killing twelve woodcutters near the mouth of the Marias.

A huge, powerful man, he became dangerous when drunk. The traders feared him so much they paid more for his buffalo robes than they paid any other Indian. Finally they determined to rid themselves of the troublesome chief by giving him poisoned whiskey. When the poison failed to affect him, a trader shot him, but Calf Shirt refused to die. He staggered out of the store and fell into a hole. The traders struck him with axes, tied him up so that he could not move, and threw him into the river. Whenever he rose to the surface they shoved him under, until at last he was seen no more.

(John C. Ewers, *The Blackfeet,* 1961.)

Camp Holmes, Treaty of, 1835. As a result of continuing warfare between Plains Indians and eastern tribes removed to their borders, a treaty was negotiated on August 24, 1835, at Camp Holmes in the territory assigned to the Creek Nation. U. S. Commissioners Matthew Arbuckle and Montfort Stokes convinced the Comanches, Wichitas, Cherokees, Creeks, Osages, Senecas, and Quapaws to agree to remain at peace with the United States and with one other. The Kiowas had been summoned to participate, but because of delays they grew impatient and returned home.

(Charles J. Kappler, ed., *Indian Affairs: Laws and Treaties, II*, 1972; Mildred P. Mayhall, *The Kiowas*, 1962.)

Canville Trading Post, Treaty of, 1865. On September 29, 1865, the Osage Indians signed a land cession treaty at Canville Trading Post, Kansas, with commissioners D. N. Cooley and Elijah Sells. A large section of the eastern portion of their reservation was purchased for $300,000. A smaller area in the northern part of their land, valued at $80,000, would be surveyed and sold for the benefit of the tribe. The Osages agreed to grant right of way for roads and railways.

(John Joseph Mathews, *The Osages*, 1961; Charles J. Kappler, ed., *Indian Affairs: Laws and Treaties, II*, 1972.)

Carondelet, Fort, Missouri. In 1794, August Chouteau received permission from the Baron de Carondelet to enjoy exclusive rights to trade with the Osage Indians. The following year he established Fort Carondelet on the Osage River at the present site of Haley's Bluff, Missouri. When it was acquired by Manuel Lisa a short time later, it fell into disrepair and was abandoned.

(John Joseph Mathews, *The Osages*, 1961; Grant Foreman, *Indians & Pioneers*, 1936.)

Carpenter, Louis H., Campaign. On September 21, 1868, Captain Louis H. Carpenter led three Tenth Cavalry troops from Fort Wallace, Kansas, to search for hostile Indians. Four days later they rescued Major George A. Forsyth's beleaguered frontiersmen on the Republican River. (See Beecher's Island, Battle of.) Afterward they marched down Beaver River and on October 18 they attacked a Cheyenne camp, killing nine Indians and wounding many more. When they returned to Fort Wallace on October 21, they had scouted 230 miles without losing a man.

George Bird Grinnell, *The Fighting Cheyennes*, 1956; William H. Leckie, *The Buffalo Soldiers*, 1967; Richard H. Dillon, *North American Indian Wars*, 1983.)

Carr, Eugene A., Indian Campaigns. Major Eugene A. Carr, a West Point graduate, began a forty-year Indian fighting career as an officer of the Regiment of Mounted Riflemen. The first of his many wounds was caused by an arrow in 1854 in Texas. In 1868, he commanded the Fifth United States Cavalry operating against the Cheyennes in eastern Colorado out of Fort Wallace. In December he commanded a column in General Phil Sheridan's campaign intended to converge on the hostiles from several directons. On December 21, he rescued General W. H.

Penrose's column, suffering from starvation while caught in a blizzard. He remained in the field until January, preventing the Cheyennes from escaping to the north and west and keeping them in the area overrun by Custer on the Washita and Colonel A. W. Evans on the Red River.

"On July 11, 1869, Carr won an important victory over the Cheyenne Dog Soldiers at Summit Springs, Colorado. With five cavalry troops and 150 Pawnee Scouts, he surprised the hostile camp, killing 50 warriors and capturing 117." (See North, Frank; Tall Bull, Cheyenne Chief.)

In 1880, Carr played a leading role in the war against the Apaches in Arizona. Ten years later he participated in the campaign in the Dakotas that ended the Indian wars at Wounded Knee. Known to the Indians as War Eagle, he retired in 1893.

(George Bird Grinnell, *The Fighting Cheyennes*, 1956; William H. Leckie, *The Buffalo Soldiers*, 1967; Robert M. Utley, *The Last Days of the Sioux Nation*, 1963.)

Carrington, Henry B. Colonel Henry B. Carrington, a scholar, teacher, lawyer, engineer, and soldier, was assigned to establish forts to protect the Bozeman Trail when miners began to travel over it in large numbers to the Montana gold fields. During the summer of 1866, he established Fort Phil Kearny at the foot of the Big Horn Mountains between Big and Little Piney Creeks in Wyoming, Fort Reno on the Powder River in Wyoming, and Fort C. F. Smith on the Bighorn River in Montana.

These forts infuriated the Indians, particularly the Sioux chief Red Cloud. All three forts were harassed constantly, and Carrington, from his headquarters at Phil Kearny, adopted a defensive position that antagonized his subordinates. When he finally sent a force out to relieve a party of woodcutters, it was wiped out by the Sioux. (See Fetterman Massacre.)

"Fetterman died because he disobeyed his chief, but a scapegoat was needed, and Carrington, who was not remotely to blame, was removed from his post and transferred to Fort Caspar."—Paul I. Wellman

(Paul I. Wellman, *Death on Horseback*, 1947; Margaret Carrington, *Ab-Sa-Ra-Ka, Home of the Crows*, 1868; Richard H. Dillon, *North American Indian Wars*, 1983; U. S. National Park Service, *Soldier and Brave*, 1963.)

Carroll, Henry, Campaign. Captain Henry Carroll, an officer in the Ninth U. S. Cavalry and an experienced Indian fighter, led 95 Buffalo Soldiers from Fort McKavett, Texas, in search of hostile Kiowas and Comanches in September, 1869. At the headwaters of the Salt Fork of the Brazos River he charged a Comanche camp of almost two hundred lodges, putting the Indians to flight and pursuing them for eight miles. About a dozen warriors were killed or wounded, and the camp was destroyed.

(William H. Leckie, *Buffalo Soldiers*, 1967.)

Carter, Lydia, Osage Child. A four-year-old Osage Indian girl was seized during a raid by the Cherokees in October 1817. Her parents were slain during the attack. As the Cherokees were returning to their own country they met a missionary who begged them to give him the child to educate at the Brainerd Indian school. Her captor refused until a substantial ransom was paid. The major contributor was a Mrs. Lydia Carter, for whom the child eventually was named.

Enrolled in the Indian school, little Lydia was adopted by the Reverend and Mrs. William Chamberlain. She enjoyed her new life, learned the English language, and succeeded with school work. In 1820, the Osages learned of Lydia's whereabouts and requested her return. The government acceded to their demands and sent an agent to the school to take her back to the tribe. But Lydia wanted to remain with her white family. She fled into the woods and ran five miles before being overtaken. Her pleas fell on deaf ears, and she became ill and died in the home of a white family during the journey to the Osage village.

(Elias Cornelius, *The Little Osage Captive,* n.d.; John Joseph Mathews, *The Osages,* 1961.)

Carter, Robert Goldthwaite. Robert G. Carter, a native of Maine, served in the Union Army as a private during the Civil War. Afterward he attended the United States Military Academy, graduating in 1870, and joined the Fourth Cavalry in Texas. Serving under General Ranald Mackenzie as a lieutenant at Fort Sill, he participated in several successful campaigns against the Comanches, Apaches, and Kickapoos before being discharged for a disability contracted in line of duty in 1876.

Carter's most noted exploit occurred in October 1871, when he led a few soldiers in pursuit of Comanches who had stolen horses from Mackenzie's camp. They had almost overtaken the raiders when they suddenly encountered several hundred warriors. A Comanche, Cohaya, related later that "when we made a charge the soldiers commenced to fire. The bullets came toward us like the roar of a sling whirling through the air. Some of the soldiers were dismounted, some mounted." Carter stood his ground with such gallantry until reinforcements arrived that he was awarded the Congressional Medal of Honor.

(*Handbook of Texas, I,* 1952; Joan Edward Weems, *Death Song,* 1976; W. S. Nye, *Carbine & Lance,* 1969.)

Casey, Edward W. Lieutenant Edward W. Casey, a young and promising member of an Army family, distinguished himself during the capture of Sioux chief Lame Deer's village in 1877. On January 7, 1891, he was slain by the Sioux during the aftermath of the Wounded Knee Massacre. While commanding a company of Cheyenne scouts, he persuaded a small band of Sioux to surrender. Afterward, accompanied by two Sioux scouts, he set out to visit Chief Red Cloud. On the way he was shot in the back by a Brulé Sioux, Plenty Horses, a graduate of Carlisle Institute. Arrested and tried for murder, Plenty Horses testified that as an educated Indian he had no standing with the Sioux and, therefore, he killed Casey to make his people proud of him. He was acquitted when the judge ruled that during time of war an Indian was justified in killing an enemy soldier.

(Joe De Barthe, *Life and Adventures of Frank Grouard*, 1958; Robert M. Utley, *The Last Days of the Sioux Nation*, 1963; Paul I. Wellman, *Death on Horseback*, 1947.)

Cass, Fort, Montana. Fort Cass was the first post established among the Crow Indians. It was built in 1832 by Samuel Tulloch for the American Fur Company on the Yellowstone River three miles below the mouth of the Bighorn. It was abandoned in 1835.

(Hiram Martin Chittenden, *The American Fur Trade of the Far West*, 1954.)

Catlin, George. George Catlin, a young Philadelphia artist and attorney, met a visiting delegation of Indians and, convinced that red men were doomed to extinction, determined to devote his life to making a visual record of their race. In 1834, he accompanied the Dodge Expedition to the Plains Indians and almost died when fever swept through the ranks. Undaunted, he painted six hundred portraits of Indian men and women, mainly on the plains and along the Missouri River.

(George Catlin, *Letters and Notes on the Manners, Customs, and Conditions of the North American Indians*, 1973; Doane Robinson, *A History of the Dakota or Sioux Indians*, 1974; Roy W. Meyer, *The Village Indians of the Upper Missouri*, 1977.)

Cato, Black Comanche. Cato, a black man who had served in the United States Army, married an Indian woman and settled near Fort Concho, Texas, in 1870. He was suspected of serving as a spy for the Comanche Indians and compelled to leave Fort Concho, but he merely moved his operations to the Fort Griffin area. A reward was posted for him dead or alive, and the Tonkawa Indians were determined to collect it. Before they tracked him down, however, he led a Comanche attack on Ledbetter's Salt Works. The defenders wounded Cato and killed four of his warriors while repulsing the attack.

Afterward, a Fourth Cavalry troop joined the Tonkawas in the pursuit of Cato and his Comanches. The scouts located the camp and the troopers attacked it at dawn. A Tonkawa shot Cato to death. Twelve Comanches were killed.

(J. Marvin Hunter, ed., *The Bloody Trail in Texas*, 1931.)

Cavagnolle, Fort, Kansas. Fort Cavagnolle was established in 1745 near the present site of Kansas City, Kansas, by the Sieur Deruisseau, a Frenchman who had been granted a monopoly by his government to trade with the Missouri River tribes. Located at the site of a Kansa Indian village, it was garrisoned by a French officer and eight soldiers. When plans to open trade with New Mexico failed and the French and Indian War adversely affected Indian trade, the post was abandoned.

(John Joseph Mathews, *The Osages,* 1961; Robert W. Frazer, *Forts of the West,* 1965.)

Cedar Bluffs Massacre. In May 1864, Major Jacob Downing led a force of Colorado Cavalry to Cedar Bluffs, 60 miles north of the South Platte River, in search of hostile Cheyennes. Unfortunately he found a friendly Cheyenne village camped in a canyon that was occupied only by women and children and a few old men. Downing made a surprise attack at dawn, killing 26 Indians and wounding some 60 others, at a loss of one man killed and one wounded. "I took no prisoners," he reported.

(George Bird Grinnell, *The Fighting Cheyennes,* 1956; John Tebbel and Keith Jennison, *The American Indian Wars,* 1960; Richard H. Dillon, *North American Indian Wars,* 1983.)

Chafee, Adna R., Expeditions Against Indians. Captain Adna R. Chafee, a veteran of the Civil War, served 27 years in the Sixth Cavalry, much of that time at war with the western Indians. In 1868, he led 62 troopers and 7 Tonkawa scouts in pursuit of Comanches who had attacked a wagon train. On March 8, they surrounded the Comanche camp on the Wichita River in northern Texas and killed seven warriors before the others broke through his line and escaped. Among the slain raiders were a Mexican and a black man.

On October 17, 1874, Chafee destroyed a hostile Indian village near the Washita River. The Indians fled and no one was killed on either side. Afterward he remained in the field through December, pursuing hostile bands and driving them toward the reservation.

Chafee fought in the Apache wars of the 1880s. On July 17, 1882, he defeated a large force of hostiles on the Mogollon Rim, in Arizona, killing 21 warriors.

(Carl Coke Rister, *Fort Griffin on the Texas Frontier,* 1956; W. S. Nye, *Carbine & Lance,* 1969; U. S. National Park Service, *Soldier and Brave,* 1963.)

Champlain, Jean Baptiste. Jean Baptiste Champlain, a Rocky Mountain trapper employed by Manuel Lisa, discovered in 1811 that the Spanish in Santa Fe were sending expeditions to trade with the Arapaho Indians along the Platte. Lisa sent him with trade goods to the Araphoes and instructed him to attempt to open trade with Santa Fe if he should encounter one of their agents. Champlain never returned, and Lisa learned later that he had been killed by the Blackfeet.

(LeRoy R. Hafen, ed., *Mountain Men and Fur Traders of the Far West*, 1982.)

Charbonneau, Toussaint. Born near Montreal about 1759, Toussaint Charbonneau became a trader for the Northwest Fur Company on the Assiniboine River at an early age. He settled among the Mandan and Hidatsa Indians on the Knife River in North Dakota about 1797. He had several Indian wives before he married Sacagawea, the Shoshoni slave girl of the Hidatsa chief, Le Borgne. Chiefly because of her knowledge of the West, the couple served as guides for the Lewis and Clark Expedition.

After the return of the expedition, Charbonneau went with William Clark to St. Louis. From there he accompanied a party of trappers to the Arkansas and Red rivers. In 1810, employed by Manuel Lisa, he visited the Mandan villages and urged the Indians of the Upper Missouri to support the Americans during the impending war with the British. After the War of 1812, he traded for Auguste Pierre Chouteau and Jules de Mun on the Rio Grande. By 1819, he returned to St. Louis and served as a guide for the Stephen H. Long Expedition. In 1823, he was at Fort Kiowa, South Dakota. From 1828 to 1834, he served as interpreter for the Indian agent on the Upper Missouri. He lived with the Mandans until his death about 1839.

(W. Raymond Wood and Thomas D. Thiessen, eds., *Early Fur Trade on the Northern Plains*, 1985; Roy W. Meyer, *The Village Indians of the Upper Missouri*, 1977; Gordon Speck, *Breeds and Half-Breeds*, 1969.)

Chardon, François A. François Chardon, a veteran trader for the American Fur Company, was bourgeois at Fort Clark, North Dakota, after 1834. He obtained huge quantities of robes by selling liquor to the Indians until they blamed him for a smallpox epidemic. Afterward, several warriors tried to kill him as revenge and he developed a fierce hatred of Indians.

In 1843, Chardon and Alexander Harvey fired a cannon at Piegan Indians who had come to Fort McKenzie to trade. At least ten Indians were killed. (See Harvey, Alexander.) This massacre made it necessary to abandon Fort McKenzie. He died in 1848.

(John C. Ewers, *The Blackfeet*, 1961; Roy W. Meyer, *The Village Indians of the Upper Missouri*, 1977.)

Charger, Sioux Chief. See Waneta, Sioux Chief

Chasca, Sioux warrior. Chasca, an educated Sioux who had adopted many ways of the white people, joined a war party during the Minnesota

Sioux uprising in 1862. He took no part in the murders, however, and saved
the lives of Dr. J. L. Wakefield's family, telling his companions that they
would have to kill him first. After the Indians surrendered, he was accused
of being present when a white man, George Gleason, was murdered and,
although Mrs. Wakefield testified in his behalf, he was condemned to
death. He was hung on December 26, 1862.

(C. M. Oehler, *The Great Sioux Uprising,* 1959.)

Chaui Indians. See Pawnee Indians

Cheyenne Indians. The Cheyenne Indians, an important Algonquian
tribe, lived in Minnesota until migrating to the Great Plains about 1700.
With the acquisition of horses they abandoned an agricultural way of life
and became nomadic buffalo hunters in the Missouri and Platte river
regions. In 1833 a division of the tribe into northern and southern divisions
occurred when many Cheyenne bands, along with their Arapaho allies,
moved to the vicinity of Bent's Fort on the Arkansas. Soon they became
dependent upon trader's goods, and their old way of life modified rapidly.
   From 1860 to 1878, the Cheyennes were fearsome raiders, fighting
alongside the Sioux in the north and the Comanches and Kiowas in the
south. It is probable that they lost more warriors in proportion to their total
population than any other tribe on the Plains. (See Sand Creek Massacre;
Cedar Bluffs Massacre; Washita, Battle of the.) During the Plains Indian
wars of the 1870s, they inflicted numerous casualties upon the whites as
well. On July 3, 1874, they attacked a wagon train and burned several
teamsters to death. They played a powerful role in assisting the Sioux to
destroy Custer's command at the Little Bighorn on June 25, 1876.
   During the summer of 1877, a large number of Northern Cheyennes
were compelled to go on the reservation at Fort Reno, Oklahoma. There
they suffered so greatly from lack of food that on September 9, 1878, Dull
Knife and Little Wolf led 300 of them northward to join the Sioux. Troops
were sent to compel their return to the reservation, and a running fight
ensued over hundreds of miles. The Indians killed some 40 settlers in
Kansas (see Sappa Creek Fights), but armed whites were converging on
them from several directions and some of the older Cheyennes and
children were suffering from the strain of the journey. Upon reaching the
South Platte, Dull Knife wanted to halt for a rest, but Little Wolf insisted
upon continuing the march as rapidly as possible. On the following
morning Dull Knife led his followers toward imprisonment at Fort Robinson while Little Wolf went on toward Montana. (See Robinson, Fort.)
Little Wolf was persuaded to surrender on March 25, 1879, and allowed
to settle his people near their former homes in the north.
   "The Cheyennes fought well," wrote George Bird Grinnell, "but they
will fight no more. Their wars have long been over. Their tribal wanderings

ceased before 1880. Since then they have been confined to two reservations, one in Oklahoma and one in Montana."

George Bird Grinnell, *The Fighting Cheyennes*, 1956; *The Cheyenne Indians*, 1972; Donald J. Berthrong, *The Cheyenne and Arapaho Ordeal*, 1976; *The Southern Cheyennes*, 1963; Peter J. Powell, *Sweet Medicine*, 1969; Francis Paul Prucha, *American Indian Policy in Crisis*, 1976; W. S. Nye, *Carbine & Lance*, 1969; Paul I. Wellman, *Death on Horseback*, 1947; David Lavender, *Bent's Fort*, 1954.)

Chicony, Comanche Chief. Chicony, a principal Comanche chief, refused to sign a treaty with Texas officials in 1836. Instead, he "swore eternal enmity to the white man."

(*Handbook of Texas, I*, 1952.)

Childs, Fort, Nebraska, Treaty of. On August 6, 1848, Fort Childs on the Platte River provided the site for treaty negotiations between Ludwell E. Powell and the Pawnee Indians. The tribe ceded an area sixty miles long on both sides of the Platte for goods valued at $2,000.

(Charles J. Kappler, ed., *Indian Affairs: Laws and Treaties, II*, 1972.)

Chisholm, Jesse. Jesse Chisholm, a Cherokee Indian, became a trader near Fort Gibson and later near the present site of Oklahoma City. He could speak fourteen Indian languages and was greatly valued as an interpreter during treaty negotiations. On several occasions he purchased the freedom of white captives. He played an important part in 1867 in persuading the Plains Indians to negotiate the Medicine Lodge Treaty. He died in 1868.

(Grant Foreman, *Advancing the Frontier*, 1933; *Handbook of Texas, 1*, 1952.)

Chivington, John Milton. Colonel John Milton Chivington of the Colorado Volunteers left two indelible marks on the history of the West. In the spring of 1862 he led the attack on a Confederate Army and sent the invaders retreating to Texas. Three years later, on November 29, 1864, he massacred more than a hundred peaceful Cheyenne Indians. (See Sand Creek Massacre.)

An elder of the Methodist Church, Chivington had political ambitions, and his detractors accused him of precipitating Indian battles in order to build a reputation as the "fighting parson" that would influence voters of the territory. After the massacre, based in large measure on his own reports, he basked as a hero in Denver. But as information about the slaughter of women and children reached the public, revulsion spread, sparking a Congressional investigation.

While Chivington is branded a villain by most historians, he does not lack for supporters, especially among historians of his own era. A case in point is his defense in J. P. Dunn's *Massacres of the Mountains,* and even modern frontier historians John Tebbel and Keith Jennison contend that he was

> the undeserved villain of the piece. In fairness to this excellent officer, who was compelled to resign his commission, it must be said that he had performed a service to his country of the first magnitude . . . It was Chivington who fashioned the victory in the Battle of Sante Fe . . . a victory that may well have decided . . . the outcome of the Civil War.

In regard to the Sand Creek Massacre, Tebbell and Jennison assert that Chivington was carrying out the orders of his superior officer, General S. R. Curtis, and the attack, " was further justified from the military view by the potential danger to Fort Lyon."

(John Tebbel and Keith Jennison, *The American Indian Wars,* 1960; J. P. Dunn, *Massacres of the Mountains,* 1958; Paul I. Wellman, *Death on Horseback,* 1947; Robert M. Utley and Wilcomb E. Washburn, *The American Heritage History of the Indian Wars,* 1977; David Lavender, *Bent's Fort,* 1954; Stan Hoig, *The Sand Creek Massacre,* 1961.)

Chivington Massacre. See Sand Creek Massacre

Chouteau, Auguste Pierre. Auguste Pierre Chouteau, eldest son of the famous fur trader Jean Pierre Chouteau, was born in St. Louis on May 9, 1786. He attended the U. S. Military Academy and became an ensign in the Second Infantry in 1806. Three years later he resigned his commission to enter the fur trade. At the close of the War of 1812, he joined Jules de Mun in a partnership to seek furs on the Platte and Arkansas rivers, but the venture failed because of Indian hostility and arrest by Spanish soldiers. Afterward he traded with the Osages in Missouri and Arkansas. In 1821, he established a trading post on Grand River, Oklahoma. Two years later he acquired a post just below the falls of the Verdigris, and he managed both establishments. Because of the long association of the Chouteau family with the Indians, he persuaded many Osages to move near his post and he frequently managed negotiations between that tribe and the Cherokees and Creeks and between the government and various Indian nations.

A. P. Chouteau built a large log home on the Grand River where he lived like a frontier nobleman, entertaining famous guests and travelers. With him were his Indian wife, Rosalie, and their several children. He also fathered children by three other Indian women. He died on December 25, 1838.

(Grant Foreman, *Indians & Pioneers,* 1936; Robert Glass Cleland, *This Reckless Breed of Men,* 1963; Hiram Martin Chittenden, *A History of the American Fur Trade of the Far West,* 1954.)

Chouteau, Jean Pierre. Jean Pierre Chouteau was born in New Orleans on October 10, 1758, and moved with his parents to St. Louis in September 1764. He lived for many years among the Osage Indians, holding—with his half brother, René Auguste—a monopoly on the trade with that tribe from 1794 to 1802. When the monopoly was transferred to Manuel Lisa, he persuaded thousands of Osages to move to his post on the Arkansas. A few years later Lisa lost the monopoly and Chouteau regained dominance of the tribe's trade. In 1809, he became a partner in the Saint Louis Missouri Fur Company. During that same year he led a force that returned the Mandan chief, Big White, through the hostile Arikaras and Sioux to his village on the Missouri. He retired from the fur trade in 1820 and died on July 10, 1849.

(LeRoy R. Hafen, ed., *Mountain Men and Fur Traders of the Far West,* 1982; Hiram Martin Chittenden, *A History of the American Fur Trade of the Far West,* 1954; Grant Foreman, *Indians & Pioneers,* 1936.)

Chouteau, Pierre (Cadet). Pierre (Cadet) Chouteau, second son of Jean Pierre Chouteau, was born in St. Louis on January 19, 1789. He became involved in his father's fur trade at the age of sixteen. He joined Julien Dubuque at the lead mines in 1808, and the following year he went on a trading expedition for the Saint Louis Missouri Fur Company. In 1813, he formed a partnership with Bartholemew Berthold, trading with the Indians until 1831, when he joined Bernard Pratte and Company. In 1834, the firm purchased the western department of the American Fur Company, and in 1838, the name was changed to Pierre Chouteau, Jr., and Company. Eventually his fur trade enterprises extended over the entire Missouri and upper Mississippi river regions. He became increasingly wealthy by extending his interests to mining, milling, and railroads, and he spent much of his time managing his enterprises in New York. He died on September 6, 1865.

(LeRoy R. Hafen, ed., *Mountain Men and Fur Traders of the Far West,* 1982; Hiram Martin Chittenden, *A History of the American Fur Trade of the Far West,* 1954.)

Chouteau, René Auguste. René Auguste Chouteau was born in New Orleans in September 1749 and moved to the Illinois country with Pierre Laclède Liguest in 1763. Although he was only fourteen, he assisted

Laclède Liguest in selecting a site for a trading post that developed into the city of St. Louis. He became the founder of a line of traders that remained the leading family of St. Louis for at least a century. From 1794 until 1802, he enjoyed a monopoly of the Osage Indian trade, making him wealthy by the standard of the times. He was trusted by both Indians and whites and served as a commissioner in negotiating treaties with the Sauks, Foxes, and Iowas. He died on February 24, 1829.

(Hiram Martin Chittenden, *History of the American Fur Trade of the Far West,* 1954; Grant Foreman, *Indians & Pioneers,* 1936; W. J. Ghent, *The Early Far West,* 1936; John Joseph Mathews, *The Osages,* 1961.)

Clark, Fort, Missouri. See Osage, Fort, Missouri

Clark, Fort, Missouri, Treaty of, 1808. On November 10, 1808, Pierre Chouteau negotiated a treaty with the Osage Indians at Fort Clark in the Louisiana Territory. The government agreed to protect the tribe from other Indians, to sell trade goods at low prices, to provide a blacksmith, and to pay damages to settlers for property destroyed by the Osages. The tribe ceded an enormous tract, including a large portion of the present states of Arkansas and Missouri. The Osages were permitted to live and hunt on the ceded lands.

(Charles J. Kappler, ed., *Indian Affairs: Laws and Treaties, II,* 1972; Grant Foreman, *Indians & Pioneers,* 1936.)

Clark, Fort, North Dakota. Fort Clark, one of the most important trading posts on the Missouri River, was founded for the American Fur Company by James Kipp about 1833. It was located about fifty miles north of the present site of Bismarck, North Dakota. Kipp was in charge until 1834.

(Hiram Martin Chittenden, *The American Fur Trade of the Far West,* 1954.)

Clark, James. Born in Tennessee and educated at the University of Virginia, James Clark became a trader to the Indians in Arkansas and Texas in 1824. His business prospered when President Jackson appointed him to deliver food to the Southern Indians removed to the present state of Oklahoma. From his post on the Red River, he served as a peace commissioner during negotiations with tribes of that region. After establishing Clarksville, Texas, in 1833 he became an effective Indian fighter. He died in 1838.

(*Handbook of Texas, I,* 1952.)

Clermont, Osage Chiefs. Clermont (Clermo, Clamore) was the name given to a succession of Osage chiefs by American officials and settlers. The first in the line was called "the Builder of Towns" by whites and

Gra-Mon by the Osages. Both he and the second Clermont were also known as Arrow-Going-Home.

The first Clermont was the hereditary chief of the Osage Nation, but during his childhood, at the instigation of Pierre Chouteau, White Hair (Pahuska) usurped leadership of the tribe. By 1787, Clermont was hostile to white invaders of Osage lands and played a part in the slaying of several Spaniards and Frenchmen. He was summoned to St. Louis on August 16, 1787, and ordered to provide hostages to guarantee the good behavior of the tribe. Whether this experience persuaded him to change his views is an open question, but by 1802, when he acceded to Chouteau's request to remove his band from the Osage River to the Arkansas, he had become a firm friend of white people.

The first Clermont's life was made increasingly difficult after moving to the Arkansas by the hostility of the Cherokees. His village suffered a savage attack by a Cherokee war party in 1818 and, although Clermont did his best to maintain peace, tribal warfare prevailed for years. His son, Mad Buffalo, was a leading war chief who killed several white hunters on the Blue River in 1823. Army officers called upon Clermont to surrender the leaders of the attack, and Mad Buffalo gave himself up to the authorities. (See Mad Buffalo.)

The first Clermont died in 1828 and was succeeded by his son, also called Clermont. Like his predecessor, he attempted to keep his people at peace with the whites. A friend to the Chouteau family and to the army officers at Fort Gibson, he was considered an arrogant man of great force. He died in 1837.

Not much is recorded of the deeds of a more recent chief known as Clermont (Claremore). He led the Osage band called the Upland-Forest-People to a conference with Indian agents in 1870.

(John Joseph Mathews, *The Osages,* 1961; Grant Foreman, *Advancing the Frontier,* 1933; *Indians & Pioneers,* 1936.)

Cobb Fort, Oklahoma. Fort Cobb was established on October 1, 1859, by Major William H. Emory to protect a reservation recently established for Indians removed from Texas. At the onset of the Civil War, the garrison abandoned the fort and Confederate officer Albert Pike negotiated a preliminary treaty there with the Kiowas and Comanches. On October 23, 1862, the Osages and other tribes wiped out a small force of Confederate soldiers there and burned most of the buildings.

After the Civil War, Indian agent Colonel W. B. Hazen used the post as his headquarters. He distributed rations there to the Kiowas and Comanches in an attempt to discourage them from joining raids by the Cheyennes.

Fort Cobb was abandoned in 1869, but it still played an occasional role in Indian affairs. On July 25, 1872, a conference was held there between chiefs of the Five Civilized Tribes and Plains Indian leaders. The Southern Indians urged acceptance of white civilization, but the Comanches and Kiowas refused to stop raiding Texas settlements or to release their captives.

(W. S. Nye, *Carbine & Lance,* 1969; De B. Randolph Keim, *Sheridan's Troopers on the Borders,* 1870; Robert W. Frazer, *Forts of the West,* 1965.)

Cody, William F. William F. (Buffalo Bill) Cody, a legendary frontiersman and showman, was born in Le Claire, Iowa, on February 26, 1846. While his exploits have been greatly exaggerated by writers of sensational stories, it is evident that he played an important role in Indian-white relations on the Great Plains for 20 years as a Pony Express rider, freighter, hunter, and scout.

Cody scouted for Major George A. Armes' Tenth Cavalry along the Saline River, Kansas, in 1867-1868. Beginning in October 1868, he served as chief of scouts for the hard-bitten Fifth Cavalry Indian fighter, Major Eugene Carr. In May 1869, he led the pursuit of the Cheyennes from Beaver Creek to Spring Creek, Kansas, which culminated in an attack by two hundred warriors on May 16. He was wounded in the scalp but volunteered to ride fifty miles to Fort Kearny with dispatches.

During the summer of 1869, Cody accompanied Carr and Frank North's Pawnee scouts in search of Chief Tall Bull's Cheyenne Dog Soldiers. They located the hostiles on July 11 (see Summit Springs, Colorado, Battle of) and killed 52 Indians, including Tall Bull. Most of Cody's many biographers believe that he killed the chief, while North's brother, Luther, who witnessed the event, has asserted that Frank fired the fatal shot.

In June, 1870, Cody killed several Sioux warriors during a fight near Red Willow Creek, Nebraska. In May 1871, he was cited for gallantry during an engagement with the Sioux on Birdwood Creek, Nebraska. In April 1872, while scouting for the Third Cavalry, he killed several warriors during a running fight on the South Fork of the Loup River, Nebraska. In July 1876, he killed Cheyenne chief Yellow Hand while scouting for the Fifth Cavalry near Hat Creek, Nebraska. (See Yellow Hand.)

After 1876, Cody curtailed his scouting activities and began a career as a showman. In 1890, however, he was called upon by General Nelson A. Miles to call upon Sitting Bull, a former member of his Wild West Show, to seek assistance in ending the Ghost Dance craze. Unfortunately, Sitting Bull was slain before Cody arrived at the reservation.

Cody died in Denver in 1917.

(Bill O'Neal, *Fighting Men of the Indian Wars,* 1991; William F. Cody, *The Life of Hon. William F. Cody,* 1978; Helen Cody Wetmore and Zane Grey, *Last of the Great Scouts,* 1918; Don Russell, *The Lives and Legends of Buffalo Bill,* 1960;

Nellie Snyder Yost, *Buffalo Bill*, 1979; John Burke, *Buffalo Bill*, 1973; Shannon Garst, *Buffalo Bill*, 1948.)

Coffee, Holland. Holland Coffee of Fort Smith, Arkansas, established a trading post in 1833 in the present Tillman County, Oklahoma. By March 1836, he built trading posts at the mouth of Cache Creek and on Walnut Bayou, Oklahoma. In 1837 he crossed the Red River into Texas and established Coffey's Station on Preston Bend. There, because of honest trading and the ability to speak several Indian languages, he not only prospered but was able to negotiate peace treaties and redeem captives as well. He was stabbed to death by an Indian in 1846.

(*Handbook of Texas, I*, 1952; Grant Foreman, *Advancing the Frontier*, 1933; J. W. Wilbarger, *Indian Depredations in Texas*, 1985.)

Coho, Arapaho Chief. Coho, a mid-nineteenth century Arapaho chief, was feared and hated by frontiersmen of the Southwest. He was considered to be the leader of hostilities along the Santa Fe Trail.

(Lewis H. Garrard, *Wah-To-Yah and the Taos Trail*, 1955; Virginia Cole Trenholm, *The Arapahoes, Our People*, 1970.)

Cohoe, William, Cheyenne Warrior. William Cohoe, whose Indian name was Water Elk, was born in Colorado in 1854. He went on numerous war parties until compelled to surrender in 1874. Imprisoned at Fort Marion, Florida, he spent his time practicing to become an artist and, in 1878-79, he attended Hampton Institute and the Carlisle Indian School. When he completed his studies he became a Christian and a farmer in Oklahoma, but before he died in 1924 he abandoned his progressive propensities to become chief of the War Dancer's Society.

(Frederick J. Dockstader, *Great North American Indians*, 1977.)

Cole, Nelson, Expedition. Colonel Nelson Cole commanded a column in General P. E. Connor's Powder River campaign of 1865. His force of 1,800 men was attacked by the Sioux and Cheyennes on several occasions. He repulsed them with cannon, killing at least two hundred warriors (according to his reports), but the Indians drove off his horses and the soldiers ran out of provisions. They had almost reached the point of starvation when Connor's Pawnee Indian scouts rescued them.

(George Bird Grinnell, *The Fighting Cheyennes*, 1956; Ruby E. Wilson, *Frank J. North, 1984.*)

Coleman, Robert M., Family of. Robert M. Coleman was born in Kentucky about 1799 and moved his family to Bastrop County, Texas, in 1832. In 1835 he commanded four companies of volunteer Indian fighters.

During the Texas Revolution he served as aide-de-camp to General Sam Houston. After the war, while commanding a regiment of Rangers, he drowned in the Brazos River in 1837.

Coleman was survived by his wife and six children. In 1839, their farm home near Webberville, Texas, was attacked by Indians. Mrs. Coleman and a five-year-old son, Thomas, ran from the garden toward the house, but an Indian seized the child while another shot the mother through the throat with an arrow as she staggered inside and barred the door. She died while extracting the arrow. Her eldest son, Albert, defended the home with a rifle while the younger children hid under a bed. He killed four Indians before they shot him to death. James Coleman and two small daughters escaped when the Indians left to attack Dr. Joel W. Robertson's home nearby.

The Indians kept Thomas Coleman until he was almost grown. Then when ransomed, he ran away and rejoined the Indians.

(John Holland Jenkins, *Recollections of Early Texas*, 1958; *Handbook of Texas, I*, 1952.)

Collins, Mary. Mary Collins, a Congregational missionary to the Sioux, competed with Sitting Bull for spiritual leadership of the Indians along the Grand River. The most dramatic event in her career was her attempt to prevent the Ghost Dances. As reported by Robert M. Utley, "she would charge into the dance circles and challenge the Great Mysterious to make good his promise, relayed by Sitting Bull, to cause the earth to swallow the unbeliever." She believed that she had caused doubts in the minds of some of the dancers, and although Sitting Bull never publicly renounced the doctrine, he admitted his lack of conviction while insisting that he had gone too far to turn back.

(Robert M. Utley, *The Last Days of the Sioux*, 1963.)

Colter, John. John Colter, a native of Staunton, Virginia, was born about 1775. In October 1803, he enlisted to accompany Lewis and Clark to the Pacific Ocean, undertaking many hazardous missions along the way. On their return journey, Colter left the expedition at the Mandan villages in order to join a party of trappers. In 1807 he guided Manuel Lisa and 40 trappers to the Crow Indian country and helped them build a trading post at the mouth of the Bighorn River. When Lisa sent Colter to explore the country of the Blackfoot Indians, a war party attacked him, but he escaped and explored Yellowstone Park before returning to Lisa's fort.

During the spring of 1808 Lisa sent Colter and John Potts to trap beaver near the Three Forks of the Missouri. They were attacked by the Blackfeet, and Potts was shot to death. Colter was captured and given the opportunity to run for his life. The Indians granted him a three-hundred-yard head start before beginning pursuit. He outran them to a river and dived under a pile of driftwood, keeping his head above water but concealed under the raft. The warriors searched for him in vain. After they abandoned the search he swam out and fled to Lisa's fort.

In September 1809, Colter guided a party of trappers to the Three Forks of the Missouri. They were attacked by Indians while building a fort and Colter decided that he had had too many narrow escapes. He retired to a farm in Missouri and died in 1813.

(John C. Ewers, *The Blackfeet,* 1961; Hiram Martin Chittenden, *The American Fur Trade of the Far West,* 1954; Thomas Froncek, ed., *Voices From the Wilderness,* 1974.)

Comanche Indians. The Comanche Indians, a powerful and predatory tribe of Shoshonean stock, are believed to have separated from the Shoshonis in eastern Wyoming and moved onto the plains of southwestern Kansas by 1700. Then, eager to acquire horses, they moved south of the Arkansas in order to facilitate frequent forays into Mexico. For many years they waged constant warfare against the Spanish settlers and the Apaches, destroying villages and ranches and replenishing losses by incorporating captive children into the tribe.

By moving southward the Comanches blocked both the Spanish expansion northeastward and the French attempt to advance toward the southwest. They were particularly determined to prevent the acquisition of European weapons by their deadly enemies, the Apaches. In 1758, when the Spaniards established the San Saba mission in Texas to serve the Apaches, the Comanches destroyed it and increased their incursions into Mexico.

The earliest Anglo-Texans established friendly relations with the Comanches by trading them superior goods for stolen horses. But by 1835 so many men from the United States had intruded on Comanche hunting grounds that the Indians turned hostile. Several sanguinary raids during the Texas Revolution caused the settlers to hate and fear the tribe. (See Parker's Fort; Beales' Texas Colony.) Sam Houston, first President of Texas, attempted to restore peace with the Comanches, but the frontier settlers and their representatives repudiated his initiatives and attempted to prevent Indian incursions by building a chain of forts facing the Comanche heartland in northwestern Texas and Oklahoma.

In 1840, an attempt to negotiate a treaty in San Antonio erupted into a slaughter of 35 Comanches. (See Council House Fight.) In retaliation, Chief Buffalo Hump led a huge war party all the way to the Gulf Coast. (See Linnville, Texas, Raid.) On their return they were intercepted and defeated by the Texans in one of the fiercest battles in South Plains history. (See Plum Creek, Battle of; Moore, John Henry.)

After Texas joined the Union, the army attempted to halt Comanche depredations, but with such little initial success that the Texas Rangers took over the task. By 1856 the army had improved its effectiveness and the Comanches and their Kiowa allies could no longer raid the settlements and retreat to the Staked Plains without fear of pursuit. In 1859, the government compelled many of the hostiles to move to a reservation in Oklahoma, but by no means did this development prevent raids into Texas. The Comanches drew their rations, slipped across the Red River, raided the settlements, and retreated to their sanctuary on the reservation. Hostilities continued until the Comanches were crushed during the final outbreak of 1875-1876. (See Adobe Walls; Palo Duro Canyon.)

"For a good 150 years, since first they had come down from the north, at first alone and later with the aid of their Kiowa allies, the Comanches had been the lords of the Southern Plains."—Ernest Wallace and E. Adamson Hoebel

(Ernest Wallace and E. Adamson Hoebel, *The Comanches*, 1952; T. R. Fehrenbach, *Comanches*, 1983; Carl Coke Rister, *Border Captives*, 1940; W. S. Nye, *Carbine & Lance*, 1969; De B. Randolph Keim, *Sheridan's Troopers on the Border*, 1870; Josiah Gregg, *Commerce of the Prairies*, 1968; John Holland Jenkins, *Recollections of Early Texas*, 1958; Charles L. Kenner, *A History of New Mexican-Plains Indian Relations*, 1969.)

Comancheros. Comancheros were traders from New Mexico who sold guns and trade goods to the Comanches and other Plains tribes on the Staked Plains of western Texas. They began their trading about 1786 and kept it up for a century. In exchange for trade goods they obtained captives and stolen horses and mules. Although they provided a service by redeeming captives, they were condemned for arming Indians who raided the settlements of Texas and New Mexico.

(Charles L. Kenner, *A History of New Mexican-Plains Indian Relations*, 1969); Frank McNitt, *The Indian Traders*, 1962; Carl Coke Rister, *Border Captives*, 1940.)

Concho, Fort, Texas. Fort Concho was established in December 1867, on the Concho River in western Texas. It was in the center of a chain of forts intended to protect the settlements from the Comanches and Kiowas in Oklahoma and the Texas Panhandle. After the defeat of the Plains Indians, troops from Fort Concho fought the Apaches. The fort was abandoned in 1889.

(National Park Service, *Soldier and Brave*, 1963; Robert W. Frazer, *Forts of the West*, 1965.)

Connor, Fort, Wyoming. Fort Connor, Wyoming, was established on the Powder River on August 14, 1865, by General Patrick E. Connor. It was intended as a supply base for Connor's Powder River Indian campaign. It was replaced by Fort Reno on the opposite side of the river the following year.

(Robert W. Frazer, *Forts of the West,* 1965.)

Connor, Patrick Edward, Indian Campaign. Patrick Edward Connor was born in County Kerry, Ireland, in 1820 and came to America as a small child. He joined the army at the age of 19 and fought in the Seminole and Mexican Wars, receiving a commission during the latter conflict. During the Civil War he assumed command of the military district of Utah. He campaigned against the Bannock and Shoshoni Indians in 1863 and in 1865 he was ordered to direct the Powder River campaign against the Cheyennes.

Connor had some 2,500 soldiers and Pawnee scouts in his command. He divided them up into three forces, commanding one of them himself. His Pawnee scouts defeated the Cheyennes, but he fought a bloody battle without victory against the Arapahoes. His other columns were hit hard by the Sioux and Cheyennes and rendered ineffective by severe winter weather.

Richard H. Dillon has noted that the expedition was a failure: "The combination of hostiles, bad terrain and filthy weather beat his unwieldy army. Worst of all, his supposedly powerful expedition, instead of chastening the Indians, only emboldened them."

(Richard H. Dillon, *North American Indian Wars,* 1983; Ruby E. Wilson, *Frank J. North,* 1984.)

Conquering Bear, Brulé Sioux Chief. Conquering Bear, a friendly Brulé chief, was caught up in 1854 in an incident that flared into a major Indian war. A member of his band killed a cow belonging to a Mormon wagon train. Lieutenant John L. Grattan, eager to attack Indians, refused Conquering Bear's offer to trade horses for the cow. The chief was shot to death while instructing his warriors not to fight the soldiers. (See Grattan, John L.)

(Robert H. Dillon, *North American Indian Wars,* 1983.)

Cook, Jim. Jim Cook, a young Texas trail driver after the Civil War, was captured by Indians and lived among them long enough to marry a maiden of the tribe. After several years of captivity he and his wife, White Swan, escaped. He served as a scout in the wars with the Plains Indians and then began ranching in the Texas Panhandle.

(*Handbook of Texas, I,* 1952.)

Coryell, James. James Coryell, an Ohio native who moved to Texas about 1829, was involved in several Indian fights before his death at their hands eight years later. In 1831, he joined Jim Bowie in his search for a lost silver mine, an expedition that ended with one of the fiercest Indian battles in Texas history. In 1836, he served with Sterling C. Robertson's Rangers, and the following year he signed on with the company of T. H. Barron. While camped near the Brazos River on May 27, 1837, he was robbing a bee tree when Indians crept up behind him and shot him to death.

(*Handbook of Texas, I*, 1952; J. W. Wilbarger, *Indian Depredations in Texas*, 1985.)

Council Ground on the Upper Missouri, Treaty of. Isaac Stevens negotiated a treaty with the Blackfoot Indians on October 17, 1855, at the council ground on the upper Missouri, near the mouth of the Judith River. The Blackfeet agreed to live in peace with citizens of the United States and with neighboring tribes. The government agreed to protect the Blackfeet from the whites. The tribe consented to safe passage and the construction of forts and roads. An annuity of $20,000 for ten years was guaranteed.

(Charles J. Kappler, ed., *Indian Affairs: Laws and Treaties, II*, 1972.)

Council Grove, Kansas, Treaties of. The Osage Indians, on August 7, 1825, and the Kansa Indians, on August 16, 1825, negotiated treaties with United States commissioners at Council Grove, Kansas. The tribes agreed to permit the building of roads through their territories in exchange for a payment of $500.

(Charles J. Kappler, ed., *Indian Affairs: Laws and Treaties, II*, 1972.)

Council House Fight. One of the most costly blunders in the history of Indian-white relations occurred at San Antonio, Texas, on March 19, 1840, when twelve Comanche chiefs, accompanied by their families, met representatives of the Texas government in and around the courthouse. The motives of the Indians in coming to this stronghold of their enemies remains a matter of dispute 150 years after the event. Mildred P. Mayhall, historian of the Texas Indian wars, asserted that Chief Muguara (Spirit Talker) wanted to make peace because his band was decimated by attacks by Texas Rangers. T. R. Fehrenbach, historian of the Comanches, contends that the chief believed the Texans desired peace and that they would pay a large ransom for each of the captives held by his band.

The intentions of the Texans in holding the conference are unclear as well. According to Mayhall, Muguara had agreed on January 9 to surrender some of their chiefs as hostages until they released all of their white captives. He had been warned that failure to keep his promise would lead to seizure of the entire delegation. Fehrenbach has pointed out that Indians regarded a council as sacred and that the Comanches "never envisioned violence or treachery." Richard H. Dillon has condemned the actions of the Texans as "treachery which recalled Jesup's seizure of Osceola in Florida."

While the intentions of the two negotiating parties are subject to varying interpretations, the sequence of events that occurred is undisputed. Sixty-five Indians arrived in San Antonio. The chiefs and warriors entered the courthouse, bringing a captive, Matilda Lockhart, while the women and children waited in the courtyard. The Texas delegates, William G. Cooke and Hugh McLeod, infuriated because Miss Lockhart had been horribly mutilated by her captors, demanded the immediate release of other captives. The Indians claimed that they held no others, but Matilda retorted that they did and that they intended to release only one at a time in order to exact a large ransom for each one. At this juncture Lieutenant Colonel William S. Fisher led an infantry detachment into the conference room and the commissioners announced that all of the Indians were hostages. A fight to the death immediately ensued.

The Comanches began shooting their bows and arrows and attempted to escape through the doors. The soldiers opened fire, killing Muguara and several Indians and whites. The battle spilled out into the square and the Indians sought cover behind houses. They tried to flee along the San Antonio River, but none escaped. Thirty-three Comanches, including all of the chiefs, were killed. The remaining 32 were captured and imprisoned. Seven Texans were killed and ten wounded. When other Indians learned of the fiasco, they tortured 13 captives to death, and the Comanches retaliated with a raid that struck terror all the way to the Gulf Coast. (See Linnville, Texas, Raid; Plum Creek, Battle of.)

(Walter Prescott Webb, *The Texas Rangers*, 1965; John Holland Jenkins, *Recollections of Early Texas*, 1958; T. H. Fehrenbach, *Comanches*, 1983; Mildred P. Mayhall, *Indian Wars of Texas*, 1965; Richard H. Dillon, *North American Indian Wars*, 1983.)

Council Springs, Texas, Treaty of, 1846. At Council Springs in Robinson County, Texas, United States commissioners P. M. Butler and M. G. Lewis negotiated a treaty on May 15, 1846, with the Comanche Indians and several other tribes. The federal government agreed to protect the tribes and to provide them with licensed traders and blacksmiths. The Indians agreed to release their captives. Criminals of either race would be punished by the courts.

(Charles J. Kappler, ed., *Indian Affairs: Laws and Treaties, II*, 1972.)

Cox, Euclid M. Euclid M. Cox, a Kentuckian, moved to Texas in 1832. After fighting in several battles during the Texas Revolution, he became a surveyor. On October 8, 1838, he participated in the so-called Surveyors'

Fight with twenty-five companions against three hundred Kickapoo Indians. The surveyors were trapped in a ravine with warriors in cottonwood trees firing at every head that showed itself above the bank. Finally Cox determined upon a dangerous plan to return fire. He climbed a tall oak, secreted himself in the foliage, and opened fire at the Indians below. For several hours he kept up a steady fire, returned tenfold by the Kickapoos, until at length a bullet shattered his spine and he fell from the tree. A companion, Walter P. Lane, dashed into the open and carried Cox into the ravine. Cox was still alive when his companions escaped under the cover of darkness. A friend offered to remain with him, but Cox, realizing that his wound was fatal, told him to save himself.

(James T. De Shields, *Border Wars of Texas,* 1976.)

Craft, Francis M. Father Francis M. Craft, a Catholic missionary to the Sioux, was severely wounded during the Wounded Knee massacre on December 29, 1890. While attempting to pursuade Big Foot's band to surrender their rifles, he sustained a warrior's lance thrust through his back and lungs. Courageously he continued to give first aid to the wounded and to administer the last rites to the dying until hostilities ended. Eventually he recovered from his wound.

(Robert M. Utley, *Last Days of the Sioux Nation,* 1969.)

Crazy Horse, Oglala Sioux Chief. Crazy Horse, one of the most celebrated war chiefs of American history, was born about 1841. His Indian name was Tashunka Witco. Son of an Oglala medicine man, he was trained in mystic arts by his father and in martial arts by Red Cloud and other prominent war chiefs. He was destined, along with Sitting Bull, to lead the Sioux in some of the bloodiest battles with the United States Army from 1866 until his death on September 7, 1877.

At the time of the Fetterman Massacre in December, 1866, Crazy Horse was beginning to build a reputation as a daring and resourceful warrior deeply hostile to white soldiers and settlers. Paul I. Wellman believes that he, rather than Red Cloud, was the real leader of the ambush that claimed the lives of 80 Fort Phil Kearny soldiers. After Red Cloud moved to a reservation, Crazy Horse assumed leadership of the Sioux and many of his wife's people, the Cheyennes.

During the early 1870s, Crazy Horse, recognized by both Indians and whites as a skilled guerrilla tactician and a fighter so fearless that he led every attack, disrupted construction of the Northern Pacific Railroad on several occasions. With the seizure of the Black Hills, he and Sitting Bull led the hostiles in the Sioux War that began in 1875. In 1876, he fought General George Crook's army on the Rosebud and Powder rivers, and on June 25 he annihilated Custer's cavalry on the Little Bighorn.

After Custer's defeat, Crazy Horse declined to accompany Sitting Bull to Canada, choosing to remain in the Big Horn Mountains. In May 1877, General Nelson A. Miles and Sioux chief Spotted Tail persuaded him to surrender at Fort Robinson. There a rumor spread that he planned to lead an outbreak. When asked to assist in a campaign against the Nez Percé Indians, he assented, but the translator, Frank Grouard, reported that Crazy Horse intended to fight for Chief Joseph rather than against him.

This misunderstanding led to Crazy Horse's arrest. When the chief realized that soldiers and Indian police planned to imprison him, he pulled a knife and attempted to escape. In the melee he was stabbed with a bayonet and died soon afterward on September 7, 1877.

> One of the most tragic and heroic figures of modern history, he combined in his own character most of the virtues of his people. Crazy Horse was an enemy of all white men but even hardbitten Indian fighters like Crook and Miles . . . yielded him ungrudging admiration.—Paul I. Wellman

(Paul I. Wellman, *Death on Horseback*, 1947; Doane Robinson, *A History of the Dakota or Sioux Indians*, 1974; Frederick J. Dockstader, *Great North American Indians*, 1977; Joe De Barthe, *Life and Adventures of Frank Grouard*, 1958; Mari Sandoz, *Crazy Horse*, 1942; Dee Brown, *Bury My Heart at Wounded Knee*, 1971.)

Crittenden, George B., Expedition. In December 1860, Colonel George B. Crittenden led 60 soldiers from Fort Union, New Mexico, to attack a Comanche village on the Cimarron River. After marching through an uncharted country in bitterly cold weather, he located a large village on January 4 and attacked at dawn. His men killed 10 Indians, burned 150 lodges, and destroyed a large quantity of buffalo robes. The Comanches fled after wounding three of the soldiers.

(Charles L. Kenner, *A History of New Mexican-Plains Indian Relations*, 1969.)

Crooked Creek, Kansas, Battle of. See Nescutunga, Battle of

Crooks, Ramsay. Ramsay Crooks was born in Scotland on January 2, 1787. In 1802, he went to Montreal to enter the fur trade. By 1806, he was living in St. Louis. There he formed a partnership with Robert McLellan to trap on the Missouri, but they were driven away by the Sioux. In 1810, he joined the Pacific Fur Company and went to Astoria, where he became so ill that he had to return to St. Louis in 1813.

In 1817, Crooks joined the American Fur Company and quickly rose to the head of the western department, which he managed for many years. He was responsible in large measure for destroying the government factory system in order to increase company profits. When John Jacob Astor sold his interest, Crooks purchased the northern department and operated it under the name of the American Fur Company. He died on June 6, 1859.

"Crooks was always open and above board in his dealings, yet a vigorous and relentless enemy when he took up a contest."—Hiram Martin Chittenden

(Hiram Martin Chittenden, *The American Fur Trade of the Far West*, 1954; Le Roy R. Hafen, ed., *Mountain Men and Fur Traders of the Far West*, 1982.)

Crow Dog, Brulé Sioux Chief. Crow Dog (Kangi Sunka), a fierce enemy of white soldiers and settlers, is best known as the murderer of Chief Spotted Tail in 1881. White citizens were enraged because he was not executed for the crime under Sioux custom and demanded that Indian reservations be placed under the jurisdiction of the United States courts. As a result he was convicted of murder and sentenced to death. An appeal was filed, however, and the Supreme Court freed him, ruling that the courts lacked jurisdiction over crimes committed on reservations. Congress considered the decision outrageous and, in the Indian Appropriation Act of 1885, extended federal jurisdiction over seven major crimes committed on reservations.

Crow Dog was a leader of the Sioux Ghost Dance in 1890. He died in 1910, at the age of 75.

(Vine Deloria, Jr., *Custer Died for Your Sins*, 1969; Wilcomb E. Washburn, *Red Man's Land/White Man's Law*, 1971; Frederick J. Dockstader, *Great North American Indians*, 1977.)

Crow-Flies-High, Hidatsa Chief. Crow-Flies-High, a medicine man and war chief, refused to bring his people to the Fort Berthold reservation until compelled by starvation in 1893. He resisted allotment of lands in severalty for many years and opposed placing Indian children in white schools.

(Roy W. Meyer, *The Village Indians of the Upper Missouri*, 1977.)

Crow Indians. The Crow Indians, an important Siouan linguistic tribe, probably constituted a division of the Hidatsas until about 1776. Both resided on the Missouri River until a dispute caused the Crows to move to the shadow of the Rocky Mountains. In 1800, they were concentrated on the Bighorn while roaming along the Powder, Platte, Yellowstone, Musselshell, and Wind rivers.

The Crows were wandering buffalo hunters, constantly at war with their more numerous neighbors, the Sioux and Blackfeet. They befriended white traders and trappers, gaining a considerable degree of wealth by their skill in acquiring furs for the market. The only instance of Crow hostility to the whites occurred in 1834, when they attempted to starve out the American Fur Company traders who were establishing a fort in

Blackfoot territory. Claiming never to have killed a white man except in self-defense, they assisted the United States Army as scouts during wars with hostile Plains Indians.

(Margaret Carrington, *Ab-Sa-Ra-Ka, Home of the Crows*, 1869; Frank B. Linderman, *American*, 1930.)

Crow Killer. See Johnston, John

Cuerno Verde, Comanche Chief. Cuerno Verde (Green Horn) was a fearsome Comanche chief in New Mexico during the period 1760-1780 Held in such high regard by his people that he was served by pages and bodyguards, he hated the Spanish for killing his father and exacted a terrifying retribution. In 1778 alone he killed 127 people along the Rio Grande.

In 1779, Governor Juan Bautista de Anza determined to end the reign of terror. At the head of 85 soldiers and 259 Pueblo Indians, he attacked Cuerno Verde's camp at Pueblo, Colorado, when the chief and most of the warriors were away on a raid. He seized 50 women and children and lay in ambush for the return of the warriors. In the fight, which occurred near Greenhorn Peak, the Comanches were outnumbered ten to one. Cuerno Verde led a last desperate assault, and he and almost all of his warriors lost their lives. "Anza's successful campaign all but ended the Comanche threat to New Mexico."—Charles L. Kenne

(Charles L. Kenner, *A History of New Mexican-Plains Indian Relations*, 1969; T. R. Fehrenbach, *Comanches*, 1983).

Culbertson, Alexander. Alexander Culbertson was born in Chambersburg, Pennsylvania, in May 1809. He became a member of the American Fur Company in 1829 and proved be a courageous trader and a capable administrator. In 1833, at Fort McKenzie, a large Assiniboin war party attacked the Blackfeet camped outside the stockade. Culbertson held open the gates for the Blackfeet to come inside while Assiniboins threatened to lance him.

In 1845, Culbertson, known to the Indians for fair dealing, was sent up the Missouri to try to recover the Blackfoot trade. While managing Fort Union he married Medicine Snake Woman, sister of the prominent Blood chief, Seen From Afar. She was tremendously helpful to him in regaining the Blackfoot trade, and she bore him five children. In 1846, the Indians brought him 21,000 buffalo robes and a large number of beaver pelts.

In 1858, Culbertson retired after managing important posts on the Missouri and the Yellowstone. He and his Indian wife built a mansion in Illinois. (See Medicine Snake Woman.) In later life he served as interpreter at Fort Belknap, Montana. He died in 1879.

(Hiram Martin Chittenden, *The American Fur Trade of the Far West*, 1954; James Larpenteur Long, *The Assiniboines*, 1961; John C. Ewers, *The Blackfeet*, 1961; Walter O'Meara, *Daughters of the Country*, 1968.)

Cureton, Jack J. Jack Cureton (Curiton) came to Texas as a soldier in the Mexican War, liked the country, and settled on Keechi Creek. He served as captain of a company of volunteer Indian fighters. In 1860 he and his followers fought a battle with Comanches on Wolf Creek, killing every member of the war party except one. That same year he led the citizen soldiers who killed the important Comanche chief Peta Nocona.

(*Handbook of Texas I;* 1953; J. W. Wilbarger, *Indian Depradations in Texas*, 1985.)

Curly, Crow Scout. Curly (Ashishishe) was a Crow warrior born about 1859. He became a noted scout for the Seventh Cavalry and brought the first news of the destruction of Custer's command at the Little Bighorn. Some writers have identified him as the sole survivor of Custer's army, but he and other Indian scouts were employed to locate the enemy and released before the battle began. It is believed that he watched the battle from a distant hill.

(Frederick J. Dockstader, *Great North American Indians*, 1977; Evan S. Connell, *Son of the Morning Star*, 1984.)

Custer, George Armstrong. General George Armstrong Custer was born at New Rumley, Ohio, on December 5, 1839. He lived at Monroe, Michigan, when appointed to attend the United States Military Academy in 1857. Graduating in 1861, he had a distinguished Civil War career, becoming General Phil Sheridan's most trusted assistant and gaining the rank of major general. After the war his rank was reduced to captain.

Custer's career as an Indian fighter began in 1866 when he was appointed colonel of the Seventh Cavalry and stationed at Fort Riley, Kansas. During the Hancock Campaign of 1867, he drove his men so hard and dealt with deserters so harshly that he was court martialed and suspended from duty for a year. When reinstated he was chosen by Sheridan to lead a winter campaign against the Cheyennes. Determined to remove the blot from his record by winning a great victory, Custer (characterized by Richard H. Dillon as "politically as well as militarily ambitious") marched through a blizzard to launch a surprise attack on Black Kettle's unsuspecting village on November 27, 1868. Some two hundred Cheyennes were slain or wounded. (See Washita, Battle of the.) Custer's losses were limited, but he abandoned a small detachment when he withdrew (see Elliott, Joel H.), and sixteen men lost their lives. This tragedy caused dissension in the Seventh Cavalry as long as Custer lived. Several of his officers detested him for his eccentricities, his long golden curls, and his buckskin costume, and they condemned him for hurrying to proclaim victory while leaving missing men in the field.

During the early 1870s, Custer was active in exploration of Sioux territory and in guarding surveyors. In 1873, he protected the Northern Pacific Railway surveyors in the Yellowstone region (see Yellowstone, Battle of the), and in 1874 he explored the Black Hills and confirmed the presence of gold. "It would be difficult," Doane Robinson wrote, "to frame language better calculated to inflame the public mind and excite men to enter this country or die in the attempt, than in the language of General Custer's official report." A rush by miners into the forbidden territory led to the catastrophic (for Custer) Indian war of 1876.

Early in 1876, Sheridan ordered a campaign against the hostile Sioux in the Yellowstone region. Custer, then in command of Fort Abraham Lincoln, was in disfavor with President Grant for political activities, and only as a result of intercession by Sheridan was he permitted to accompany the expedition as a subordinate to General Alfred H. Terry. Terry sent him to locate the hostiles, and when he found an enormous encampment on the Little Bighorn, he charged the Indians without waiting for reinforcements. The result was the destruction of Custer's entire command. (See Little Bighorn, Battle of the.)

In a perceptive paragraph avoiding the controversy that lingers over Custer's motives and tactics, editors of the National Park Service's *Soldier and Brave* observed that

> an aura of mystery surrounds the annihilation of Custer and the five troops that he personally led. It is an enigma that spurs students of military history to infinite speculations over exactly why and how Custer met such a catastrophe. But one thing is certain. By suffering one of the worst defeats in the history of the Indian wars, he won for himself and his regiment an immortality that no victory, however brilliant and decisive, could have achieved.

Custer's wife, Elizabeth, spent the remainder of her life writing books and articles defending the actions of her adored spouse. Her view that he was innocent of disobeying orders, operating under Terry's permission to act in accordance with the dictates of the situation, has gained credence among many historians of today.

(Elizabeth B. Custer, *Boots and Saddles,* 1961; U. S. National Park Service, *Soldier and Brave,* 1963; Paul I. Wellman, *Death on Horseback,* 1947; Robert H. Dillon, *North American Indian Wars,* 1983; Doane Robinson, *A History of the Dakota or Sioux Indians,* 1974; Evan S. Connell, *Son of the Morning Star,* 1984; Bruce A. Rosenberg, *Custer and the Epic of Defeat,* 1974; Frederic F. Van de Water, *Glory Hunter,* 1963; W. A. Graham, *The Story of the Little Big Horn,* 1959.)

Cut Nose, Sioux Warrior. Cut Nose, whose name was acquired when Chief John Otherday bit off the tip of his nose, was one of the most ferocious warriors during the Minnesota Sioux uprising of 1862. Before he was hung, he boasted of murdering 23 settlers.

(C. M. Oehler, *The Great Sioux Uprising,* 1959.)

-D-

Dakota Indians. See Sioux Indians

Darlington, Brinton. Brinton Darlington, a Quaker, was appointed agent to the Cheyenne and Arapaho Indians on the Canadian River in accordance with President Grant's peace policy in 1869. He made a determined effort to induce the Indians to farm and to persuade them to send their children to school. He was greatly disappointed in their lack of response and felt when replaced in 1872 that he had failed. But he had accomplished more than he realized. He was regarded with affection by fierce warriors and, wrote Flora Seymour, "he is still remembered in their lodges." He died in 1872.

(Flora Warren Seymour, *Indian Agents of the Old Frontier*, 1975; Virginia Cole Trenholm, *The Araphoes, Our People*, 1970.)

Davidson, John W. Colonel John W. (Black Jack) Davidson, a West Point graduate, served in the Mexican War, the Civil War, and several Indian wars. In 1864, he was appointed Chief of Cavalry, Military Division of the West. In 1873, he assumed command of Fort Sill, bringing most of the Tenth Cavalry to the post to guard the Indian frontier. In 1874, he led the Buffalo Soldiers in the fight known as the Anadarko Affair. (See Anadarko, Oklahoma, Hostilities.) Later that year he participated in the major campaign called the Red River War, capturing almost four hundred Indians without losing a man. In 1875, he assumed command of Fort Griffin, Texas, but he returned to Fort Sill in 1878.

(William H. Leckie, *The Buffalo Soldiers*, 1967; W. S. Nye, *Carbine & Lance*, 1969.)

Davidson, Robert. Robert Davidson was born in Kentucky in 1799 and moved to Texas in 1825. In 1834, he settled on a headright on Little River. During the Texas Revolution the settlers were threatened by the Mexican Army on one side and hostile Indians on the other. The Davidsons and their neighbors fled toward the small community of Nashville, Texas. Enroute they were attacked by two hundred Indians. Davidson and a Baptist minister, Jasper Crouch, were killed. The other settlers made a stand in a grove of timber, and the Indians withdrew after several warriors were slain.

(James T. De Shields, *Border Wars of Texas*, 1976.)

Davis, Daniel. Daniel Davis, a native of Tennessee, came to Texas as a buffalo hunter in 1818. He ventured repeatedly into Comanche and Kiowa country on both sides of the Red River until the Indians killed him in 1838.

(*Handbook of Texas, I*, 1952.)

Day, Martha. See Diaz, Martina

Delauney, David. David Delauney, an unscrupulous promoter, visited the Osage Indians in 1827, representing himself as a United States Army officer, and persuaded twelve of them to go to France with him. Half of them turned back near New Orleans, but the others sailed with him to Paris. The Osages were unaware that their public appearances were intended to raise money for Delauney and that he planned to abandon them as soon as the venture was no longer profitable. Left to their own devices, they were destitute until French civil and religious officials contributed funds to send them home in 1830. Two of them died of smallpox while crossing the Atlantic.

(John Joseph Mathews, *The Osages*, 1961.)

Denig, Edwin Thompson. Edwin Thompson Denig was born in Pennsylvania in 1812. He became a fur trader in 1833, being employed at Fort Union and other Missouri River posts for 23 years. Credited with understanding Indians better than any trader on the Missouri, he wrote about tribal customs and collected materials for display at the Smithsonian Institution. He had two Indian wives at the same time, fathered four children, and sent them east to be educated. When he retired, he and his families lived with the Metis at Red River settlement in Canada.

(Walter O'Meara, *Daughters of the Country*, 1968; James Larpenteur Long, *The Assiniboines*, 1961; Edwin Thompson Denig, *Five Indian Tribes of the Upper Missouri*, 1961.)

Diaz, Martina, Captivity of. Martina Diaz (Martha Day), a sixteen-year-old Mexican girl, was captured by Comanche Indians in 1870 while traveling from Laredo to San Antonio, Texas. Her captor, a cruel warrior called Black Beard, beat her frequently, and she determined to attempt to escape, even though it could cost her her life.

On December 4, 1872, the Comanches camped near Fort Sill. Martina, ordered to watch the horse herd, fled to the Indian agency at midnight. As the agent, Lawrie Tatum, was asleep, she sat on his porch until he found her at dawn and hid her inside. Soon Black Beard and other warriors surrounded the house and demanded her return, but Tatum refused. That night he put her on the stage to Texas, and when Black Beard returned the following day, she was well beyond reach.

(Carl Coke Rister, *Border Captives*, 1940; Hugh D. Corwin, *Comanche & Kiowa Captives in Oklahoma and Texas*, 1959.)

Dixon, Billy. Billy Dixon was born in Virginia in 1850 and moved to the Great Plains as a youth. He worked as a mule skinner in Kansas, Nebraska, and Colorado before becoming a buffalo hunter in the Texas Panhandle. A famous marksman, he occasionally served as a hunting guide for easterners and Europeans.

In 1874, during the Battle of Adobe Walls, he shot a Cheyenne chief off his horse at a distance of almost a mile. Later that year, while carrying dispatches for Genenal Nelson A. Miles, he was awarded the Congressional Medal of Honor for his role in rescuing soldiers besieged by the Indians. (See Buffalo Wallow Fight.) Afterward he served as a guide for military operations against the Comanches. About 1900 he established a homestead in Cimarron County, Oklahoma, and died there in 1913.

(Paul I. Wellman, *Death on Horseback*, 1947; Mildred P. Mayhall, *Indian Wars of Texas*, 1965.)

Dodge, Henry, Plains Expeditions. In 1834, Colonel Henry Dodge accompanied a military expedition from Fort Gibson to the Plains Indians. Known as the Dragoon Expedition, it was commanded by General Henry Leavenworth until fever swept through the column, killing Leavenworth and many of his men. Dodge assumed command, met the Wichitas, Kiowas, and Comanches, and arranged for their representatives to attend a peace conference. As a result, a peace treaty was negotiated with the Plains Indians in 1835 that temporarily halted hostilities along the Santa Fe Trail and provided a respite in wars with the Civilized Tribes.

In 1835 Dodge led his dragoons along the Platte River as far as the Rocky Mountains, returning by way of the Sante Fe Trail. He met the Arikara Indians near the forks of the Platte, persuaded them to make peace with the Arapahoes and Cheyennes, and urged them to settle near the Pawnees.

(W. S. Nye, *Carbine & Lance*, 1969; U. S. National Park Service, *Soldier and Brave*, 1963; Hiram Martin Chittenden, *The American Fur Trade of the Far West*, 1954; Roy W. Meyer, *The Village Indians of the Upper Missouri*, 1977; John Joseph Mathews, *The Osages*, 1961.)

Dog Soldiers. During the Indian War of 1864, the military society called Dog Soldiers ravaged the western plains. "The Dog Soldiers, composed principally of Cheyennes, were an organized band made up of the turbulent and uncontrollable spirits of all the tribes' men who were never satisfied unless they were at war."—Virginia Cole Trenholm

(Virginia Cole Trenholm, *The Araphoes, Our People,* 1970; Paul I. Wellman, *Death on Horseback,* 1947.)

Dohasan, Kiowa Chief. Dohasan, one of the most prominent Kiowa chiefs, was born about 1805. During the 1840s, he fought white men who invaded tribal hunting lands. Afterward he signed the Treaty of Fort Atkinson, promising peace in exchange for an annuity; and the Treaty of Little Arkansas, agreeing to live on a reservation. He died in 1866.

(Mildred P. Mayhall, *The Kiowas,* 1962; Frederick J. Dockstader, *Great North American Indians,* 1977.)

Dorman, Isaiah. Isaiah Dorman, a black frontiersman who was a freed-man or a runaway slave, served as an army courier in the Dakotas in 1865. Two years later he married a Sioux woman, went to live with the tribe, and became a friend of Sitting Bull. In 1871, he was employed as an interpreter at Fort Rice. A guide with Custer's army in 1876, he was captured and tortured to death at the Battle of the Little Bighorn.

(Evan S. Connell, *Son of the Morning Star,* 1984; William Loren Katz, *Black Indians,* 1986.)

Doroin, Pierre, Sr. Pierre Doroin, Sr., was born in Quebec and moved to the Illinois country about 1780. In 1782, he married a Yankton Sioux woman and went to live with her tribe. For many years he traded along the Missouri and other western rivers. He served as an interpreter for the Lewis and Clark Expedition and was assigned by Lewis to escort a delegation of Sioux chiefs to Washington.

Doroin married more than one Indian woman and fathered several children, two of whom, Pierre, Jr., and Baptiste, became prominent guides. He served as Indian agent for Missouri tribes and spent his last days at Fort Pierre, South Dakota.

(Gordon Speck, *Breeds and Half-Breeds,* 1969; Bernard De Voto, ed., *The Journals of Lewis and Clark,* 1953.)

Dougherty, John. John Dougherty, government agent for the Pawnee Indians, learned in 1833 that the Skidis were preparing to sacrifice a Cheyenne captive girl to the Morning Star. With five other white men, he attempted to prevent the sacrifice, seizing the intended victim and endeavoring to escort her from the village. As they forced their way through the crowd, a medicine man shot the girl with an arrow. She fell from her horse and the Skidis prevented Dougherty from going to her rescue. They sacrificed her and tore her limb from limb while Dougherty and his men were compelled to flee for their lives.

(George E. Hyde, *The Pawnee Indians*, 1974.)

Drexel Mission. Immediately after the Wounded Knee Massacre in South Dakota in 1890, some Sioux warriors congregated near the Drexel Mission in White Clay Valley. While nuns offered them food, warriors seeking revenge set fire to one of the mission buildings. Seeing the smoke from a distance, Colonel James W. Forsyth led a regiment to the scene to investigate. Indians on a bluff attacked the troops and kept them pinned down throughout the day. Finally a detachment of Buffalo Soldiers, led by Colonel Guy V. Henry, arrived at the scene and compelled the Sioux to withdraw. Several of Forsyth's men were killed or wounded.

(Robert M. Utley, *The Last Days of the Sioux Nation*, 1963; Joe De Barthe, *Life and Adventures of Frank Grouard*, 1958; William H. Leckie, *The Buffalo Soldiers*, 1967.)

Drips, Andrew. Andrew Drips was born in Ireland in 1789 and emigrated to Pennsylvania at an early age. He fought in the War of 1812 and entered the fur trade soon afterward. As an employee of the American Fur Company, he was in charge of the mountain expeditions from 1836 to 1840. In 1842, he was appointed Indian agent for the upper Missouri tribes, a post he held for four years. During his tenure he made a determined but not entirely successful effort to prevent the sale of liquor to Indians.

Drips married an Oto Indian woman and they had several children. He died in 1860.

(Hiram Martin Chittenden, *The American Fur Trade of the Far West*, 1954; Le Roy Hafen, ed., *Mountain Men and Fur Traders of the Far West*, 1982.)

Drouillard, George. Little is known of the early life of George Drouillard, a French-Pawnee mixed blood hunter who was recommended to the Lewis and Clark Expedition by George Rogers Clark. He proved to be a tremendous asset to the explorers, keeping them supplied with meat during their transcontinental journey. While passing through Blackfoot country, he shot a warrior who was attempting to steal his rifle, an incident that caused the tribe to be hostile toward Americans for many years.

In 1807, Drouillard worked for Manuel Lisa, leading his trading expedition to regions he had visited with Lewis and Clark. He was instrumental in getting them past the hostile Arikaras on the Missouri and in establishing Fort Raymond at the mouth of the Bighorn River, a highly successful post in the Crow Indian trade.

In March 1810, Drouillard guided Andrew Henry and Pierre Menard to the Three Forks of the Missouri to establish trade with the Blackfeet.

While hunting near the post they established, he was slain by the Black-feet.

(John C. Ewers, *The Blackfeet*, 1961; Gordon Speck, *Breeds and Half-Breeds*, 1969; Hiram Martin Chittenden, *The American Fur Trade of the Far West*, 1954.)

Dull Knife, Cheyenne Chief. Dull Knife (Tamela Pashme) was born in Montana in 1810. He became a prominent war chief who fought the United States Army at the battles of the Little Bighorn and Red Fork. His village was destroyed by Colonel Ranald Mackenzie in 1876. He surrendered in 1877 and was removed with his people to Oklahoma. In 1878, when the Northern Cheyennes were starving, he and Little Wolf led an outbreak in a desperate attempt to return to their homeland. When they crossed the South Platte the two chiefs quarreled over Dull Knife's desire to stop for a rest. Their forces split up, and Dull Knife and his followers surrendered to the Third Cavalry. They were imprisoned at Fort Robinson and ordered to return to the Indian Territory.

Dull Knife refused to return and, as a consequence, the Cheyennes were denied food and fuel to keep them from freezing to death. On January 10, 1879, they broke out of the guard house. Most of them were killed or recaptured, but Dull Knife escaped to a Sioux village. After the Northern Cheyennes were given a reservation on the Rosebud, he was permitted to remain there. He died in 1883.

(Frederick J. Dockstader, *Great North American Indians*, 1977; Paul I. Wellman, *Death on Horseback*, 1947; George Bird Grinnell, *The Fighting Cheyennes*, 1956; Homer W. Wheeler, *Buffalo Days*, 1925.)

Duluth, Daniel Greysalon, Sieur. Daniel Greysalon, Sieur Duluth (Dulhut), was born in France in 1636, a member of a royal family. He went to Canada in 1672 and became a *coureur de bois*. While exploring Lake Superior in 1678, he persuaded the Sioux to make peace with the Chippewas. In 1679, he visited a Sioux village in Minnesota, where he negotiated an alliance between the Sioux and the French government and claimed the territory for his king. In 1684 and 1687, he led expeditions to punish the Iroquois. In 1690, he commanded Fort Frontenac. He retired to Montreal in 1695 and died in 1710.

(Louise Phelps Kellogg, *The French Régime in Wisconsin and the Northwest*, 1968.)

Dunbar, John Brown. John Brown Dunbar, a Protestant minister, went to the Grand Pawnees as a missionary in 1834. He lived with Chief Sharitarish to master the language and went with him on an extended buffalo hunt. In 1837, he brought his wife to Bellevue, Nebraska, to live at the agency. He attempted to induce the Indians to become farmers, but with scant success. In 1846, he prevented a Sioux war party from entering the mission stockade by barring the gate with his body. Soon afterward, regarding his mission a failure, he moved to Missouri.

(George E. Hyde, *The Pawnee Indians,* 1974.)

Durgan, Millie, Captivity of. Millie Durgan, a one-year-old, was captured by the Kiowa Indians during a raid in Young County, Texas, in 1864. (See Elm Creek Raid.) After the murder of her mother, the house was set on fire, and Millie was pulled from the flames by the warrior Aperian Crow and raised as his daughter. Quickly assimilated, she married a warrior named Goombi at age 16, and they had many children.

In 1930, after more than sixty years as a Kiowa, she was restored to her relatives in Texas. Two years later, with a son serving as interpreter, she toured Texas schools to tell her life story.

(Mildred P. Mayhall, *The Kiowas,* 1962; *The Indian Wars of Texas,* 1965; Benjamin Capps, *The Warren Wagontrain Raid,* 1974.)

Du Tisne, Claude-Charles. Claude-Charles Du Tisne, a native of Paris, France, was sent to Canada as a military officer about 1705. In 1714, promoted to lieutenant, he built forts at Natchez and on the Wabash. In 1719, he visited the Osages, Pawnees, and Missouris, introducing French trade goods and establishing friendly relations. In 1723, he commanded Fort de Chartres in the Illinois country. In 1729, he was mortally wounded there by a Fox Indian warrior.

(John Joseph Mathews, *Wah' Kon-Tah,* 1932; John Anthony Caruso, *The Mississippi Valley Frontier,* 1966.)

-E-

Eagle Ribs, Blackfoot Chief. Eagle Ribs (Petohpeekiss) was one of the most formidable Backfoot chiefs during the early nineteenth century. In 1832, he visited Fort Union, exhibited eight scalps, and boasted that they were lifted from American traders and trappers.

(George Catlin, *Letters and Notes on the Manners, Customs, and Conditions of the North American Indians*, 1973; John C. Ewers, *The Blackfeet*, 1961.)

Eastlick, John, Family of. The John Eastlick family lived in the Lake Shetak, Minnesota, settlement during the Sioux uprising of 1862. They and their neighbors attempted to flee, but were overtaken by a war party led by an Indian called Pawn. They hid in a pond full of rushes, where the Sioux fired upon them, killing John Eastlick and wounding his wife, Lavinia. After all of the men were slain, the women and children surrendered. Mrs. Eastlick's sons, Freddy and Frank, were beaten to death.

Since Mrs. Eastlick believed that she was fatally wounded, she handed her 15-month-old son, Johnny, to her 11-year-old son, Merton, and instructed him to take care of the child as long as they lived. Although shot in the back by Pawn, beaten over the head, and left for dead, she managed to rise to her feet and struggle away from the scene. Several days later she was found by August Garzine, a mail carrier who took her in a buggy toward New Ulm. Forty miles away from the massacre scene they found Merton, still carrying the baby. An emaciated skeleton, his bare feet lacerated by brambles, he had carried Johnny every step of the way, hiding during daylight and subsisting on berries. Mrs. Eastlick and both boys recovered.

(Charles S. Bryant, *A History of the Great Massacre by the Sioux Indians in Minnesota*, 1868; Paul I. Wellman, *Death on Horseback*, 1947.)

Eastman, Charles Alexander. Charles Alexander Eastman (Ohiyesa), a Santee Sioux, was born at Redwood Falls, Minnesota, in 1858. He was educated in mission schools, graduated from Dartmouth College in 1877, and completed medical school at Boston University in 1890.

Eastman was appointed physician at the Pine Ridge Reservation in 1890. He was there at the time of the Wounded Knee massacre and saved the lives of some of the Indians shot by the soldiers. He married Elaine Goodale, a teacher at the agency, and they wrote several books that increased understanding between Indians and whites. In 1903, he supervised allotments of Sioux lands, and during the 1920s he served as Indian inspector. He died in 1939.

(Frederick J. Dockstader, *Great North American Indians*, 1977; Robert M. Utley, *The Last Days of the Sioux Nation*, 1963; Charles A. Eastman, *Indian Boyhood*, 1972.)

Eastman, John. John Eastman, brother of Dr. Charles A. Eastman, was born at Shakopee, Minnesota, in March, 1849. After studying with the Rev. A. L. Riggs, he was ordained a Presbyterian minister at Flandreau, Minnesota, in 1876. He served as Sioux school supervisor as well as a minister and a model farmer.

(F. W. Hodge, ed., *Handbook of American Indians, I*, 1912.)

Eayre, George, Expedition. In April 1864, Lieutenant George Eayre set out from Camp Weld, near Denver, in pursuit of Cheyennes who had stolen some cattle. Failing to find the culprits, he attacked the camps of two friendly Cheyenne chiefs, Crow Chief and Racoon, near the Republican River, killing a score of Indians.

(Paul I. Wellman, *Death on Horseback*, 1977; George Bird Grinnell, *The Fighting Cheyennes*, 1956.)

Edmunds, Newton. Newton Edmunds, former governor of the Dakota Territory, was an experienced treaty negotiator with the Plains tribes when appointed in 1882 to persuade the Sioux to part with large portions of their great reservation. He headed a commission that sought a cession of half of the reservation in exchange for clear title to five smaller reserves. Edmunds

> brought intense pressure to bear, made much of the many advantages to the Indians, and barely mentioned that he was asking them to part with half of their remaining land. They grew dizzy at his avalanche of words. At each agency the chiefs held out as long as they could, but someone always started a stampede and they lined up to sign.—Robert M. Utley

When the agreement was accepted in 1883, many Sioux protested that they had been cheated. Indian rights organizations joined the outcry, and Congress voided the agreement because it conflicted with the Treaty of 1868.

(Robert M. Utley, *The Last Days of the Sioux Nation*, 1963; Doane Robinson, *A History of the Dakota or Sioux Indians*, 1974; Dee Brown, *Bury My Heart at Wounded Knee*, 1971.)

Ekhaka Sapa, Oglala Sioux Medicine Man. See Black Elk, Oglala Sioux Medicine Man

Eldridge, Joseph C., Expedition. Joseph C. Eldridge moved to Texas from Connecticut in 1837. During most of the decade that he remained in the republic and state he frequently was involved in Indian affairs. His most important service in that regard occurred in 1843 when he headed a peace commission that visited the Comanche country.

Accompanied by Hamilton Bee and Thomas Torrey, he located the band of Chief Pahayuca on the upper Canadian River in August and returned two Comanche children who had been captured and held since 1840. (See Hockley, Bill.) Eldridge was advised by his three Delaware Indian guides that the Comanches were debating in council whether to kill the commissioners. At one time every chief at the council advocated a death sentence except Pahayuca. The principal chief persuaded a majority to respect the flag of truce and agreed to attend a peace conference at Bird's Fort.

(Ernest Wallace and E. Adamson Hoebel, *The Comanches,* 1952; W. S. Nye, *Carbine & Lance,* 1969; J. W. Wilbarger, *Indian Depredations in Texas,* 1985.)

Elliott, Joel H. Major Joel H. Elliott, a young Seventh Cavalry officer who had been severely wounded during the Civil War, led three troops during Custer's attack on the Cheyennes on November 27, 1868. (See Washita, Battle of the.) A gap occurred in the cavalry line and Chief Little Rock and a few followers fled through it. Yelling "here goes for a brevet or a coffin," Elliott and nineteen troopers rode recklessly in pursuit. Little Rock was slain protecting the retreat of the women and children, but the noise of the conflict alerted the Kiowas and Araphoes camped nearby. Led by Little Raven and Satanta, these fierce warriors, while rushing to the battlefield, encountered Elliott's men and killed them all.

Elliott and his followers were missing at the end of the battle, and Custer made little attempt to determine their fate when he withdrew from the field. This action was condemned as a gross abandonment by some of his officers and by historians as well. Others have defended Custer on grounds that he was outnumbered and out of supplies.

(De B. Randolph Keim, *Sheridan's Troopers on the Borders,* 1870; Frederick F. Van de Water, *Glory Hunter,* 1963; Evan S. Connell, *Son of the Morning Star,* 1984.)

Ellis, Fort, Montana. Fort Ellis was built in 1867 near the site of the present Bozeman, Montana. It was intended as a bulwark against the Sioux, and troops quartered there fought in the Indian wars until 1881. It was abandoned in 1886.

(Robert W. Frazer, *Forts of the West,* 1965.)

Ellison Springs Fight. On August 9, 1864, seven soldiers led by Corporal James L. Head were attacked by 40 Indians in Eastland County, Texas. They retreated to the Gilbert ranch, recruited five cowboys, and pursued the war party to Ellison Springs. There a fierce battle was fought that cost the lives of two whites and several Indians.

(*The Handbook of Texas, I*, 1952.)

Elm Creek, Texas, Raid. In October 1864, a Comanche and Kiowa war party led by Chief Little Buffalo raided Young County, Texas. They attacked Fort Murray, a Confederate outpost, and killed five soldiers. Then they passed a few miles west of Fort Belknap and swept along Elm Creek, killing 11 ranchers and capturing their wives and children.

Peter Harmonson and his son, Perry, were pursued by several hundred warriors to the mouth of Elm Creek. There they dismounted in a thicket and fought so courageously that the Indians departed in search of easier prey. Raiders attacked the McCoy ranch, killing McCoy and his son and capturing two women. Then they encountered a detachment of Texas Cavalry, fought a brief battle, and lost the McCoy women, who reached safety at Fort Murray.

Seven hundred warriors advanced along both sides of Elm Creek, plundering almost every house and driving away horses and cattle. At the home of widow Elizabeth Fitzpatrick, they found only women and children. Susan Durgan, Mrs. Fitzpatrick's grown daughter, and a young black boy, Charles Johnson, tried to defend the house, and both were slain. The raiders captured Mrs. Fitzpatrick; her son, Joe; her granddaughters, Lottie and Milly; and Mrs. Britt Johnson and her children, Jube and Cherry. (See Johnson, Britton; Durgan, Millie.)

At the George Bragg ranch, a few men led by Thornton Hamby defended the house against a horde of raiders. Hamby killed Little Buffalo during a fight that lasted all afternoon and, soon afterward, the Indians withdrew. Britt Johnson followed them to the Canadian River where he recovered Mrs. Fitzpatrick. Later he redeemed his wife and children and Lottie Durgan.

(T. R. Fehrenbach, *Comanches,* 1983; Mildred P. Mayhall, *The Kiowas,* 1962; Benjamin Capps, *The Warren Wagontrain Raid,* 1974.)

Eubank, William, Family of. On August 7, 1864, Cheyennes raided the Eubank stage station in southeastern Nebraska Territory, killing William Eubank and several of his relatives. Mrs. Eubank, her three-year-old daughter, Isabelle, and her infant son were captured, along with sixteen-year-old Laura Roper. After a year of captivity, Mrs. Eubank was carried to Wyoming and sold to the Sioux chiefs Two Face and Black Foot. They brought her to Fort Laramie, hoping to prove their friendship or receive a reward, but they were seized by the soldiers, condemned to death by General P. E. Connor, and hanged. Laura Roper and the Eubank children were redeemed from captivity by Major E. W. Wynkoop at Fort Lyon.

(Ruby E. Wilson, *Frank J. North*, 1984; Carl Coke Rister, *Border Captives*, 1940.)

Evans, John. John Evans, a physician from Ohio, was appointed territorial governor of Colorado on March 26, 1862. Immediately upon assuming the post he began negotiating with the Cheyenne and Arapaho Indians in an initially successful attempt to prevent attacks on settlers and Ute Indian villages. Upon the outbreak of the Indian war of 1864, however, he refused to meet chiefs brought to Denver by Major E. W. Wynkoop in the interest of peace, asserting that hostile bands must be punished first. This decision was a contributing factor to the Sand Creek Massacre.

(Virginia Cole Trenholm, *The Arapahoes, Our People*, 1970; John Tebbel and Keith Jennison, *The American Indian Wars*, 1960.)

Evea, Comanche Chief. Evea, a principal Comanche chief, signed a peace treaty with Governor Juan María Vicencio de Ripperda at San Antonio, Texas, in 1772. Afterward he became hostile to Spanish settlers and led several raids in the East Texas area.

(F. A. Hodge, ed., *Handbook of American Indians, I*, 1912; *Handbook of Texas, I*, 1952.)

F

Faulkenberry, David and Evan. David Faulkenberry and his son, Evan, settled at Parker's Fort, Texas, in the spring of 1836. On May 19, they were in fields two miles away when an Indian war party destroyed the fort. They rescued several settlers who had escaped to the woods and helped them reach safety at Fort Houston. (See Parker's Fort.)

On January 28, 1837, the Faulkenberrys and several companions left Fort Houston in search of hogs. In the Trinity River bottoms they encountered thirty hostile Indians who opened fire with rifles and bows and arrows. David was mortally wounded, but he managed to swim the river before he died. Evan Faulkenberry and Abraham Anglin sought protection behind trees, and while David attempted to hold the Indians at bay, Anglin ran toward Fort Houston for help. Wounded several times, he staggered into the fort and sent a relief party to the scene of the battle. Searchers found the bodies of all the men except Evan, who was never seen again. Many years later an Indian reported that Evan Faulkenberry "fought like a demon, killing two of his assailants, wounded a third, and when scalped and almost cloven asunder, jerked away from them, threw himself into the river and swam as far as midstream, where he sank from view."

(James T. De Shields, *Border Wars of Texas,* 1976.)

Fetterman Massacre. Captain William J. Fetterman, twice brevetted for bravery during the Civil War, reported for duty at Fort Phil Kearny in November 1866. A reckless and self-confident officer who asserted that a company of cavalrymen could whip a thousand Sioux, he was contemptuous of the cautious tactics of his commanding officer, Colonel Henry B. Carrington, who permitted the Sioux and Cheyennes to keep the fort in a virtual state of siege.

On December 6, Fetterman led 40 troopers to rescue a wagon train, while Carrington took 25 men to attack the Indians from the rear. A fierce fight ensued, and Fetterman lost seven men before Carrington arrived and drove the Indians away.

On December 21, a large war party attacked a wood train near the fort and Carrington acceded to Fetterman's demand to lead a force to the rescue. Fearing that Fetterman's recklessness would cause him to fall into a trap, Carrington ordered him to refrain from crossing Lodge Trail Ridge, where he would be out of sight of the fort. But Fetterman ignored the order and led his 80 men over the ridge and into an ambush.

A few warriors rode so close, shouting derisively, that, wrote Paul I. Wellman, the hot impulse to pursue could not be denied. How was he to know that, in the ravines running from each side of the draw, hid the Sioux and Cheyennes in hundreds, their mounted men clustering at the mouth of the ravine, to close the door of the trap, while others in scores lay in the grass across the line of march?

Led by Crazy Horse and Red Cloud, the Indians annihilated the command to the last man.

(Paul I. Wellman, *Death on Horseback,* 1947; J. W. Vaughan, *Indian Fights,* 1966; Margaret Carrington, *Ab-Sa-Ra-Ka, Home of the Crows,* 1868; Doane Robinson, *History of the Dakota or Sioux Indians,* 1974; Richard H. Dillon, *North American Indian Wars,* 1983.)

Fisher, Rebecca (Gilleland). See Gilleland, Johnstone, Family

Fitzpatrick, Thomas. Thomas Fitzpatrick, one of the foremost guides for parties crossing the Great Plains and Rocky Mountains, was born in Ireland about 1799. He received a good education before coming to America as a youth to enter the Indian trade. In 1823, he joined William Ashley's company of trappers and fought in both battles with the Arikara Indians on the Missouri River. He spent the winter of 1823-1824 among the Crow Indians.

Fitzpatrick continued to trap for many years. In 1830, he joined Jim Bridger and Milton Sublette in organizing the Rocky Mountain Fur Company. Afterward he trapped for the American Fur Company until the beaver trade expired in 1840.

Fitzpatrick, who had already discovered South Pass and guided several clergymen to their missions west of the Rocky Mountains, began leading emigrant trains in 1841 when he brought the Bidwell-Bartleson expedition to Fort Hall and escorted Father Pierre Jean De Smet to the Flathead Indian country. Returning to Fort Laramie, he met Dr. Elijah White's emigrant train and guided it to Fort Hall. In 1843, he served as guide for John C. Fremont's second expedition, leading them to California and returning to Bent's Fort on the Arkansas. In 1845, he guided the S. W. Kearny expedition to the South Pass and Bent's Fort, where he was detached from Kearny to serve as a guide for J. W. Abert's explorations of the Comanche country along the Canadian River.

Fitzpatrick was appointed Indian agent for the Arkansas-Platte region on August 6, 1846, a career in which he quickly excelled. David Lavender has observed that "in the dismal role of America's corrupt and blundering Indian agents, his name is one of few that leave no sour taste." He served fairly and wisely for eight years, gaining the respect of the Plains Indians as well as the settlers. In 1850, he married a mixed-blood Arapaho woman, Margaret Poisal. The following year he arranged the Fort Laramie Council, and in 1853, he persuaded the Kiowa and Comanches to sign a peace treaty. From his headquarters at Bent's Fort, he proved to be a formidable force for peace along the Santa Fe Trail. He frequently escorted Indians to visit the President in Washington, and in 1854, he died in that city of pneumonia.

(Le Roy R. Hafen, *Broken Hand*, 1973; Hiram Martin Chittenden, *The American Fur Trade of the Far West*, 1954; David Lavender, *Bent's Fort*, 1954; Robert M. Utley and Wilcomb E. Washburn, *The American Heritage History of the Indian Wars*, 1977; Virginia Cole Trenholm, *The Arapahoes, Our People*, 1970.)

Flandrau, Charles E. Charles E. Flandrau was born in New York City on July 15, 1828, son of Aaron Burr's law partner. After attending law school he established a practice at St. Paul and Traverse des Sioux, Minnesota. In 1856, he was appointed Indian agent to the eastern Sioux. During his tenure he played a significant role in rescuing female captives taken by the Sioux during the Spirit Lake Massacre of 1857. (See Gardner, Rowland.) Soon afterward he served as a Minnesota Supreme Court judge.

An organizer of the St. Peter Frontier Guards, he led the defense of New Ulm, Minnesota, during the Sioux uprising of 1862. "Athletic, eloquent, and alert, respected, an intelligent leader, he had great natural aptitude for the responsibilities to which the citizen soldiers elected him."—C. M. Oehler

In a day-long battle the defenders drove off the huge war party. (See New Ulm.) Before his death in 1903, Flandrau wrote valuable histories of frontier life in Minnesota.

(Charles E. Flandrau, *The History of Minnesota and Tales of the Frontier*, 1900; C. M. Oehler, *The Great Sioux Uprising*, 1959.)

Fletcher, Lizzie, Captivity of. Lizzie Fletcher was captured by Arapaho Indians in 1865 at the age of two. By the age of 15 she was completely assimilated and had married General Crook's scout, John Broken Horn. When seen by an Indian agent in 1878, she insisted that she was not white. She remained with the tribe her entire life.

(Virginia Cole Trenholm, *The Arapahoes, Our People*, 1970.)

Foley, Tucker. In August 1840, when the Comanche Indians made a massive raid to the Gulf Coast (see Linnville, Texas, Raid), they encountered Tucker Foley and Dr. Joel Ponton near the present town of Halletsville. Foley, son of a wealthy planter, was riding a race horse, and 27 warriors, eager to obtain the prized animal, dashed in pursuit. Ponton, riding a slow horse, was quickly overtaken and struck by a lance. He fell to the ground, feigning death, while the Indians kept on after Foley. Afterward he fled to the nearest settlement to give the alarm.

Foley was hemmed in after a two-mile chase. He tried to hide in a creek, but warriors dragged him out, shot him, scalped him, and cut off the soles of his feet.

(Walter Prescott Webb, *The Texas Rangers*, 1965; John Holland Jenkins, *Recollections of Early Texas*, 1958.)

Ford, John Salmon. John Salmon (Rip) Ford was born in South Carolina on May 26, 1815. He moved to Texas in June 1836, and served in the Republic of Texas Army until 1838. Afterward he became a physician and newspaper editor in San Augustine and Austin. During the Mexican War he served as adjutant to John Coffey Hays.

In 1849, Ford and R. S. Neighbors blazed a trail from San Antonio to El Paso. Upon his return he was appointed captain of a Texas Ranger company on patrol between the Nueces and Rio Grande. In that thinly settled region he participated in several fights with Comanche Indians, in one of which he was shot in the hand by a poisoned arrow.

Ford was promoted to senior captain of state military forces in 1858 and instructed to chastise hostile Indians wherever he could find them. On May 12, at the head of 102 Rangers and 113 friendly Indians from the Brazos Reserve, he attacked Iron Jacket's camp on the Canadian River. The Comanches suffered a costly defeat, losing 76 warriors and a large horse herd. Only two Texans were killed. Ford's campaign convinced the Comanches that they could no longer reach safety from pursuit by crossing the Red River. Afterward Ford became a prominent politician.

While most historians regard Ford as a hero of the Indian wars, William Loren Katz holds an opposite view:

Seminole families had hardly settled down when in 1851 U. S. outlaw John 'Rip' Ford rode into Mexico with a band of four hundred men. Wildcat and John Horse were called upon to drive out the bandits, former Texas Rangers and unemployed Texans. Sixty Seminoles drove back the Texans without a casualty.

(John Salmon Ford, *Rip Ford's Texas*, 1963; Walter Prescott Webb, *The Texas Rangers*, 1965; William Loren Katz, *Black Indians*, 1986.

Forest City, Minnesota, Raid. During the Minnesota Sioux uprising of 1862, Chief Sacred Rattle led a raid on the Forest City community. Outside the town they murdered Jack Adams, captured his wife, and bashed his baby's brains out. Other citizens took refuge in a stockade while warriors burned most of the town.

(C. M. Oehler, *The Great Sioux Uprising*, 1959.)

Forsyth, George A. Major George A. Forsyth began his military career as a private and advanced all the way to brigadier general during the Civil War. He devised a winter campaign against the Sioux and Cheyennes in 1868, a plan that was adopted by General Sheridan. To keep the hostiles reeling, he recruited 50 experienced scouts and Indian fighters and led them in a campaign that culminated in the Battle of Beecher's Island. During the bloody battle he was wounded three times and developed blood poisoning. As a result he was incapacitated for two years. (See Beecher's Island, Battle of.) Afterward he fought in the Apache wars.

(Richard H. Dillon, *North American Indian Wars*, 1983; Paul I. Wellman, *Death on Horseback*, 1947.)

Forsyth, James W. Colonel James W. Forsyth of the Seventh Cavalry was dispatched from Fort Riley to the Pine Ridge Reservation in 1890 to keep an eye on the Ghost Dance unrest that was sweeping through the Sioux nation. A distinguished veteran of the Civil War, he knew little about Indians. On December 29 he attempted to disarm Chief Big Foot's Sioux warriors, and their resistance resulted in the slaughter of Indians at Wounded Knee. (See Wounded Knee Massacre.)

(Robert M. Utley, *The Last Days of the Sioux Nation*, 1963; Dee Brown, *Bury My Heart at Wounded Knee*, 1971.)

Four Bears, Mandan Chief. See Mato Tope, Mandan Chief

Fraeb, Henry. Henry Fraeb (Frapp), a German, was one of the most active Indian traders on the plains and in the mountains from 1830 to 1841. As a brigade leader of the Rocky Mountain Fur Company, he participated in numerous Indian fights, including the Battle of Pierre's Hole. In 1841, while associated with Jim Bridger, he was killed in a battle between 60 trappers and a large war party of Sioux and Cheyennes on the St. Vrain branch of the Yampah River in southern Wyoming.

(Hiram Martin Chittenden, *A History of the American Fur Trade of the Far West*, 1954; Le Roy R. Hafen, *Broken Hand*, 1973.)

Frapp, Henry. See Fraeb, Henry

Fremont's Orchard Fight. In April 1864, some Southern Cheyenne Dog Soldiers on their way to join a Northern Cheyenne war party were attacked by the First Colorado Cavalry on the South Platte River near the community of Fremont's Orchard. Two of the soldiers were killed and two wounded.

(George Bird Grinnell, *The Fighting Cheyennes*, 1956.)

Friday, Cheyenne Chief. In 1831, Thomas Fitzpatrick found a starving Cheyenne child on the Santa Fe Trail, took him to St. Louis, and arranged for him to go to school. Named Friday because he was found on that day, he returned to his people before 1840 and became chief of a small band. In 1851, he visited Washington with a delegation of chiefs. In 1864, he tried to prevent his followers from taking part in the war against the whites and when they went to the reservation he helped them to adjust to the new way of life. On several occasions he served as interpreter during treaty negotiations. He died in 1881.

(Le Roy R. Hafen, *Broken Hand*, 1973.)

Friend, Temple, Captivity of. On February 6, 1868, a Comanche war party attacked the home of John S. Friend in the Legion Valley, near Llano, Texas. They wounded and scalped Mrs. Friend, leaving her for dead, and captured seven women and children. All of the captives were murdered soon afterward except two small children, Temple Friend and Melinda Cordle. Temple's grandfather, the Reverend L. S. Friend, traveled fifteen thousand miles through Texas, New Mexico, and Arizona, offering a $1,000 reward for information about the child's whereabouts, but without success. Melinda Cordle was recovered by Agent E. W. Wynkoop.

In 1873, Quaker Indian agent Lawrie Tatum redeemed Temple Friend when the Comanches were compelled to surrender their captives. He had forgotten his name and spoke only the language of his captors, but when Tatum sent for his grandfather, they recognized each other immediately.

(Lawrie Tatum, *Our Red Brothers,* 1970; Carl Coke Rister, *Border Captives,* 1940).

Galbraith, Thomas J. Major Thomas Galbraith was appointed agent to the Minnesota Sioux in 1861. He was living with his family at the Yellow Medicine Agency in 1862 when the Sioux revolted over the government's failure to provide food as promised by treaty. On August 4, some hungry Indians broke into the warehouse and Galbraith gave them all the food he had.

When the Sioux began murdering settlers, Galbraith was away recruiting men to fight for the Union in the Civil War. Chief John Otherday escorted Mrs. Galbraith and her three children to safety through a country swarming with hostile Sioux. Galbraith and his recruits participated in the battles of Fort Ridgely and Birch Coulee. After the outbreak was quelled, bitter because he was blamed for conditions beyond his control that inflamed the Indians, he moved to Montana and became a judge.

(C. M. Oehler, *The Great Sioux Uprising*, 1959; Flora Warren Seymour, *Indian Agents of the Old Frontier*, 1975.)

Gall, Hunkpapa Sioux Chief. Gall (Pizí) was born in South Dakota about 1840. An orphan, he was adopted by Sitting Bull and fought beside his chief in many battles against Indian enemies and whites. During the winter of 1865-1866, while visiting Fort Berthold, he was bayoneted by a soldier and left for dead, but he survived and exacted revenge by killing a considerable number of troopers during the next decade.

At the beginning of the Battle of the Little Bighorn, Major Reno's soldiers killed several of Gall's relatives. He retaliated, wrote Evan S. Connell, by riding "through Custer's desperate troopers like a wolf through a flock of sheep." A giant of a man, he wielded his war axe with skull-shattering effect. After the annihilation of Custer's command, he withdrew to Canada with Sitting Bull.

In 1880, Gall abandoned warfare, settled on the Standing Rock Reservation, and became an advocate of the white man's way. In 1889, he signed a land cession treaty and was appointed to the Indian judiciary. He opposed the Ghost Dance in 1890 and afterward served his people as an envoy to Washington. He died on December 5, 1895.

(Frederick J. Dockstader, *Great North American Indians*, 1977; Robert M. Utley, *The Last Days of the Sioux Nation*, 1963; Evan S. Connell, *Son of the Morning Star*, 1984.)

Galvanized Yankees. *Galvanized Yankees* was a term applied to captured Confederate soldiers who were released from prison after swearing allegiance to the United States and agreeing to fight in the Union Army against hostile Indians in the West. In 1864 and 1865, more than six thousand ex-Confederates were inducted, many of them manning forts on the Great Plains. Others served as guards for stage coaches and wagon trains.

Perhaps the most unfortunate of the Galvanized Yankees were stationed at Fort Connor during the winter of 1864-1865. Red Cloud's Sioux warriors cut off supplies for the fort, and many of the soldiers died of malnutrition, scurvy, or pneumonia before they were relieved on June 28.

(Dee Brown, *Galvanized Yankees,* 1963.)

Gantt, John. Captain John Gantt (Gant, Gaunt), who has been charged with turning the Cheyennes into a nation of drunkards, was an Army officer at Fort Atkinson when the western fur trade began. He participated in the battle against the Arikaras in 1823. In 1829, he was dismissed from the Army and is believed to have been trading on the Arkansas by 1830. In 1831, he led an unsuccessful brigade of trappers from St. Louis to the Laramie River. The following year he and his partner, Jefferson Blackwell, trapped in Colorado. Some of his men, including Kit Carson, fought a battle with the Comanches, but Gantt built a post on the upper Arkansas, where he became the first trader to establish friendly relations with the Arapahoes.

In 1835, his business having failed despite his debauchery of the Indians, Gantt served as guide for Dodge's dragoons during the Army's first penetration of the Great Plains. In August, he made a major contribution to the expedition by persuading the Arapahoes and Gros Ventres to attend a peace council with Dodge at Bent's Fort.

(David Lavender, *Bent's Fort,* 1954; Hiram Martin Chittenden, *A History of the American Fur Trade of the Far West,* 1954; Kit Carson, *The Story of Kit Carson's Life and Adventures,* 1874.)

Gardner, J. W. J. W. Gardner, a native of Louisiana, settled in Frio County, Texas, in 1855. In this frontier region he became a cowboy and a prominent Indian fighter. In 1871, he was wounded and taken captive by Indians at Lago Cocheno. He was rescued after a brief captivity by his brother, A. G. Gardner.

(*Handbook of Texas, I,* 1952.)

Gardner, Rowland, Family of. In March 1857, a renegade Sioux chief, Inkpaduta, massacred many of the settlers of the Spirit Lake region near the Iowa-Minnesota boundary. On March 8 they murdered Mr. and Mrs. Rowland Gardner and their daughter, Mrs. Harvey Luce, her two children, and Rowland Gardner, Jr. A thirteen-year-old daughter, Abbie, was taken captive. A few weeks later two friendly Sioux chiefs, John Otherday and Paul Mazakutamani, secured her release for a reward of $400. (See Spirit Lake Massacre.)

(Abbie Gardner-Sharp, *History of the Spirit Lake Massacre*, 1900; Charles E. Flandrau, *The History of Minnesota*, 1900; Doane Robinson, A *History of the Dakota or Sioux Indians*, 1974.)

German Sisters, Captivity of. In 1874, a band of Cheyenne Dog Soldiers attacked a family named German near Fort Hays, Kansas. The father, mother, son, and eldest sister were slain, while four daughters fell into captivity. The two youngest girls, Julia (7) and Adelaide (5), were rescued during Major Frank Baldwin's attack on a Cheyenne camp on November 8, 1874. Catharine (17) and Sophia (12) were held until the next spring, when Chief Stone Calf took them under his care and brought them to safety at Fort Reno. Colonel Nelson A. Miles adopted the girls and provided for their education.

(Carl Coke Rister, *Border Captives*, 1940; W. S. Nye, *Carbine & Lance*, 1969.)

Gervais, Joseph. Joseph Gervais was one of the first traders to live among the Pawnee Indians. In 1802, he attempted to establish trade between the tribe and the Spanish in New Mexico. The following year he led a delegation of Pawnees to visit the Spanish, but little was achieved.

(George E. Hyde, *The Pawnee Indians*, 1974.)

Ghost Dance Religion. The Ghost Dance religion, which originated among the Paiutes in Nevada, had its greatest impact on the Indians of the northern plains. In 1889, Indians on reservations were demoralized by future prospects, and they welcomed a religion that they believed offered the opportunity to return to the wild, free life they had so recently enjoyed. While Wovoka, founder of the religion, advocated peaceful relations, the Plains Indians seized upon his promise that dancing would make the whites disappear as an incentive to reassert their warlike propensities.

Adorned in "ghost shirts" that they believed would stop bullets, and led by such war chiefs as Sitting Bull, the Sioux, Cheyennes, Arapahoes, and others danced and sang all night, alarming Indian agents and other whites near the reservations.

In 1890, Frank Grouard, a scout who had lived with Sitting Bull, was sent to the Rosebud Reservation to investigate. He became convinced that widespread hunger was the cause of the unrest and that if left alone, the Ghost Dance would pass without leading to violence. Nevertheless, a panicky Sioux agent called for military intervention, and the result was the Wounded Knee Massacre.

(Dee Brown, *Bury My Heart at Wounded Knee*, 1971; Robert M. Utley, *The Last Days of the Sioux Nation*, 1963; Paul I. Wellman, *Death on Horseback*, 1947; Joe De Barth, *Life and Adventures of Frank Grouard*, 1958; Angie Debo, *A History of the Indians of the United States*, 1970; L. G. Moses, *The Indian Man*, 1984.)

Gibson, Fort, Treaties of. Two Indian treaties were negotiated at Fort Gibson with the Plains tribes. On May 26, 1837, A. P. Chouteau and Montfort Stokes persuaded the Kiowas to permit passage across their lands in exchange for a large quantity of gifts. On January 11, 1839, Matthew Arbuckle persuaded the Osages to abandon claims within the limits of their reservation that had been assigned to other tribes by the government. In return, the Osages received an annuity of $20,000 to extend over 20 years.

(John Joseph Mathews, *The Osages*, 1961; Charles J. Kappler, ed., *Indian Affairs: Laws and Treaties, II*, 1972.)

Gibson, Isaac T. Isaac T. Gibson, a Quaker appointed Osage agent in 1869 under Grant's peace policy, found no peace when he assumed the assignment. So much hostility existed between Osages and white settlers encroaching on tribal lands that he had to call for troops to prevent warfare. In order to protect the Osages, he removed them from Kansas to Oklahoma. He resigned in 1876 after failing to persuade Osage parents to send their children to school.

(John Joseph Mathews, *The Osages*, 1961.)

Gilleland, Johnstone, Family of. Johnstone Gilleland and his wife and two children moved from Pennsylvania to the vicinity of Refugio, Texas, in 1837. In 1840, Mr. and Mrs. Gilleland were killed by Comanche Indians and their two small children, William and Rebecca, were captured. After a brief captivity they were rescued by General Albert Sidney Johnston and a detachment of the Matagorda Riflemen. Rebecca, seven years old when captured, described her experiences:

> A white man, with all the cruel instincts of the savage, was with them. Several times they threatened to cut off our hands and feet if we did not stop crying. . . . Slowly and stealthily they pushed their way through the settlement to avoid detection, and just as they halted for the first time time the settlers suddenly came upon them and firing commenced. As the battle raged the Indians were forced to take flight. Thereupon, they pierced my little brother through the body, and striking me with some sharp instrument on the side of the head, they left us for dead.

Both children recovered, and Rebecca, after her marriage to Methodist minister Orceneth Fisher, became so prominent in civic affairs that she was known as the "Mother of Texas."

(*Handbook of Texas, I*, 1952; James T. De Shields, *Border Wars of Texas*, 1976.

Gillis, J. L. Judge J. L. Gillis of Pennsylvania was appointed Pawnee Indian agent in 1859. A jovial man of seventy, he was called grandfather by the Indians, who loved and admired him. In 1860, when a Sioux war party attacked the agency, he armed himself with pistols, mounted his horse, and led a counter attack, "banging away," wrote George E. Hyde, "and lustily cheering his Pawnees on."

Before his removal in 1861, Gillis organized a tribal police force and persuaded some of the Pawnees to stop raiding other tribes for horses. He was less successful, however, in removing white squatters from Indian lands.

(George E. Hyde, *The Pawnee Indians*, 1974; Ruby E. Wilson, *Frank J. North*, 1984.)

Glass, Hugh. Hugh Glass, a legendary trapper, was born in Pennsylvania. His age is unknown, but he was described as an old man in 1823. In his youth he had been a sailor, serving at one time with Jean Lafitte's buccaneers. On the Texas coast he was captured by Indians who took him to St. Louis and gave him his freedom. There he joined the second expedition of William Ashley's trappers in 1823 and was wounded in a battle with the Arikara Indians. Later that year he accompanied Andrew Henry's party to the Yellowstone River. There he was mauled by a grizzly bear and, abandoned by his companions, he crawled more than a hundred miles to Fort Kiowa.

After his recovery, Glass trapped over most of the Great Plains and Rocky Mountains, surviving countless Indian encounters. Finally, in 1833, he and two companions were ambushed and slain while crossing the frozen Yellowstone River. According to some accounts they blew themselves up with gunpowder to avoid being tortured to death.

(Hiram Martin Chittenden, *The American Fur Trade of the Far West*, 1954; Thomas Froncek, ed., *Voices From the Wilderness*, 1974.)

Goacher, James, Family of. James Goacher (Gocher, Gotcher, Gotier), a native of Alabama, brought his family to Robb's Creek in Lee County, Texas, in 1828. He blazed a trail from there to Bastrop County and established a cotton plantation in 1835. In February, 1837, Indians attacked his home, killing Goacher, his wife, his son, and his son-in-law. His married daughter, Mrs. Jane Crawford, and her two sons and a daughter were captured and treated brutally until the distraught mother gained their respect by felling one of their tormentors with a tree limb. After two years of captivity, Jane and her children were taken to Holland Coffee's trading post and purchased from the Indians by Charles Spaulding. Afterward Mrs. Crawford and Spaulding were married.

(James T. De Shields, *Border Wars of Texas,* 1976; J. W. Wilbarger, *Indian Depredations in Texas,* 1985; John Holland Jenkins, *Recollections of Early Texas,* 1958.)

Godfrey, Sioux Warrior. Godfrey, a mulatto, was a member of a Sioux war party that murdered Minnesota settlers during the outbreak of 1862. Present during the murder of Francis Patoile and the capture of three white women, he claimed later that he was compelled by the Sioux to accompany the raiders. The son of a French trader and a black mother, he had married a Sioux woman and lived with her people at the time of the uprising.

Arrested and convicted of murder, Godfrey testified against several warriors for committing crimes against the settlers. As a result they were hung while his life was spared.

(Charles S. Bryant, *A History of the Great Massacre by the Sioux Indians in Minnesota,* 1863; C. M. Oehler, *The Great Sioux Uprising,* 1959.)

Gra-Mon, Osage Chief. See Clermont, Osage Chief

Grand Island Fight. Grand Island, Nebraska, near Fort Kearny, was the site of a Cheyenne Indian encampment in August 1856. A mail driver on his way to the fort fired upon two warriors who attempted to stop him to beg for tobacco. He missed, but one of the infuriated Indians wounded him with an arrow. In retaliation, on the following morning 41 troopers led by Captain G. H. Stewart attacked the village, killing ten Indians and seizing the pony herd. The surviving Cheyennes fled on foot.

(George Bird Grinnell, *The Fighting Cheyennes,* 1956.)

Grand Pawnee Village, Treaty of. On October 9, 1833, the Pawnee Indians ceded their lands located below the Platte River as a result of a treaty negotiated for the government by Henry L. Ellsworth. The several Pawnee bands divided an annuity of $4,600. Provision was made to establish schools among the Pawnees and to provide them with agricultural instructors, blacksmiths, tools, and domestic animals.

(Charles J. Kappler, ed., *Indian Affairs: Laws and Treaties, II,* 1972.)

Grant, Ulysses S., Peace Policy. In 1869, when Grant became president, he was besieged by humanitarian reformers who sought to insure just treatment for Indian tribes. At the suggestion of Quaker petitioners, the president appointed Indian agents nominated by religious leaders in an attempt to eliminate the corruption rampant on the reservations and to promote Christian morality by good example. He was moved to take this major policy shift by the Iroquois chief and Civil War officer Ely S. Parker, and by congressional criticism of the massacre of the Cheyennes at Sand Creek. The policy failed because of the Plains Indian's love of the ways of his ancestors and belief by hostile chiefs that kindness was a sign of weakness.

(Francis Paul Prucha, *American Indian Policy in Crisis*, 1976; *The Great Father*, 1984; Robert Wooster, *The Military and United States Indian Policy*, 1988; Robert Winston Mardock, *The Reformers and the American Indian*, 1971; Robert M. Utley, *The Indian Frontier of the American West*, 1846-1890, 1983.)

Grass, John, Teton Sioux Chief. John Grass (Pezi) was one of the most important peace chiefs during the final epoch of Plains Indian warfare. Born about 1837, he was promoted to chief as a result of pressure applied on the demoralized Sioux by Indian agent James McLaughlin. On the Standing Rock Reservation he demonstrated the importance of agriculture to the nonprogressives. After the Battle of Wounded Knee he played an important part in the restoration of peaceful relations between the races. He was respected by all when he died in 1918.

(Dee Brown, *Bury My Heart at Wounded Knee*, 1971; Robert M. Utley, *The Last Days of the Sioux Nation*, 1963.)

Grattan, John L. Lieutenant John L. Grattan, an inexperienced officer with a strong contempt for Indians, was primarily responsible for starting a war with the Sioux in 1854. A sick cow, abandoned by a Mormon immigrant, was killed by the Sioux, and the owner demanded the help of the military at Fort Laramie in recovering his loss. Grattan led 30 men, backed by two howitzers, to the Indian camp, determined, he boasted, to "conquer or die." The Sioux offered to pay for the animal, but Grattan was spoiling for action. One of the soldiers fired, the Indians retaliated, and the howitzers blasted the camp. A fierce fight compelled the troops to retreat, but they were cut off by encircling Sioux. Every soldier in the detachment was killed.

The Grattan incident led to Sioux raids on the Oregon Trail. Hostilities increased steadily and during the following year the Harney Expedition was sent to punish the Sioux.

(Fairfax Downey, *Indian Wars of the U. S. Army*, 1963; Richard H. Dillon, *The American Indian Wars*, 1983; George Bird Grinnell, *The Fighting Cheyennes*, 1956; Robert M. Utley and Wilcomb E. Washburn, *The American Heritage History of the Indian Wars*, 1977.)

Great Nemowhaw, Treaty of. John Dougherty, commissioner for the United States, negotiated a treaty with the Iowa tribe at the Great Nemowhaw agency on October 19, 1838. The Iowas ceded a large tract of land in exchange for the government's offer to invest $157,000 for the benefit of the tribe.

(Charles J. Kappler, ed., *Indian Affairs: Laws and Treaties, II*, 1972.)

Great Walker, Iowa Chief. See Big Neck, Iowa Chief

Griffin, Fort, Texas. Fort Griffin was constructed on the Clear Fork of the Brazos River in July, 1867. Garrisoned by Sixth Cavalry soldiers, it provided protection against Indian attack for settlers, surveyors, cowboys, and buffalo hunters. It was abandoned in 1881.

(Carl Coke Rister, *Fort Griffin on the Texas Frontier*, 1956.)

Gros Ventre Indians. See Atsini Indians, Hidatsa Indians

Grouard, Frank. Frank Grouard was born in the South Pacific on the Island of Paumotu on September 20, 1850. His mother was a native of the island, his father a Mormon elder. He moved with his father to California in 1852. While living with Addison Pratt, he was taken to Beaver, Utah. He ran away at age fifteen to become a mule skinner.

While riding a mail route near the Milk River in 1869, he was captured by the Sioux. For several years he lived in Sitting Bull's lodge, closely guarded at first, but soon becoming an adopted member of the family. He remained six years with the Sioux. Then, in 1875, he became a scout for the Army, fighting in the Battles of Powder River, the Rosebud, Slim Buttes, and others. He served also as interpreter, and he has been blamed for a misinterpretation that led to the death of Chief Crazy Horse. After the Sioux War he was a scout at Fort McKinney, Wyoming. He died on August 15, 1905.

"All in all, he was probably as valuable a scout as the frontier army ever knew. General Crook considered Grouard's services to be so valuable that he said he would rather lose one-third of his command than be deprived of them."—Edgar T. Stewart

(Joe De Barthe, *Life and Adventures of Frank Grouard*, 1958; Stanley Vestal, *Sitting Bull*, 1957.)

H

Ham, Caiaphas K. Caiaphas K. Ham, born in 1803, was an associate of Jim Bowie in Louisiana and Texas. In 1830, he joined the Comanche Indians in order to obtain horses to sell in Louisiana. Adopted by Chief Incorroy, he remained with the Comanches until Bowie recruited him to help in the search for the lost San Saba silver mine. He was in Bowie's party of eleven men that fought a bloody battle with more than a hundred Indians near the San Saba in November 1831. Ham shot the chief, and four braves who rushed to remove his body lost their lives in the attempt. Ham survived the battle and returned with Bowie to San Antonio.

(James T. De Shields, *Border Wars of Texas,* 1976.)

Hamleton, William, Family of. William Hamleton married the widow of James Myres in Tarrant County, Texas, about 1861. By 1867, they had two children of their own in addition to six Myres children. In April, while Hamleton and the eldest boy were away, Kiowas led by Satanta and Satank attacked their cabin, killing Mrs. Hamleton and capturing the three youngest children, Sarina Myres, Mary Hamleton, and Gus Hamleton. The other children, at work in the fields, escaped.

Mary, about five years old, became so sick on the trail to the Kiowa village that she was left for dead. Sarina and the infant, Gus, were ransomed a few months later, and Sarina reported that her half-sister had died. She was unaware that a warrior, Hahbayte, had returned for Mary, restored her to health, and given her to his daughter for adoption. Mary grew up as an Indian, forgot her native language, and could not recall her own name. At age seventeen she married a Mexican captive called Calisy, and they had seven children.

Late in life Mary became a Christian. After 57 years as an Indian, she died in 1924 and was buried at the Rainy Mountain Baptist Mission.

(Wilbur Sturtevant Nye, *Bad Medicine & Good,* 1962.)

Hancock's War. Major General Winfield Scott Hancock, a Civil War hero but an inept Indian fighter, was military commander of the Department of the Missouri in 1867. The Indians of the central plains—Cheyennes and Arapahoes—were peaceful, but Hancock suspected that an uprising was imminent and was determined to forestall it. Several chiefs conferred with him at Fort Larned to profess peaceful intentions, but to no avail.

Taking the field in April, Hancock announced his intention "to feel the temper of the Indians and to separate the sheep from the goats." He marched his men toward an Indian village on the Pawnee Fork of the Arkansas, putting the friendly inhabitants to flight. Custer's cavalry pursued but failed to overtake them, while Hancock destroyed 140 Sioux and 111 Cheyenne tipis. In retaliation, the Indians initiated a reign of terror around the Smoky Hill River region of Kansas.

> Hancock campaigned busily for four full months. During that time, his 1400 men killed four Indians—two of them friendlies.—Stanley Vestal

> Hancock's campaign brought disastrous results. He failed to overawe a single Indian, and he provoked a full-scale war which he was unable to control.—William H. Leckie

> All that was needed to break a good number of eggs was for some clumsy-footed fool to walk through the scene at this point. And just such a person was on hand: Major General Winfield Scott Hancock. —Ralph K. Andrist

(Stanley Vestal, *Warpath and Council Fire*, 1948; William H. Leckie, *The Buffalo Soldiers*, 1967; Ralph K. Andrist, *The Long Death*, 1964; Wilbur Sturtevant Nye, *Plains Indian Raiders*, 1968; Robert Wooster, *The Military and United States Indian Policy*, 1988; Robert M. Utley and Wilcomb E. Washburn, *The American Heritage History of the Indian Wars*, 1977; Virginia Cole Trenholm, *The Arapahoes, Our People*, 1970; George Bird Grinnell, *The Fighting Cheyennes*, 1956.)

Hard Heart, Iowa Chief. Hard Heart, an Iowa Indian medal chief, was a friend of the United States after meeting President Madison in 1809. When the Iowas fought on the British side during the War of 1812, he left them to live with the Otoes. In 1819, he rejoined his people and they recognized him as principal chief.

(Martha Royce Blaine, *The Ioway Indians*, 1979.)

Hard Rope, Osage Chief. Hard Rope, war chief of the Heart-Stays Osage band, was a friend of the whites and a scout for the U. S. Cavalry. While scouting for Custer he located the Cheyenne camp preceding the Battle of the Washita in 1868.

(John Joseph Mathews, *The Osages*, 1961; W. S. Nye, *Carbine & Lance*, 1969.)

Hare, William Hobart. William Hobart Hare, a Protestant Episcopal missionary, was born at Princeton, New Jersey, on May 17, 1838. Educated at the Academy of the Protestant Episcopal Church and at the University of Pennsylvania, he was ordained in May 1862. During the following year he visited Michigan and Minnesota and became interested in Indian welfare. His missionary career began in 1871 when he was appointed secretary and general agent of the Foreign Committee of the Board of Missions.

In 1872, Hare was elected bishop of the Sioux Indian country north of the Niobara River, beginning a service of 37 years. Under his administration schools and missions were established over a wide area of the present state of South Dakota. His headquarters during most of his tenure was at Sioux Falls, and long before he died there on October 23, 1909, he was called the "Apostle to the Sioux."

Bishop Hare was convinced that the Sioux, in order to survive, must abandon their roving life-style and learn the ways of the white man. He advocated the breakup of the Great Sioux Reservation and the cession of much of that territory to the government for settlement by whites, but in 1883 he objected to the methods used to that end by the Newton Edmunds Commission. He was a strong advocate, as well, of the movement to make Indians on reservations subject to the criminal justice system of the United States. He served as chairman of a committee of investigation that exonerated Indian agents of wrong doing on the Sioux reservations and recommended the stationing of troops at the agencies for the protection of government personnel.

(Francis Paul Prucha, *American Indian Policy in Crisis,* 1976; Flora Warren Seymour, *Indian Agents of the Old Frontier,* 1975; Robert M. Utley, *The Last Days of the Sioux Nation,* 1963.)

Harney, William S., Sioux Expedition. Colonel William S. Harney led a punitive expedition against the Brulé Sioux in the summer of 1855 as the result of the Grattan incident. (See Grattan, John L.) In the first major engagement fought between the U. S. Army and the Sioux, Harney's 1,200-man army, infantry and dragoons, attacked Chief Little Thunder's village in the Bluewater Creek Valley on September 3, killing 85 Indians and capturing 70 women and children. (See Ash Hollow, Battle of.) After the battle Harney demanded that hostile chiefs surrender. Spotted Tail and others who complied were jailed at Fort Leavenworth. Harney, known to the Sioux as "the Butcher," marched through the Sioux country seeking battle, but the Indians avoided him.

(Doane Robinson, *A History of the Dakota or Sioux Indians,* 1974; Richard H. Dillon, *North American Indian Wars,* 1983.)

Harvey, Alexander. Alexander Harvey, characterized by Hiram Martin Chittenden as "one of the boldest men and most reckless desperados known to the frontier," was born in St. Louis. Employed as a youth by the American Fur Company, he served many years at Forts McKenzie and Union. In 1843, he perpetrated an incident known in frontier history as the "Blackfoot massacre." When his superior at McKenzie, François A. Chardon, determined to seek revenge for the slaying of a servant by the Indians, Harvey pointed a cannon at the front gate and fired into the first band of Blackfeet that came to the fort to trade. Ten Indians were killed and three wounded. On another occasion he shot to death a wounded and helpless warrior begging for his life.

Harvey, a dangerous man to his fellow traders when drunk, finally became too much of a liability to remain in the employ of the American Fur Company. Some members of the company attempted to murder him, but he escaped and organized a rival firm, Harvey, Primeaux and Company, that traded in the west for several years.

(Hiram Martin Chittenden, *A History of the American Fur Trade of the Far West*, 1954.)

Haskell Institute, Lawrence, Kansas. Haskell Institute was established in 1884 to train Indian students in manual arts and to prepare them to succeed in the strange new world of the white man. It opened with 22 students, and enrollment increased tenfold during the first year of operation. By 1906, students from 60 tribes attended Haskell. Still included in the Federal Indian school system, it offers both academic and vocational training through high school.

(U. S. National Park Service, *Soldier and Brave*, 1963.)

Haworth, James. James Haworth, a Quaker, succeeded Lawrie Tatum as Indian agent to the Comanches and Kiowas on March 31, 1873. He immediately dismissed the agency's military guard, but within a month he had to ask for their return to keep the more turbulent warriors in check. In June 1873, he released the hostile warriors who had been captured by Colonel Ranald S. Mackenzie, and some of them resumed raiding without delay.

In 1874, shipments of food to the agency at Fort Sill were delayed by the weather and Haworth had to reduce Indian rations by half. Many families were compelled to eat their horses to avoid starvation. As a result, some of them fled from the reservation to rejoin their kinsmen who remained free on the plains. By 1876, Haworth resorted to holding a roll call every third day in an attempt to keep a record of desertions.

When reservation Indians were caught crossing the Red River to raid in Texas, Haworth attempted to prevent military authorities from punishing them. He forgave them for stealing his own livestock, and, as one old warrior observed with a chuckle, "he used to pray for us all the time." He resigned for health reasons in 1878.

(W. S. Nye, *Carbine & Lance*, 1969; Ernest Wallace and E. Adamson Hoebel, *The Comanches*, 1952; T. R. Fehrenbach, *Comanches*, 1983.)

Hayfield Fight. On August 1, 1867, a Cheyenne war party consisting of 500 hostiles attacked 20 soldiers and 6 civilians working in a hayfield less than three miles from Fort C. F. Smith in southern Montana. The defenders forted up in a log corral and, armed with superior breech-loading rifles, repulsed the first charge, inflicting heavy losses on their assailants. The only officer present, Lieutenant Sigmund Sternberg, was killed, but a former Confederate officer, Al Colvin, took command, and under his leadership charge after charge was turned away. Finally the warriors set fire to the grass, but the flames failed to reach the corral. After sustaining heavy losses, the Indians withdrew.

(Dee Brown, *Bury My Heart at Wounded Knee,* 1971; Richard H. Dillon, *North American Indian Wars,* 1983; U. S. National Park Service, *Soldier and Brave,* 1963.)

Hays, Fort, Kansas. Fort Hays was established in 1865 and rebuilt near the present Hays, Kansas, in 1867 after a flood destroyed the original facility. It was intended to protect emigrants using the Smoky Hill Trail and construction workers on the Kansas Pacific Railway. General George A. Custer was stationed at Fort Hays from 1867 to 1870. It was the staging ground for Custer during the Hancock Campaign of 1867 and the Forsyth Campaign of 1868 (see Beecher's Island) and Sheridan's headquarters during the winter campaign of 1868-1869. It was abandoned in November 1869.

(Robert W. Frazer, *Forts of the West,* 1965; U. S. National Park Service, *Soldier and Brave,* 1963; George Bird Grinnell, *The Fighting Cheyennes,* 1956.)

Hays, John Coffee. John Coffee Hays was born in Tennessee in 1817 and moved to San Antonio, Texas, in 1837 to survey the frontier for the Republic. In 1840, he was appointed captain of Texas Rangers and assigned to guard the San Antonio-Nueces River region against attacks by Indians or Mexicans. In 1841, with 35 Rangers, he pursued a Comanche war party from near San Antonio to the Uvalde Canyon, attacked the hostiles in a thicket, and killed or captured a dozen warriors. From that time until the onset of the Mexican War he fought Comanches at Enchanted Rock in 1841, Bandera Pass in 1842, and elsewhere. A pioneer in the use of Colt revolvers, he employed them with deadly effect against amazed Indians.

Hays served as a colonel in the Texas Mounted Volunteers during the Mexican War, distinguishing himself at Monterrey and Mexico City. In 1849, he led a wagon train of gold miners to California and remained in that state to serve as sheriff of San Francisco County and Surveyor General of California. His last Indian fight occurred in Nevada in 1860.

Among the old settlers his memory is revered. They cannot forget he once stood upon the frontier as a tower of strength. They trusted him in the dark days of weakness, danger, and peril, and

he responded with efficient fidelity and a full measure of success.—John Salmon Ford

(T. R. Fehrenbach, *Comanches*, 1983; John Salmon Ford, *Rip Ford's Texas*, 1963;
Walter Prescott Webb, *The Texas Rangers*, 1965; John Holland Jenkins, *Recollec-
tions of Early Texas*, 1958; James T. De Shields, *Border Wars of Texas*, 1976; J.
W. Wilbarger, *Indian Depredations in Texas*, 1985.)

Hazen, William B. Colonel W. B. Hazen, a West Point graduate in 1855,
served in Oregon and Texas before the Civil War. Afterward he served
many years on the plains in the 38th and then in the 6th Infantry. In 1868,
he was loaned to the Indian Department to act as agent at Fort Cobb for
the Comanche and Kiowa tribes. In that capacity he prevented Custer from
attacking a Kiowa camp in 1868. Custer accused him of falsely asserting
that the Kiowas were remaining peacefully at the agency when they were
departing frequently to raid the settlements. "How," Custer wondered,
"could an officer such as Hazen with wide experience fighting Indians,
even suffering a wound at their hands, be so easily deceived?" Hazen, who
seemed embroiled in controversy throughout his career, refuted Custer's
account of the incident in a written report at a later time.

Hazen was relieved as agent by Lawrie Tatum in 1869. A pioneer in
the Indian rights movement, he testified against the Indian Ring and was
instrumental in establishing the Board of Indian Commissioners.

(W. S. Nye, *Carbine & Lance*, 1969; Flora Warren Seymour, *Indian Agents of the
Old Frontier*, 1975; George Armstrong Custer, *Wild Life on the Plains*, 1969.)

Henry, Andrew. Andrew Henry, the first fur trapper to establish a post
west of the Continental Divide, was born in Pennsylvania about 1775. He
moved to Missouri as a youth and became a partner in the St. Louis
Missouri Fur Company upon its incorporation in 1809. In the spring of
1809, he led the company's first expedition up the Missouri to establish a
post at the Three Forks. He wintered with the Crow Indians and, accompanied by partner Pierre Menard, built the post early the following spring.
Beginning on April 12, Blackfoot Indians began attacking the trappers and
work became impossible. In the fall Henry abandoned the fort, led the
survivors across the Divide, and established a post on the Snake River.
Game was scarce, however, and his men became so discouraged that many
deserted. In the spring of 1811, Henry abandoned the venture and returned
to Missouri.

Henry became involved with General William H. Ashley in mining
activities, and at the onset of the War of 1812 he served as a major under
Ashley in the Missouri Territorial Militia. At the end of the war he
continued his association with Ashley, and in 1822 they founded the
Rocky Mountain Fur Company. Henry led an expedition that departed up
the Missouri in April to trap at the Three Forks. Their horses were stolen

by the Assiniboins, however, and they were compelled to winter with the Crow Indians. In the spring of 1823, they acquired horses and set out toward the Three Forks. Near Great Falls, however, they were attacked by the Blackfeet and driven back to the mouth of the Yellowstone. There Henry learned of Ashley's battle with the Arikaras and led most of his men to join his partner at the mouth of the Cheyenne River. Ashley and Henry fought in Colonel Henry Leavenworth's battle with the Arikaras. After the Arikaras abandoned their villages, Henry led most of Ashley's men to the Yellowstone. Attacked by Indians along the way, he finally constructed a fort at the mouth of the Bighorn River. There, while acquiring a large number of furs, he sent Étienne Provost to explore west of the Rockies, crossing the Divide at the South Pass.

In 1824, Henry brought the furs to St. Louis and, on October 21, he began his return journey to the mountains. But years of Indian fighting had taken their toll. He resigned from the partnership with Ashley soon afterward and died in Missouri in 1832.

(Hiram Martin Chittenden, *A History of the American Fur Trade of the Far West*, 1954; Le Roy R. Hafen, ed. *Mountain Men and Fur Trappers of the Far West*, 1982.

Henry, Guy V. Guy V. Henry, a native of New York, graduated from West Point in 1856. During the Civil War, while serving as colonel in the 40th Massachusetts Infantry, he earned the Congressional Medal of Honor for bravery at the Battle of Cold Harbor. At war's end he served as captain of the First Artillery until transferring to the Third Cavalry in 1870.

While commanding the left wing of General Crook's army at the Battle of the Rosebud on June 17, 1876, Henry was wounded by a bullet that knocked out an eye and smashed his nose. Warriors charged in an attempt to kill him, but he was rescued by an Indian scout, Yute John. Ignoring his wound, Henry stayed in the saddle to set an example for his hard-pressed troopers. After the battle he was hauled a long distance on a litter drawn by mules. Once he fell over a twenty-foot bluff into a stream and almost drowned, but Henry refused to die during that terrible journey, and he survived to fight again and again.

In 1881, Henry joined the 9th Cavalry (Buffalo Soldiers) as colonel. He was with the forces called to South Dakota during the Ghost Dance unrest in 1890, and he rescued Colonel James W. Forsyth's Seventh Cavalry troopers who were pinned down by the Sioux near the Drexel Mission on December 30, following the Wounded Knee massacre.

Henry retired as a major general in 1898. No officer was held in higher esteem by his men.

(Robert M. Leckie, *The Buffalo Soldiers*, 1967; Robert M. Utley, *The Last Days of the Sioux Nation*, 1963; Evan S. Connell, *Son of the Morning Star*, 1984; Joe De Barthe, *Life and Adventures of Frank Grouard*, 1958.)

Hibbons, Sarah, Family of. In 1828, John McSherry and his wife, Sarah, Creath McSherry, moved from Illinois to the Guadalupe Valley, present De Witt County, Texas. Their first child, John, was born in 1829. Later that year McSherry was killed by Indians while hauling water from the river. Sarah witnessed his death from the cabin, barred the door, and stood off the Indians with her husband's rifle until they withdrew.

After a brief time as a widow, Sarah married John Hibbons, a neighbor. Soon after the birth of her second child she and the children visited her parents in Illinois. They returned by boat, accompanied by her brother, George Creath, to Columbia on the Brazos River. There Hibbons met them with an ox cart. When they were about 15 miles from home, 13 Comanches attacked them, killed Hibbons and Creath, and captured Sarah and the children.

When the Hibbons infant could not stop crying, a warrior bashed its head against a tree. Then the Indians camped for the night on the Colorado River near the present site of Austin without posting guards. As soon as she was sure all the warriors slept, Sarah fled into the darkness. Fortunately she found a Texas Ranger camp ten miles to the south and begged the men to rescue little John. Led by Reuben Hornsby, the Rangers trailed the Indians to their camp on Walnut Creek, made a surprise attack, and rescued the child.

In 1837, Sarah married Claiborne Stinnett, the sheriff of Gonzales County. A few months later Stinnett was murdered by escaping prisoners. In 1840, she married Phillip Howard, and while moving from the Guadalupe to San Antonio they were attacked by Indians. They managed to escape unharmed, but young John McSherry narrowly avoided a second captivity.

(Walter Prescott Webb, *The Texas Rangers*, 1965; James T. De Shields, *Border Wars of Texas*, 1976; J. W. Wilbarger, *Indian Depredations in Texas*, 1985; John Holland Jenkins, *Recollections of Early Texas*, 1958.)

Hidatsa Indians. The Hidatsa Indians, a Siouan-speaking tribe, lived on the Missouri between the Little Missouri and Heart rivers. Also known as the Minitaris, they numbered about 2,500 in 1740 when visited by French traders. Fifty years later, when met by the Spanish and Americans, they became middlemen in trading horses and firearms to tribes to the north and west. They were a prosperous agricultural people when visited by Lewis and Clark, but increasing white contacts proved to be disastrous, for most Hidatsas died of smallpox in 1837. The survivors moved to the Fort Berthold reservation in 1845, where their descendants still live.

(John R. Swanton, *Indian Tribes of North America*, 1952; Ray W. Meyer, *The Village Indians of the Upper Missouri*, 1977; W. Raymond Wood and Thomas D. Thiessen, eds., *Early Fur Trade of the Northern Plains*, 1985.)

High-Backed Wolf, Cheyenne Chief. High-Backed Wolf, the first Cheyenne chief well known by white men, attempted to keep his people at peace. In 1825, he signed a treaty with General Henry Atkinson. George Catlin painted his portrait in 1832 and characterized him as "a man of honour and strictest integrity." He was slain during a family quarrel in 1834.

A second High-Backed Wolf was killed during the Battle of Platte Bridge in 1865.

(Stan Hoig, *Peace Chiefs of the Cheyennes,* 1980.)

Hinman, Samuel D. Samuel D. Hinman, an Episcopal missionary for many years, came to Bishop Henry B. Whipple of Minnesota as an orphan and became one of his divinity students. In 1860, he was ordained and became a missionary to the Santee Sioux at the Lower Agency. On the Sunday before the Minnesota Sioux outbreak of 1862, he preached a sermon to which Chief Little Crow listened intently before assuming the lead in the uprising.

Hinman was at work at his desk when he heard gunshots. An Indian warned him that all whites were in danger of death, and he removed his family safely across the Minnesota River. On the way to Fort Ridgely, he met John Marsh's soldiers advancing to the Lower Agency. He warned them to turn back, but they continued on their way and blundered into an ambush at Redwood Ferry.

After the uprising was quelled, Hinman baptized many of the hostiles held at Fort Snelling. A gang of irate citizens beat him senseless for this service to the hated Sioux. When the tribe was removed to Dakota territory, he continued as their missionary.

Hinman played an important and controversial role in opening Indian land to white settlement. He recruited Indian scouts for Custer's Black Hills expedition and served on a commission that urged the Sioux to surrender these sacred lands. In 1882, he acted as interpreter for the Newton Edmunds Commission that sought to open the Great Sioux Reservation to settlement, and he threatened the Indians with loss of rations and removal to Oklahoma if they refused. (See Edmunds, Newton.) In addition, he was active in the attempt to persuade the Poncas to move to the Osage Reservation. "An old hand at stealing Indian lands," Dee Brown asserted, "Hinman believed the Indians needed less land and more Christianity."

(Dee Brown, *Bury My Heart at Wounded Knee,* 1971; Henry Benjamin Whipple, *Lights and Shadows of a Long Episcopate,* 1900; C. M. Oehler, *The Great Sioux Uprising,* 1959; Francis Paul Prucha, *American Indian Policy in Crisis,* 1976; Flora Warren Seymour, *Indian Agents of the Old Frontier,* 1975.)

Hishkowits, Cheyenne Translator. Hishkowits, also known as Harvey Whiteshield, was born in Oklahoma in 1867. He attended Carlisle and Hampton Institute and became a teacher at Cantonment, Oklahoma. He assisted Mennonite missionaries in translating the Bible and compiling a Cheyenne dictionary.

(F. W. Hodge, ed., *Handbook of American Indians, I,* 1912.)

Hoag, Enoch. Enoch Hoag, a Quaker, was appointed to direct the Central Superintendency (Cheyenne-Arapaho area) under President Grant's peace policy. He was a great friend of the Indians and tried to protect raiders from military retaliation. He defended the Kiowas and Comanches who were making devastating attacks on ranches south of the Red River, contending that the tribes were merely asserting their rights to their homelands in Texas. When the German sisters (see German Sisters, Captivity of) were redeemed from captivity, Hoag refused "to accept any responsibility in connection with them. He was too busy trying to save the Indians."—W. S. Nye

(Flora Warren Seymour, *Indian Agents of the Old Frontier,* 1975; W. S. Nye, *Carbine & Lance,* 1969.)

Hockley, Bill. In 1840, Republic of Texas troops captured two children of a principal Comanche chief who had been killed during the Battle of Plum Creek. The fourteen-year-old boy was adopted by Colonel G. W. Hockley and given the name Bill Hockley. His eleven-year-old sister, Nosacooiash, was adopted by another white family and called Maria.

In 1843, the Texans, desiring peace with the Comanches, sent Bill and Maria with the Joseph C. Eldridge expedition far out on the plains. During the peace negotiations with Chief Pahayuca, Bill eagerly rejoined his people. But Maria, who no longer remembered the Comanche language, begged Eldridge not to leave her with the Indians. Disregarding her pleas, the commissioners turned her over to her relatives and she became an interpreter at councils with the Comanches.

(J. W. Wilbarger, *Indian Depredations in Texas,* 1985; J. Norman Heard, *White Into Red,* 1973.)

Hollow-Horn Bear, Brulé Sioux Chief. Born about 1850 in Nebraska, Hollow-Horn Bear was an important Brulé war chief who participated in the destruction of Fetterman's troopers and fought in several battles in Wyoming, Montana, and the Dakotas. He made peace with the whites in 1873 and joined the Indian police on the Rosebud Reservation. There he tried to resolve misunderstandings between Indians and whites. He occasionally visited Washington, rode in President Theodore Roosevelt's inaugural parade in 1905, and was buried there in 1913.

(Frederick J. Dockstader, *Great North American Indians*, 1977; Dee Brown, *Bury My Heart at Wounded Knee*, 1971; F. W. Hodge, ed., *Handbook of American Indians*, 1912.)

Hood, John B. Indian Campaign. John B. Hood, later a famous Confederate general, is less known as an Indian fighter, in spite of the fact that Comanches almost cut short his military career several years before the Civil War. Born in Kentucky in 1831, he entered West Point in 1849. After graduation he served in New York and California before joining Robert E. Lee's Second Cavalry in Texas.

In July 1857, Hood led 24 troopers out of Fort Mason, Texas, on the trail of hostiles heading toward Mexico. On July 20, he located the camp of 50 Comanches near the headwaters of the Devil's River. The Indians charged, and two warriors tried to wrestle Hood off his horse, but he managed to kill them both. A third warrior shot an arrow that pinned Hood's hand to his bridle.

Hood's men could have been annihilated had it not been for the lamentations of Comanche women over the mounting death toll of their men. After losing 19 of their people, the warriors heeded the pleas of the women and withdrew from the field. Hood had two troopers killed and several seriously wounded. The survivors returned to Fort Mason on August 8.

Hood was partially incapacitated by his wound for two years. In 1861, he resigned his commission and joined the Confederate army.

(T. R. Fehrenbach, *Comanches*, 1983; James T. De Shields, *Border Wars of Texas*, 1976.)

Horn, Mrs. Sarah Ann, Captivity of. Mrs. Sarah Ann Horn was born in Huntington, England, in 1809. In 1835, she, with her husband, John, and two small children, joined the colony of Dr. John C. Beales on Las Moras Creek, near its juncture with the Rio Grande in southwestern Texas. When the Texas Revolution began in 1836, they abandoned the colony and fled through the sand hills. Intercepted by Comanche Indians on April 4, she and the children were captured while witnessing the death of their husband and father.

The captives were treated with great cruelty. Tied to the backs of mules and seldom permitted to eat or drink, they suffered terrible tortures while their captors rode rapidly toward the Staked Plains. When they arrived at the Indian village her sons John, aged five, and Joseph, aged four, were taken from her, and she never saw them again. Later she learned that John had frozen to death and Joseph had been adopted.

After more than a year of captivity, Mrs. Horn was ransomed by a trader at San Miguel, New Mexico. Broken-hearted over the loss of her family and ill from abuse, she did not long survive her ordeal.

(Carl Coke Rister, *Comanche Bondage,* 1955; *Border Captives,* 1940.)

Hornsby, Reuben, Family of. Reuben Hornsby, a native of Rome, Georgia, joined Stephen F. Austin's Texas colony in 1830, settling at Hornsby's Bend of the Colorado River in Travis County. A ranger in the Republic of Texas Army, he was, said James T. De Shields, "the outside sentinel of American civilization."

Hornsby and his wife, the former Sarah Morrison, had ten children. Several of his sons became celebrated Indian fighters. One of them, Smith Hornsby, died of wounds received in the Battle of Tehuacana Spring in 1835. In 1836, three Hornsby boys, Malcolm, Bill, and Reuben, Jr., were attacked by a dozen Comanches while working in the fields. They swam the river and concealed themselves in a thicket. Reuben, Sr., his wife, and their daughters (dressed as men) marched around the stockade with rifles, giving the appearance of a strongly defended home, and the Indians withdrew after stealing the livestock.

In 1843, Joe Hornsby, then living in Austin, rescued Alexander Coleman from Comanche captivity by charging a war party while armed only with a single-shot pistol. (See Bell, William, murder of.) In 1845, Daniel, the youngest son, and a friend were fishing when attacked by Comanches. They tried to escape by swimming the river, but Daniel drowned and his friend was shot to death.

(J. W. Wilbarger, *Indian Depredations in Texas,* 1985; John Holland Jenkins, *Recollections of Early Texas,* 1958.)

Horseback, Comanche Chief. Horseback, principal chief of the Noconee Comanches, was generally a friend of white people. He signed the Medicine Lodge Treaty in 1867, he tried to keep his warriors from raiding, and he was active in restoring white captives. Angered, however, by the slaughter of buffalo, he participated in the second Battle of Adobe Walls, sustaining two wounds at the hands of the hunters.

In 1875, Horseback and the Kiowa chief, Kicking Bird, turned in to authorities a number of warriors who had murdered whites. As a result, he was "thrown away" by his people, and he camped near Fort Sill, suffering from tuberculosis, unable to hunt, and subsisting on food given to him by army officers. In 1876, the government built a house for him. He still lived in it as late as 1878.

(W. S. Nye, *Carbine & Lance,* 1969; Mildred P. Mayhall, *Indian Wars of Texas,* 1965.)

Howard, George Thomas. George Thomas Howard, a native of Washington, D. C., went to Texas in 1836 to fight in its revolution. After the war, with the rank of captain, he was stationed in San Antonio to guard against hostile Indians. In the spring of 1839, he maneuvered a band of Comanches into a trap at Opossum Creek. Seven warriors were killed. In March 1840, he led his troops into the courthouse at San Antonio, precipitating the famous Council House Fight, and he was stabbed by a Comanche when he blocked the doorway. A few months later he was cited for bravery during the battle with Comanches at Plum Creek.

In November 1840, Howard led 200, regulars and volunteers, to raid the Comanche stronghold. On Las Moras Creek, near the present town of Brackettville, Texas, they surrounded a large Comanche camp and captured it in a surprise attack. Most of the warriors were away on a raid into Mexico. Four or five Indians were killed and several captives were recovered.

Howard's Indian-fighting career was interrupted by participation in the Texan Santa Fe Expedition, the Somervell Expedition, and the Mexican War. Afterward he served as Indian Agent from 1850 to 1855. He died at Washington, D. C., in 1866.

(*Handbook of Texas, I*, 1952; John Holland Jenkins, *Recollections of Early Texas*, 1958; J. W. Wilbarger, *Indian Depredations In Texas*, 1985.)

Howard Wells, Texas, Massacre. On April 20, 1872, Chief Big Bow led a Kiowa war party in an attack on a government wagon train at Howard Wells, a waystation on the road from San Antonio to El Paso. The train had no military escort, and a hundred warriors easily overran the defenders. Nineteen teamsters were slain, eight of them being burned to death tied to wagon wheels. In addition, several children were killed and a woman was captured.

After the massacre the Kiowas carried away the contents of the wagons and camped within sight of Howard Wells. A few hours later, a detachment of Ninth Cavalry troopers led by Captain Michael Cooney arrived at the massacre scene and trailed the Kiowas to their camp. The soldiers attacked at once, but were driven back to Howard Wells by withering fire from warriors concealed on rocky slopes. The woman captive managed to escape during the battle.

(W. S. Nye, *Carbine & Lance*, 1969; William H. Leckie, *The Buffalo Soldiers*, 1967.)

Howling Wolf, Cheyenne Artist. Howling Wolf (Honanist-to), a noted Cheyenne artist, was born about 1850. A leader of war parties in his youth, he surrendered in 1875 and was sent to Fort Marion, Florida. While in prison he spent his time drawing pictures that attracted the attention of St. Augustine citizens and soldiers alike. In 1878, he was released to the Darlington Agency in Oklahoma. There he became a farmer and was converted to Christianity. Three years, later, however, he became leader of the Dog Soldiers and opposed the attempts of white people to induce the Indians to adopt their way of life.

(Frederick J. Dockstader, *Great North American Indians*, 1977.)

Hudson, Charles L., Expedition. On December 9, 1873, Lieutenant Charles L. Hudson led 41 Fourth Cavalry troopers on patrol from Fort Clark, Texas. He caught up with a Comanche and Kiowa war party on the West Fork of the Nueces River in Edwards County, Texas. The Indians spread out along a ridge top and began firing guns at the soldiers at long range. Hudson and his men, still mounted, climbed the rocky slope with great difficulty, never returning fire until they reached the top. Then they dismounted and opened fire at close range. After ten minutes of battle some of the warriors fled. Hudson remounted his men and charged the remaining Indians, scattering them and pursuing as long as a survivor could be found. At least nine hostiles were killed, including the son of the Kiowa war chief, Lone Wolf.

(W. S. Nye, *Carbine & Lance*, 1969; William H. Leckie, *The Buffalo Soldiers*, 1967.)

Hump, Miniconjou Sioux Chief. Hump, whose Indian name was Etokeah, was a formidable enemy of the U. S. Army for more than thirty years. He led a charge on the soldiers during the Fetterman massacre near Fort Phil Kearny on December 21, 1866. Afterward he participated in several battles against Generals Custer and Crook, but after he surrendered to General Miles in 1877 he became a government scout in the Nez Percé war and an Indian policeman at the Cheyenne River Reservation.

In 1889, at the onset of the Ghost Dance excitement, Hump came under the influence of Kicking Bear, leader of the Sioux dancers, and discarded his police uniform to don a ghost shirt. He became the leading dancer at Cheyenne River, and his band of 600 joined in the frenzy. But General Miles and Captain Ezra P. Ewers met with him on December 9 and persuaded him to rejoin the Indian scouts. During the Wounded Knee massacre he remained peacefully on the Pine Ridge Reservation.

(Frederick J. Dockstader, *Great North American Indians*, 1977; Robert M. Utley, *The Last Days of the Sioux Nation*, 1963; Dee Brown, *Bury My Heart at Wounded Knee*, 1971.)

Humphrey, Philander, Family of. Dr. Philander Humphrey, government physician at the Lower Agency, had to flee with his family at the onset of the Minnesota Sioux outbreak of 1862. They attempted to reach Fort Ridgely but, unfortunately, they stopped to rest at the cabin of a settler who had hurriedly abandoned it a few hours earlier. There a Sioux war party found them, murdered the physician, and burned down the house with his wife and children inside. The only survivor was a small boy who had gone to a spring for water and hid when he saw the Indians approaching.

(C. M. Oehler, *The Great Sioux Uprising*, 1959.)

Hungate Family Massacre. In the spring of 1864, Cheyenne Indians attacked a family named Hungate on Box Elder Creek, 30 miles east of Denver. They killed Mr. and Mrs. Hungate and their two children. When their mutilated bodies were discovered in a well, a panic occurred in Denver. The incident caused fury among Colorado settlers that culminated in the Sand Creek massacre.

(George Bird Grinnell, *The Fighting Cheyennes*, 1956; John Tebbel and Keith Jennison, *The Indian Wars*, 1960.)

Hunkpapa Indians. The Hunkpapa Indians, a division of the Teton Sioux, lived in the area around the Cheyenne and Yellowstone rivers. Led by their great chief, Sitting Bull, they fought many battles against the U. S. Army and were among the last of the Sioux to live on a reservation.

(F. W. Hodge, ed., *Handbook of American Indians, I*, 1912.)

Hunkpatina Indians. The Hunkpatina Indians, a division of the Yanktonai Sioux, lived in eastern South Dakota during frontier times. Afterward they settled on the Crow Creek Reservation.

(F. W. Hodge, ed., *Handbook of American Indians, I*, 1912.)

Hunter, John F., Family of. John F. Hunter settled in Fannin County, Texas, in 1838. Five years later Indians raided his ranch home, killing his mother and several other persons and capturing his sister, Lavicia. The young lady was carried to western Texas, where an Indian called Delaware Frank redeemed her for $750. Hunter devoted the next thirteen years to Indian hunting.

(A. J. Sowell, *Rangers and Pioneers of Texas*, 1964.)

Hutchinson, Minnesota, Raid. During the Sioux uprising of 1862, Chief Little Crow and a war party attacked the little town of Hutchinson. More than twenty buildings, including Hutchinson Academy, were destroyed, but the residents rushed inside their stockade and stood off the raiders until they withdrew, taking all the livestock and a great deal of plunder.

Little Crow was killed by a farmer near Hutchinson the following year.

(C. M. Oehler, *The Great Sioux Uprising*, 1959.)

Immell, Michael. Michael Immell and Robert Jones, veteran trappers of the Missouri Fur Company, agreed to work the dangerous streams bordering Blackfoot country in 1821. They obtained thirty packs of beaver from the Crow Indians and returned safely to company headquarters. The following year, with several companions, they made an expedition to the mouth of the Bighorn River. There they acquired thirty packs of beaver, waited out the winter, and trapped the Three Forks country in the spring. On May 30, they were ambushed by the Blackfeet and Immell, Jones, and five of their men were hacked to pieces.

(David Lavender, *Bent's Fort*, 1954; Hiram Martin Chittenden, *The American Fur Trade of the Far West*, 1954; John C. Ewers, *The Blackfeet*, 1961.)

Inkpaduta, Sioux Chief. Inkpaduta (Scarlet Point), son of a Sioux war chief named Wamdesapa, was born in South Dakota about 1815. In 1828, Wamdesapa murdered another Sioux chief and his band was outlawed by the tribe. When Wamdesapa died in 1848, Inkpaduta became chief of the outlaws, and he had several fights with both Indians and whites.

In 1857, Inkpaduta's band camped near Spirit Lake, Iowa, not far from the Minnesota boundary. One of his warriors killed a settler's dog that had bitten him, the owner attacked the Indian, and Inkpaduta's infuriated followers began murdering white people. Before the massacre ended, 47 settlers were dead and four women carried into captivity. (See Spirit Lake Massacre; Gardner, Rowland.) Pursued by soldiers and friendly Sioux Indians, Inkpaduta managed to evade capture and punishment.

After the Minnesota Sioux uprising of 1862, Inkpaduta joined other hostile bands on the plains. He led them in engagements with General Alfred Sully's army, losing many of his followers during the battles of Big Mound, Whitestone Hill, and Killdeer Mountain. His last battle was against Custer at the Little Bighorn. Afterward he went to Canada, and it is believed that he died there about 1878.

(Doane Robinson, *A History of the Dakota or Sioux Indians*, 1974; Charles E. Flandrau, *The History of Minnesota*, 1900; Frederick J. Dockstader, *Great North American Indians*, 1977; U.S. National Park Service, *Soldier and Brave*, 1963.)

Iowa Indians. The Iowa Indians, a small Siouan tribe related to the Winnebagos, were located at the mouth of the Blue River in Minnesota when first visited by French explorers about 1675. Later they moved to northwestern Iowa. By 1760 they lived along the Mississippi between the Iowa and Des Moines rivers. Never prominent in warfare with whites, the Iowas began ceding their lands during the early nineteenth century.

Between 1824 and 1836 they ceded territory in Missouri, Iowa, and Minnesota in exchange for a reservation in Kansas and Nebraska. Some of them moved to Oklahoma after the Civil War and were given allotments in severalty. The others arrived in Oklahoma in 1883 and received allotments in 1890.

(Martha Royce Blaine, *The Ioway Indians*, 1979; Muriel H. Wright, *A Guide to the Indian Tribes of Oklahoma*, 1951.)

Iron Eye, Omaha Chief. See LaFlesche, Joseph

Iron Jacket, Comanche Chief. Iron Jacket (Pobishequasho), a prominent Comanche chief and medicine man, wore a Spanish coat of mail when he rode into battle against Texans or Indian enemies. His followers believed that he had power to blow away bullets or arrows with his breath. His medicine failed him, however, during a battle on the South Canadian River in 1858 with Texas Rangers and Brazos Reserve Indians. A Shawnee Indian, Doss, shot him out of the saddle and an Anadarko chief, Pockmark, finished him off. (See Antelope Hills, Battle of.)

(John Salmon Ford, *Rip Ford's Texas*, 1963; Walter Prescott Webb, *The Texas Rangers*, 1965.)

Iron Tail, Oglala Sioux Chief. Iron Tail (Sinte Maza) was born in South Dakota about the mid-nineteenth century. A feared warrior in his youth, at the close of the Indian wars he toured Europe with Buffalo Bill Cody's Wild West Show. He lived until 1916.

(Frederick J. Dockstader, *Great North American Indians*, 1977.)

Ishatai, Comanche Medicine Man. Ishatai (Coyote Droppings) was a fierce enemy of white hunters and settlers. After amazing the Indians by correctly predicting the advent of a comet, he claimed to have acquired the ability to stop bullets while lifted into the clouds to commune with the Great Spirit. He organized the first Comanche sun dance in 1874.

Ishatai schemed to unite the southern plains Indians into a force—protected by his power over bullets—that would wipe out white invaders and bring back the buffalo. Chief Quanah Parker suggested an attack on the buffalo hunters at Adobe Walls, and many Comanches, Kiowas, Cheyennes, and Arapahoes flocked to the Texas Panhandle to participate. After nine warriors had been killed, the Indians concluded reluctantly that Ishatai's magic had failed and gave up the fight. (See Adobe Walls, Battles of.)

(Ernest Wallace and E. Adamson Hoebel, *The Comanches*, 1952; W. S. Nye, *Carbine & Lance*, 1969.)

Isimanica, Comanche Chief. Inflamed by the slaughter of Indians during the Council House Fight, Isimanica led three hundred Comanche warriors to San Antonio, Texas, on March 28, 1840. Leaving the war party on the outskirts of the city, he and a single warrior rode back and forth along Commerce Street, shaking their lances and daring any or all citizens to come forth and fight.

Informed that the soldiers were quartered at the San José mission, Isimanica rode there and challenged the commanding officer to come out and fight. Captain William D. Redd replied that a truce was in effect to exchange prisoners and that when it ended the troops would fight the war party. The chief hurled insults, wheeled his horse, and rode off.

Some of the soldiers were so angry that they had to be herded into the church to prevent them from pursuing Isimanica. Captain Lysander Wells called Redd a coward, and they killed each other in a duel.

(Mildred P. Mayhall, *Indian Wars of Texas*, 1965.)

Itscheabine Indians. The Itscheabine Indians, an Assiniboin band, lived near the boundary between the United States and Canada. The Lewis and Clark Expedition visited them in 1804.

(F. W. Hodge, ed., *Handbook of American Indians, I*, 1912.)

-J-

James, Fort, North Dakota. See Berthold, Fort, North Dakota

Jesseaume, René. See Jusseaume, René

Jock, Jemmy. Jemmy Jock, a Hudson's Bay Company trapper, was sent by his superiors to learn the language of the Blackfoot Indians. He fell in love with a chief's daughter, married her by Indian custom, and remained with the tribe thirty years. In time he gained great influence over the Blackfeet and was chosen to be a chief.

(Walter O'Meara, *Daughters of the Country*, 1968.)

Johnson, Big Nose, Tonkawa Chief. A. J. Sowell, a Texas Ranger who knew Big Nose at Fort Griffin, Texas, wrote of him:

> Big Nose Johnson was the war chief of the tribe (in 1870), and was a powerfully-made man, standing nearly seven feet in his moccasins, with broad shoulders and deep chest. He was a terror to the Comanches, and a match for half a dozen common warriors. . . . On one occasion he went with the soldiers after the Comanches, and surprised them in their camp, and defeated them, although in considerable force, and outnumbering the soldiers and a few Tonks, which Johnson had with him. On this occasion he was fearful to behold; running from place to place, shouting his war cry, and overcoming all opposition, killing and scalping his enemies as he came to them; sometimes tearing the scalp off before they were dead, and came out of the fight with seven scalps dangling at his belt. He was often wounded, and they said his broad breast bore many scars.

(A. J. Sowell, *Rangers and Pioneers of Texas*, 1964.)

Johnson, Britton, Family of. Britton (Britt) Johnson, a free Negro, was born on the Moses Johnson ranch and remained with the family when they moved to the northwest Texas frontier during his youth. He was such a valuable hand that he gained a partial ownership of the Johnson ranch and served as foreman of Elizabeth Fitzpatrick's cattle business. In addition, he worked as an orderly and a freighter at Fort Belknap.

In October 1864, while Johnson was away with the wagons, Kiowa and Comanche Indians attacked the Fitzpatrick house in which his own wife and children lived. (See Elm Creek Raid.) When he returned he found the bodies of his eldest son and Mrs. Fitzpatrick's daughter. His wife, Mary, and his children, Cherry and Jube, had been taken captive along with several members of the Fitzpatrick and Durgan families. Britt Johnson set out alone across the Red River to redeem them.

Johnson spied around the Comanche villages until he located Mrs. Fitzpatrick and her granddaughter, Lottie Durgan. Then he rode into the camp, showed no fear when warriors danced around him, and exhibited such skill as a horseman and marksman that some of the Indians wanted to adopt him. He ransomed the two captives and learned that his own family was held elsewhere by the Kiowas. He made three trips to hostile villages and redeemed two other captives before he located Mary, Cherry, and Jube. Then he slipped into the village, rescued them with the help of a friendly Comanche, and outran the Kiowas back to the Fitzpatrick ranch.

In 1871, Johnson and three other black freighters encountered a Kiowa war party near Flat Top Mountain while hauling freight to Fort Griffin. They put up a terrific fight before being overridden and slain. The Indian leader, Mamanti,

> retold the story about the tough fight the men had put up and how one (Johnson) had almost refused to die even though he had arrows sticking in him from every direction. In fact, with his nose and ears cut off and his bowels cut open that one would not admit he was dead, but had shown the nerve to pull out a fistful of a Kiowa warrior's hair. . . . —Benjamin Capps

(Benjamin Capps, *The Warren Wagontrain Raid*, 1974; Mildred P. Mayhall, *The Kiowas*, 1962; T. R. Fehrenbach, *Comanches*, 1983.)

Johnson, Liver-Eating. See Johnston, John

Johnston, Albert Sidney, Indian Campaigns. Albert Sidney Johnston, renowned in history as a prominent Confederate Army general, was equally as effective as an Indian fighter. Born in Kentucky on February 2, 1803, he graduated from the United States Military Academy in 1826. He was regimental adjutant in the Black Hawk War, resigned his commission in 1834, and came to Texas to fight in its revolution in 1836. In 1837, he was appointed senior brigadier general of the Texas Army and fought several engagements with the Comanche Indians. (See Gilliland, Johnstone, Family of.) In 1838, he was appointed Secretary of War for the Republic of Texas, and he led the expedition against the Cherokees that expelled them from the new nation. In addition, he devised the strategy that proved highly effective of employing Tonkawas and Lipan Apaches to scout against the Comanches.

During the Mexican War, Johnston served as colonel of the First Texas Rifle Volunteers. Afterward he was appointed paymaster for United States Army troops guarding the Texas frontier. In 1855, he accompanied Harney's expedition against the Sioux and soon afterward returned to

Texas as commanding officer of the U. S. Second Cavalry, a regiment that produced more general officers than any other in American history. T. R. Fehrenbach has noted that as all other soldiers in Texas were in the infantry,

> almost the entire burden of the active defense (against Indians) fell on the cavalry. Colonel Johnston welcomed this, and relished the orders received from the war secretary to patrol, pursue, and punish any wild Indians found in Texas because the regiment was out to prove . . . the effectiveness of horse soldiers.

> He kept patrols constantly in the field that disrupted Comanche hostilities. (See Hood, John B.)

At the onset of the Civil War, Johnston became a Confederate General and was killed at Shiloh on April 6, 1862.

(T. R. Fehrenbach, *Comanches*, 1983; James T. De Shields, *Border Wars of Texas*, 1976.)

Johnston, John. John Johnston (Liver-Eating Johnson), a native of New Jersey who became a legendary figure in the western fur trade, began his career in 1843. Tutored in the trade by such veteran trappers as John Hatcher, Chris Lapp, and Del Gue, the powerful young mountain man soon learned to fight Indians as well as kill animals along the Musselshell River in Montana and in the Big Horn Mountains.

In May 1847, Johnston married Swan, a daughter of the Flathead chief, Bear's Head. He took her to his camp on the Musselshell, taught her to shoot a rifle, and then crossed the continental divide to live in his cabin on the Little Snake River. He left his pregnant bride there for the winter while he trapped in the Uintah Mountains. Before he returned in the spring, a Crow Indian warrior tomahawked her. When Johnston discovered the tragedy, he identified the tribe of the murderer by a feather found at the scene. He "swore a merciless oath that he would be avenged—and mightily—upon the Crows."—Raymond W. Thorp and Robert Bunker

In 1848, according to legend that spread throughout the mountains, so many Crow warriors were killed and their livers removed that Johnston became known as Crow Killer and Liver-Eating Johnson. How many warriors he killed, or whether he ate their livers, has been the subject of much speculation:

> Alone and unaided, mountain men asserted, he tracked down and killed Crow until that nation of valiant warriors appointed twenty braves to destroy him or die in the attempt. Johnson killed them

all, hand to hand. Before his terrible thirst for revenge was satisfied, he had accounted for three hundred Crow warriors and had eaten their livers.—Walter O'Meara

There are two stories of how the name was earned. One is that he threatened to kill and eat the liver of the first Indian who bothered him, and old-timers insist that he did. The other is that he "bluffed out" a young easterner . . . who wished to accompany him on a trip by pretending that he had just killed an Indian and was cooking the liver for supper.—Edgar I. Stewart

As most historians of the Indian wars make no mention of Johnston, it is plain that they consider the legend to be greatly exaggerated.

Johnston left the mountains in 1863 to fight for the Union. When he returned in 1865 he resumed his life as a hunter of men and beasts. He joined other trappers in battles with Blackfeet, Nez Percé, Sioux, and Cheyenne Indians. He served as a scout for the Army and, late in life, he was sheriff of Red Lodge, Montana. He died in January 1900.

(Raymond W. Thorp and Robert Bunker, *Crow Killer*, 1958; Joe DeBarthe, *Life and Adventures of Frank Grouard*, 1958; Walter O'Meara, *Daughters of the Country*, 1968.)

Jones, Horace P. Horace P. Jones was an interpreter and farmer-instructor to the Comanches at Fort Cobb as early as 1859. At the onset of the Civil War he became an interpreter at Fort Cobb while the Confederacy controlled it. In October 1862, he had to leap out a window and run for his life when Indians destroyed the agency. After the war he interpreted for United States Army officers and treaty negotiators. In 1885, he accompanied a delegation of Indian chiefs to Washington to help them gain permission to lease tribal lands to cattlemen. In later life he became a farmer on land given him near Fort Sill.

(W. S. Nye, *Carbine & Lance*, 1969; Mildred P. Mayhall, *The Kiowas*, 1962.)

Jones, John B. John B. Jones was one of the most proficient Texas Rangers in protecting frontier settlements from Indian attacks. In 1874, while serving as major of the Frontier Battalion, he led an attack on a Kiowa and Comanche war party near Jacksboro, Texas. The following year his five Ranger companies fought 18 battles, killing 27 warriors. His success in guarding the northwestern Texas frontier prevented the abandonment of several counties.

(*Handbook of Texas*, *I*, 1952; J. W. Wilbarger, *Indian Depredations in Texas*, 1985; Walter Prescott Webb, *The Texas Rangers*, 1965.)

Jones, Robert. See Immell, Michael

Julesburg, Colorado, Indian Attacks. In retaliation for the Sand Creek massacre, a war party of Cheyennes and Arapahoes, accompanied by some Sioux warriors, attacked Camp Rankin on the outskirts of Julesburg on January 7, 1865. Repulsed by the soldiers, the hostiles sacked Julesburg. A few weeks later, while residents and soldiers forted up at Camp Rankin, too weak numerically for a sortie, the Indians returned and burned all of the buildings in town.

(Eugene F. Ware, *The Indian War of 1864*, 1960; George Bird Grinnell, *The Fighting Cheyennes*, 1956.)

Jusseaume, René. René Jusseaume, a Canadian, lived with the Mandan Indians as early as 1789. An independent trader, he traveled between the Mandan villages and Canadian posts in Saskatchewan and Manitoba, and in 1794 he established a post at the mouth of Knife River for the North West Company. He was a guide and interpreter for the David Thompson expedition to the Missouri in 1797. In 1804, he served as interpreter to the Mandans for Lewis and Clark, and he accompanied the explorers to Washington on their return from the Pacific Coast. In 1807, he was wounded by the Sioux while attempting with the Nathaniel Pryor party to return the Mandan chief, Big White, to his people. Afterward he traded among the Mandans for Manuel Lisa until 1820.

In spite of Jusseaume's association with leading explorers and traders, he was regarded unfavorably by most Americans. Thompson regarded him as a poor guide and interpreter. Lewis and Clark considered him to be a liar and cheat. Alexander Henry the Younger, who met him at the Mandan villages in 1806, commented that "this man . . . has a wife and family who dress and live like the natives. He retains the outward appearance of a Christian, but his principles, as far as I could observe, are much worse than those of the Mandans."

(W. Raymond Wood and Thomas D. Thiessen, eds., *Early Fur Trade of the Northern Plains*, 1985; Walter O'Meara, *Daughters of the Country*, 1968; Roy W. Meyer, *The Village Indians of the Upper Missouri*, 1977; Gordon Speck, *Breeds and Half-Breeds*, 1969.)

Kainah Indians. See Blackfoot Indians

Kansa Indians. The Kansa (Kaw) Indians, a Siouan-speaking tribe closely related to the Osages, were visited on the Kansas River by French traders as early as 1700. Their population at that time was estimated at 1,500. Although other tribes considered them to be great warriors, they never played an important role in Indian-white affairs on the frontier.

The Kansa signed a treaty of peace and friendship with the United States on October 28, 1815. On June 3, 1825, by signing the Treaty of St. Louis, they ceded their lands in northern Kansas and southeastern Nebraska and abandoned claims to territory in Missouri, while reserving for tribal use a tract on the Kansas River. Another treaty was negotiated on January 14, 1846, by which the tribe ceded 2 million acres and accepted a reservation twenty miles square at Council Grove, Kansas, on the Neosho River. As the new reservation was rapidly overrun by white settlers, they ceded a large portion of it in 1859. The remainder was disposed of by 1880, and the tribe moved to a reservation of 100,000 acres in Oklahoma adjoining the Osages. By 1902, all of their lands were allotted in severalty.

(F. W. Hodge, ed., *Handbook of American Indians, I*, 1912; Muriel H. Wright, *A Guide to the Indian Tribes of Oklahoma*, 1951.)

Karnes, Henry Wax. Henry Wax Karnes, a native of Tennessee, moved to Texas in 1835 and played a prominent part in the Revolution and in Indian affairs of the Republic. In 1838, he was appointed captain and authorized to raise eight companies of Rangers to protect exposed settlements from Comanche attacks.

On August 10, 1839, while scouting the Arroyo Seco with 20 men, Karnes was attacked by 200 Comanches. The Rangers dismounted and took cover in a ravine. Firing by alternate platoons, they killed 20 Indians and wounded so many that the war party abandoned the attack. Karnes was so severely wounded that it caused his death a year later.

On January 9, 1840, Karnes received a delegation of three Comanche chiefs at his headquarters in San Antonio. The chiefs announced that the Comanches wanted peace, and Karnes agreed upon condition that they bring all of their white captives to San Antonio. When Karnes reported on the agreement to his superior, Albert Sidney Johnston, he stated that he had no faith in Indian promises and recommended that troops be stationed in position to seize the chiefs if they failed to release all of the captives. Johnston agreed, and the result was a battle in and around the courthouse that led to many years of hostility. (See Council House Fight.)

"Karnes, like most Texans, could never see a Comanche, even under the most friendly conditions, without visualizing the barbarities the Indian had done, or might do under different circumstances."—T. R. Fehrenbach

(T. R. Fehrenbach, *Comanches,* 1983; James T. De Shields, *Border Wars of Texas,* 1976; Walter Prescott Webb, *The Texas Rangers,* 1965.)

Kaw Indians. See Kansa Indians

Kearny, Fort, Nebraska. Fort Kearny was established in May, 1846, fifty miles below Omaha on the Missouri River. It was abandoned two years later and reconstructed on the Platte, near the present site of Kearny, Nebraska, on land purchased from the Pawnee Indians. Intended to protect travelers on the Oregon Trail, it marked the end of the first leg of their journey. It was abandoned in 1871 after railroad construction terminated its usefulness.

(Robert W. Frazer, *Forts of the West,* 1965; U.S. National Park Service, *Soldier and Brave,* 1963.)

Kelly, Fanny, Captivity of. On July 12, 1864, Fanny Kelly, nineteen-year-old bride of Josiah Kelly, was captured by the Oglala Sioux while enroute to Idaho in a wagon train. The attack on the train occurred near Little Box Elder Creek, Colorado. Her husband escaped, but a small girl, Mary, that the couple had adopted, was captured. During the ride to the Sioux village three hundred miles to the north, Fanny instructed the child to hide in bushes beside the trail, and they never saw each other again.

Fanny was taken into the lodge of an aged chief, Silver Horn, to serve his six wives. She was well treated until her captors learned that General Alfred Sully had mounted the heads of slain Sioux warriors on poles as a warning. While fleeing from Sully, the Sioux held a council to decide Fanny's fate. Most of the chiefs wanted to kill her, but she was saved by Silver Horn's plea that she should not be held responsible for the acts of soldiers.

In October 1864, the Oglalas sold Mrs. Kelly to Brings Plenty, a Hunkpapa Sioux chief who took her to his village on the Grand River in South Dakota. Major E. A. House at Fort Sully heard of her situation and sent some Blackfoot Sioux Indians, led by Chief Crawler, to try to redeem her. Brings Plenty declined to give her up, but Crawler seized her at pistol point and took her to his own village to rest. Then they resumed the journey to Fort Sully, accompanied by a large number of Indians who, according to Crawler, hoped to share in a reward. Mrs. Kelly was convinced, however, that they planned to attack the fort, and she sent a warning by a warrior who had fallen in love with her. As soon as she entered the fort, the gates were slammed in the faces of the Indians. After rejoining her husband, she received a $5,000 reward from Congress for saving Fort Sully.

(Fanny Kelly, *My Captivity Among the Sioux Indians,* 1872; Howard H. Peckham, *Captured by Indians,* 1954; Frederic Drimmer, *Scalps and Tomahawks,* 1961.)

Kenny's Fort, Texas. Kenny's Fort, consisting of a few houses surrounded by a stockade, was built in Williamson County, Texas, in 1839. In August 1840, the settlers of the area gathered in the fort and withstood an Indian attack, killing several warriors.

(James T. De Shields, *Border Wars of Texas,* 1976; *Handbook of Texas, I,* 1952.)

Keogh, Fort, Montana. Fort Keogh was established on the Yellowstone River near the present site of Miles City by General Nelson A. Miles. Intended to help conquer the Indians of the northern plains, it served as headquarters for Miles in his campaigns against the Sioux and Cheyennes. It was closed in 1900.

(Robert W. Frazer, *Forts of the West,* 1965; U. S. National Park Service, *Soldier and Brave,* 1963.)

Kicking Bear, Teton Sioux Medicine Man. Kicking Bear, a medicine man at the Cheyenne River Reservation, played the leading role in introducing the Ghost Dance to the Sioux. Born about 1850, he had been a fearsome warrior who had fought with distinction at the battles of the Rosebud, Slim Buttes, and the Little Bighorn. An Oglala by birth, he had married a niece of Chief Big Foot and thereby became a Miniconjou. "Uncompromising hatred of the white man and all his ways, refusal to adjust to the new life, mystical leanings, and rank and reputation, made Kicking Bear a natural leader in the quest for the old life." —Robert M. Utley

In 1890, Kicking Bear learned of the teachings of the Paiute prophet, Wovoka. Hopeful that the Paiute would prove to be the Indian Messiah, Kicking Bird, Short Bull, and several other Sioux rode the train as far as it went, then obtained horses to complete the pilgrimage to Wovoka's cabin at Walker Lake, Nevada. Wovoka taught them the dance that would rid the country of white people and bring back the ghosts of Indian ancestors.

When Kicking Bear returned to the Sioux, he encountered so much skepticism that he went to Wyoming to visit the Ghost Dancers among the Arapahoes. The new religion had made such a profound impression on that tribe that Kicking Bear was able to transmit their enthusiasm to his own people. Soon Cheyenne River became the center of the Ghost Dance, and Sioux from other reservations flocked there to seek inspiration. When the dance swept the Standing Rock Reservation, agent James McLaughlin instructed Sitting Bull to evict Kicking Bear. The great chief refused, and McLaughlin's Indian police escorted the Miniconjou medicine man from the reservation.

After the massacre of Big Foot's band at Wounded Knee, Kicking Bear surrendered to General Nelson Miles. He was confined in a military prison for a time and, after release, he joined Buffalo Bill Cody's Wild West Show.

(Dee Brown, *Bury My Heart at Wounded Knee*, 1971; Robert M. Utley, *The Last Days of the Sioux Nation*, 1963.)

Kicking Bird, Kiowa Chief. Kicking Bird, a Kiowa chief noted for his advocacy of peace with white people, was born about 1835. He accepted a treaty in 1865 establishing a reservation and two years later signed the Treaty of Medicine Lodge. As a result, many of his people turned against him.

In 1870, stung by taunts that he had lost his warrior spirit, Kicking Bird led a hundred braves on a raid into Texas. On July 12, the war party encountered a detachment of 53 Sixth Cavalry troopers, led by Captain Curwen B. McClellan, near Seymour, Texas. Kicking Bird lanced a soldier while leading a charge, and the attack was sustained for the entire afternoon. Three troopers were killed and twelve wounded before Kicking Bird, believing himself vindicated in the eyes of the Kiowas, broke off the battle.

The fight with McClellan was Kicking Bird's final battle against soldiers or settlers. He realized that the Plains Indians could not prevail over the numerous and powerful invaders and tried to prepare his people for a new way of life. He supported the efforts of Thomas A. Battey to educate the Kiowa children, and he worked closely with religious and military leaders to prevent raids by the more warlike chiefs of the tribe. When Lone Wolf and his followers surrendered in 1875, Kicking Bird, then recognized as principal chief, was ordered to select 74 hostiles to be imprisoned in Florida. One of those chosen for exile was the medicine man, Mamanti, who retaliated by placing a curse on the chief. After the train departed for Florida, Kicking Bird drank a cup of coffee, collapsed, and died on May 3, 1875.

(Frederick J. Dockstader, *Great North American Indians*, 1977; Mildred P. Mayhall, *The Kiowas*, 1962; W. S. Nye, *Carbine & Lance*, 1969; Lawrie Tatum, *Our Red Brothers*, 1899; Thomas C. Battey, *The Life and Adventures of a Quaker Among the Indians*, 1876.)

Kidder, L. S., Expedition. On June 29, 1867, Lieutenant L. S. Kidder and ten troopers of the Second Cavalry were sent by General Sheridan from Fort Sedgwick, Colorado, to deliver dispatches to General Custer, believed to be campaigning along the Republican River. Led by a Sioux scout, Red Bead, the detachment encountered Chief Pawnee Killer's hostile Sioux and Cheyenne Dog Soldiers, and every man in the detachment was slain. Custer, who discovered the bodies a few days later, reported that they had been "so brutally hacked and disfigured as to be beyond recognition" and several had been burned to death.

(Paul I. Wellman, *Death on Horseback*, 1947; George Bird Grinnell, *The Fighting Cheyennes*, 1956.)

Killdeer Mountain, Battle of. In 1864, General Alfred Sully led an army of 2,200 soldiers, cavalry, and artillery, in pursuit of hostile Sioux bands. On July 28, 1864, he attacked Chief Inkpaduta's 1,600 warriors at Killdeer Mountain in Dunn County, North Dakota. The Indians took a position at the south base of the mountain, and Sully ordered his men to charge. After the troops had killed or wounded about 100 hundred warriors, Inkpaduta and his survivors fled from the field.

(Doane Robinson, *A History of the Dakota or Sioux Indians*, 1974; Robert H. Dillon, *North American Indian Wars*, 1983; U. S. National Park Service, *Soldier and Brave*, 1963.)

Kinney, Henry Lawrence. Henry L. Kinney, a native of Pennsylvania, established a ranch on Corpus Christi Bay, Texas, in 1841. This exposed position was attacked frequently by Indians, but Kinney and his cowboys invariably prevailed. On one occasion when attacked by 17 Comanches on the prairie, Kinney and 11 of his men dismounted and a battle ensued at close range. Kinney was lanced while assisting one of his men, but he survived and slew his assailant. The Indians withdrew after losing seven warriors. Kinney had three men killed, and all of the survivors were wounded. Kinney fought in the Mexican War, served in the Texas legislature, filibustered in Latin America, and was killed during a revolution in Mexico.

(J. W. Wilbarger, *Indian Depredations in Texas*, 1985; *Handbook of Texas, I*, 1952.)

Kiowa Dutch, Captivity of. In 1837, a Kiowa war party raided the Matagorda Bay area of Texas and massacred a German family. The Indians spared an eight-year-old boy and carried him into captivity. He remained with them for sixty years. The boy grew into a fearsome warrior, known throughout the Texas frontier as Kiowa Dutch. An enormous blond, no amount of exposure to the sun could make him resemble his Indian companions, but culturally he was as much a Kiowa as if he had been born into the tribe.

In August 1866, an Army wagon train was attacked by the band of the famous raider, Satanta, near the Llano River in Central Texas. A severe fight lasted most of the day. Finally the Indians broke off the engagement, fight lasted most of the day. Finally the Indians broke off the engagement, but before they left the scene Kiowa Dutch rode close enough to the wagons to curse the soldiers in English, spoken with a German accent. He warned them that he would get their scalps before they reached Buffalo Gap.

In 1890, the Kiowas were living peacefully on the reservation in Oklahoma. There an Indian agent interviewed Kiowa Dutch. The captive recalled attending school in Germany for one year and then moving with his family to Texas, where they settled on a river near the Gulf of Mexico. After the Kiowas killed his family he had never felt any desire to return to white civilization. He could not recall his family name.

(Clarence Wharton, *Satanta*, 1935.)

Kiowa, Fort, South Dakota. Fort Kiowa was built about 1822 for the American Fur Company on the Missouri River near the present site of Chamberlain, South Dakota. In 1825, General Henry Atkinson negotiated a treaty of friendship and trade at Fort Kiowa with the Teton, Yankton, and Yanktonai Sioux. The fort was abandoned after the decline of the fur trade.

(Hiram Martin Chittenden, *The American Fur Trade of the Far West*, 1954.)

Kiowa Indians. The Kiowa Indians, a small but powerful and predatory tribe of a distinctive language stock, were located in prehistoric times near the headwaters of the Missouri River. Pushed southward by northern plains tribes, they found a home in western Oklahoma and the Texas Panhandle. There they became allies of the Comanches about 1790, and the two tribes held the area under their control for eighty years.

The Kiowas were known by the Spanish as early as 1732. After acquiring Spanish horses from the Crow Indians, they began raiding over a vast area of Mexico, sometimes going all the way to the Gulf of California. When immigrants from Europe and the United States began settling in Texas, the Kiowas included them in their raids. In proportion to their own numbers, they caused more casualties to white settlers than any other tribe. They captured so many Mexican children and incorporated them into the tribe that by the time they stopped raiding, few pure-blood Kiowas could be found. (See Elm Creek Raid; Hamleton, William; Kiowa Dutch; Howard Wells Massacre; Satanta; Setangya; White Horse; Big Tree; Mamanti; Warren WagonTrain Raid.)

The first treaty between the Kiowas and the United States was negotiated in 1837. Thirty years later the Treaty of Medicine Lodge removed them to a reservation. In neither case, however, did raiding cease for long, for Kiowas and Comanches using the reservation as sanctuary continued to attack Texans until the destruction of the buffalo herds and campaigns by the military compelled them to live in peace after 1875.

Their lands on the reservation in southwestern Oklahoma were allotted in severalty in 1901 and the remainder opened to settlement.

(Mildred P. Mayhall, *The Kiowas*, 1962; W. S. Nye, *Carbine & Lance*, 1969; Grant Foreman, *Advancing the Frontier*, 1933; Clarence Wharton, *Satanta*, 1935; Carl Coke Rister, *Border Captives*, 1940; Lawrie Tatum, *Our Red Brothers*, 1899; Thomas C. Battey, *The Life and Adventures of a Quaker Among the Indians*, 1876; David Lavender, *Bent's Fort*, 1954; J. W. Wilbarger, *Indian Depredations in Texas*, 1985; Benjamin Capps, *The Warren Wagontrain Raid*, 1974.)

Kiowa-Apache Indians. The Kiowa-Apache Indians, an Athapascan-speaking tribe closely related to the Lipans, accompanied the Kiowas when they moved southward along the eastern slope of the Rockies to the southern plains. They were known to early explorers by a variety of names, including Gattaca (La Salle), Quataquois (La Harpe), and Kataka. They were fierce raiders who frequently accompanied the Comanches on forays into Mexico and Texas. With a population of around 300, they were placed on the Kiowa Reservation in southwestern Oklahoma in 1867.

"The Kiowa Apache are remarkable merely as an example of a tribe incorporated into the social organization of another tribe of entirely alien speech and origin."—John R. Swanton

(John R. Swanton, *Indian Tribes of North America*, 1952; Wildred P. Mayhall, *The Kiowas*, 1962.)

Kipp, James. James Kipp was a prominent Indian trader along the Missouri River for thirty years. Little is known of his early life, but he arrived on the Missouri with Columbia Fur Company traders in 1822. There he built Tilton's Fort among the Mandans, married a member of the tribe, and fathered several children. Because of the hostility of the neighboring Arikara Indians, he was compelled to abandon it in 1825 and move to the mouth of the White Earth River.

In 1831, Kipp, upon instruction of Kenneth McKenzie, established Fort Piegan among the Blackfoot Indians on the Marias River. The Blood Indians, a Blackfoot division, attacked the post soon afterward, instigated, it was suspected, by British traders with the Hudson's Bay Company. Kipp, after repulsing the Bloods, won the Blackfoot trade by the liberality of his presents. In the words of Hiram Martin Chittenden, historian of the fur trade, Kipp "poured into them incessant charges of alcohol until the whole band was utterly vanquished and surrendered body and soul to the incomparable trader."

In 1833, Kipp was in charge of Fort Clark, North Dakota, managing it for the American Fur Company. In 1845, he established Fort Berthold near the mouth of the Little Missouri. In 1846, he was living on a farm near Independence, Missouri, with a white wife and children, but he soon returned to the Missouri, for in 1851, when Rudolph Kurz visited him at Fort Berthold, he found him living with his Mandan family.

(Hiram Martin Chittenden, *The American Fur Trade of the Far West*, 1954; John C. Ewers, *The Blackfeet*, 1961; W. Raymond Wood and Thomas D. Thiessen, eds., *Early Fur Trade of the Northern Plains*, 1985; Roy W. Meyer, *The Village Indians of the Upper Missouri*, 1977; Walter O'Meara, *Daughters of the Country*, 1968.)

Kitkehahki Indians. See Pawnee Indians

Koozer, Gottlieb, Family of. In July 1870, the dangerous Kiowa raider White Horse led a war party to the Texas farm home of Gottlieb Koozer. The father went forth to meet them, offering his hand in friendship, but he was instantly shot to death. The raiders captured Mrs. Koozer and her three sons and two daughters, along with a boy named Martin Kilgore, and returned to the reservation. Agent Lawrie Tatum threatened to cut off Kiowa rations unless the raiders released their captives. The Kiowas demanded arms and ammunition, but finally settled for the $100 per captive ransom that Tatum offered. They were the last captives for whom a ransom was ever paid.

(A. C. Green, *The Last Captive*, 1972; Mildred P. Mayhall, *The Kiowas*, 1962; W. S. Nye, *Carbine & Lance*, 1969.)

Korn, Adolph, Captivity of. Adolph Korn, son of a San Antonio, Texas, candy maker, was captured by Comanche Indians at the age of eight. He became completely assimilated and developed into one of the fiercest warriors in his band. He and another captive, Clinton Smith, would enter a town and steal horses from stables while warriors watched from the woods.

When the Comanche band was compelled to go to the reservation at Fort Sill, Adolph and Clinton were sent to San Antonio under troop escort. Turned over to his father, Adolph stole a horse at the first opportunity and returned to the Indians.

(J. Norman Heard, *White into Red*, 1973.)

Krieger, Justina. Justina Krieger was born in Posen, Germany, in 1835. In 1862, she settled with her husband, Frederick, and nine children on the Minnesota River. On August 8, 1862, neighbors warned the Kriegers that the Sioux were murdering settlers, and twelve families attempted to flee to Fort Ridgely. Halfway to the fort they were attacked by 22 warriors. Few of the settlers were armed, and all of the men and some of the women were killed. Justina whispered to her children to drop out the back of the wagon, and eight of them escaped into the woods. The last daughter to leave was seen by the Sioux and beaten to death.

Justina was shot in the back and lay unconscious for several hours. She awoke to find an Indian cutting off her dress and feigned death while the knife ripped a gash in her stomach. After the Indians left, too weak to walk, she began crawling toward Fort Ridgely. Twelve days later she was found by Captain Hiram Grant's soldiers, who placed her lying down in a wagon. She lay there throughout the Battle of Birch Coulee and was not hit while two hundred bullets tore through the wagon. Afterward she was taken to St. Paul, where she recovered. Two months later she married John Meyer, whose entire family had been slain by the Sioux.

Seven of Mrs. Krieger's children eventually reached safety at Fort Ridgely. The eighth starved to death in the wilderness.

(Charles S. Bryant, *A History of the Great Massacre by the Sioux Indians in Minnesota,* 1868; C. M. Oehler, *The Great Sioux Uprising,* 1959.)

La Barge, Joseph. Captain Joseph La Barge became a Missouri River steamboat pilot in 1832 when he left his home at St. Louis at the age of 17. For many years he steered through hostile Indian country to deliver supplies to American Fur Company posts. In 1847, while he was delivering annuity goods for distribution to the Indians at Fort Pierre, an angry mob of Yankton warriors boarded the boat when it docked at their village for wood. After one of the boatmen was slain, La Barge cleared the decks by pointing a small cannon at the hostiles.

(Hiram Martin Chittenden, *The American Fur Trade of the Far West*, 1954; Doane Robinson, *A History of the Dakota or Sioux Indians*, 1974.)

La Flesche, Francis. Francis La Flesche, son of Omaha Indian chief Joseph La Flesche, was taught tribal traditions and dances before attending a mission school. For a quarter of a century he helped Alice C. Fletcher study Omaha civilization. In 1910, he was employed by the Bureau of American Ethnology to study Osage tribal traditions and ceremonials. He died in 1932 at the age of seventy-five.

(Frederick J. Dockstader, *Great North American Indians*, 1977.)

La Flesche, Joseph, Omaha Chief. Joseph La Flesche, last recognized chief of the Omaha tribe, was the son of Joseph La Flesche, a wealthy young Frenchman who had run away to Canada to work as a trader for the Hudson's Bay Company. His mother was an Omaha Indian, and he grew up to manhood as a member of that tribe. Speaking French as well as several Indian languages, he quickly attained a prominent position in tribal affairs and eventually was elected chief. He married Mary, daughter of Army surgeon John Gale and an Indian woman, and reared his children to appreciate the best of both civilizations.

(Dorothy Clark Wilson, *Bright Eyes*, 1974.)

La Flesche, Susan. Susan La Flesche was born on June 17, 1865, at Omaha, Nebraska. Daughter of the Omaha chief Joseph La Flesche, she attended Hampton Institute and the Pennsylvania Women's Medical College before becoming the first female Indian medical doctor. In 1894, she married a Sioux mixed-blood, Henri Picotte. At their home at Bancroft, Nebraska, she treated the sick of both races. In 1905, she became a missionary and worked toward inducing Indians to send their children to school and to live on individual homesteads. She died on September 18, 1916.

(L. G. Moses and Raymond Wilson, eds., *Indian Lives*, 1984; Frederick J. Dockstader, *Great North American Indians*, 1977.)

La Flesche, Susette. Susette La Flesche (Bright Eyes) was born on the Omaha Indian Reservation in 1854. Daughter of the half-French, half-Indian Omaha chief Joseph La Flesche, she received a good education at mission schools and at the Institute for Young Ladies at Elizabeth, New Jersey, before becoming a teacher. She is best known as an advocate of Indian rights, and between 1879 and 1881 she advanced the cause significantly during a speaking tour of eastern cities with the Ponca chief, Standing Bear. Soon afterward she married a newspaper reporter, Thomas H. Tibbles, who shared her dedication to Indian affairs. In 1886, they lectured extensively in England and Scotland, where audiences were amazed by her eloquence. In addition, she spoke convincingly before Congressional committees about Indian grievances. She died on May 26, 1903.

(Thomas Henry Tibbles, *Buckskin and Blanket Days*, 1958; Dorothy Clark Wilson, *Bright Eyes*, 1974.)

Lame Bull, Piegan Blackfoot Chief. Lame Bull, principal chief of the Piegan Indians, was important in Blackfoot history both as a warrior and a diplomat. On August 28, 1833, while camped just outside the walls of Fort McKenzie, he and his warriors, with the help of white traders, fought off an attack by six hundred Assiniboins and Crees. In 1855, by means of Lame Bull's Treaty, he agreed to permit white persons to settle in or transverse the tribe's territory.

(John C. Ewers, *The Blackfeet*, 1961.)

Lame Deer, Miniconjou Sioux Chief. Lame Deer, a prominent participant in the Battle of the Little Bighorn, refused to join the hostiles who fled to Canada. On May 7, 1877, near the Rosebud River, he attempted to surrender to General Nelson A. Miles. He was handing his rifle to Miles when a scout rode up and acted as if he intended to shoot the chief. Retrieving his rifle, Lame Deer fired at Miles, the general dodged, and the bullet killed a trooper nearby. In the ensuing battle Lame Deer and 13 warriors, as well as 4 soldiers, lost their lives.

(Richard H. Dillon, *North American Indian Wars*, 1983; Paul I. Wellman, *Death on Horseback*, 1947; George Bird Grinnell, *The Fighting Cheyennes*, 1956.)

Lane, Walter P. Walter P. Lane was born in Ireland on February 18, 1817, and arrived in Texas on March 1, 1836, to fight in the revolution. Afterward he worked on the frontier as a surveyor. In 1838, he was wounded in a bloody battle with Kickapoo Indians. (See Battle Creek Fight.) Beginning in 1845 he served in the Texas Rangers, fighting Indians alongside famous frontiersman John Coffee Hays. He was a Mexican War hero and a brigadier general in the Confederate Army. He died on January 22, 1892.

(James T. De Shields, *Border Wars of Texas*, 1976; *Handbook of Texas, II*, 1952.)

Lapham, Moses. Moses Lapham, a native of Rhode Island, was born on October 16, 1808, and settled in Texas in 1831. A frontier surveyor, he and three companions were killed by Comanche Indians in Fort Bend County on October 20, 1838.

(*Handbook of Texas, II*, 1952.)

Laramie, Fort, Wyoming. Fort Laramie was constructed in 1834 near the junction of the Laramie and North Platte rivers. Originally a trading post, it was purchased by the Army in 1849. It proved to be in an excellent position to control the Sioux and Cheyennes and protect wagon trains enroute to Oregon. Several important councils and treaty negotiations were conducted at Fort Laramie. The arrival of General Henry B. Carrington's army in 1866 broke up one such council and caused Red Cloud to declare war.

(Robert W. Frazer, *Forts of the West*, 1965; Paul I. Wellman, *Death on Horseback*, 1947; Doane Robinson, *A History of the Dakota or Sioux Indians*, 1974; Margaret Carrington, *Ab-Sa-Ra-Ka, Home of the Crows*, 1868.)

Laramie, Fort, Treaty of, 1851. On September 17, 1851, Superintendent of Indian Affairs David D. Mitchell and Indian agent Thomas Fitzpatrick negotiated a treaty at Fort Laramie with several Plains Indian tribes. The Indians ceded an enormous territory in Montana, Wyoming, and North Dakota for an annuity of $50,000. Each tribe agreed to live within the boundaries of a specified territory and to permit the construction of roads and forts. Safe passage of travelers was guaranteed.

> For the privilege of building roads and military posts in the ancient lands of these Indians, which it fully meant to do in any case, the government agreed to pay $50,000 a year for fifty years. When this treaty went to the Senate, the phrase "ten years" was substituted for "fifty years"; the Indians, of course, were never told.—John Tebbel and Keith Jennison

The treaty was never ratified by the tribes.

(Richard H. Dillon, *North American Indian Wars*, 1983; Charles J. Kappler, ed., *Indian Affairs: Laws and Treaties, II*, 1972; John Tebbel and Keith Jennison, *The American Indian Wars*, 1960.)

Laramie, Fort, Treaty of, 1868. One of the most amazing events in American frontier history occurred at Fort Laramie in April 1868, when United States commissioners, including generals William T. Sherman, William S. Harney, and Alfred H. Terry, agreed to abandon their forts along the Bozeman Trail. This withdrawal was a great victory for Red Cloud, the leader of the Sioux, Cheyennes, Araphahoes, and Crows who signed the treaty. Northern Wyoming and the Black Hills were forbidden to white settlement.

(Paul I. Wellman, *Death on Horseback*, 1947; Charles J. Kappler, ed., *Indian Affairs: Laws and Treaties, II*, 1972.)

La Ramie, Jacques. Jacques La Ramie, a French fur trapper, was one of the first Europeans to penetrate the southeastern section of Wyoming in 1821. He was killed near the Laramie River by the Arapaho Indians. Both the river and Fort Laramie were named for him.

(Virginia Cole Trenholm, *The Arapahoes, Our People*, 1970.)

Larned, Fort, Kansas. Fort Larned was established on the Pawnee River near its junction with the Arkansas on October 22, 1859. It was intended to guard the Santa Fe Trail and to provide a distribution center for annuities to be paid to the central and southern Plains Indians. The Cheyenne and Arapaho agency was located at the post during a period of sustained Indian hostility.

In 1864, the Kiowa Indians held a scalp dance just outside the post. The famous raider Satanta strode toward the gate, and when a sentry ordered him to halt, the chief shot him to death with an arrow. A battle began and the Kiowas managed to steal most of the horse herd. Later Satanta sent word to the quartermaster that he was disappointed in the inferior quality of army mounts.

In 1868, the agency was removed to Indian Territory. The fort was abandoned on July 19, 1878.

(Robert W. Frazer, *Forts of the West*, 1965; U. S. National Park Service, *Soldier and Brave*, 1963; W. S. Nye, *Carbine & Lance*, 1969.)

La Vérendrye Explorations. Pierre Gaultier de Varennes, Sieur de la Vérendrye, son of the French governor of Three Rivers, Canada, was born in 1685 and entered the army at the age of 12. He fought in the colonial wars and participated in the Deerfield, Massachusetts, raid in 1704. He and his four sons, Jean Baptiste, Pierre, François, and Louis Joseph, became prominent explorers during the first half of the eighteenth century.

In 1726, La Vérendrye assumed command of the French fort at Lake Nipigon. There, after hearing Indians describe rich territories to the west, he applied for a monopoly of the fur trade in regions that he explored. His request was granted in 1729 and he was instructed to search for the western sea. With the assistance of his sons, he built a chain of trading posts extending from Lake Superior to the Saskatchewan River. In 1736, while constructing a fort on the Lake of the Woods, his eldest son, Jean Baptiste, was slain by a Sioux war party. In 1738, he established trade with the Mandan Indians, and the tribe adopted him as "father."

In 1742, Pierre or his sons explored western Minnesota, the Dakotas, and as far westward as the Big Horn Mountains, opening a vast territory to French fur traders and showing the way to the Pacific. Their explorations ended in 1744 when he lost his command.

(Roy W. Meyer, *The Village Indians of the Upper Missouri,* 1977; W. Raymond Wood and Thomas D. Thiessen, eds., *Early Fur Trade in the Far West,* 1985.)

Lawrence, James. James Lawrence entered the Indian Service in his youth, serving first among the Poncas and Sioux as a clerk in Nebraska. In 1876, he was appointed Indian agent to the Poncas. Popular with the Poncas, he was called Little Brave Heart after he saved the life of a white man attacked by an Indian and then saved the Indian from other members of the tribe.

In 1877, Lawrence accompanied a band of Poncas to Oklahoma to evaluate Osage land to which the government wanted to remove the tribe. He rejected the plan because of Osage hostility, but he agreed that the Poncas could settle on land owned by the friendly Quapaws. After most of the Poncas refused to leave their lands, Lawrence was appointed agent to the Sioux on the Niobara River. A dispute with the Secretary of the Interior about distribution of goods to the Sioux resulted in his resigning his position soon afterward.

(Flora Warren Seymour, *Indian Agents of the Old Frontier,* 1975.)

Lean Bear, Cheyenne Chief. Lean Bear (Starving Bear) was a Cheyenne peace chief. In 1861, he signed the Treaty of Fort Wise and two years later visited President Lincoln in Washington to receive a peace medal and a certificate stating that he was a friend of white people. When war broke out on the plains in 1864, he led his people far south of the Platte to avoid hostilities. In mid-May, however, he learned that soldiers had attacked Cheyennes south of the Platte and, seeking safety in numbers, he brought his people northward to join Black Kettle's Cheyennes.

While hunting buffalo on the Smoky Hill River, Lean Bear discovered troops with cannon approaching. He hung his medal outside his coat, held his government papers in his left hand, and rode forward alone to shake hands. He was unaware that Lieutenant George S. Eayre had been ordered by Colonel John M. Chivington to kill Indians on sight.

When Lean Bear was within thirty yards, the troops opened fire, knocking him from his horse. As he lay helpless on the ground, a soldier rode forward and shot him in the head. Furious Cheyennes rushed to the scene, a battle ensued, and several men on each side were slain before Black Kettle ordered the warriors to stop shooting and the soldiers retreated.

(Dee Brown, *Bury My Heart at Wounded Knee,* 1971; George Bird Grinnell, *The Fighting Cheyennes,* 1956; Stan Hoig, *The Peace Chiefs of the Cheyennes,* 1980.)

Leavenworth, Fort, Kansas. Fort Leavenworth, established about twenty miles above the mouth of the Kansas River on May 8, 1827, played an important role in the Plains Indian wars. Originally called Cantonment Leavenworth, it was occupied briefly by the Kickapoo Indians in 1829 when troops were withdrawn temporarily.

Located near the jump-off areas of the Oregon and Santa Fe Trails, Fort Leavenworth served as a base for settlers moving west, military expeditions against the tribes, and headquarters of the Upper Missouri Indian agency. It was the scene of several important Indian-white negotiations.

(Robert W. Frazer, *Forts of the West,* 1965; Hiram Martin Chittenden, *The American Fur Trade of the Far West,* 1954; U. S. National Park Service, *Soldier and Brave,* 1963.)

Leavenworth, Fort, Treaty of, 1836. William Clark negotiated the Treaty of Fort Leavenworth on September 27, 1836, with the Iowa Indians and some Sauks and Foxes. The tribes ceded territory between the boundary of the state of Missouri and the Missouri River in exchange for land south of the Missouri and $7,500. The government promised to build houses for the Indians and to provide them with rations, livestock, and instructors.

(Charles J. Kappler, ed., *Indian Affairs: Laws and Treaties, II,* 1972.)

Leavenworth, Henry. General Henry Leavenworth was born in New Haven, Connecticut, on December 10, 1783. After studying law he decided upon a military career and achieved the rank of major during the War of 1812. In 1819, he began a long career on the frontier by building Fort Snelling at the junction of the Minnesota and Mississippi rivers. He assumed command of the Sixth Infantry in 1821 at Fort Atkinson, Nebraska.

When informed in 1823 of an attack by the Arikara Indians upon Ashley's fur brigade, Leavenworth led a force of 220 soldiers, 120 mountain men, and some 500 Sioux Indians to punish the offenders. The hostiles were compelled to abandon their villages (see Arikara Indians), but Leavenworth's conduct in this first major battle involving the U. S. Army and Plains Indians has drawn the censure of historians:

> Colonel Leavenworth's prompt and energetic action, when he received the news of Ashley's disaster, was most creditable. . . . But from this point on the conduct of Colonel Leavenworth was so vacillating and ineffectual . . . that he disgusted the Indian allies, forfeited their friendship and cooperation, and excited the contempt and amazement of the trappers and mountaineers.— Hiram M. Chittenden

> The campaign was an entire failure. The whites had lost the respect of the Sioux and had intensified the enmity of the Arikaras, who thereafter for many years were to prove a scourge to traders and trappers. . . . —W. J. Ghent

In 1827, Leavenworth built the important fort in Kansas that bears his name. Two years later, he assumed command of Jefferson Barracks. Early in 1834, in command of the southwestern frontier, he led the Dragoon Expedition intended to establish peace with the southern Plains Indians, but he died of fever on July 21, 1834.

(Hiram Martin Chittenden, *The American Fur Trade of the Far West*, 1954; W. J. Ghent, *The Early Far West*, 1936; Grant Foreman, *Pioneer Days in the Early Southwest*, 1926.)

Leavenworth, Jesse H. Jesse H. Leavenworth, son of General Henry Leavenworth, was a West Point graduate. After service as a colonel in the Union Army, he was sent to the frontier to attempt to establish peace with the southern Plains Indians. In April, 1865, he held a conference with the Comanches and Kiowas at Fort Zarah, Kansas, but the Indians threatened him and made off with his mules. In October he achieved his objective (see Little Arkansas, Treaty of) when the tribes agreed to live on reservations and to maintain peace. Afterward he was appointed Indian agent to the Kiowas and Comanches.

Leavenworth was a sincere friend of the Indians and a severe critic of the military policy toward them. He assumed his duties at Fort Cobb with every expectation of civilizing his charges and transforming them from hunters to farmers. But his good intentions were doomed by failure of the government to provide rations as promised and by the raiding and wandering propensities of the Plains Indians. In 1868, the discouraged idealist resigned and departed from the Indian country.

(W. S. Nye, *Carbine & Lance*, 1969.)

Le Borgne, Hidatsa Chief. Le Borgne, a fearsome Hidatsa chief, was a dominant figure among the Mandans as well as his own people at the beginning of the nineteenth century. In 1800, he sold his slave, the teenaged Sacajawea, to Toussaint Charbonneau, and the pair served as guides for the Lewis and Clark Expedition. Although he was condemned as a monster by some whites, he apparently treated them courteously. In 1813, Clark reported that Le Borgne had been deposed by the Hidatsas and planned to fight for the British in the War of 1812.

(Roy W. Meyer, *The Village Indians of the Upper Missouri,* 1977; Gordon Speck, *Breeds and Half-Breeds,* 1969; Walter O'Meara, *Daughters of the Country,* 1968.)

Lee, Abel, Family of. On June 9, 1872, a Kiowa war party led by White Horse raided along the Clear Fork of the Brazos River near Fort Griffin, Texas. The Indians crept up to the Abel Lee home, found the owner rocking on the porch, and shot him to death. Rushing through the front door, they shot Mrs. Lee with an arrow, scalped her, and cut off an arm and both ears. The Lee children ran out the back door, but Susanna (17), Millie (9), and John (6), were captured, while Frances (14) was killed by an arrow as she fled through a vegetable garden.

The captives were taken to a Kiowa village, compelled to participate in a scalp dance, and given to Indian families. A month later the Kiowas demanded ransom, but Indian Agent Lawrie Tatum refused. When he threatened to call for troops and to refuse to issue rations, the captors gave them up. The Lee children were the first captives surrendered by the Kiowas without receiving ransom.

(W. S. Nye, *Carbine & Lance,* 1969; Carl Coke Rister, *Border Captives,* 1940).

Lee, Nelson. Nelson Lee emigrated to Texas from New York in 1840. He became a Texas Ranger, serving against Indians and Mexicans under such prominent captains as Ben McCulloch, Jack Hays, and Samuel H. Walker. In 1855, he and 25 companions undertook the task of driving a large horse herd from San Patricio County, Texas, to California. On April 2, near El Paso, a Comanche war party killed 21 of the men and captured Lee and three others. Soon afterward the other captives were tortured to death, and Lee survived only because his large alarm watch fascinated the Comanche chief. After three years of captivity, Lee escaped and was taken in by a band of Comancheros. He returned to New York in 1858.

Lee's captivity narrative, written in 1859, has been condemned by some historians as a fabrication. Walter Prescott Webb, who edited the 1957 edition of the narrative, was convinced of its authenticity, however, and Carl Coke Rister wrote that "so far as the author has been able to ascertain, the only white man ever to be taken captive by Comanches, and later to escape, was Nelson Lee . . . "

(Nelson Lee, *Three Years Among the Comanches,* 1957; Carl Coke Rister, *Border Captives,* 1940.)

Left Hand, Arapaho Chief. Left Hand, a peace chief who died as a result of his friendship with the whites, was born about 1820. During his youth his family traded extensively at Bent's Fort, and his sister married John Poisal, one of Bent's traders, in 1833. As a result, Left Hand became fluent in English. When hostility arose between Indians and whites a few years later, Left Hand urged the Arapahoes to remain at peace. He visited white settlements and miner's camps, offered his friendship, and studied their way of life.

In 1864, after the murder of Chief Lean Bear by Colorado soldiers, Left Hand visited Fort Wise to offer help in recovering cavalry mounts stolen by Kiowas. He displayed a white flag, but the soldiers fired at him. As a result, many of his followers joined the hostiles, but Left Hand asserted that he would never fight the whites. He led his remaining followers to join Black Kettle's peace-seeking Cheyennes at Sand Creek and was shot at the onset of hostilities while running toward Chivington's soldiers giving the peace sign. (See Sand Creek Massacre.) His wife and children were killed at the scene, but he survived just long enough to reach the Cheyenne camp on the Smoky Hill River.

(Margaret Coel, *Chief Left Hand,* 1981; David Lavender, *Bent's Fort,* 1954; George Bird Grinnell, *The Fighting Cheyennes,* 1956.)

Lehmann, Herman, Captivity of. Herman Lehmann was born of German immigrant parents in Gillespie County, Texas, in 1859. He was captured by Apache Indians in May 1870, and lived with them four years, becoming substantially assimilated. Then he killed an Apache medicine man, fled to join the Comanches, and was adopted into their tribe. He participated in many raids on white settlements and regarded the Indians as his own people.

When Lehmann had been with the Comanches four years, his chief, Quanah Parker, led the band to live on a reservation. Herman avoided revealing himself as white to the authorities and spent his final years with the Indians as an adopted member of Quanah's family. Finally, under Quanah's persuasion, he agreed to rejoin his white family. He made the trip from Fort Sill, Oklahoma, to Loyal Valley, Texas, under military guard. During his first year of redemption he was watched constantly to prevent his running away. But in time he ceased longing for the Indian way of life, settled down with a wife, and became a farmer.

(Herman Lehmann, *Nine Years Among the Indians,* 1927; A. C. Green, *Last Captive,* 1972.)

Lincoln, Fort. See Abraham Lincoln, Fort

Linnville, Texas, Raid. Linnville was established on Lavaca Bay by John Linn in 1831. Unfortunately it became the target of a great Comanche raid in retaliation for the Council House Fight in San Antonio of March 19, 1840. Determined to prove their ability to drive all the way to the Gulf Coast, a force estimated at five hundred to a thousand warriors led by Buffalo Hump rode southward from their villages on the plains, keeping just westward of the settlements during the first week of August. On August 6, they burned several buildings at Victoria and then moved on to Linnville, arriving about dawn on August 8.

Upon the appearance of the Indians, most of the citizens rushed to small boats and rowed out into the bay. Others found safety on the steamer *Mustang*. Several were captured before they could reach the shore, including Captain H. O. Watts, collector of customs. Watts was killed, but his recent bride was among the women and children carried away as captives.

From their boats in Lavaca Bay, the citizens watched the pillage and destruction of Linnville:

> After looting the wholesale houses and stores . . . the warriors put on the coats, the chiefs the tall hats, and they plaited the bright ribbons and calicos from the warehouses into their horses' manes and tails, making gay streamers as the riders dashed about. . . . Thus far they had killed and captured not less than 20 or 25 people, and they must have felt that the murder of the chiefs in San Antonio had been avenged. They withdrew from the town after nightfall of August 8, returning to their western haunts by the broad trail they had made coming down. They carried with them between two and three thousand horses and mules, many of them loaded with the plunder of Linnville, encumbering them too much.—Walter Prescott Webb

The war party was attacked and defeated by Texas citizen soldiers four days later. (See Plum Creek, Battle of.)

(Walter Prescott Webb, *The Texas Rangers*, 1965; Donaly E. Brice, *The Great Comanche Raid*, 1987; James T. De Shields, *Border Wars of Texas*, 1976; J. W. Wilbarger, *Indian Depredations in Texas*, 1985.)

Lions, Warren. See Lyons, Warren

Lisa, Fort, Nebraska. Fort Lisa was founded, probably in the spring of 1813, near the present site of Omaha by Manuel Lisa. It was an important trading post for the Omaha Indians and neighboring tribes, and Lisa used it as a base in keeping them in the American interest during the War of 1812. The post was abandoned in 1822.

(Hiram Martin Chittenden, *The American Fur Trade of the Far West*, 1954.)

Lisa, Manuel. Manuel Lisa, a giant of the fur trade, was born in New Orleans of Spanish parents on September 8, 1772. With his father, a Spanish government official, he moved to St. Louis about 1790. Soon afterward he became a trader, piloting his own boat to trade with Indians and settlers along the Mississippi and Ohio rivers. In 1796, he established a store at Vincennes. In 1802, he received a five-year monopoly of the Osage trade.

The Lewis and Clark Expedition alerted Lisa to the tremendous fur trade opportunities along the Missouri River and in the Rocky Mountains. With Pierre Ménard and William Morrison, he organized and led an expedition up the Missouri and Yellowstone rivers in 1807. Confronted by hostile Arikaras and Assiniboins along the way, he cowed both tribes by threatening to shoot them with his boat's swivel guns. He built Manuel's Fort at the mouth of the Bighorn and reaped a rich fur harvest by trading with the friendly Crow Indians.

Lisa returned to St. Louis in the spring of 1808 and organized the St. Louis Missouri Fur Company. His attempt to establish trade with the Spanish at Santa Fe was thwarted by Indian hostility (see Champlain, Jean Baptiste), so he determined to develop the industry on the upper Missouri. Each spring through 1812 he ascended the river to trade, sometimes wintering at Manuel's Fort, sometimes at the Arikara or Mandan villages. In 1813, he established Fort Lisa near the present site of Omaha and undertook the task of holding the tribes of that region in the American interest during the War of 1812. Appointed subagent for the Missouri River tribes, he organized raids by Indians under his control against those allied with the British. In March 1813, enemy tribes attacked one of his posts and killed 15 of his men. Escaping from the burning fortress, Lisa removed to Cedar Island, South Dakota, where he treated the destitute Sioux so kindly that they resisted the attempts of British agents to gain their allegiance.

In 1817, Lisa resigned his commission and returned to the fur trade, becoming president of the Missouri Fur Company. Always a fierce competitor, he made many enemies among rival traders, but, wrote Hiram M. Chittenden, he "was as far master of the art of conciliating the good will of the Indians as was any trader that ever ascended the river." In 1820, he made his last trip up the Missouri, fell ill, and died on August 12.

(Hiram Martin Chittenden, *The American Fur Trade of the Far West*, 1954; LeRoy R. Hafen, ed., *Mountain Men and Fur Traders of the Far West*, 1982; W. J. Ghent, *The Early Far West*, 1936; Dale Van Every, *The Final Challenge*, 1964.)

Little Arkansas River, Treaties of. In October 1865, a series of treaties was negotiated on the Little Arkansas River with the southern Plains tribes through the efforts of their agent, Jesse H. Leavenworth. Commissioners Kit Carson, William Bent, William S. Harney, Thomas Murphy, and John B. Sanborn signed similar treaties on October 14 with the Araphoes and Cheyennes, on October 17 with the Kiowa-Apaches, and on October 18 with the Kiowas and Comanches. Peace was established between the tribes and the United States, and the Indians agreed to live within more restricted areas and to release their captives. The Kiowas and Comanches abandoned claims to Kansas, Colorado, and New Mexico and agreed to remove south of the Arkansas River. The tribes granted permission for the construction of forts and roads on the reservations and promised to cease molesting travelers on the Santa Fe Trail. The government agreed to spend $40 per capita for Indians who lived on the reservation.

"None of the parties lived up to the agreement."—T. R. Fehrenbach

(Charles J. Kappler, ed., *Indian Affairs: Laws and Treaties, II,* 1972; Mildred P. Mayhall, *The Kiowas,* 1962; T. R. Fehrenbach, *Comanches,* 1983; Virginia Cole Trenholm, *The Arapahoes, Our People,* 1970.)

Little Assiniboin, Sioux Chief. Little Assiniboin, an eleven-year-old Assiniboin boy, saw his parents and brothers and sisters killed by the Sioux on the frozen Missouri River in 1857. He showed such bravery that Sitting Bull adopted him as a brother. He grew into a brave warrior and chief of the Strong Heart Society.

He remained loyal to the Sioux, defended Sitting Bull on many occasions, and died trying to save him when the famous chief was killed by Indian police on December 15, 1890.

(Stanley Vestal, *Sitting Bull,* 1957; Joe De Barth, *Life and Adventures of Frank Grouard,* 1958.)

Little Bighorn, Battle of the. The Battle of the Little Bighorn, the Plains Indians' greatest victory over the United States Cavalry, was fought on June 25, 1876, on the Little Bighorn River in southeastern Montana. Disregarding the warning of scouts that an enormous Indian concentration too powerful for his Seventh Cavalry force of 700 to defeat was camped for miles along the river, George A. Custer made a fateful decision to divide his forces and attack without delay. The result was the destruction of five cavalry companies, at least 230 men, while less than 50 Indians were killed.

Custer sent Captain Frederick Benteen with three companies to scout the bluffs west of the Indian villages, a move that Benteen characterized later as a "wild goose chase." He ordered Major Marcus A. Reno to charge the southern end of the concentration with three companies, while he planned to lead five companies around the camps and attack from the north. Reno's charge was met and thrown back by a swarm of Sioux and Cheyenne warriors before Custer was in position to launch his attack. Taking refuge on a bluff and joined later by Benteen, he dug in and fought a defensive action for two days, making no sustained attempt to break out and go to Custer's assistance.

Custer, meanwhile, failed to reach the opposite end of the Indian encampment. Crossing a shallow ford, he led his troopers to the attack at a point nearer the center of the village. Warriors who had been fighting Reno's force pulled back and rode rapidly to meet Custer's assault, and the general discovered for the first time that he faced an enormous force of Indians led by the ablest and most courageous chiefs on the plains. He ordered a retreat, but the command came too late to extricate his five companies from encirclement.

Paul I. Wellman has provided a graphic account of the action.

Part of the Sioux galloped down the left bank of the river and dashed across the ford in front of the village. . . . Another big division rode up a dry coulee which ran close by the hill where Custer had halted. Still others must have gone around behind the bluffs to the east where they cut off the white men from retreat later in the battle. . . . The Indians swirled up the hill and around them. Gall was on one side; Crazy Horse on the other, and they were followed by a fighting mad horde of Sioux and Cheyennes. Pushed back by the mass of savages, Custer crossed a deep gulch and climbed a hill on the other side which looked like a good place for defense. . . . But he never got to the top. . . . Custer and many of his officers died there on the slope. . . . Within an hour all the white soldiers were down.

Reno and Benteen were saved when the Indians withdrew, warned of the approach of General Alfred H. Terry's army. Custer has been censured for attacking without waiting for Terry. Many modern historians assert, however, that Terry had authorized him to exercise his own judgment. Reno and Benteen have been blamed for failing to go to Custer's assistance, but it is likely that if they had done so, their troopers would have joined those of the general in death upon the hill. General Sherman, in his official report, indicated that Custer's decision to divide his forces in the face of a numerically superior enemy caused the disaster: "Separated as it was into three distinct detachments, the Indians had largely the advantage, in addition to their overwhelming numbers." (See Custer, George A.; Reno, Marcus A; Benteen, Frederick; Sitting Bull; Crazy Horse; Gall.)

(Paul I. Wellman, *Death on Horseback,* 1947; Richard H. Dillon, *North American Indian Wars,* 1983; George Bird Grinnell, *The Fighting Cheyennes,* 1956; Bruce A. Rosenberg, *Custer and the Epic of Defeat,* 1974; Frederic F. Van de Water,

Glory Hunter, 1963; Evan S. Connell, *Son of the Morning Star,* 1984; Walter Mason Camp, *Custer in '76,* 1976; Mari Sandoz, *The Battle of the Little Bighorn,* 1966; David Humphreys Miller, *Custer's Fall,* 1957; Thomas B. Marquis, *A Warrior Who Fought Custer,* 1931.)

Little Buffalo, Comanche Chief. In October 1864, thousands of Comanches and Kiowas camped along the Canadian and Red rivers. Little Buffalo, an ambitious Comanche chief, circulated among the camps recruiting warriors for a raid into Texas. On October 13, 1,000 warriors struck the area near Fort Belknap. (See Elm Creek Raid.) Little Buffalo and 20 of his warriors were killed.

(T. R. Fehrenbach, *Comanches,* 1983; Mildred P. Mayhall, *Indian Wars of Texas,* 1965.)

Little Crow, Mdewakanton Sioux Chief. Little Crow, leader of the Minnesota Sioux uprising of 1862, was born near St. Paul about 1820. After the death of his father he became principal chief of the Mdewakantons in spite of his reputation among his people as an irresponsible wastrel. He had 6 wives and 22 children.

Little Crow was condemned by many Sioux as a "cut-hair" (progressive). He ceded Sioux lands in Minnesota by signing the Treaty of Mendota in 1851. He permitted the establishment of Protestant missions at the agency and attended Christian services. He adopted white men's clothing, lived in a frame house, and became a farmer.

Charles Flandrau, Sioux agent, thought highly of Little Crow, appointing him captain of his personal bodyguard and designating him as negotiator with other tribes. In 1856-1857, Flandrau sent him as leader of an Indian police force to seize Chief Inkpaduta and a band of Sioux outlaws for perpetrating the Spirit Lake Massacre, but Inkpaduta evaded them.

At the onset of the uprising of 1862, the Sioux asked Little Crow to lead them. He warned the Indians that they were suicidal fools but, since they insisted, he agreed to lead and die with them. He led the unsuccessful attack on Fort Ridgely on August 20 and, disregarding a wound received in that action, he fought in most of the battles that followed. Although he did not sanction the murder of women and children, his warriors massacred many before the outbreak was quelled. (See Minnesota Sioux Uprising.)

After the defeat of the Sioux, Little Crow fled to Canada but, failing to obtain a land grant, he returned to Minnesota in 1863. On July 3, he was shot to death by a settler, Nathan Lampson, near Hutchinson, Minnesota.

(Frederick J. Dockstader, *Great North American Indians*, 1977; C. M. Oehler, *The Great Sioux Uprising*, 1959; Paul I. Wellman, *Death on Horseback*, 1947; Doane Robinson, *A History of the Dakota or Sioux Indians*, 1974.)

Little Dog, Piegan Blackfoot Chief. Little Dog (Many Horses) led attacks upon wagon trains during his youth. By the time he became principal chief, however, he befriended the whites, signing treaties with the government in 1855 and 1865. He was murdered by his own people in 1866.

"This man was one of the noblest and bravest chiefs living at that day. He . . . killed four of the under chiefs of his tribe for warring against the whites."—George Bird Grinnell

(George Bird Grinnell, *Beyond the Old Frontier*, 1976; John C. Ewers, *The Blackfeet*, 1961.)

Little Paul, Sisseton Sioux Chief. See Mazakutemani, Sisseton Sioux Chief

Little Raven, Arapaho Chief. Little Raven, son of the hereditary chief of the southern Arapahoes, was born in Nebraska about 1817. He succeeded his father in 1855 and attempted to lead his people along the path of peace with the whites. In 1857, realizing that wild game soon would be gone, he requested farm implements for his people. In 1861, he signed the Treaty of Fort Wise. In 1864, sadly convinced that the whites were ignoring treaty provisions, he led raids on Kansas settlements. During the following year, however, he made permanent peace. He signed the Treaty of Medicine Lodge in 1867, and his band was the first to go on the reservation. In 1871, he made a tour of eastern cities, speaking eloquently about Indian rights. He died in 1891.

"A born leader, admired for his intelligence, oratorical skill, and impressive appearance, he guided his people through one of the most difficult periods of their history."—Frederick J. Dockstader

(Frederick J. Dockstader, *Great North American Indians*, 1977; Virginia Cole Trenholm, *The Arapahoes, Our People*, 1970.)

Little Six, Mdewakanton Sioux Chiefs. See Shakopee, Mdewakanton Sioux Chiefs

Little Thunder, Brulé Sioux Chief. Little Thunder became principal chief of the Brulé Sioux in 1854 when Singing Bear was slain during the Grattan massacre. He fought General Harney during the Battle of Ash Hollow in 1855.

(F. W. Hodge, ed., *Handbook of American Indians, I*, 1912; Doane Robinson, *A History of the Dakota or Sioux Indians*, 1974.)

Little Wolf, Cheyenne Chief. Little Wolf, one of the great Northern Cheyenne war chiefs, was born in Montana about 1820. In 1865, after the Sand Creek Massacre, he became a leader of war parties that fought white soldiers and settlers. In 1866, he was one of the ten warriors chosen to decoy Fetterman's detachment into a death trap. He was a prominent participant in several major battles, including the Rosebud and the Little Bighorn.

After the victory over Custer, Little Wolf's band was attacked in the Powder River valley by General Ranald S. MacKenzie. Little Wolf led the women and children to a side canyon. While bullets smashed into the cliffs beside him, he remained at his post, directing the noncombatants until all of them had reached safety.

In 1876, the Northern Cheyennes were compelled to remove to the Indian Territory. So many of them died there of malaria that Little Wolf and Dull Knife led them in a desperate outbreak, attempting to return to their northern homeland. There were only 79 warriors in the band, but they fought their way through thousands of soldiers. When they reached the Niobara River in Nebraska, the women and children were so exhausted that the band divided. Dull Knife led the weakest to surrender at Fort Robinson, while Little Wolf brought the others to safety in Montana. During the following spring he was persuaded to make peace by Lieutenant W. P. Clark, upon assurance that he could remain in his homeland. He lived on the Tongue River Reservation until his death in 1904.

" . . . he was what few Indians have been—an organizer. His march north from the Indian Territory in 1878 showed him to be a great general."—George Bird Grinnell

(George Bird Grinnell, *The Cheyenne Indians*, 1972; *The Fighting Cheyennes*, 1956; Paul I. Wellman, *Death on Horseback*, 1947.)

Lockhart, Matilda, Captivity of. Matilda Lockhart, aged 13, was captured by Comanche Indians near Gonzales, Texas, in October 1838, while gathering pecans along the Guadalupe River. Her father, Andrew Lockhart, led two unsuccessful expeditions in an attempt to recover her, being seriously wounded by the Indians during the second. She was held in captivity until March 19, 1840, when the Comanches surrendered her under treaty terms at San Antonio. Matilda was terribly bruised, and her nose had been burned off. Her condition so angered the Texans that they violated the peace treaty and massacred the Indians. (See Council House Fight.)

(A. J. Sowell, *Rangers and Pioneers*, 1964; Mildred Mayhall, *Indian Wars of Texas*, 1965.)

Loisel's Post. Régis Loisel established a trading post on the Missouri River 35 miles below Fort Pierre on Cedar Island by 1802. The first post in Sioux territory along the Missouri, it was provided with goods by Manuel Lisa and Pierre Ménard. Loisel was in charge of the post until his death in 1805.

(Doane Robinson, *A History of the Dakota or Sioux Indians*, 1974; Mildred P. Mayhall, *The Kiowas*, 1962; Hiram Martin Chittenden, *The American Fur Trade of the Far West*, 1954.)

Lone Wolf, Kiowa Chief. Lone Wolf (Guipago), born about 1820, was one of the fiercest Kiowa chiefs during the Indian wars of the southern plains. He signed the Medicine Lodge Treaty of 1867 and made two visits to Washington, but he was never impressed by the power of white people.

Lone Wolf attempted to kill General W. T. Sherman when a fight erupted at Fort Sill in 1871, but Chief Satanta ended the fray by surrendering to authorities. In 1873, his son was killed during a raid in Texas. Afterward he harried the Texas settlements, leading the Kiowas at the Battle of Adobe Walls and refusing to go on the reservation until defeated by General Ranald S. Mackenzie in 1875. He was imprisoned at Fort Marion, Florida, until shortly before his death in 1879.

(Frederick J. Dockstader, *Great North American Indians*, 1977; Benjamin Capps, *The Warren Wagontrain Raid*, 1974; Mildred P. Mayhall, *The Kiowas*, 1962; W. S. Nye, *Carbine & Lance*, 1969.)

Long Horn, Kiowa Warrior. Long Horn, a Yaqui Indian, was captured by Comanches in Mexico while a small boy. While still a youth he was sold to the Kiowas and soon proved his value by his skill in stealing horses. He married the daughter of Chief Satanta and accompanied him on many raids, but after the tribe was established on the reservation he became a model farmer and stockman. The government built a home for him about 1866, and he joined the Saddle Mountain Baptist Church in 1896. He died in 1916 at the age of 76.

(W. S. Nye, *Bad Medicine & Good*, 1962; Hugh D. Corwin, *Comanche & Kiowa Captives in Oklahoma and Texas*, 1959.)

Long, Stephen H., 1819-1820 Expedition. In 1819, Major Stephen H. Long of the Topographical Engineers and a team of scientists set out to explore and study the southern plains region. A detachment going up the Kansas River was attacked by the Pawnees, losing horses and baggage. When Long learned of the attack he prohibited traders from going to the

Pawnees. The Indians needed to trade before beginning their winter hunt and reluctantly returned most of the plunder.

After wintering near the present site of Omaha, Long explored the Platte and the southern Rockies, learning much about the civilization of the Plains Indians.

(George S. Hyde, *The Pawnee Indians,* 1974.)

Lookout, Fort, Treaty of. On June 22, 1825, Henry Atkinson and Benjamin O'Fallon negotiated a treaty with the Yankton, Yanktonai, and Teton Sioux at Fort Lookout, South Dakota. The government offered protection to the tribes in exchange for their promise to reject the offers of foreign traders.

(Doane Robinson, *A History of the Dakota or Sioux Indians,* 1974; Charles J. Kappler, ed., *Indian Affairs: Laws and Treaties, II,* 1972.)

Lookout Point Fight. In September, 1869, seven Comanche warriors raided the ranches in Hood County, Texas, stealing horses. Ten cowboys pursued them to Lookout Point, where the Indians took refuge in a deep ravine. During the day a large number of whites rode up, reinforcing the cowboys until the Comanches were outnumbered ten to one. The whites rushed the ravine and killed all of the warriors in a brief battle. One white man was fatally wounded.

(J. W. Wilbarger, *Indian Depredations in Texas,* 1985.)

Lost Valley Raid. In July 1874, a Kiowa war party led by Lone Wolf and Mamanti struck Lost Valley in western Texas. They ambushed a party of 25 Texas Rangers led by Major John B. Jones, but the defenders dismounted in a ravine and defended themselves with great determination. After killing two Rangers the Indians withdrew.

(W. S. Nye, *Carbine & Lance,* 1969; Walter Prescott Webb, *The Texas Rangers,* 1965.)

Lyman, Wyllys, Wagon Train. In September, 1874, Captain Wyllys Lyman led an Army wagon train to deliver supplies to Colonel Nelson A. Miles. Near the Washita River he was attacked by a Kiowa war party. He circled his 36 wagons and stood off several furious charges. The Indians kept up their attacks for three days (see Botalye), withdrawing when Major William E. Price arrived to rescue the besieged teamsters. Only one soldier was killed.

(W. S. Nye, *Carbine & Lance,* 1969.)

Lynd, James W. James W. Lynd was an agency employee of Nathan Myrick at the time of the Minnesota Sioux uprising of 1862. Married to a Sioux woman and a sincere friend of the Indians, it is ironic that he was the first white man killed at the Redwood Agency during the outbreak.

(Doane Robinson, *A History of the Dakota or Sioux Indians*, 1974; C. M. Oehler, *The Great Sioux Uprising*, 1959.

Lyon, Fort, Colorado. Fort Lyon, originally called Fort Fauntleroy and then Fort Wise, was established in 1860 on the Arkansas River near the site of the present city of La Junta, Colorado. (See Wise, Fort, Treaty of.) Named for Brigadier General Nathaniel Lyon on June 25, 1862, it was damaged so severely by a flood in 1867 that the site was abandoned and the fort reestablished near the mouth of the Purgatoire River. This new Fort Lyon remained in use until 1889, when the close of the Indian wars made in unnecessary.

(Robert W. Frazer, *Forts of the West*, 1965; David Lavender, *Bent's Fort*, 1954.)

Lyons, Warren, Captivity of. Warren Lyons (Lions) was born in Ohio in 1876 and moved with his family to join Stephen F. Austin's Texas colony. Mr. and Mrs. Lyons and their five children settled in Lavaca County in 1835. In the summer of 1837 a band of Comanche Indians attacked them, killed Mr. Lyons, and captured Warren. He remained with the Indians 11 years, became substantially assimilated, and acquired two Comanche wives. In 1848, he accompanied a Comanche band to San Antonio to trade. There he was recognized by friends of the family and urged to return to his home. He protested that he did not want to leave his wives, but after receiving many presents he agreed to visit his mother. He had every intention of rejoining the Indians, but finally he was persuaded to join the Texas Rangers by a brother who belonged to that organization.

Lyons proved to be a valuable scout and interpreter for the Rangers. Serving in John S. (Rip) Ford's company along the Nueces River, he participated in 1851 in a fight between 8 Rangers and 14 Comanches. Ford reported that Lyons "came at his old compañeros in true Indian style—jumping, stooping down, and changing positions in various ways." The Indians had four warriors killed and eight wounded before fleeing from the field after shooting more than two hundred arrows at Lyons and his companions.

Lyons married Lucy Boatwright soon afterward and raised a family. He died in 1870.

(John Holland Jenkins, *Recollections of Early Texas*, 1958; John Salmon Ford, *Rip Ford's Texas*, 1963; James T. De Shields, *Border Wars of Texas*, 1976; J. W. Wilbarger, Indian Depredations in Texas, 1985.)

McClellan Creek Fight. The Battle of McClellan Creek was fought in the Texas Panhandle on September 29, 1872, between Colonel Ranald Mackenzie's troopers and Mow-Way's Comanche warriors. Mackenzie set out from Fort Griffin with 222 soldiers and several Tonkawa scouts. The scouts located Mow-Way's village of 262 lodges near the mouth of Blanco Canyon, and Mackenzie attacked it with complete surprise. In a fight that was over in half an hour, the soldiers killed more than 20 warriors, captured 130 women and children, rescued two white boys from captivity, and seized 3,000 horses and mules. Only four soldiers were killed.

On September 30 the Indians stampeded the herd and recovered their horses, but Mackenzie had broken the fighting spirit of Mow-Way's band. The chief promised to cease hostilities and soon returned to the reservation.

(Carl Coke Rister, *Fort Griffin on the Texas Frontier*, 1956; W. S. Nye, *Carbine & Lance*, 1969; Ernest Wallace and E. Adamson Hoebel, *The Comanches*, 1952.)

McCulloch, Ben. Ben McCulloch, a native of Tennessee, came to Texas to fight in the revolution and remained to become one of her foremost Rangers and Indian fighters. After the Linnville raid of 1840, McCulloch recruited men to follow the huge Comanche war party, skirmished with them at Victoria, rode around them to warn settlers in their path, and joined in the successful attack on them at Plum Creek.

McCulloch served in John Coffee Hays' Ranger company and accompanied that famous frontiersman in fights with both Indians and Mexicans. He fought in the Mexican War as leader of a spy company for General Zachary Taylor. In the Civil War, as a brigadier general in the Confederate Army, he guarded the Indian Territory against invasion by Federal troops. He was killed during the battle of Elk Horn Tavern on March 7, 1862.

(Walter Prescott Webb, *The Texas Rangers*, 1965; J. W. Wilbarger, *Indian Depredations in Texas*, 1985.)

McCusker, Phillip. Phillip McCusker was a prominent scout and interpreter in the Indian Territory. Because he was married to a Comanche woman, he was the only white man permitted to enter their villages near Fort Cobb in 1859. During the Indian attack on the agency on October 23-24, 1862, he narrowly escaped and fled to Texas. He served as interpreter during the Medicine Lodge Treaty negotiations in 1867. During the 1870s, he accompanied several expeditions that fought against the southern Plains tribes.

(Mildred P. Mayhall, *The Kiowas,* 1962; W. S. Nye, *Carbine & Lance,* 1969.)

McElroy, John R., Family of. In June 1868, Comanche Indians captured Ellen, Jake, and W. D. McElroy, children of John R. McElroy of Montague County, Texas. They were held in a village near the Wichita Mountains until their father found them. He sold his cattle herd for $1,950 and ransomed his children at Fort Cobb.

(Carl Coke Rister, *Border Captives,* 1940.)

McGillycuddy, Valentine T. Dr. Valentine T. McGillycuddy was one of the more effective Indian agents, serving among the Sioux at the Pine Ridge Agency from 1879 to 1886. He was convinced that in order to transform warriors into farmers it would be necessary to undermine the power of the chiefs, and he undertook this basic change by issuing rations directly to families and working through progressive chiefs to employ Indians as freighters or stockmen. He had a difficut time with Red Cloud, but by 1882 he had convinced the chief that he must adhere to government rules and permit the children to attend school regularly. By 1883, he had influenced Indians to build 625 houses for their families.

In 1886, McGillycuddy, exasperated by government red tape, resigned from the Indian Service. Had he remained, some historians believe, much of the ensuing hostility could have been averted.

> It may safely be assumed that had Dr. McGillycuddy been at the helm there would have been no bloodshed . . . Taking charge of these Indians when they had come in fresh from the warpath, he managed them for seven years without a soldier nearer than sixty miles away. Relying on Indians themselves, he introduced the principle of home rule by organizing a force of fifty Indian police . . . With these he was able to . . . maintain authority and start the Indians well on the road to civilization.—Doane Robinson

With the onset of the Ghost Dance crisis, McGillycuddy was sent to Pine Ridge in 1890 to assess the situation. He recommended permitting the dances to continue and warned that if troops were not withdrawn, trouble would follow. His view did not prevail, and the Wounded Knee massacre followed.

(Flora Warren Seymour, *Indian Agents of the Old Frontier,* 1975; Doane Robinson, *History of the Dakota or Sioux Indians,* 1974; Robert M. Utley, *The Last Days of the Sioux Nation,* 1963; Dee Brown, *Bury My Heart at Wounded Knee,* 1971.)

McKenzie, Fort, Montana. In 1832, Kenneth McKenzie of the American Fur Company sent David Mitchell up the Missouri River to establish a post among the Blackfoot Indians. Mitchell built Fort McKenzie near the mouth of the Marias River and enjoyed great success in competing with the Hudson's Bay Company for the Blackfoot fur trade.

On August 28, 1833, a large number of Piegan Indians were attacked by the Assinboins and Crees just outside the stockade. The fur traders helped the Piegans drive their enemies away. Nine years later, however, a blunder by the post commander, François Chardon, led to the abandonment of Fort McKenzie. In retaliation for the murder of one of his men by a hostile Indian, Chardon and Alexander Harvey fired a cannon at a friendly band that had come to trade. The post was abandoned in the winter of 1843-1844 and burned by the Indians soon afterward.

(Hiram Martin Chittenden, *The American Fur Trade of the Far West,* 1954; John C. Ewers, *The Blackfeet,* 1961.)

McKenzie, Kenneth. Kenneth McKenzie was born in Scotland on April 15, 1797. He went to Canada in 1816 and began a career in the fur trade. In 1822 he moved to St. Louis, where he established the Columbia Fur Company, which merged with the American Fur Company five years later. In 1828-1829, he built Fort Union at the mouth of the Yellowstone River and secured a large share of the trade with the Assiniboin Indians. Soon afterward, at Fort Piegan, he embarked on the Blackfoot trade. In 1831, he negotiated peace between the Assiniboins and the Blackfeet.

McKenzie's experience in Canada helped him to establish the Canadian system of trade on the Missouri. Instead of relying upon white trappers, he encouraged the Indians to bring furs to the posts, where they traded them for trinkets, tools, and liquor. In order to gain trade advantages, he married an Indian woman and encouraged his employees to do the same. "McKenzie was the hard-driving chief of the American Fur Company's Upper Missouri outfit. From Fort Union the so-called King of the Missouri presided over a far flung trading network that did business with the Blackfeet, Assiniboins, Crows, Crees and other northern plains tribes."—Robert M. Utley

In 1832, McKenzie got into serious trouble, violating United States law to build a distillery at Fort Union. As a result, the company almost lost its charter and McKenzie took an enforced vacation in Europe. Afterward he closed his affairs with the American Fur Company and formed a new firm, Chouteau and McKenzie, devoting most of his time to the wholesale liquor business. He died in St. Louis on April 26, 1861.

(Hiram Martin Chittenden, *A History of the American Fur Trade of the Far West,* 1954; John C. Ewers, *The Blackfeet,* 1961; Robert M. Utley and Wilcomb E. Washburn, *The American Heritage History of the Indian Wars,* 1977; Ray Allen

Billington, *The Far Western Frontier,* 1956; Dale Van Every, *The Final Challenge,* 1964.)

Mackenzie, Ranald S. Colonel Ranald S. Mackenzie, one of the most successful military officers fighting Indians on the Great Plains, was born in New York in 1840. He attended West Point and was commissioned second lieutenant in 1862. After surviving four wounds as a Union officer in the Civil War, he was appointed to command the Fourth Cavalry and assigned to duty on the Texas frontier. Between 1871 and 1876, he led several campaigns that resulted in the defeat of the powerful Comanche and Kiowa Indians. (See McClellan Creek; Palo Duro Canyon; Red River War.)

In 1876, Mackenzie was transferred to the northern plains to punish the Indians who had annihilated Custer's command. He located the Cheyennes in the Powder River Valley on November 25 and destroyed their villages, causing great suffering and eventually leading to their surrender. (See Red Fork, Battle of; Little Wolf, Cheyenne Chief.) This was Mackenzie's last Indian battle, but he remained on duty in the West until he retired on March 24, 1884. He died on January 19, 1889.

> Like Custer a war hero and brevet general . . . Colonel Ranald S. Mackenzie commanded the 4th Cavalry with a diligence and discipline that made it the best of all the cavalry regiments. Intense, nervous, short-tempered—his career would end in insanity—Mackenzie nevertheless won the loyalty and energetic support of his men.—Robert M. Utley

(Paul I. Wellman, *Death on Horseback,* 1947; Richard H. Dillon, *North American Indian Wars,* 1983; W. S. Nye, *Carbine & Lance,* 1969; Carl Coke Rister, *Fort Griffin on the Texas Frontier,* 1956; Robert M. Utley and Wilcomb E. Washburn, *The American Heritage History of the Indian Wars,* 1977.)

McKnight, John. John McKnight went to Santa Fe in 1821 to obtain the release of his brother, Robert, a trader who had been imprisoned in Mexico for nine years. After bringing his brother back to the states, John established a trading post on the Canadian River in 1823. He had been in business only a few months when a Comanche warrior shot him to death.

(R. L. Duffus, *The Santa Fe Trail,* 1975.)

McLaughlin, James. James McLaughlin, one of the most influential agents of the U.S. Indian Service, was born in Canada on February 12, 1842. He established residence in Minnesota in 1863 and became assistant agent to the Sioux at Fort Totten, North Dakota, in 1871. Promoted to agent on July 4, 1876, he succeeded in suppressing the Sun Dance among the Sioux at the agency.

In 1881, McLaughlin was appointed agent at Standing Rock, where five thousand Sioux lived, including many who had fought at the Little Bighorn. He encountered strong resistance when he attempted to persuade them to abandon their tribal life-style, but he received a great deal of assistance from his wife, a woman of partial Sioux ancestry. As a result, schools were opened, an Indian police force was established, and a court of Indian offenses was inaugurated. Some of the Indians undertook farming after the last big buffalo hunt was held in 1882.

In 1883, Sitting Bull appeared at Standing Rock to challenge McLaughlin for mastery of the tribe's way of life. This contest lasted until December 1890, when McLaughlin ordered the chief to curtail his harmful influence. When Sitting Bull held his ground and advocated the Ghost Dance religion, McLaughlin had him arrested by the Indian police. A scuffle ensued, and Sitting Bull was shot to death by two policemen, Bullhead and Red Tomahawk.

After Sitting Bull's death, McLaughlin was able to influence two other prominent chiefs, Gall and John Glass, to assist him in advocating the white man's road. He was called upon frequently to negotiate agreements with various tribes. In 1895, he was promoted to inspector, traveling to reservations throughout the nation and reporting on tribal conditions to the Secretary of the Interior. He died on July 28, 1923.

(Flora Warren Seymour, *Indian Agents of the Old Frontier*, 1975; Robert M. Utley, *The Last Days of the Sioux Nation*, 1963; Stanley Vestal, *Sitting Bull*, 1957.)

McLellan, Robert. Robert McLellan was a prominent St. Louis fur trader during the period of the trade's early expansion to the upper Missouri. A veteran frontiersman who had fought under Anthony Wayne in the early Indian wars, he was described by H. M. Chittenden as "a man of many perilous exploits and hairbreath escapes, a sure shot, a daring hunter, and altogether a superb example of frontier manhood."

McLellan traded with the Omaha Indians in 1805. In 1807, as partner to Ramsay Crooks, he began fur trading along the middle Missouri. Two years later he established a post among the Sioux. In 1811, he joined the Pacific Fur Company and accompanied Wilson P. Hunt on his overland expedition. He returned to St. Louis in 1813 and died there three years later.

(Hiram Martin Chittenden, *A History of the American Fur Trade of the Far West*, 1954.)

McSherry, John. See Hibbons, John, Family of

Mad Buffalo, Osage Chief. Mad Buffalo (Bad-Tempered Buffalo, Skitock) was a determined opponent of settler occupation of Osage lands. On November 17, 1823, he led an attack on a party of white hunters on the

Blue River in Oklahoma. Five hunters, including Major Curtis Welborn, were killed and beheaded. Upon learning that the Arkansas militia was preparing to retaliate, Mad Buffalo and four other Osages surrendered at Fort Gibson in an attempt to avert an attack on the tribe. In a trial held at Little Rock, Mad Buffalo and Little Eagle were condemned to death while the others were acquitted. The execution was postponed several times and, finally, on March 21, 1825, President John Quincy Adams, upon the recommendation of Colonel Matthew Arbuckle, granted them a pardon in order to improve relations with the Osages.

(Grant Foreman, *Indians & Pioneers*, 1936; John Joseph Mathews, *The Osages*, 1961.)

Mallet, Pierre and Paul. Pierre and Paul Mallet, Canadian traders, were among the first to attempt to open trade with the Spanish at Santa Fe. In 1739, with six companions and a packtrain of merchandise, the brothers set out from the Missouri, paused to visit the Pawnee villages, then crossed Nebraska, Kansas, and Colorado before arriving at Santa Fe on July 22, 1739. Although they were kept under close surveillance, it is believed that they were permitted to trade their goods at a profit. On May 1, 1840, they departed from Santa Fe. Three members of the party returned to the Pawnee villages while the others followed the Arkansas River to the Mississippi and proceeded downriver to New Orleans. After reporting to Governor Bienville, the Mallet brothers resumed their trade with the Indians from the Arkansas Post.

(Hiram Martin Chittenden, *A History of the American Fur Trade of the Far West*, 1954; W. J. Ghent, *The Early Far West*, 1936; *Handbook of Texas, II*, 1952.)

Mamanti, Kiowa Medicine Man. Mamanti (Dohate, Sky-Walker, Owl Prophet), a Kiowa chief who became a powerful medicine man, led most of his tribe's raids during the early 1870s. In 1871, a vision informed him that if he led a hundred warriors into Texas they would meet two parties of whites, a small one not to be attacked and a large one that would provide them with much glory and plunder. As a result they held off while General W. T. Sherman passed by on his way to Fort Sill and then captured a wagon train in one of the fiercest Indian fights in Texas history. (See Warren Wagon Train Raid.) In 1874, he led the war party that attacked 25 Texas Rangers led by Major John B. Jones. (See Lost Valley Raid.)

On February 26, 1875, Mamanti came to the reservation with Lone Wolf's band, promising to cease hostilities. At General Sheridan's command, Kicking Bird selected 74 chiefs and warriors to be imprisoned at Fort Marion, Florida. Mamanti was included, and it was widely believed by the Indians that the medicine man put a deadly curse on the chief.

Kicking Bird died before the train departed for Florida, and Mamanti died before it reached its destination.

(W. S. Nye, *Carbine & Lance*, 1969; Mildred P. Mayhall, *The Kiowas*, 1962.)

Man Afraid of His Horses. See Young Man Afraid of His Horses, Ogalala Sioux Chief

Mandan, Fort, North Dakota. Fort Mandan was built by Lewis and Clark a few miles below the mouth of the Knife River as the expedition's winter quarters in 1804-1805. It was located not far from the Mandan Indian villages.

(Bernard De Voto, ed., *The Journals of Lewis and Clark*, 1953.)

Mandan Indians. The Mandan Indians, an important Siouan-speaking tribe, are believed to have settled upon the Missouri River about the eleventh century. An agricultural people with a population of about 3,600, they lived in large fortified villages near the mouth of the Knife River when the French explorer, Sieur de la Vérendrye, visited them in 1738. Even before their first white contacts they received European goods from the Cree and Assiniboin Indians, and their strategic location assisted them to prosper as middlemen in the trade with Plains tribes, bartering horses and firearms at a tremendous profit.

An unusually light-skinned people, the Mandans were believed by early English and French visitors to be of European origin. The beauty of their women attracted men of the Lewis and Clark Expedition and induced traders and trappers to live in their villages. Tragically for the Mandans, diseases brought by the visitors decimated the tribe, especially the small-pox epidemic of 1837. The effects of disease, demoralization of their social structure, and attacks by the Sioux forced them to abandon their villages and flee to the Hidatsas for protection.

In 1845, the handful of Mandan survivors (probably less than two hundred) settled at Fort Berthold. They participated in the Fort Laramie Treaty of 1851 that defined tribal boundaries, and in 1866 they accepted a proposal for the allotment of lands in severalty.

(Roy W. Meyer, *The Village Indians of the Upper Missouri*, 1977; W. Raymond Wood and Thomas C. Thiessen, eds., *The Early Fur Trade of the Northern Plains*, 1985; George Catlin, *Letters and Notes on the Manners, Customs, and Conditions of the North American Indians*, 1973; Bernard De Voto, ed., *The Journals of Lewis and Clark*, 1953.)

Mandan Village, Treaties of. In July and August 1825, a series of similar treaties was negotiated by Henry Atkinson and Benjamin O'Fallon with the Hidatsa, Mandan, and Crow Indians. The government agreed to

158 Handbook of the American Frontier

provide the tribes with licensed traders, and the Indians promised to refuse to trade with representatives of other nations. The United States placed the tribes under its protection.

(Charles J. Kappler, ed., *Indian Affairs: Laws and Treaties, II*, 1972.)

Mankato, Mdewakanton Sioux Chief. Mankato was one of the most influential Minnesota Sioux chiefs. He was a negotiator of the Treaty of Washington in 1858 and a leader of the Sioux outbreak of 1862. When war parties massacred settlers, he tried to recall them in order to make a unified attack on military installations. He and Little Crow led the attack on Fort Ridgely, and he participated in the battles of Birch Coulee and New Ulm. He was killed by a cannon shot at the Battle of Wood Lake on September 23, 1862.

(C. M. Oehler, *The Great Sioux Uprising*, 1959.)

Manuel's Fort, Montana. Manuel's Fort was built by Manuel Lisa at the junction of the Yellowstone and Bighorn rivers in 1807. It was the first trading post on the upper river system and the first building erected in Montana. It served as the base for several trapping expeditions before attacks by the Blackfoot Indians forced its abandonment in 1811.

(Hiram Martin Chittenden, *A History of the American Fur Trade of the Far West*, 1954.)

Many Horses, Blackfoot Chief. See Little Dog, Blackfoot Chief

Maria, Daughter of Comanche Chief. See Hockley, Bill

Marias Massacre. One of the most controversial campaigns in western American history was conducted in January 1870, by Colonel E. M. Baker against the Piegan Indians of Montana. Lands assigned to the Piegans, Bloods, and Blackfeet by an 1855 treaty were invaded by ranchers and miners, causing the Piegans to commit depredations, and Baker was ordered to punish them. General Philip M. Sheridan's instructions were, "If the lives and property of citizens of Montana can best be protected by striking the Indians, I want them struck. Tell Baker to strike them hard." The depredations had been made by the bands of Mountain Chief, Bear Chief, and Red Horn. Baker was ordered to avoid battle with the bands of Heavy Runner and other friendly chiefs.

Baker departed from Fort Ellis on January 6 with four companies of the Second Cavalry. At Fort Shaw he was reinforced by two companies of mounted infantry. They marched toward the Marias River through extremely cold weather, finally reaching a Piegan camp on January 23. Paul I. Wellman asserted that it was the winter camp of the hostile chief,

Red Horn. John C. Ewers contends that it was Heavy Runner's camp that bore the brunt of Baker's onslaught and that the friendly chief came out alone to meet the troops, only to be shot dead before he could identify himself.

All sources agree that the camp contained 37 lodges and that the Piegans were stricken by smallpox when the soldiers attacked them. The Indians offered little resistance while 173 were slain and 140 captured. Only nine escaped. One soldier was killed.

The point of greatest controversy is centered around the sex and age of the slain Indians. Baker reported killing 120 warriors and 53 women and children. The Piegan agent, Lieutenant W. B. Pease, relying upon Indian information, asserted that only 33 warriors were killed, along with 90 women and 50 children.

The attack on the Piegans was reported in the East as the "Marias massacre." It was condemned in Congress in the strongest terms, one member censuring an Indian policy that sends "the sword and the fagot into their midst when they are in their lodges, in the dead of winter; to strike them when dying of disease, sparing neither mother nor babe, till the scream of the last expiring infant shall be heard. . . . " Indignation over the massacre put an end, for the time, to a movement that would have transferred the Indian Bureau to the War Department.

(J. B. Dunn, *Massacres of the Mountains,* 1958; John C. Ewers, *The Blackfeet,* 1961; J. W. Schultz, *My Life as an Indian,* 1935.)

Martin, Gabriel N. In 1834, Judge Gabriel N. Martin of Miller County, Arkansas, and his 9-year-old son, Matthew Wright Martin, joined a party of hunters who went up the Red River to the present site of Madill, Oklahoma. They were attacked by Indians, Judge Martin was shot to death, and Matthew was captured. A few months later Colonel Henry Dodge redeemed the boy from captivity by trading three Indian girls held by the Osages to the Wichitas for him.

(James T. De Shields, *Border Wars of Texas,* 1976; Hugh D. Corwin, *Comanche & Kiowa Captives in Oklahoma and Texas,* 1959; Mildred P. Mayhall, *The Kiowas,* 1962.)

Martin, Matthew Wright. See Martin, Gabriel N.

Martínez, Andres, Captivity of. Andres Martínez was captured by Apache Indians near Las Vegas, New Mexico, in 1866. He was about eight years old when taken. The Apaches turned him over to a Kiowa warrior, Heap-o-Bears, who adopted him and treated him kindly. Within a few years he became greatly assimilated.

As soon as he was old enough he became a warrior and married a Kiowa girl.

After the Kiowas ended their raids, Andres returned to his family, but he decided that his place was with the Indians. He became a blacksmith on the reservation.

(J. J. Methvin, *Andele*, 1899.)

Mason, Fort, Texas. Fort Mason was established on July 6, 1851, in Mason County, Texas, on the San Antonio-El Paso road. It played an important role in protecting the German settlers of the area from Indian attack. It was abandoned in March 1869.

(Robert W. Frazer, *Forts of the West*, 1965.)

Mato Tope, Mandan Chief. Mato Tope (Four Bears), was born about 1800 in the Mandan village on the upper Missouri. He became a famous warrior against the Sioux and other Indians, but he was a friend of white explorers and traders. George Catlin characterized him as "the most extraordinary of nature's noblemen."

Mato Tope turned against the whites as a result of the smallpox epidemic of 1837. On the day of his death, July 30, 1837, he called upon his warriors to kill all white people.

(Frederick J. Dockstader, *Great North American Indians*, 1977; George Catlin, *Letters and Notes on the Manners, Customs, and Conditions of the North American Indians*, 1973; Roy W. Meyer, *The Village Indians of the Upper Missouri*, 1977.)

Maxey, Jesse, Family of. On September 5, 1870, Comanche Indians attacked the cabin of Jesse Maxey (Moxie) in Montague County, Texas, while he was away from home. They killed his father and shot an arrow through his wife's breast, piercing the skull of a nursing infant. Mrs. Maxey was scalped and left for dead, but she eventually recovered.

John Valentine Maxey, age five, and his little sister were carried into captivity. The girl was killed the first night because she wouldn't stop crying. John Valentine Maxey was held in captivity three years, forgetting his name and native language. Eventually he was ransomed and returned to his parents.

(W. S. Nye, *Carbine & Lance*, 1969; Hugh D. Corwin, *Comanche & Kiowa Captives in Oklahoma and Texas*, 1959.)

Mazakutemani, Sisseton Sioux Chief. Mazakutemani was born in Minnesota in 1806. A friend to white settlers, he was converted to Christianity in 1855 and became an assistant to the missionary, Stephen R. Riggs. At the onset of the Minnesota Sioux uprising of 1862, he helped 62 white people escape from the war parties who murdered some 800 settlers.

(Charles E. Flandrau, *A History of Minnesota,* 1900; Doane Robinson, *A History of the Dakota or Sioux Indians,* 1974.)

Mdewakanton Sioux Indians. The Mdewakanton Indians, a division of the Santee Sioux, lived around Mille Lacs in Minnesota when first encountered by explorers and missionaries. Afterward they established villages along the Minnesota and upper Mississippi rivers. They were eager participants in the Minnesota Sioux uprising of 1862. When the outbreak failed, they were removed to the Crow Creek Reservation in Dakota and subsequently to the Santee Reservation in Nebraska.

(F. W. Hodge, ed., *Handbook of American Indians, II,* 1912.)

Medicine Lodge Creek, Treaties of. Two of the most important treaties in the history of the Great Plains were negotiated on Medicine Lodge Creek, Barbour County, Kansas, in October 1867. They became major underpinnings for President Grant's Peace Policy of 1869, but they failed to put an end to Plains Indian warfare.

On October 21, 1867, after receiving enormous stores of presents, the Comanches, Kiowas, and Kiowa-Apaches conferred with U.S. commissioners C. C. Auger, J. B. Henderson, William S. Harney, Samuel F. Tappan, Alfred H. Terry, John B. Sanborn, and Nathaniel G. Taylor. The tribes agreed to cease hostilities and to live on a large reservation. The government promised to provide schools, mills, farm implements, seeds, clothing, doctors, blacksmiths, and carpenters. The Indians were permitted to hunt on the ceded lands, and they agreed to the construction of forts, roads, and railways on the reservations. Indian families could obtain lands in severalty upon request. Annuities provided under the Treaty of the Little Arkansas would extend for thirty years. The Apache Indians would share in all benefits.

One week later the same commissioners negotiated a similar treaty with the Cheyenne and Arapaho Indians. A large reservation was established for them, and they could not live elsewhere, but they could continue to hunt on coded lands.

> The treaty represented the last effort of the United States to reach a settlement of disputes with all the hostile tribes south of the Platte River. Clearly outlined was the beginning of a system that would eventually confine the Indians to specific reservations, by force if necessary, and included for the first time in an Indian treaty were provisions for civilizing the tribes. . . . There would no longer be attempts to place the tribes in far corners and allow them to live as they pleased.—Douglas C. Jones

(Douglas C. Jones, *The Treaty of Medicine Lodge*, 1966; Charles J. Kappler, ed., *Indian Affairs: Laws and Treaties, II,* 1972; Mildred P. Mayhall, *The Kiowas*, 1962; Ernest Wallace and E. Adamson Hoebel, *The Comanches*, 1952; W. S. Nye, *Carbine & Lance*, 1969; George Bird Grinnell, *The Fighting Cheyennes*, 1956; Virginia Cole Trenholm, *The Arapahoes, Our People*, 1970.)

Medicine Man, Arapaho Chief. Medicine Man was an Arapaho chief who opposed warfare against the whites and held many conferences with them in an attempt to keep his people at peace. He signed the Treaty of Fort Laramie of 1868 and died there three or four years later.

(Virginia Cole Trenholm, *The Arapahoes, Our People*, 1970.)

Medicine Snake Woman, Blackfoot Woman. Medicine Snake Woman, daughter of a Blood Indian chief, married Alexander Culbertson, an American Fur Company trader.

"She was young, beautiful, vivacious and . . . although only fifteen years old she was capable of assuming a mature dignity that befitted the wife of the most important bourgeois in the West."—Walter O'Meara

She was tremendously helpful to Culbertson's business, traveling hundreds of miles with him to visit Indian villages and establish trade. In addition, she was influential in discouraging the Blackfeet from attacking trappers and traders.

In 1858, Culbertson retired from the fur trade and built a mansion near Peoria, Illinois. Medicine Snake Woman entertained distinguished guests there in style. Several times each year, however, she erected her tipi on the grounds and lived in the manner of her ancestors for weeks at a time.

(John C. Ewers, *The Blackfeet*, 1961; Walter O'Meara, *Daughters of the Country*, 1968.)

Ménard, Pierre. Pierre (François) Ménard was the first French trader to live with the Mandan Indians, arriving about 1780. He explored a large area of the Great Plains and Rocky Mountains, and reports of his experiences aroused great interest among later fur traders. In 1803, he was murdered by Assiniboin Indians.

(Roy W. Meyer, *The Village Indians of the Upper Missouri*, 1977.)

Mendota, Minnesota, Treaty of. On August 5, 1851, Alexander Ramsey and Luke Lea negotiated the Treaty of Mendota with the Minnesota Sioux. The Indians ceded an enormous territory in Minnesota and Iowa for

$1,410,000. Most of the money was to be invested with five percent interest to be paid over a period of fifty years.

(Charles E. Flandrau, *The History of Minnesota,* 1900; Doane Robinson, *A History of the Dakota or Sioux Indians,* 1974; Charles J. Kappler, ed., *Indian Affairs: Laws and Treaties, II,* 1972.)

Mento Indians. French explorers of the seventeenth and early eighteenth centuries described the Mentos as a concentration of several tribes on a branch of the Arkansas River. They were reputed to be fierce enemies of the Spanish in New Mexico.

(F. W. Hodge, ed., *Handbook of American Indians, I,* 1912.)

Methodist Mission, Kansas, Treaty of. Under terms of the Treaty of the Methodist Mission, signed on January 14, 1846, the Kansa Indians ceded 2 million acres for $202,000, most of it invested with interest to be paid to the tribe for thirty years. Some of the money was designated for training in agriculture and other educational programs. Government negotiators were Richard W. Cummins and Thomas H. Harvey.

(Charles J. Kappler, ed., *Indian Affairs: Laws and Treaties, II,* 1972.)

Metzger, Anna, Captivity of. Anna Metzger was the daughter of Peter Metzger, a German settler of Gillespie County, Texas. In 1864, at the age of 11, she was captured by Kiowa Indians. Her sister was killed during the raid. Although Anna was treated with cruelty, she became greatly assimilated in less than a year, learning the Indian sign language and forgetting how to speak German. She was ransomed by a trader in 1865.

(J. Marvin Hunter, *Horrors of Indian Captivity,* 1937.)

Meusebach, John O., Comanche Treaty. In 1847, John O. Meusebach, commissioner general of the German Colonization of Texas Association, negotiated a treaty with Comanche chief Buffalo Hump that guaranteed the safety of settlers in the area between the Colorado and Llano rivers and permitted the Indians to visit white settlements. The agreement was reached on March 1-2 and ratified in Fredericksburg a few weeks later. In return for numerous gifts and a promised payment of more than $1,000, the Comanches permitted the Germans to survey lands in the San Saba area.

"The treaty was essential to the success of German colonization plans because it afforded the long-range stability required for the establishment of towns, businesses, and industry."—Glen E. Lich

(Glen E. Lich, *The German Texans,* 1981; T. R. Fehrenbach, *Lone Star,* 1983.)

Miles, John D. John D. Miles, a courageous Quaker, was appointed agent to the Cheyenne and Arapaho Indians in 1872. Two years later a major Indian war erupted and troops were sent to the Upper Arkansas Agency to protect the employees. Miles believed that theft by whites of Indian horses was largely to blame for the hostilities.

After the army compelled the Indians to return to the reservation, Miles began to make progress in leading them along the white man's road. He reduced the power of the chiefs by issuing rations directly to families, and he tried with some success to prevent the liquor traffic.

After the Northern Cheyennes were compelled to move to the agency, Miles encountered increasing hostility. In 1880, he was attacked because rations were late in arriving. In 1882, a second attempt was made on his life. In 1884, he resigned for health reasons.

(Flora Warren Seymour, *Indian Agents of the Old Frontier,* 1975; Virginia Cole Trenholm, *The Arapahoes, Our People,* 1970.)

Miles, Nelson A., Plains Campaigns. Born in 1839, General Nelson A. Miles gained a reputation as a fierce fighter during the Civil War. Afterward he was sent to the West to fight Indians, and his campaigns on the Plains were so successful that he eventually became commanding general of the U. S. Army.

In 1874, Miles commanded one of four columns in a campaign planned by General Sheridan to converge on the villages of the hostile Indians. On August 30, he encountered the Cheyennes near the headwaters of the Washita River, attacked them with cavalry and Gatling guns, and compelled them to flee to the Staked Plains.

After the Battle of the Little Bighorn, Miles was ordered to harass the Sioux and to try to prevent them from escaping into Canada. In October 1876, he captured about 2,000 hostiles and compelled them to settle on reservations. He kept his troops in the field during a severe winter, inflicting heavy losses on the Sioux. On January 8, 1877, he defeated Crazy Horse's band. The hostiles were freezing and almost out of ammunition, and soon afterward they surrendered. (See Wolf Mountain, Battle of.)

During the Ghost Dance hostilities, Miles ordered the arrest of Sitting Bull in December 1890, a decision that led to the death of the chief at the hands of the Indian police. After the Wounded Knee massacre, he condemned Colonel James W. Forsyth for an attack that upset carefully developed plans to induce all the hostiles to surrender without bloodshed. He relieved Forsyth of command of the Seventh Cavalry and charged him with the indiscriminate slaying of noncombatants, but a Court of Inquiry cleared the officer of the charge. For thirty years Miles advocated compensation for Sioux survivors of Wounded Knee, but without success.

(Paul I. Wellman, *Death on Horseback,* 1947; Robert M. Utley, *The Last Days of the Sioux Nation,* 1963; Richard H. Dillon, *North American Indian Wars,* 1983.)

Miller, Daniel. Daniel Miller, one of the least successful Plains Indian agents, was appointed to work with the Pawnees in 1842. A pro-slavery advocate from Missouri, he held all nonwhites in contempt and opposed the efforts of missionaries to educate the Indians at a pace that might have succeeded. His harsh measures led to his removal in a short time, but he had already caused the destruction of missions among the Pawnees.

(George E. Hyde, *The Pawnee Indians,* 1974.)

Miller, James. James Miller of New Hampshire was appointed governor of Arkansas in 1819. A dedicated public servant, he labored for several years to bring about peace between the Osages and Cherokees, but the two tribes continued to wage bloody warfare upon each other in spite of his strenuous efforts.

(Grant Foreman, *Indians & Pioneers,* 1936; John Joseph Mathews, *The Osages,* 1961.)

Millier, Hubert. Hubert Millier, a ferry operator at the Redwood Agency, was a hero during the Minnesota Sioux uprising of 1862. Surrounded by Sioux war parties massacring settlers, he could have fled to safety, but he continued to operate the ferry until most of the settlers were safely across the Minnesota River. Finally the Indians discovered that he was still at his post and put him to death.

(C. M. Oehler, *The Great Sioux Uprising,* 1959.)

Mills, Anson. Anson Mills was born in Indiana in 1834. After failing to graduate from the U. S. Military Academy, he moved to Texas in 1857 and surveyed the site of El Paso. He joined the Union Army at the onset of the Civil War and afterward continued in military service for 54 years, much of it spent in fighting Indians. After the Battle of the Little Bighorn, he played an important part in the Rosebud campaign. He burned Crazy Horse's village, led a charge at Tongue River, checked the Sioux on the Rosebud bluffs, and defeated them at Slim Buttes.

Mills was promoted to colonel in 1892 and lived in Washington, D.C., until his death in 1924.

(Paul I. Wellman, *Death on Horseback,* 1947; Robert H. Dillon, *North American Indian Wars,* 1983.)

Miniconjou Sioux Indians. The Miniconjou Indians, a warlike division of the Teton Sioux, were first mentioned by Lewis and Clark in 1804 as living on both sides of the Missouri north of the Cheyenne River. For more than a half century thereafter they were characterized by traders and government officials as one of the "most unruly and troublesome of the Teton tribes." They signed the peace treaties of Fort Sully in 1865 and Fort Laramie in 1868, but in 1869 General D. S. Stanley reported that of their 2,000 people, only 400 were peaceful. After the close of the Indian wars they settled on the Cheyenne River Reservation in South Dakota.

(F. W. Hodge, ed., *Handbook of American Indians, I,* 1912; Doane Robinson, *A History of the Dakota or Sioux Indians,* 1974.)

Minnesota Sioux Uprising. In August 1862, the Santee Sioux in Minnesota began a major outbreak (see Acton, Minnesota, Murders), and within 40 days they massacred not less than 800 settlers. (See New Ulm; Sacred Heart Creek; Redwood Ferry; Birch Coulee; Hutchinson; Wood Lake; Ridgely, Fort.) Led by Chief Little Crow, the Indians launched a sneak attack in retaliation for the government's failure to provide rations as promised. After their defeat most of the leaders fled to Canada or to join the Sioux in the Dakotas. Of those who surrendered, 307 were tried and condemned to death, but President Lincoln spared all except 38.

"It was the bloodiest Indian massacre the West ever knew, ten times as deadly as the Fetterman disaster, and with four times the fatalities of Custer's tragedy. Most of the victims were unarmed civilians."—C. M. Oehler

(C. M. Oehler, *The Great Sioux Uprising,* 1959; Charles E. Flandrau, *The History of Minnesota,* 1900; Paul I. Wellman, *Death on Horseback,* 1947; Doane Robinson, *A History of the Dakota or Sioux Indians,* 1974; Charles S. Bryant, *A History of the Great Massacre by the Sioux Indians in Minnesota,* 1868; Richard H. Dillon, *North American Indian Wars,* 1983.)

Missouri, Camp, Nebraska. See Atkinson, Fort, Nebraska

Missouri Fur Company. See Saint Louis Missouri Fur Company

Missouri Indians. The Missouri Indians, a Siouan-speaking tribe, were located on the Missouri River near the mouth of the Grand when visited by the early French explorers. Because of Sauk and Fox Indian hostilities and smallpox, they abandoned this location in 1798 and settled south of the Platte River, where they were found by Lewis and Clark. Soon afterward, their numbers dwindling as a result of disease, they were absorbed by the Oto and Iowa tribes.

(John R. Swanton, *Indian Tribes of North America,* 1952; Muriel H. Wright, *A Guide to the Indian Tribes of Oklahoma,* 1951.)

Mitchell, David D. David D. Mitchell was born in Virginia in 1806 and entered the western fur trade at an early age. He was employed as a clerk by the American Fur Company and then became a partner in its Upper Missouri division. He built Fort McKenzie in the territory of the Blackfoot Indians in 1832 and traded with that powerful tribe for seven years, enjoying much success in weaning them away from the Hudson's Bay Company.

In 1841, Mitchell was appointed Superintendent of Indian Affairs, Central Division, with headquarters at St. Louis. He held that post until the Mexican War, in which he served as Lieutenant Colonel of the Missouri Mounted Volunteers in the Doniphan Expedition. Afterward he was reappointed superintendent. In 1849, his recommendation that a council of all Plains tribes be held to establish boundaries and deal with grievances led to the Fort Laramie Treaty of 1851. He was a stabilizing influence during the negotiations and a signer of the document. He held his position until 1852 and died in 1861.

(Hiram Martin Chittenden, *The American Fur Trade of the Far West*, 1954; Le Roy R. Hafen, *Broken Hand*, 1973; John C. Ewers, *The Blackfeet*, 1961.)

Mitchell, Robert B. General Robert B. Mitchell was in command of the Military District of Nebraska during the Plains Indian war of 1864. In June 1864, the Sioux, who had been friendly until that time, made a raid on the Pawnees and attacked some whites, probably because they mistook them at night for Pawnees. A few whites were killed, and Mitchell sent troops to punish the attackers. As a result, the Sioux joined the other tribes in raiding the settlements. In January 1865, Mitchell sought to avenge the attack on Julesburg, Colorado, but his scouts failed to locate the hostiles while they were devastating the Platte road.

(George Bird Grinnell, *The Fighting Cheyennes*, 1956.)

Moanahonga, Iowa Chief. Bee Big Neck, Iowa Chief

Mohongo, Osage Woman. Mohongo, a beautiful Indian woman, was a member of an Osage group that visited Europe under the sponsorship of a promoter who hoped to enrich himself during the tour. (See Delauney, David.) When the promoter was arrested in France for debt, Lafayette paid for their passage back to America. Her husband died of smallpox during the voyage.

(Thomas L. McKenney and James Hall, *Biographical Sketches of Ninety-Five of 120 Principal Chiefs From the Indian Tribes of North America*, 1838.)

Moore, John Henry. John Henry Moore was born in Tennessee in 1800 and moved to Texas in 1818. In 1821, he was one of the first settlers on the upper Colorado River. During the ensuing three years he participated in several fights with Indians along that river. In 1828, having received a land grant near the present site of La Grange, he constructed Moore's Fort to guard his family and neighbors against the Tawakoni and Waco Indians.

Moore's campaigns against the Comanches began in January, 1839, when he led 60 volunteers to attack an Indian village on the San Saba River. Penetrating an area believed to be safe from Texan invasion, he made a surprise attack at dawn on February 14, firing into the tipis and killing Comanches of all ages and both sexes. The Indians rallied and drove Moore's men into a ravine. There they withstood repeated charges, lost most of their horses, and finally had to withdraw on foot.

"The Texans only held off the buzzing Comanches with the accuracy of their long rifles; shielded by a thin cavalry patrol, the little army was forced to make a humiliating march back down the Colorado."—T. R. Fehrenbach

In 1840, Moore made up for the failure of his earlier expedition by leading 90 frontiersmen and 12 Lipan Indian scouts in pursuit of Comanches who had survived the Battle of Plum Creek. On October 24 they located the village of 60 lodges on a small river west of the Red Fork of the Colorado. During the night Moore sent a detachment across the river to cut off escape. At dawn his main force charged on horseback, riding through rows of tipis and shooting down startled Comanches as they emerged. The Indians fled to the river, where they were shot at point-blank range.

"Moore spared neither age nor sex," Fehrenbach noted, "and he made no attempt to burden himself with prisoners. He operated under clear orders: this was a punitive expedition for Linnville and Victoria and a dozen roasted victims. The firing ceased only when the last Comanche was dead or had crawled away." More than 130 Indians were killed without the loss of one of Moore's men.

In 1842, Moore recruited 200 volunteers to guard the western Texas frontier. They fought battles with Comanche raiders in August and November.

(T. R. Fehrenbach, *Comanches,* 1983; Ernest Wallace and E. Adamson Hoebel, *The Comanches,* 1952; John Holland Jenkins, *Recollections of Early Texas,* 1958; J. W. Wilbarger, *Indian Depredations in Texas,* 1985.)

Morgan, Mrs. James S., Captivity of. Mrs. James S. Morgan, age 24, was captured by the Cheyenne Indians in 1867. She and Miss Sarah White were held for more than a year. Finally General George A. Custer obtained their release by threatening to hang Dull Knife and two other chiefs. The women had been passed from camp to camp, and both of them gave birth to half-Indian children.

(Frederic F. Van de Water, *Glory Hunter*, 1963; Elizabeth B. Custer, *Following the Guidon*, 1966.)

Morgan, John. John Morgan was a particularly bloodthirsty Indian hater. He murdered four Piegan Indians who paid him a friendly visit in the Sun Valley.

(John C. Ewers, *The Blackfeet*, 1961.)

Mortimer Fort, North Dakota. Fort Mortimer was established at the abandoned site of Fort William (present site of Fort Buford) in 1842 by the Union Fur Company. After three years of inability to compete with the American Fur Company, it was abandoned in 1845.

(Hiram Martin Chittenden, *The American Fur Trade of the Far West*, 1954.)

Mountain Chief, Blackfoot Chief. Mountain Chief, last hereditary chief of the Blackfoot nation, was born in 1848. Usually friendly to the whites, he visited Washington on several occasions and signed treaties ceding a huge area of tribal land. He died in 1942.

(Frederick J. Dockstader, *Great North American Indians*, 1977.)

Mow-Way, Comanche Chief. Mow-Way (Shaking Hand), a Comanche chief who was inclined toward peace with the whites, was compelled to leave the reservation by the hostility of his followers. In 1872, Colonel Ranald Mackenzie destroyed his village in the Texas Panhandle (see McClellan Creek Fight), and Mow-Way had more than adequate reason to lead his people back to the reservation.

(T. R. Fehrenbach, *Comanches*, 1983; Mildred P. Mayhall, *Indian Wars of Texas*, 1965.)

Moxie, John Valentine. See Maxey, Jesse, Family of

Mud Springs Ranch Fight. On February 5, 1865, a Cheyenne war party attacked the Mud Springs ranch near the present site of Simla, Nebraska. The cowboys forted up in the ranch house, firing through loopholes for several hours. About noon the Indians drove off the horse herd and temporarily abandoned the attack. They returned the following morning and found that more than a hundred soldiers from Fort Laramie had arrived.

Two hundred Cheyennes crept up near the ranch house and began to shoot fire arrows from the cover of a ravine. So many men and horses were wounded that the soldiers carried out a successful sally, drove the Indians from the ravine, and dug a rifle pit on a hill that commanded the field. The

Indians began retiring during the early afternoon, pursued by the troops toward the Black Hills.

(George Bird Grinnell, *The Fighting Cheyennes*, 1956.)

Munroe, Daniel. In 1828, Daniel Munroe, a trader from Franklin, Missouri, accompanied a caravan to Santa Fe. On the return trip he and a young companion became weary of plodding along with the caravan and rode ahead to a creek. There they drank water and stretched out on the bank to wait for the wagons. Incredibly they fell asleep, and Comanche Indians killed them with their own guns. Milton Sublette, leader of the caravan, buried the murdered men and named the stream McNees Creek for Munroe's companion. Soon afterward six Comanches rode up and requested a parley. Seeking revenge, the teamsters opened fire, killing five of the warriors.

(Hiram Martin Chittenden, *The American Fur Trade of the Far West*, 1954; David Lavender, *Bent's Fort*, 1954.)

Myrick, Andrew. Andrew Myrick, a trader at the Lower Sioux Agency, played a part in causing the Minnesota uprising of 1862. When government rations were late in arriving because of the Civil War, he reportedly said that "if the Indians are hungry let them eat grass!" Infuriated Indians made him one of their first victims and stuffed his mouth with grass.

(C. M. Oehler, *The Great Sioux Uprising*, 1959.)

Nacheninga, Iowa Chief. Nacheninga (No Heart), an influential Iowa chief, succeeded his father as leader of his nation in 1832. He visited Washington in 1837 and was so greatly impressed by the marvels he observed that he encouraged his people to send their children to school. He signed the Treaty of St. Louis in 1837.

(Martha Royce Blaine, *The Ioway Indians,* 1979.)

Napeshneeduta, Mdewakanton Sioux Chief. Napeshneeduta (Joseph Napeshnee) was a friend of the white settlers of Minnesota. On February 21, 1840, he became the first full-blooded Sioux to accept Christianity. During the Sioux uprising of 1862, when 800 settlers were slain, he served as a scout for the U. S. Army in operations that ended the massacres. He died in 1870.

(F. W. Hodge, ed., *Handbook of American Indians, II,* 1912.)

Nawat, Arapaho Chief. See Left Hand, Arapaho Chief

Neal, Alpheus D. Alpheus D. Neal was one of the most resolute Texas Rangers during the mid-nineteenth-century Indian wars. In 1850, with two Ranger companions, he was attacked by thirty Indians near the Nueces River. Neal was wounded eight times, lost consciousness, and was left for dead by the Indians. His captain, John S. (Rip) Ford, has described his determination to survive:

> He managed to extract several arrows from his body and, in his efforts, broke 2 or 3. He was naked. In this condition, with a nearly tropical August sun pouring its rays upon him, he began to drag himself in the direction of San Patricio. The heat of the sun blistered him from head to foot . . . his festering wounds agonized him; hunger tormented him; the anguish of unquenched thirst rendered him quite frantic; yet the dauntless, indomitable ranger wended his way, with a will nothing but death could overcome. Sustained by a courageous determination savoring of the superhuman, he pursued his weary and painful way for sixty-five miles, when his eyes were gladdened by the humble edifices of San Patricio.

Remarkably, Neal recovered sufficiently to resume his career. In spite of the fact that he carried an arrowhead lodged in his lung, he fought in the Civil War. He was murdered soon after the war ended.

(John Salmon Ford, *Rip Ford's Texas*, 1963.)

Neill, James Clinton. James Clinton Neill, a native of North Carolina and an Indian fighter under Andrew Jackson, was wounded during the Battle of Horseshoe Bend. He moved to Texas in 1831, fought in the Texas Revolution, and resumed his role as a frontier fighter. In 1835, he served as adjutant during an expedition against the Tawakoni Indians. Six warriors were captured, and Neill inoculated one of them with smallpox virus and sent him back to his people to spread the infection. In 1842, he led a campaign against the tribes on the upper Trinity River. Two years later he served on a commission to negotiate peace with the Indians. He died in 1845.

(John Holland Jenkins, *Recollections of Early Texas*, 1958.)

Neomonni, Iowa Chief. Neomonni was a formidable war chief while fighting other tribes, but he was generally friendly to whites. He signed the treaties of Prairie du Chien in 1830, Fort Leavenworth in 1836, and St. Louis in 1837. He was taken with several other chiefs to visit England in 1843.

(F. W. Hodge, ed., *Handbook of American Indians, II*, 1912.)

Neosho, Treaty of the. On August 10, 1825, Chief White Hair's Little Osages signed a treaty permitting the construction of a road across their lands leading toward New Mexico. For the privilege of using this road, the Indians were paid $5,000. U. S. negotiators were Thomas Mather and Benjamin H. Reeves.

(John Joseph Mathews, *The Osages*, 1961.)

Nescutunga, Battle of. In 1859, Captain Earl Van Dorn led four companies of the Second U. S. Cavalry to Crooked Creek, near the Cimarron River in southern Kansas. On May 13, he attacked a Comanche war party, killing 49 Indians, wounding 5, and capturing 32 women. He reported that the Indians "fought till not one was left to bend a bow." Van Dorn's casualties were 2 troopers and 4 scouts killed and 11 men wounded.

(Robert H. Dillon, *North American Indian Wars*, 1983; W. S. Nye, *Carbine & Lance*, 1969; Mildred P. Mayhall, *Indian Wars of Texas*, 1965.)

New Ulm, Minnesota, Battle of. The Battle of New Ulm was fought on August 23, 1862, when 650 Sioux warriors led by Little Crow attacked the town. New Ulm, a community of approximately a thousand recent emigrants from Germany, was poorly prepared for defense, as few citizens owned or knew how to use firearms. Moreover, many refugees fled into the town at the onset of the Minnesota Sioux uprising, spreading terror with accounts of massacres throughout the countryside.

Fortunately for the little community, Judge Charles E. Flandrau and a few veteran Indian fighters rode into New Ulm before the war party attacked. The citizens elected Flandrau to lead the defense, and he recruited about 250 men to meet the invaders on the prairie a half mile west of town. The warriors charged on horseback, putting the defenders to flight and seizing the houses on the edge of town. Soon the Sioux were firing at citizens from the cover of their own homes.

Flandrau, a courageous leader who once had been an Indian agent, rode back and forth, rallying his men while bullets whined around him. The defense stiffened, and the Sioux halted their advance toward the center of town. After several hours of fierce fighting, Judge Flandrau led a charge that drove the Indians out of the houses. Immediately he put the buildings to the torch, depriving the Indians of cover. The Sioux attempted one more charge, but the defenders drove them back with heavy losses. The town was surrounded throughout the night, but on the following morning the Indians withdrew.

During the Battle of New Ulm, some 34 settlers were killed and 60 wounded. Almost 200 buildings were burned. Sioux losses are unknown.

(C. M. Oehler, *The Great Sioux Uprising,* 1959; Charles E. Flandrau, *The History of Minnesota,* 1900; Paul I. Wellman, *Death on Horseback,* 1947.)

No Heart, Iowa Chief. See Nacheninga, Iowa Chief

Noble, Mrs., Spirit Lake, Iowa. Mrs. Noble, a twenty-year-old bride, was captured by the Sioux chief, Inkpaduta, during the Spirit Lake, Iowa, massacre of March 8, 1857. She was murdered by Inkpaduta's son, Roaring Cloud, because she resisted his advances. Afterward the Indians used her scalped body for target practice.

(Doane Robinson, *A History of the Dakota or Sioux Indians,* 1974.)

Nocona, Comanche Chief. See Peta Nocona, Comanche Chief

North, Frank J. Major Frank J. North, a famous scout and Indian fighter, was born in Ludlowville, New York, on March 10, 1840. He moved to Nebraska in 1856, and the family settled near the Pawnee villages on the Loup Fork of the Platte in 1858. He was quick to master the Pawnee language and the Indian sign language and, in 1860, he was employed by the Indian agent as an interpreter, clerk, and sawmill instructor on the reservation.

North's career as leader of Indian scouts began in 1864 when General S. R. Curtis appointed him lieutenant in a newly established band of

Pawnee volunteers to participate in a campaign against hostile Indians. In October 1864, Curtis authorized him to enlist a regular Pawnee scout company. With North as captain, the Pawnees scouted for General Patrick Connor on the Powder River and fought in the Battle of Tongue River.

The role of the Pawnee scouts expanded the following year when General C. C. Augur authorized North to enlist four companies to protect the construction of the Union Pacific Railroad. On August 17, North, then serving as major, led them against the Cheyennes at the Battle of Plum Creek, Nebraska.

North's most famous exploit occurred on July 11, 1869, during the Battle of Summit Springs, Colorado. He and his Pawnee scouts led the charge into Chief Tall Bull's Cheyenne village. He shot Tall Bull to death when the chief raised his head above the rim of a ravine to fire at the Pawnees.

During the early 1870s, North was interpreter at Fort D. A. Russell, Wyoming, and Sidney Barracks, Nebraska. On several occasions he served as guide for scientific expeditions. In 1876, he recruited a hundred Pawnee scouts for General George Crook's winter campaign against the Sioux. On November 25, they led the attack on Dull Knife's Northern Cheyennes. Afterward they participated in the pursuit of Crazy Horse.

When his military service ended in 1877, North pioneered cattle ranching in the Nebraska Sandhills as Buffalo Bill Cody's partner. Later he was injured performing in Cody's Wild West Show, and he never completely recovered. He died in 1885.

"Major Frank North . . . knew the Pawnees better than any other white man in the period 1860-76."—George Hyde

(George E. Hyde, *The Pawnee Indians*, 1974; Ruby E. Wilson, *Frank J. North*, 1984; Luther North, *Man of the Plains*, 1961; George Bird Grinnell, *Two Great Scouts and Their Pawnee Battalion*, 1928.)

North, Luther. Captain Luther North, younger brother of Major Frank North, served in the Second Nebraska Cavalry against the Sioux and Cheyennes in 1864. When Frank North organized the Pawnee scouts, he called on Luther to assist him. Luther led the Pawnees in several campaigns during the Great Plains Indian wars.

(Luther North, *Man of the Plains*, 1961; George Bird Grinnell, *Two Great Scouts and Their Pawnee Battalion*, 1928.)

North, Robert. Robert North married a woman of the Northern Arapaho tribe and became a renegade and outlaw. In 1853, he led a band of outlaws that participated in the murders of ten miners. In 1866, he led the Arapahoes during the Fetterman massacre. He and his wife were captured and hung in 1869.

(Virginia Cole Trenholm, *The Arapahoes, Our People,* 1970; George Bird Grinnell, *The Fighting Cheyennes,* 1956.)

Northern Pacific Railway Battles. Surveyors for the Northern Pacific Railway recommended in 1871 that the track should be laid through Sioux lands that had been set aside for Indian use by the Treaty of Fort Laramie. Disregarding the protests of the Sioux, the United States government provided military escorts and built forts to protect the men constructing the line.

The Sioux began their attacks on August 14, 1872, near Pryor's Fork, Montana. Eight cavalry troops defeated the war party, killing a dozen braves while losing one soldier. Other battles occurred on August 26 and October 2, but the Indians were too lacking in ammunition to halt construction of the Northern Pacific.

(Doane Robinson, *A History of the Dakota or Sioux Indians,* 1974.)

Oglala Sioux Indians. The Oglalas, largest band of the Sioux nation, first came to notice when Lewis and Clark visited them on the Missouri River in the present state of South Dakota. The center of their territory was around the mouth of the Bad River, where a trading post was established by 1825. They were generally friendly toward white people until the Sioux were attacked by United States soldiers in 1854. (See Grattan, John L.) Afterward they were fierce enemies, attacking wagon trains crossing the plains, boats on the Missouri, and troops on patrol. After the Battle of the Little Bighorn, many of them went to Canada, but most returned eventually and lived on the Pine Ridge Reservation. They participated in the Ghost Dance in 1889-1890, but took little part in the Wounded Knee hostilities. (See Red Cloud, Sioux Indians.)

(George E. Hyde, *Red Cloud's Folk,* 1937; Robert M. Utley, *The Last Days of the Sioux Nation,* 1963.)

Old Strike, Yankton Sioux Chief. See Struck-by-the-Ree, Yankton Sioux Chief

Old Tobacco, Cheyenne Chief. Old Tobacco (Senemone, Cinemo) was friendly to white people throughout his life, and he died in an attempt to save a wagon train from ambush. In 1847, aware that wagons on the Santa Fe Trail were nearing a large Comanche war party, he rode forward to warn them. Before he could speak, a teamster opened fire, mortally wounding him. With his dying words he ordered his people not to avenge him because the white men were friends who had failed to recognize him.

(Stan Hoig, *Peace Chiefs of the Cheyennes,* 1980.)

Omaha Indians. The Omaha Indians, a Siouan tribe, moved from their ancestral homes along the Ohio and Wabash rivers about 1500 and settled on the Missouri River in northeastern Nebraska by the time of first contact with French explorers. In 1775, they had a population of almost 3,000 and, under Chief Blackbird, they were terrors to traders along the Missouri. In 1801, however, smallpox killed Blackbird and half of his people, destroying their power and making them easy prey for their Sioux enemies.

The Omahas signed treaties with the United States in 1830 and 1836, and in 1854 they sold most of their lands as a result of the Treaty of Washington. Eleven years later they gave up the northern part of their remaining lands to the Winnebago tribe. In 1882, they were granted citizenship and their reservation lands were allotted in severalty.

(F. W. Hodge, ed., *Handbook of American Indians, II*, 1912; Thomas Henry Tibbles, *Buckskin and Blanket Days*, 1958; J. P. Kinney, *A Continent Lost—a Civilization Won*, 1937.)

One-Eyed Sioux. See Tamaha, Mdewakanton Sioux Chief

Oohenopa Sioux Indians. The Oohenopa (Two Kettle) Indians, a division of the Teton Sioux, were located along the Missouri and Cheyenne rivers when first encountered by explorers and missionaries. They were generally friendly toward whites. They signed the Treaty of Fort Sully in 1865 and settled on the Cheyenne River Reservation in South Dakota.

(F. W. Hodge, ed., *Handbook of American Indians, II*, 1912.)

Orleans, Fort, Missouri. Fort Orleans, the first post on the Missouri River, was built in 1723 by the French in order to protect their allies, the Missouri Indians, from Spanish attacks. The Sieur de Bourgmont chose a site on an island 25 miles above the mouth of the Missouri. It remained in use until 1728, and its fate is a matter of some disagreement.

"There is a tradition that when Bourgmont left the fort a year or two later to go down to New Orleans, the Indians attacked it and massacred every inmate."—H. M. Chittenden

"There seems to be no basis for the tradition that the post was wiped out and the garrison massacred by the Indians."—Robert W. Frazer

"The fact is now known that it was peaceably evacuated in 1728."—W. J. Ghent

(H. M. Chittenden, *The American Fur Trade of the Far West*, 1954; Robert W. Frazer, *Forts of the West*, 1965; W. J. Ghent, *The Early Far West*, 1936.)

Osage, Fort, Missouri. Fort Osage, known earlier as Fort Clark, was established in 1808 on the Missouri River near the present site of Sibley, Missouri. Intended to control the Osage, Kansa, and Iowa Indians, it was a government Indian factory as well as a military post. The fort was abandoned in 1813 but regarrisoned three years later. The factory was closed in 1822 and the fort in 1827.

(Robert W. Frazer, *Forts of the West*, 1965.)

Osage Indians. The Osage Indians, a powerful and warlike tribe of Siouan linguistic stock, were encountered by French explorers on the Mississippi before 1700. Because of constant warfare with both plains and woodland tribes from Michigan to Texas, they formed an alliance with the French in order to acquire the firearms they needed. They murdered traders on occasion, but the French overlooked it because the tribe provided a powerful buffer against the Spanish and English. During the 1790s, they killed many Americans on the Mississippi River.

Before 1802, the tribe was divided into two bands—the Great Osages living near the mouth of the Marmaton River in present Vernon County, Missouri, and the Little Osages, living a few miles west of the Little Osage River. In 1802, the powerful Chouteau trading family persuaded some members of both bands to move to the Arkansas River near the mouth of the Verdigris. (See Chouteau, Auguste Pierre; Clermont; White Hair.) They became known as the Arkansas band.

The Osages signed a treaty with the United States in 1808 ceding most of the state of Missouri and a large portion of Arkansas. (See Clark, Fort, Missouri, Treaty of.) Afterward the Great and Little Osages removed to the Neosho Valley in Neosho County, Kansas. In 1825, these Neosho lands became a reservation under terms of a treaty signed at St. Louis, and their other lands were ceded to the U.S. government. The Arkansas band eventually moved to the reservation because of the hostility of the Cherokees. The size of the reservation was reduced by the Treaty of Fort Gibson in 1839.

During the Civil War, the Great Osages fought on the side of the Confederacy, while the Little Osages provided men for the Indian Brigade of the Union Army. The reservation was overrun by both armies, causing much suffering, and after the war the government opened it to settlement, selling the land for the benefit of the tribe. In 1870, the proceeds were used to establish a new reservation in Osage County, Oklahoma. Both Protestant and Catholic schools were opened on the reservation, and members of the tribe advanced rapidly along the white man's road. When oil was discovered on their lands during the first decade of the twentieth century, the Osages became the wealthiest of Indian tribes.

(Muriel H. Wright, *A Guide to the Indian Tribes of Oklahoma*, 1951; John Joseph Mathews, *The Osages*, 1961; Grant Foreman, *Advancing the Frontier*, 1933; Victor Tixier, *Tixier's Travels on the Osage Prairies*, 1940; Gilbert C. Din and A. P. Nasatir, *The Imperial Osages*, 1983.)

Otherday, John, Wahpeton Sioux Chief. John Otherday was born in 1801 at Swan Lake, Minnesota. Converted to Christianity by missionary Thomas S. Williamson, he married a white woman and adopted many of the ways of her people. A man of tremendous courage and resourcefulness, "he was one of the best friends the settlers ever had during the Spirit Lake outbreak in Iowa in 1857 and the Minnesota Sioux uprising of 1862."— Charles E. Flandrau

After the Spirit Lake massacre, Otherday rescued a young girl, Abbie Gardner, from captivity. (See Gardner, Rowland, Family of.) Five years later, in an official report regarding the Sioux uprising, Major Thomas J. Galbraith wrote of the chief's rescue of 62 settlers·as follows:

Led by the noble Other Day, they struck out on the naked prairie, literally placing their lives in this faithful creature's hands, and guided by him, and him alone. After intense suffering and privation, they reached Shakopee, on Friday, the 22nd of August, Other Day never leaving them for an instant. . . . Afterward, without stopping to rest, he returned to the scene of hostilities to attempt to save more lives.

During the remainder of the Sioux outbreak, Otherday served as a scout for General Sibley. For this service he received a reward of $2,500. Afterward he settled on the Sisseton Reservation in South Dakota. He died there in 1871.

(Frederick J. Dockstader, *Great North American Indians*, 1977; C. M. Oehler, *The Great Sioux Uprising*, 1959; Charles E. Flandrau, *The History of Minnesota*, 1900; Charles S. Bryant, *A History of the Great Massacre by the Sioux Indians in Minnesota*, 1868; Doane Robinson, *A History of the Dakota or Sioux Indians*, 1974.)

Oto Indians. The Oto Indians, a small Siouan tribe closely related to the Winnebagos and Iowas, were united with the Missouris until a quarrel between chiefs led to division. In 1680, they visited La Salle in Illinois, and French traders were among them by 1690. Although they were an agricultural people, they wandered a great deal during the years of early white contact, being met at the mouth of the Iowa in 1690 and on the Blue Earth River in Minnesota in 1700. Later they lived on the Missouri and the Platte. During the early nineteenth century, their population greatly reduced by smallpox and attacks by other Indians, they settled near their friends, the Pawnees, for protection.

The Oto and Missouri tribes signed a peace treaty with the United States in 1817. In 1830, 1833, 1836, and 1854, they ceded all of their lands except for a reservation on the Blue River in Nebraska. In 1881, they were removed to a new reservation in the Indian Territory.

(Muriel H. Wright, *A Guide to the Indian Tribes of Oklahoma*, 1951.)

Oto Village, Treaty of, 1833. The Treaty of the Oto Village was negotiated by Henry L. Ellsworth with the Oto and Missouri Indians on September 21, 1833. The Indians ceded a large part of their lands for a ten-year extension of their $2,500 annuity, $500 for schools, provision of agricultural instructors, and the promise of cattle and a grist mill if they agreed to desist from fighting and hunting.

(Charles J. Kappler, ed., *Indian Affairs: Laws and Treaties, II*, 1972.)

Pahayuca, Comanche Chief. Pahayuca was a peaceably inclined Comanche civil chief during the period of the Republic of Texas. President Sam Houston sent peace emissaries to his band in 1843, and he saved them from death by fire when the tribal council voted to kill them. He agreed to meet with Houston at Torrey's Station, but peace negotiations failed because the president could not meet his demand for a permanent boundary and Pahayuca lacked authority to speak for all Comanches.

> The best Houston could do . . . was to pledge friendship at their final meeting in 1844, and commit himself to establishing trading houses and Indian agents. . . . Pahayuca agreed to halt raiding, to return any white captives . . . and to return to annual councils. The Texas government then dispensed its gifts. It is perfectly clear from the statements made that the Comanches did not believe themselves fully bound by these promises because the central issue—the boundary—was never resolved.—T. R. Fehrenbach

(T. R. Fehrenbach, *Comanches,* 1983; Ernest Wallace and E. Adamson Hoebel, *The Comanches,* 1952; Mildred P. Mayhall, *Indian Wars of Texas,* 1965.)

Palo Duro Canyon, Battle of. Palo Duro Canyon, a few miles southeast of the present site of Amarillo, Texas, was one of the last strongholds of the southern Plains Indians. During the autumn of 1874 the Indians, chiefly Comanches, Cheyennes, and Kiowas, were camped for three miles along the floor of the canyon, protected on both sides by sheer walls extending hundreds of feet upward to the surrounding plains. Assured of safety by their medicine man, Mamanti, they paid little regard to the danger of an attack by Colonel Ranald S. Mackenzie and eight companies of the Fourth Cavalry, searching for hostiles in the Texas Panhandle.

On September 27, Mackenzie's Seminole and Tonkawa scouts discovered the camp, and the colonel ordered his troopers to descend and attack as quickly as possible. After proceeding a mile or more along the rim without detection from below, the column discovered a narrow zig-zag trail leading down the side of the cliff. It was impossible to descend on horseback, so the soldiers scrambled down the trail in single file, leading their mounts. Three companies reached the canyon floor before the hostiles discovered their presence. Finally a Kiowa fired a warning shot. Immediately the Indians fled, abandoning their belongings in a wild dash along the canyon floor. A few warriors took cover behind rocks along the sides and fired at the troopers in an attempt to give the women and children time to escape. A bugler was wounded, but not a single soldier died in the brief battle.

After destroying the Indian villages and shooting 1,400 captured ponies, Mackenzie withdrew from the region. The battle proved to be a devastating blow to the Indians. Facing winter without food or horses, their will to resist disintegrated when they realized that there remained no sanctuary safe from invasion.

(Bill O'Neal, *Fighting Men of the Indian Wars*, 1991; W. S. Nye, *Carbine & Lance*, 1969, Paul I. Wellman, *Death on Horseback*, 1947.)

Parker, Cynthia Ann, Captivity of. On May 19, 1836, a war party of 800 Comanches, Kiowas, and Wichitas attacked a citizen's fort in east central Texas (see Parker's Fort), killing five men and taking four captives. Among those carried into captivity was nine-year-old Cynthia Ann Parker. The little girl was raised by the Comanches and became completely assimilated. By 1846, she had married a Comanche war chief (see Peta Nocona), and they had two sons and a daughter. One of her sons became the famous chief called Quanah Parker.

Captain Randolph B. Marcy, who investigated her situation in 1850, reported as follows:

> This woman has adopted all the habits and peculiarities of the Comanches; has an Indian husband . . . and children, and cannot be persuaded to leave them. The brother . . . was sent back by his mother for the purpose of endeavoring to prevail upon his sister to leave the Indians, and return to her family; but he stated to me that on his arrival she refused to listen to the proposition, saying that her husband, children, and all that she held most dear, were with the Indians, and there she should remain.

In 1860, Cynthia Ann was recovered by Texas Ranger Captain L. S. Ross during a surprise attack on a Comanche camp. With her was an infant daughter, Topsannah. Cynthia Ann cried bitterly when forcibly removed from the Indians and restored to her white relatives. She tried to run away to rejoin the Indians and had to be watched constantly. Topsannah (Prairie Flower) died in 1864 and the heart-broken Cynthia Ann succumbed a few weeks later.

(Carl Coke Rister, *Border Captives*, 1940; James T. De Shields, *Cynthia Ann Parker*, 1934; J. W. Wilbarger, *Indian Depredations in Texas*, 1985; Mildred P. Mayhall, *Indian Wars of Texas*, 1965; Randolph P. Marcy, *Exploration of the Red River . . . in the Year 1852*, 1854.)

Parker, John, Captivity of. John Parker, seven-year-old brother of the famous captive, Cynthia Ann Parker, was captured by Comanche Indians during the fall of Parker's Fort, Texas, on May 19, 1836. He was held in captivity until 1842. When redeemed by General Zachary Taylor, he could no longer speak his native language and was terrified of white people.

(Carl Coke Rister, *Border Captives,* 1940.)

Parker, Quanah, Comanche Chief. Quanah, son of the Comanche chief Peta Nocona and a white captive, Cynthia Ann Parker, was born on the western Texas plains about 1845. He became chief of the Kwahdi Comanches, wildest division of the nation, upon the death of his father. His band refused to go to the reservation after the signing of the Medicine Lodge Treaty of 1867, and he continued to raid his mother's people, the Texans, until 1874. He led the Indian attack on a band of buffalo hunters (see Adobe Walls) and lanced one of the defenders before being shot from his horse. While taking refuge behind the carcass of a buffalo, a second bullet struck him between his neck and shoulder blade. One of his warriors rode to his rescue, Quanah mounted behind him, and they raced out of range.

After the Comanche defeat at Palo Duro Canyon in 1874, Quanah finally consented to settle down with his six wives on the reservation in Oklahoma. He adopted many of the white man's ways, became a successful farmer, and rode in President Theodore Roosevelt's inaugural parade. A popular figure at frontier celebrations, on one occasion he almost lost his life by blowing out the gas light before going to bed in Fort Worth's finest hotel. He died at Cache, Oklahoma, on February 21, 1911.

(Frederick J. Dockstader, *Great North American Indians,* 1977; Richard H. Dillon, *North American Indian Wars,* 1983; Mildred P. Mayhall, *Indian Wars of Texas,* 1965; William T. Hagan, *United States-Comanche Relations,* 1976; T. R. Fehrenbach, *Comanches,* 1983.)

Parker's Fort, Texas. Parker's Fort was established in 1834 near the headwaters of the Navasota River by Elder John Parker and his sons Benjamin, Silas M., and James W. Parker. The private fort, consisting of cabins for several families surrounded by a stockade, provided a bullet-proof refuge for 38 settlers of central Limestone County. Trouble arose when white men, perhaps including Parker's Fort residents, attempted to steal horses from the Indians.

On May 19, 1836, a party of 800 Indians, predominantly Comanches, approached Parker's Fort under a flag of truce. Benjamin Parker went out to parley, and the Indians chopped him to death. While the murder was taking place, most of the settlers fled into the woods. One group, led by James W. Parker and consisting mainly of women and children, hid in a thicket until the Indians departed. Another, led by David Faulkenberry, reached safety at Fort Houston. Most of the other settlers were killed or captured in the stockade, where little resistance was made, or overtaken and slain in the woods. Among those who died that day were Elder John Parker, Silas M. Parker, Samuel M. Frost, and Robert Frost. Mrs. John (Granny) Parker was lanced and left for dead, but she clung to life for a few months. The Indians captured Mrs. Rachel Plummer and her small son, James; Mrs. Elizabeth Kellogg; Cynthia Ann Parker and little John Parker. Mrs. Kellogg was ransomed by General Sam Houston a few months later, while the others remained in captivity for periods ranging from two to twenty-five years. (See Parker, Cynthia Ann; Parker, John; Plummer, Rachel.)

(T. R. Fehrenbach, *Comanches*, 1983; A. J. Sowell, *Rangers and Pioneers of Texas*, 1964; James T. De Shields, *Border Wars of Texas*, 1976; J. W. Wilbarger, *Indian Depredations in Texas*, 1985; Carl Coke Rister, *Border Captives*, 1940.)

Parraocoom, Comanche Chief. Parraocoom (Bull Bear) was a chief of the Kwahadi Comanches during the early 1870s. He was a fearsome raider who greatly enjoyed hand-to-hand combat with white men. In 1872, following the McClellan's Creek fight, he surrendered at Fort Sill and released his captives. (See Presleano.) He died of pneumonia during the Battle of Adobe Walls in 1874.

(W. S. Nye, *Carbine & Lance*, 1969; Mildred P. Mayhall, *Indian Wars of Texas*, 1965.)

Pawhuska, Osage Chief. See White Hair, Osage Chief

Pawnee Fork Council. In 1854, at the Pawnee Fork of the Arkansas River, a council of Plains Indian tribes was held to discuss measures of dealing with eastern Indians who had been removed to their borders. Representatives of the Arapaho, Cheyenne, Comanche, Kiowa, Osage, Sioux, and Apache tribes attended, forming a camp of some 1,500 lodges. The council decided on a united effort to drive the immigrant Indians from the plains, but the war party that was organized met defeat at the hands of the Sauks and Foxes.

(Virginia Cole Trenholm, *The Arapahoes, Our People*, 1970.)

Pawnee Indians. The Pawnee Indians, a powerful tribe of Caddoan linguistic stock, included four divisions: The Grand or Chaui, the Republican or Kitkehahki, the Tappage or Pitahauerat, and the Wolf or Skidi Pawnees. They were among the first Plains Indians to encounter Europeans, having been visited by Coronado in 1541. An agricultural people, their corn fields along the Platte and Republican rivers were constantly plundered by neighboring tribes. In spite of continuing warfare with enemy Indians, they had a population estimated at 10,000.

The Pawnees were allies of the French against the Spanish during the early eighteenth century. They raided New Mexico for horses and Apache slaves to sell to the French and, in 1720, instigated by French traders, the Skidi Pawnees vanquished a Spanish expedition that visited one of their villages on the Platte or the Republican. (See Villasur, Pedro de.) These early contacts introduced European diseases that greatly reduced Pawnee population and power.

As a result of the Louisiana Purchase, American-Pawnee relations began in the early 1800s. They proved to be friendly, and the Pawnees have asserted that the tribe never waged war against citizens of the United States. One source of difficulty, however, was the Skidi practice of sacrificing captives to the Morning Star, and American officials did all that they could to stamp out the practice. (See Petalésharo; Dougherty, John.)

In 1818, the Pawnees signed their first treaty with the United States at their trading center, St. Louis, on June 18-22. On September 25, 1825, under the Treaty of Fort Atkinson, they recognized United States suprem- acy and agreed to submit grievances to the government. After smallpox wiped out 3,000 Pawnees in 1833, the demoralized survivors were per- suaded to cede their lands south of the Platte and to settle on the Loup. (See Grand Pawnee Village, Treaty of.) Missionaries settled among them in 1834 and assisted them to practice agricultural methods favored by the whites. Progress was impeded greatly, however, by frequent Sioux attacks that threatened even the mission and agency property. (See Gillis, J. L.) On August 6, 1848, by the Treaty of Fort Childs, Nebraska, they sold additional land on the Platte. On September 24, 1857, in exchange for annuities and a guarantee of protection from the Sioux, they ceded all of their remaining land except for a reservation on the Loup.

In 1864, at the onset of a major Indian war on the plains, the Pawnees agreed to assist the United States Army to track down hostile Sioux and Cheyennes. Even after they ceded their reservation in Nebraska and agreed to remove to Oklahoma, they continued to serve in a battalion known as the Pawnee Scouts. (See North, Frank J.) Finally, in April 1877, they were mustered out by order of General Sheridan. In 1892, the tribe ceded their Oklahoma reservation and accepted land allotments in sever- alty.

(George E. Hyde, *The Pawnee Indians*, 1974; John Treat Irving, Jr., *Indian Sketches Taken During an Expedition to the Pawnee Tribes*, 1955; Grant Foreman, *Advancing the Frontier*, 1933; Luther North, *Man of the Plains*, 1961; Ruby E. Wilson, *Frank J. North*, 1984; George Bird Grinnell, *Two Great Scouts and Their Pawnee Battalion*, 1928; Muriel H. Wright, *A Guide to the Indian Tribes of Oklahoma*, 1951.)

Pawnee Rock, Kansas. Pawnee Rock, an important landmark on the Santa Fe Trail, was a favorite Plains Indian hiding place from which to ambush wagon trains. It was used for that purpose on several occasions by the dangerous Kiowa war chief, Satanta.

(Paul I. Wellman, *Death on Horseback,* 1947.)

Pawnee Scouts. See North, Frank J.

Perrin du Lac. An astute French traveler and trader in 1802 was a Frenchman known as Perrin du Lac. With a company of ten men, he went up the Missouri, trading with the Osages, Kansas, Pawnees, Poncas, Cheyennes, Kiowas, Arikaras, and other tribes. On the Cheyenne River he offered gun powder to the Cheyennes in exchange for buffalo meat, but the warriors had never seen a white man and did not know what to do with gun powder. He spent three months on the Missouri and then traded on the Arkansas. His short book about his experiences provides valuable information about Plains Indian culture.

(Perrin du Lac, *Travels Through the Two Louisianas,* 1807; Mildred P. Mayhall, *The Kiowas,* 1962.)

Perry, Rufus. Rufus Perry was born in Alabama on August 23, 1822, and moved with his parents to Bastrop, Texas, at the age of 11. He began a career as a Mexican and Indian fighter by participating in the siege of Bexar at the age of 13. In 1836, he served in Captain W. W. Hill's company of Texas Rangers. He was wounded during John H. Moore's expedition against the Comanche Indians in 1839. He fought against Mexican forces that invaded Texas in 1842 and invaded Mexico with the Somervell Expedition later that year.

Perry, whose first name was Cicero but was generally known as "old Rufe," had his most desperate experiences as an Indian fighter while a member of the Jack Hays' Texas Ranger company, serving between the Nueces River and the Rio Grande in 1844. On one occasion he was attacked by Comanches and struck by arrows in the shoulder, hip, and temple. He managed to hide in a thicket and to pull the arrow from his hip before fainting from loss of blood. When he regained consciousness, the Indians were gone. Surprised that he could stand, he staggered 120 miles to San Antonio, arriving a week later.

After recovering from his ordeal, Perry settled at Bastrop, but he continued to answer the call for volunteers during periods of Indian hostilities. In 1865, he fought Indians in Concho County, and he served in the Frontier Battalion in 1874. Having survived twenty bullet, arrow, and lance wounds, he died of natural causes on October 7, 1898.

(John Holland Jenkins, *Recollections of Early Texas,* 1958.)

Peta Nocona, Comanche Chief. Peta Nocona (Nawkohnee) was one of the Kwahadi Comanches' most active raiders during the Texas Indian wars. He led the attack on Parker's Fort in 1836, captured Cynthia Ann Parker, and married her as soon as she attained womanhood. They had three children, one of whom became the last Kwahadi war chief, Quanah Parker.

Cynthia Ann and her infant daughter were seized by Rangers during an attack on Peta Nocona's camp on December 17, 1860, while the chief was away hunting. Both of them died in 1864, Cynthia Ann of a broken heart. Peta Nocona survived them only a few months, expiring as a result of an infected wound.

(Frederick J. Dockstader, *Great North American Indians,* 1977; T. R. Fehrenbach, *Comanches,* 1983; Mildred P. Mayhall, *Indian Wars of Texas,* 1965.)

Petalésharo, Pawnee Chiefs. There were several important chiefs named Petalésharo (Peta La Shar). They were brave men who defied the ancient Skidi Pawnee practice of sacrificing captives to the Morning Star god. The first in the line, known as Knife Chief, saved a Mexican captive from sacrifice. His son, Man Chief, who was born about 1796, saved a Comanche girl captive at the risk of his own life in 1817, putting an end to the practice of sacrifice that the Skidis believed prevented crop failures.

Accounts of young Petalésharo's exploit made him famous. In 1821, he toured eastern cities, welcomed as a hero wherever he went. In 1825, he signed a treaty assuring the whites that his people would not attack travelers on the Santa Fe Trail. It is believed that he died about 1832.

The last Petalésharo signed peace treaties in 1833 and 1857. He was known for his friendship with the whites and peaceful leadership of all the Pawnee bands. In 1874, he protested removal of the Pawnees to Oklahoma, but to no avail, and he was shot to death while leading his people away from their former reservation on the Loup River.

(Frederick J. Dockstader, *Great North American Indians,* 1977; George E. Hyde, *The Pawnee Indians,* 1974; Ruby E. Wilson, *Frank J. North,* 1984.)

Phantom Hill, Fort, Texas. Fort Phantom Hill was established near the present site of Abilene, Texas, on November 14, 1851, by Major John Joseph Abercrombie of the Fifth Infantry. Intended to protect the Fort Smith-Santa Fe Road, it proved to be an important link in a chain of forts along the Indian frontier between the Red River and the Rio Grande. It was abandoned as a post in 1854, but it continued to serve as a Butterfield Overland Stage station until the Civil War. Between 1867 and 1880 it was used as a picket station for Fort Griffin.

(Robert W. Frazer, *Forts of the West,* 1965.)

Phil Kearny, Fort, Wyoming. Fort Phil Kearny was established by Colonel Henry B. Carrington at the foot of the Big Horn Mountains near the present site of Buffalo, Wyoming, on July 13, 1866. Its purpose to protect the Bozeman Trail aroused the fury of Sioux chief Red Cloud, and he determined to destroy it. The Sioux and Cheyennes kept the fort under virtual siege, attacking wagon and wood trains that attempted to enter or leave it and killing so many men that Carrington sent for reinforcements on July 24. By December 31, the Indians had slain 154 soldiers and civilians, most notably on December 21, when 80 men lost their lives in an ambush. (See Fetterman Massacre.) A measure of revenge was gained on August 2, 1867. (See Wagon Box Fight.)

As a result of the Fort Laramie Treaty of April 29, 1868, Red Cloud compelled United States commissioners to agree to withdraw from Fort Kearny and other posts on the Bozeman Trail. The 600-by-800 foot stockade was abandoned on July 31, 1868, and burned by the Sioux immediately afterward.

(Margaret Carrington, *Ab-Sa-Ra-Ka,* 1868; Paul I. Wellman, *Death on Horseback,* 1947; Richard H. Dillon, *North American Indian Wars,* 1983; Doane Robinson, *A History of the Dakota or Sioux Indians,* 1974; J. P. Dunn, Jr., *Massacres of the Mountains,* 1958; George Bird Grinnell, *The Fighting Cheyennes,* 1956; Dee Brown, *Bury My Heart at Wounded Knee,* 1971.)

Piegan, Fort, Montana. James Kipp established Fort Piegan for the American Fur Company in 1831 near the juncture of the Missouri and Marias rivers. The traders obtained a large quantity of furs from the Piegan Indians, fought off an attack by the Bloods, and departed for St. Louis the following spring. Indians destroyed the fort at the first opportunity.

(Hiram Martin Chittenden, *A History of the American Fur Trade of the Far West,* 1954; John C. Ewers, *The Blackfeet,* 1961.)

Piegan Indians. See Blackfoot Indians

Piegan War. See Marias Massacre

Pierre, Fort, South Dakota. Fort Pierre, named for Pierre Chouteau, Jr., was established at the site of the present Pierre, South Dakota, in 1832, by Bernard Pratte and Company. It replaced Fort Tecumseh, which was threatened with destruction by the Missouri River. Except for Fort Union, it became the most important trading post on the upper Missouri, because it was located in the heart of Sioux lands and controlled the commerce of a vast territory from the upper Platte to the Black Hills.

Fort Pierre was purchased by the government for use by the Army in 1855. It was abandoned in 1857.

(Robert W. Frazer, *Forts of the West,* 1965; George Catlin, *Letters and Notes on the Manners, Customs, and Conditions of North American Indians,* 1973; Hiram Martin Chittenden, *A History of the American Fur Trade of the Far West,* 1954.)

Pike, Albert, Indian Affairs. Albert Pike, a writer, lawyer, soldier, and Indian manager, was born in Massachusetts on December 29, 1809. After teaching in New England, he moved to the West in 1831, visiting Santa Fe with a party of traders and settling in Arkansas in 1833. He became a newspaper editor and published many articles and poems.

At the onset of the Civil War, Pike sided with the Confederacy and was sent by that government to negotiate treaties with the tribes west of the Mississippi. In August 1861, he negotiated peace treaties with the Comanches, Kiowas, and Wichitas. The Confederacy promised to furnish the Indians with cattle and supplies, but the treaty had little effect because the Wichita reservation soon was overrun by Indians supporting the Union, and the Comanches and Kiowas seized the opportunity to raid the hated Texas settlements while the men were away fighting in the east.

Pike was more successful in recruiting Indians removed from the southern states, and many warriors agreed to defend their territory against invasion by the Union Army. Pike, commissioned a brigadier general, commanded an Indian brigade at the Battle of Pea Ridge, and he was criticized so harshly when his warriors committed atrocities that he resigned his commission in July 1862. In 1865, Pike was called upon to try to enlist the Comanches and Kiowas to fight against the Union, but the war ended before he was able to arrange a council with them.

(T. R. Fehrenbach, *Comanches,* 1983; Ernest Wallace and E. Adamson Hoebel, *The Comanches,* 1952; W. S. Nye, *Carbine & Lance,* 1969.)

Pike, Zebulon Montgomery. Lieutenant Zebulon M. Pike was born on January 5, 1779. While still in his boyhood, he enlisted in the Army to serve as a cadet under the command of his father. He was promoted to lieutenant at the age of twenty and assigned to service on the Indian frontier.

In August 1805, Pike was ordered by General James Wilkinson to seek the source of the Mississippi River and to demonstrate to the British and Indians that the United States was determined to control that area. With 20 men in a keelboat, he ascended the Mississippi from St. Louis to the mouth of the Minnesota River. There he encountered 150 Sioux warriors, gained their friendship, and persuaded the chiefs to sell 100,000 acres for $2,000. He built a fort near the present site of Little Falls, Minnesota and believed (incorrectly) that he had discovered the source of the Mississippi before returning to St. Louis in April 1806.

In July 1806, Wilkinson sent Pike to explore the headwaters of the Arkansas and Red rivers with the intent to pave the way for an invasion of New Mexico. He attempted unsuccessfully to obtain the help of the Pawnees in persuading the Comanches to participate in the venture. He built a fort in New Mexico, where, in 1807, he was arrested by Spanish authorities and marched to Santa Fe. After spending a few months in Mexican jails, he was released on July 1, 1807. He returned to the Army and was killed during the War of 1812.

(Zebulon M. Pike, *Zebulon Pike's Arkansas Journal*, 1972; George E. Hyde, *The Pawnee Indians*, 1974; Theodore Roosevelt, *The Winning of the West*, 1889; Dale Van Every, *The Final Challenge*, 1964; W. J. Ghent, *The Early Far West*, 1936; Frederick L. Paxon, *History of the American Frontier*, 1924.)

Pilcher, Joshua. Joshua Pilcher, a prominent fur trader and Indian agent, was born in Virginia on March 15, 1790. He grew up in Kentucky and moved to St. Louis about 1815. He entered the fur trade in 1819 and became the manager of the Missouri Fur Company after Manuel Lisa's death in 1820. During the following year he established Fort Benton on the upper Missouri, but the enterprise ended in disaster because of the hostility of the Blackfeet. (See Immell, Michael.) In 1822, he established Fort Vanderburgh among the Mandan Indians.

In 1823, Pilcher played a prominent part in Leavenworth's campaign against the Arikaras, returning afterward to his post at Council Bluffs. After the Missouri Fur Company became bankrupt, he organized Pilcher and Company in 1825. His new company failed in 1828 and he joined the American Fur Company, serving first on the Columbia River and finally at Council Bluffs. He abandoned the fur trade in 1830 and settled at St. Louis.

In 1838, Pilcher succeeded William Clark as Superintendent of Indian Affairs at St. Louis. He saved the lives of many Sioux by vaccinating them against smallpox. He held the office until his death on June 5, 1847.

"Pilcher seems to have been a dedicated and conscientious public servant with a sincere interest in the welfare of the Indians."—Roy W. Meyer

(Roy W. Meyer, *The Village Indians of the Upper Missouri*, 1977; David Lavender, *Bent's Fort*, 1954; Hiram Martin Chittenden, *A History of the American Fur Trade of the Far West*, 1954.)

Pitalesharo, Pawnee Chief. See Petalésharo, Pawnee Chief

Platte Bridge, Battle of. The Battle of Platte Bridge was fought on July 26, 1865. In retaliation for the Sand Creek Massacre and the Battle of Killdeer Mountain, 3,000 thousand Sioux, Cheyenne, and Arapaho warriors attacked a military outpost guarding a bridge where the Oregon Trail crossed the Platte River. They skirmished with the defenders, Kansas and Ohio cavalrymen, and tried to draw them outside the stockade, but the defenders refused to fall into the trap. Then the Indians discovered that a supply train was approaching, crossed the river, and waited in ambush.

Lieutenant Caspar Collins led a troop of cavalrymen across the bridge to assist the teamsters, but warriors led by Roman Nose surrounded the detachment. Unable to reach the wagons, Collins ordered a retreat, the troopers trying to slash through the Indian line with their sabers. He and four of his men were killed, but the remainder, though wounded, escaped across the bridge. All 25 men with the wagons were shot or burned to death. Indian losses were 60 killed and 130 wounded.

(Richard H. Dillon, *North American Indian Wars*, 1983; Paul I. Wellman, *Death on Horseback*, 1947; J. W. Vaughan, *The Battle of Platte Bridge*, 1963.)

Plenty Coups, Crow Chief. Plenty Coups was born near the present Billings, Montana, about 1849. He was a brave warrior against enemy Indians but a good friend to white people. He was instrumental in assisting the Northern Pacific Railway to obtain the right of way across tribal lands, and he served as a scout for General Crook during his campaign against the Sioux. A prosperous farmer and rancher, he died in Montana on May 3, 1932.

(Frederick J. Dockstader, *Great North American Indians*, 1977.)

Plum Creek, Texas, Battle of. The Battle of Plum Creek was fought between one of the largest Comanche war parties ever assembled and a force of Texas volunteer Indian fighters. It occurred near the present town of Lockhart, Texas, on August 12, 1840. It culminated a series of events that began more than a year earlier when the Comanches captured Matilda Lockhart and released her so badly disfigured that it led to the slaughter of Indians at San Antonio. (See Council House Fight.) The Comanches retaliated by raiding Victoria and Linnville, and on their return journey to the Staked Plains they were intercepted by 200 Texans at Plum Creek.

The volunteers were led by General of the Militia Felix Huston, Colonel Edward Burleson, Captain Mathew Caldwell, and Ranger Ben McCulloch. Chief Buffalo Hump led the Comanches, and he arranged his warriors in formation for a running fight while trying to protect the women and children and to prevent the whites from recovering the enormous herd of stolen horses. One of the Texans, a Baptist minister named Z. N. Morrell, wrote a first-hand account of the action:

> The Indians had just started their pack-mules and were preparing to follow, when they were attacked by the Texans. The Indians hastily retreated; as they could not carry off their prisoners they shot them. . . . One of these daring chiefs . . . was riding a very fine horse . . . with a ribbon eight or ten feet long, tied to the tail

of his horse. He was dressed in elegant style from the goods stolen at Linnville. . . . This Indian, and others, would charge toward us and shoot their arrows, then wheel and run away. . . . Colonel Burleson with his command on the right wing, was ordered around the woods, and Captain Caldwell, on the left with his command, charged into the woods. Immediately they began howling like wolves, and there was a general stampede and a vigorous pursuit. Some 14 or 15 Indians were killed before the retreat and a great many more were killed afterward.

Their defeat at Plum Creek was a severe blow to the Comanches. Some 80 Indians were killed, and the plunder of Linnville, including 3,000 horses, was recovered. Never again did they send such a large war party against the settlements.

(Walter Prescott Webb, *The Texas Rangers*, 1965; A. J. Sowell, *Rangers and Pioneers of Texas*, 1964; James T. De Shields, *Border Wars of Texas*, 1976.)

Plum Creek Station, Nebraska, Massacre. On August 7, 1864, an Oglala Sioux war party led by Chief Big Bow attacked a wagon train near Plum Creek Station, Nebraska, killing thirteen people and capturing a woman and a small boy. The captives were ransomed the following spring.

(Ruby E. Wilson, *Frank J. North*, 1984.)

Plummer, Rachel, Captivity of. Rachel (Mrs. L. T. M.) Plummer, daughter of James W. Parker, was captured by the Comanche Indians on May 19, 1836. (See Parker's Fort, Texas.) Her 15-month-old son, James Pratt Plummer, was taken from her, and she never saw him again. Five months after her capture, she gave birth to a child which the Indians murdered in spite of her frantic efforts to save it. Given as a slave to an old Comanche couple, she was terribly abused until she struck the old woman with a club. Afterward she was better treated and called "the fighting squaw." During her three years of captivity, her father made five trips to the Indian country trying to rescue her.
Finally Mrs. Plummer was redeemed by New Mexico trader William Donoho. But the terrors of her captivity had destroyed her will to live. She died a few months after writing a book about her experiences. Her son, thoroughly assimilated, was redeemed in 1842.

(Rachel Plummer, *Rachel Plummer's Narrative*, 1977; Carl Coke Rister, *Border Captives*, 1940; T. R. Fehrenbach, *Comanches*, 1983.)

Pobishequasho, Comanche Chief. See Iron Jacket, Comanche Chief

Pochanaquarhip, Comanche Chief. See Buffalo Hump, Comanche Chief

Ponca Indians. The Ponca Indians, a small Siouan-speaking tribe, played a relatively insignificant role in frontier history, but they gained considerably in importance because of controversy regarding their removal. Originally encountered by Europeans on the Niobara River, they had a population of about 800, but by the time they were seen by Lewis and Clark their numbers had dwindled to 200 as a result of smallpox.

In 1858, with their population back to original size, they ceded most of their lands to the government and agreed to live on a reservation near the mouth of the Niobara. In 1865, they ceded a part of the reservation and received guaranteed title to the remainder. The government broke its word three years later by ceding the Poncas' lands to the Sioux. The numerous and powerful Sioux overran the land, appropriating their stock and killing Poncas who resisted. Chief Standing Bear protested, but to no avail.

Finally, in 1876, Congress ordered the removal of the Poncas to Oklahoma. Some refused to go, asserting that they would rather die in defense of their homeland, but troops removed the majority. They settled for a time with the Quapaws in 1877 but, not liking the country, they moved the following year to a reservation of 100,000 acres on the Salt Fork of the Arkansas.

Standing Bear and others (see White Eagle; La Flesche, Susette; Tibbles, Thomas Henry) spoke movingly to eastern and European audiences about Indian rights and, in 1880, the government made a special appropriation to the Poncas in restitution for their wrongs.

(Muriel H. Wright, *A Guide to the Indian Tribes of Oklahoma,* 1951; Francis Paul Prucha, *American Indian Policy in Crisis,* 1976; Charles LeRoy Zimmerman, *White Eagle,* 1941; Thomas H. Tibbles, *Buckskin and Blanket Days,* 1958.)

Pope, John, Indian Affairs. General John Pope, a prominent Union officer in the Civil War, lost his command after his defeat at Bull Run and was transferred to the Military Department of the Northwest to deal with the Minnesota Sioux uprising of August-September, 1862. Upon arrival he ordered Colonel H. H. Sibley to quell the outbreak by exterminating the hostiles if necessary. After the Sioux surrendered, however, he referred Sibley's request for permission to hang all warriors convicted of crimes to President Lincoln. (See Minnesota Sioux Uprising.)

Most of the hostile Minnesota Sioux fled to their kinsmen on the Plains for protection. Pope planned a two-pronged expedition against them, one led by Sibley and the other by General Alfred Sully. The Sioux suffered severely (see Whitestone Hill; Killdeer Mountain) during these campaigns.

In 1865, Pope assumed command of the Department of the Missouri. While he directed campaigns against hostile Indians, he developed sympathy for the plight of the tribes, sought to relieve the sufferings of the survivors, and protected them from settlers attempting to seize their lands.

(C. M. Oehler, *The Great Sioux Uprising,* 1959; Francis Paul Prucha, *American Indian Policy in Crisis,* 1976.)

Porcupine Bear, Cheyenne Chief. Porcupine Bear was chief of the Cheyenne Dog Soldiers during the middle of the nineteenth century. In 1837, he killed his cousin, Little Creek, in a drunken fight. As a result the Cheyennes declared him to be an outlaw and banished him from the tribe. "It was Porcupine Bear's banishment that changed the Dog Soldiers from a society of warriors to an outlawed tribal division."—Stan Hoig

(Stan Hoig, *The Peace Chiefs of the Cheyennes,* 1980; George Bird Grinnell, *The Fighting Cheyennes,* 1956.)

Post Oak Springs, Texas, Ambush. In May 1837, five Texas Rangers— Dave Farmer, Aaron Collins, Clabe Neil, Sterrett Smith, and Jesse Bailey—went in wagons from Nashville, Texas, to transport Milam County settlers to safety from Indian attacks. They drove into a Comanche ambush at Post Oak Springs, and all 5 were killed.

(James T. De Shields, *Border Wars of Texas,* 1976.)

Powder River, Battle of. One of the more controversial battles of the western Indian wars was fought on Powder River, near the site of the present town of Moorhead, Montana, on March 17, 1876. Hundreds of Sioux and Cheyennes were wintering on the Powder River in Montana and Wyoming, and when ordered to bring their people to the reservation, Crazy Horse and other chiefs replied that it was impossible until the intense cold abated. Military leaders rejected the excuse and sent out the cavalry.

One of the villages, containing both Sioux and Cheyennes, was attacked by six troops of cavalry led by Colonel Joseph J. Reynolds. The Indians, taken by surprise, fled to the surrounding bluffs, regrouped, and fired down on the troops who were destroying the village and seizing their pony herd. Reynolds ordered a retreat, the warriors pursued and recaptured their horses. Despite a great deal of spent ammunition, casualties on both sides were light. Two troopers were killed and six wounded. Few Indians died, but the band was made destitute.

Historians disagree on several points regarding the Powder River engagement. Most of them are convinced that Crazy Horse's village was attacked. Others assert his camp was so far away that it required days for the Indians of the destroyed village to reach it. Once they arrived, he took them in and provided for their needs.

The conduct of Reynolds has been widely disputed. General George Crook, commander of the expedition, preferred charges against him for mishandling both the attack and the retreat. His defenders point out that firing from the high ground and explosions of powder kegs in the village, as well as the danger of being cut off, made a retreat necessary. After 36 hours in the saddle in weather well below zero, the troops were exhausted. They expected to meet Crook's army at Lodge Pole Creek, and if he had arrived on schedule, the captured horse herd could have been saved. Reynolds was court-martialed and suspended for a year, but President Grant remitted the sentence.

Crook claimed that the village was a "perfect magazine of ammunition, war material and general supplies that the Indians had obtained on their reservations in exchange for proceeds of their raids upon the settlements." An Indian agent at Red Cloud retorted that only "five pounds of powder, twenty of lead, and six boxes of percussion caps comprised all the ammunition that was found in the abandoned camp."

Most historians agree that with or without Crazy Horse, the Indians won the Battle of Powder River. As a result, thousands of Sioux and Cheyennes left their agencies in the spring to join the camps of Crazy Horse and Sitting Bull.

(Joe De Barthe, *Life and Adventures of Frank Grouard,* 1958; Dee Brown, *Bury My Heart at Wounded Knee,* 1971; J. P. Dunn, Jr., *Massacres of the Mountains,* 1958; George Bird Grinnell, *The Fighting Cheyennes,* 1956; Paul I. Wellman, *Death on Horseback,* 1947; Richard H. Dillon, *North American Indian Wars,* 1983; Robert M. Utley and Wilcomb E. Washburn, *The American Heritage History of the Indian Wars,* 1977.)

Prescott, Philander. Philander Prescott, a government interpreter, lived with the Minnesota Sioux for forty-five years and married a member of the tribe. Seventy years old at the time of the Sioux uprising of 1862, he was warned to flee for his life by Chief Little Crow. The hostiles rode him down within a few miles of his home and while he begged for his life they shot him to death.

(Doane Robinson, *A History of the Dakota or Sioux Indians,* 1974; Charles S. Bryant, *A History of the Great Massacre by the Sioux Indians in Minnesota,* 1868.)

Presleano, Captivity of. Presleano, a young Mexican boy, was captured in Mexico and adopted by a fierce Comanche chief, Parraocoom. After Colonel Ranald Mackenzie defeated the Comanches at McClellan Creek, capturing 230 women and children, the tribe was compelled to surrender their captives. Parraocoom was so deeply affected by the loss of his adopted son that tears rolled down his cheeks.

(W. S. Nye, *Carbine & Lance*, 1969; Lawrie Tatum, *Our Red Brothers*, 1970.)

Pryor, Nathaniel. Captain Nathaniel Pryor, a member of the Lewis and Clark Expedition, was the leader of the party that attempted to return Mandan chief Big White to his people in 1807. (See Big White.) He resigned from the Army in 1810 to enter the Indian trade on the upper Mississippi, but after being robbed by the Winnebagos and barely escaping with his life, he reenlisted in 1813 and served with distinction at the Battle of New Orleans. At the conclusion of the war he established a trading post on the Verdigris River, married an Osage woman, and lived with her tribe.

Pryor was an effective Indian diplomat, particularly active in attempting to prevent hostilities between the Osages and Cherokees. In 1828 he was appointed acting subagent for the Arkansas Osages. He died in 1831.

(John Joseph Mathews, *The Osages*, 1961; W. J. Ghent, *The Early Far West*, 1936; Grant Foreman, *Indians & Pioneers*, 1936.)

Putnam, Mitchell, Family of. Mitchell Putnam homesteaded in the Guadalupe valley near Gonzales, Texas, in 1836. In October 1838, four of his children, accompanied by the daughter of his neighbor, Andrew Lockhart (see Lockhart, Matilda) were captured by Comanche Indians while gathering pecans. Putnam and Lockhart and a Ranger posse pursued them to the mountains of western Texas before losing the trail.

James Putnam, four years old when taken, was carried by his captors throughout the Southwest, frequently watching the Comanches attack wagon trains along the Santa Fe Trail. After eight years of captivity, he was ransomed by traders and returned to his parents. Completely assimilated, he refused at first to sit on a chair, sleep in a bed, or eat with a knife and fork. He finally adjusted, however, and eventually married a widow whose husband had been killed by the Indians.

Rhoda, the eldest Putnam girl, about 13 years old when taken, married a chief and refused all offers to redeem her. Elizabeth, the youngest girl, was surrendered by the Indians some 18 months after her capture. She had been adopted by a Comanche family and therefore was spared when the band murdered most of their captives in retaliation for the massacre of Indians in San Antonio on March 19, 1840. (See Council House Fight.) Judy Putnam, the second daughter, was held by the Indians for 14 years. Finally she was purchased by an Indian agent, but she could not remember her name. Her family identified her by marks on her body.

(Carl Coke Rister, *Border Captives*, 1940; A. J. Sowell, *Rangers and Pioneers of Texas*, 1964; J. W. Wilbarger, *Indian Depredations in Texas*, 1985; Mildred P. Mayhall, *Indian Wars of Texas*, 1965.)

- Q -

Quaker Peace Policy. See Grant, Ulysses S., Peace Policy

Quanah, Comanche Chief. See Parker, Quanah, Comanche Chief

Quitan, Esteban. Esteban Quitan, son of a Mexican soldier, was captured by Comanches in Chihuahua about 1852. After six years of captivity, he was sold to the Kiowas and grew into one of their most daring raiders. He, along with Mamanti, led the Texas raid that resulted in the deaths of Britton Johnson and his companions in 1871. He married the sister of Big Bow, a prominent war chief.

(W .S. Nye, *Carbine & Lance,* 1969; *Good Medicine & Bad,* 1962.)

Radziminski, Camp, Oklahoma. Camp Radziminski was established in Tillman County, Oklahoma, in 1858 by Captain Earl Van Dorn. It was used by both soldiers and Texas Rangers as a rallying point for the pursuit of hostile Indians. (See Rush Springs, Battle of.)

(W. S. Nye, *Carbine & Lance*, 1969.)

Rain-in-the-Face, Hunkpapa Sioux Chief. Rain-in-the-Face, a famous Hunkpapa Sioux war chief, was born about 1835 in North Dakota. He fought in many of the most important battles on the northern plains, including the Fetterman massacre, but his fearsome reputation resulted in large part from his own claims of murdering prominent white men. In 1868, he was wounded during an attack on Fort Totten, North Dakota. He raided many mining camps near the Black Hills and, in 1873, he admitted murdering a veterinarian and a sutler who were collecting fossils while accompanying a surveying party of the Northern Pacific Railway Company.

After these murders, which some historians believe he did not commit, he was arrested at the Standing Rock Reservation by Captain Tom Custer and imprisoned at Fort Abraham Lincoln. In 1874, he escaped and joined the hostiles led by Sitting Bull. He fought in the Battle of the Little Bighorn and claimed that he killed General George A. Custer, but it is more likely that his victim was the general's brother, Tom, hated by Rain-in-the-Face because of his imprisonment.

After the battle, Rain-in-the-Face accompanied Sitting Bull to Canada. He returned in 1880 and surrendered to General Nelson A. Miles. Afterward he lived on the Standing Rock Reservation until his death on September 14, 1905.

(Frederick J. Dockstader, *Great North American Indians*, 1977; Doane Robinson, *A History of the Dakota or Sioux Indians*, 1974; Elizabeth B. Custer, *Boots and Saddles*, 1961; John P. Dunn, Jr., *Massacres of the Mountains*, 1958.)

Rankin, Camp, Colorado. See Sedgwick, Fort, Colorado

Ravoux, Augustin. Father Augustin Ravoux, A Roman Catholic missionary, arrived in Minnesota in 1841. He ministered to the spiritual needs of both the Sioux and the French settlers of Mendota, St. Paul, St. Croix, and Lake Pepin. After the Sioux uprising of 1862, he worked among the warriors who were condemned to death, baptizing a majority of them. He said the final prayer before 38 of them were hung at Mankato.

(Charles E. Flandrau, *History of Minnesota*, 1900; C. M. Oehler, *The Great Sioux Uprising*, 1959; Stephen R. Riggs, *Mary and I*, 1971.)

Red Cloud, Oglala Sioux Chief. Red Cloud, one of the greatest statesmen in the history of the Sioux nation, rose as a result of leadership abilities to displace the hereditary chief of the Oglalas. His origins are obscure, and there is some doubt as to his father's identity. According to his own account, he was born in 1821 on Bluewater Creek, near the North Platte, in Nebraska, but the reliable Indian scholar Frederick J. Dockstader reports that he was born on September 20, 1822. In spite of the undistinguished character of his forebears, he rose to prominence through prowess on the battlefield (he is said to have counted 80 coups), personal bravery, remarkable intelligence, and unflagging determination to preserve Sioux lands from white intruders.

After the Minnesota Sioux uprising of 1862 was crushed and the survivors fled to the plains, Red Cloud determined that his mission in life was to preserve remaining hunting grounds by preventing the passage of roads and railways through the Powder River country. He and his young warriors virtually halted all traffic on the Bozeman Trail, and when the Army built forts to protect this passageway to the Montana mines, he harassed them until the government agreed to abandon them. (See Phil Kearny, Fort; Smith, C. F., Fort; Reno, Fort, Wyoming; Fetterman Massacre; Wagon Box Fight; Laramie, Fort, Treaty of, 1868.)

> The treaty that the great Sioux chief Red Cloud imposed on the white men in 1868 is the only admission of defeat the United States ever signed. Until the forts of the Bozeman Road had been abandoned, until the garrisons had withdrawn from Indian country, Red Cloud would not even consent to talk with the peace commissioners.—Frederic F. Van de Water

> After two years of resistance, Red Cloud had won the war.—Dee Brown

In 1870, Red Cloud visited Washington to protest treaty violations. He was received as a great chief and formidable adversary. His remaining years were spent on the Pine Ridge Reservation, where he refused to accept the ways of the white man but kept his followers from fighting the soldiers during the Indian war of 1876. He shunned the Ghost Dance on the reservation in 1890, but because of his determined opposition to change he was suspected of supporting the unrest. After the Wounded Knee massacre, the Brulé Sioux compelled him to leave the reservation, but he slipped away at the first opportunity and returned. He died there on December 10, 1909.

(Frederick J. Dockstader, *Great North American Indians*, 1977; James C. Olson, *Red Cloud and the Sioux Problem*, 1965; Katharine C. Turner, *Red Men Calling on the Great White Father*, 1951; Herman J. Viola, *Diplomats in Buckskins*, 1981; Dee Brown, *Bury My Heart at Wounded Knee*, 1971; Frederic F. Van de Water, *Glory Hunter*, 1963; Paul I. Wellman, *Death on Horseback*, 1947; Robert M. Utley, *The Last Days of the Sioux Nation*, 1963; Richard H. Dillon, *North American Indian Wars*, 1983.)

Red Fork, Battle of the. In November 1876, Colonel Ranald S. Mackenzie led 1,100 troopers and Indian scouts in pursuit of Crazy Horse in the Powder River country. He failed to find his quarry, but his scouts led him to Dull Knife's Cheyenne village on the Red Fork of the Powder and he charged it at dawn on November 25. Led by the Pawnee scouts, Mackenzie's men were among the lodges while most of the villagers still slept. Most of the warriors managed to reach the side of the Red Fork canyon, however, and mounted a desperate defense to allow the women and children time to escape. (See Little Wolf.)

Mackenzie destroyed 173 lodges and all of the village's supplies. Moreover, his scouts captured 500 ponies, leaving more than a thousand Cheyennes on foot in the mountains without food or shelter. Some of the people froze to death and others found succor with Crazy Horse. Most of the survivors returned to the reservation. Mackenzie's losses were 6 killed and 26 wounded.

(Paul I. Wellman, *Death on Horseback*, 1947; Richard H. Dillon, *North American Indian Wars*, 1983; Joe De Barthe, and *Life and Adventures of Frank Grouard*, 1958.)

Red Horn, Piegan Blackfoot Chief. Red Horn, a Piegan Blackfoot chief, was leader of a band that was massacred by Colonel E. M. Baker's army on the Marias River in Montana on January 23, 1870. He and 173 of his people were slain. (See Marias Massacre.)

(F. W. Hodge, ed., *Handbook of American Indians, II*, 1912.)

Red Middle Voice, Sioux Chief. Red Middle Voice was one of the chief instigators of the Minnesota Sioux outbreak of 1862. When several members of his Rice Creek band committed the first murders, he called Chief Little Crow a coward for advising restraint and shamed him into leading the outbreak. Members of his band took little part in fighting soldiers, spending their time searching for defenseless families to attack. At the end of the uprising, he attempted to flee to Canada, but on his way he was slain by Chippewa Indians.

"No calamity in the nation's frontier history affected as many civilians or exceeded in horror the massacre engineered by Red Middle Voice."—C. M. Oehler.

(C. M. Oehler, *The Great Sioux Uprising*, 1959; John Tebbel and Keith Jennison, *The American Indian Wars*, 1960.)

Red River Indian War. The so-called Red River War refers to a series of campaigns conducted in 1874 against hostile Comanches, Cheyennes, and Kiowas who had left their reservations in Oklahoma and Kansas to raid the settlements and ranches of northwestern Texas. Armies were dispatched from Fort Union, New Mexico, Fort Sill, Oklahoma, and forts Concho and Griffin, Texas, to converge on the Indians on the Staked Plains.

The first battle of the Red River War was fought near the Antelope Hills on August 30, when Nelson A. Miles attacked a band with Gatling guns and pushed them westward to the Staked Plains. On September 27, Ranald Mackenzie punished the hostiles severely in the Texas Panhandle. (See Palo Duro Canyon.) There were 14 engagements in all, and the relentless pursuit so discouraged the Indians that by 1875 the last of them had returned to their reservations.

> The importance of the Red River War in the history of our nation is undisputed. It saw the final subjugation of three of the most famous and powerful tribes accompanied by the most massive use of troops ever thrown against Indians to that time.—James L. Haley

(James L. Haley, *The Buffalo War*, 1976; Richard H. Dillon, *North American Indian Wars*, 1983; Ernest Wallace and E. Adamson Hoebel, *The Comanches*, 1952.)

Red Tomahawk, Teton Sioux Policeman. Red Tomahawk, a progressive Sioux at the Standing Rock Reservation, served the agency as Sergeant of Indian Police. He was a leader of the arresting officers who attempted in 1890 to seize Sitting Bull during the Ghost Dance activities at Standing Rock. A fight broke out in which 14 Indians, Sitting Bull included, lost their lives. Red Tomahawk claimed that it was his bullet that killed the chief. He died in 1931 at the age of 78.

(Frederick J. Dockstader, *Great North American Indians*, 1977; Stanley Vestal, *Sitting Bull*, 1957.)

Redwood Agency Massacre. The Redwood Sioux Agency on the Minnesota River was attacked by Indians on the first day of the uprising of 1862. The war party split up into small groups, each one surrounding a house or store and attacking the white people inside. Some 13 citizens were slain, while others escaped across the river on a ferry. (See Millier,

Hubert.) Several women and children were made captives. The agency buildings were destroyed.

(C. M. Oehler, *The Great Sioux Uprising*, 1959.)

Redwood Ferry, Battle of. Soon after the onset of the Minnesota Sioux uprising of 1862, Captain John Marsh led 46 soldiers from Fort Ridgely to the Redwood Agency. Hostile Indians hid themselves on both sides of the ferry landing and attacked the troops as they were about to board the boat. Soldiers not killed in the first fire took refuge in a thicket, and some of them escaped eventually under the cover of the river bank. Marsh and 24 of his men were slain. Only one Indian died in the fight.

(C. M. Oehler, *The Great Sioux Uprising*, 1959.)

Ree Indians. See Arikara Indians

Reno, Fort, Oklahoma. Fort Reno was established near the present city of El Reno, Oklahoma, in July 1874. It was intended to protect the Darlington Indian Agency during the Cheyenne hostilities of 1874. Troops from the fort pursued the Cheyennes who fled from the agency in 1879. The fort was abandoned in 1908.

(Robert W. Frazer, *Forts of the West*, 1965.)

Reno, Fort, Wyoming. Fort Reno, Wyoming, was established on the Powder River near the present town of Kaycee on June 28, 1866. Intended to protect the Bozeman Trail, it was garrisoned by former Confederate soldiers (Galvanized Yankees). The post was harassed by the Sioux, and all supplies from Fort Phil Kearny were prevented from reaching it. Several soldiers died during the winter of malnutrition and disease, and others deserted, convinced that their chances of survival were better among the Indians. In June 1867, the remaining soldiers were relieved by a detachment of Colonel Carrington's army. The fort was abandoned on August 18, 1868, as a result of the Treaty of Fort Laramie, and burned by the Indians soon afterward.

(Robert W. Frazer, *Forts of the West*, 1965; Dee Brown, *Bury My Heart at Wounded Knee*, 1971.)

Reno, Marcus A. Major Marcus A. Reno, a West Point graduate twice decorated for valor during the Civil War, was an officer in General George A. Custer's Seventh Cavalry in 1876. Shortly before the Battle of the Little Bighorn, he scouted the Rosebud River region and located the trail of the Sioux and Cheyennes.

When Custer determined to attack the enormous concentration of hostiles camped along the Little Bighorn River, he sent Reno with three troops (112 men) to attack one end of the camp while he rode around the Indians to strike the other. Reno charged as ordered, but Custer crossed the river well short of the point he proposed to attack. Reno's advance was halted by a swarm of warriors, and he took refuge first in an oxbow and then on the bluffs across the river. Thirty-two of his men were killed during the retreat, and he had to abandon 15 others who were wounded or missing.

On the bluffs, Reno was reinforced by Major Frederick Benteen and three cavalry troops. With Custer under heavy attack, Benteen and other officers urged Reno to ride to his assistance, but the major refused to move. After annihilating Custer, the Indians attempted to do the same to Reno's command. Heavy fighting prevailed on the bluffs with so many Indians involved that not all could find room on the hill at the same time. During a three-hour battle 18 soldiers were killed and 43 wounded.

The fighting broke off at night but resumed the following morning when a large force of Indians charged from the north and very nearly overran Reno's entrenchments. They finally were repulsed and spent most of the day firing at long range. As evening approached, the entire Indian concentration departed from the scene of destruction.

Reno's role in the Custer disaster has remained a matter of controversy for more than a century. At a court of inquiry, some of his officers accused him of cowardly behavior, setting a poor example for the troops, and being drunk. Benteen testified, however, that Reno was "cool and collected" throughout the battle. The court decided in Reno's favor, convinced that if he had not halted the charge and assumed a defensive position, all of his men would have been slain.

After the Battle of the Little Bighorn, Reno became such a heavy drinker that he was dishonorably discharged. He died in 1889. Years after his death the matter was reopened and it was ruled that he had been dismissed without sufficient cause.

(Edgar I. Stewart, *Custer's Luck*, 1955; Evan S. Connell, *Son of the Morning Star*, 1984; Richard H. Dillon, *North American Indian Wars*, 1983; Paul I. Wellman, *Death on Horseback*, 1947.)

Renville, Gabriel, Sisseton Sioux Chief. Gabriel Renville, a mixed-blood Sioux chief, was born in South Dakota in 1824. The son of Victor Renville, a trader, he supported the whites during the Minnesota Sioux uprising of 1862. In 1866, the War Department appointed him chief of the Sissetons. He died at the Sisseton Agency in 1902.

(F. W. Hodge, *Indians of North America, II*, 1912.)

Renville, Joseph, Sisseton Sioux Chief. Joseph Renville, son of a French trader and a Sioux mother, was born at St. Paul, Minnesota, in 1779. While his early life was spent as an Indian, his father took him to Canada as a youth to be educated. In 1805, he served as a guide for Zebulon Pike's explorations of the upper Mississippi. He was appointed captain in the British Army during the War of 1812, recruited 150 warriors to fight the Americans, and participated in the attacks on Forts Meigs and Stephenson.

After the war, Renville became a highly successful trader. He organized the Columbia Fur Company in 1821, a most profitable enterprise at the time. In 1828, he withdrew from the company and established a trading business at Lac qui Parle, Minnesota, where he remained until his death in 1846.

Renville, a Christian, played a major role in bringing missionaries to serve the Minnesota Sioux. He assisted the Reverend S. R. Riggs to translate the Bible into the Sioux language.

(Doane Robinson, *A History of the Dakota or Sioux Indians,* 1974; Hiram Martin Chittenden, *The American Fur Trade of the Far West,* 1954.)

Renville Rangers. The Renville Rangers, a force of Minnesota French-Sioux halfbloods, was organized early in the Civil War to fight for the Union. Upon the outbreak of the Minnesota Sioux hostilities in 1862, however, they were sent to help defend Fort Ridgely against an attack by Little Crow's hostiles. Upon arrival some of them spiked the fort's cannon and deserted to fight on the side of the Sioux. A majority fought for the whites, however, during the successful defense of the fort.

(Doane Robinson, *A History of the Dakota or Sioux Indians,* 1974.)

Reshaw, John. See Richard, John

Reshaw, Louis. See Richard, Louis

Reynolds, Charlie. "Lonesome" Charlie Reynolds was born in Illinois in 1842 and went on the Pike's Peak gold rush in 1860. During the next 15 years he was a trapper, buffalo hunter, and guide. He met General George A. Custer in 1869, became his favorite white scout, and helped him explore the Black Hills. In 1873, he served as chief of scouts for the Northern Pacific Railway. He was killed and beheaded while scouting for Marcus A. Reno during the Battle of the Little Bighorn.

(Evan S. Connell, *Son of the Morning Star,* 1984; Frederic F. Van de Water, *Glory Hunter,* 1963.)

Rice, Fort, North Dakota. Fort Rice was established on July 11, 1864, on the Missouri River near the present town of Fort Rice. It was intended to guard the frontier during Sioux hostilities and to protect steamboat traffic on the Missouri. It was abandoned as no longer needed in 1878.

(Robert W. Frazer, *Forts of the West,* 1965.)

Richard, John. John Richard (Reshaw) was one of the most ruinous traders on the central plains during the 1840s. Virginia Cole Trenholm, historian of the Arapahoes, has noted that he is "credited with introducing liquor among the Platte River Indians and causing them so much turmoil that he could be traced by following the trail of dead Indians, killed in a drunken brawl, he left in his wake."

(Virginia Cole Trenholm, *The Arapahoes, Our People,* 1970.)

Richard, Louis. Louis Richard (Reshaw), half-French, half-Indian, was one of the most skillful guides on the Great Plains during the Indian wars of the 1870s. His daughter married the Sioux chief Crazy Horse. He and another scout, Ben Arnold, brought the first news of Custer's defeat. On several occasions he served as a message carrier for Sitting Bull. In later life he was an interpreter at the Red Cloud Agency.

(Joe De Barthe, *Life and Adventures of Frank Grouard,* 1958; Dee Brown, *Bury My Heart at Wounded Knee,* 1971; Paul I. Wellman, *Death on Horseback,* 1947.)

Richardson, Fort, Texas. Fort Richardson was established in January 1866, near Jacksboro, Texas. It was intended to protect the north Texas frontier, the cattle trade, and the Butterfield Stage route. Troops stationed at the fort fought in the Red River War and the Battle of Palo Duro Canyon in 1874. The post was abandoned four years later.

(*Handbook of Texas, I,* 1952; Robert W. Frazer, *Forts of the West,* 1965.)

Rickaree Indians. See Arikara Indians

Ridgely, Fort, Minnesota. Fort Ridgely was established near the Minnesota River some twenty miles northwest of New Ulm on April 29, 1853. Intended to guard frontier settlements against Indian attacks, it proved to be of tremendous importance during the Sioux uprising of 1862. When hostilities began at the Lower Sioux Agency, 15 miles away, refugees poured into the fort.

Led by Lieutenant Timothy J. Sheehan, 180 soldiers and civilian fighting men repulsed an attack by 400 Sioux warriors on August 20, using rusty cannon and "a heterogeneous collection of misfit cannon balls, canister, and solid shot."—Paul I. Wellman

Two days later a second attempt was made to capture the fort. Little Crow led 800 Sioux warriors against the fort's outbuildings, only to be driven back by cannon and rifle fire. After a hundred warriors were shot down, a wounded Little Crow called off the attack.

After the uprising was defeated and the Sioux driven or removed to the Great Plains, Fort Ridgely was no longer needed. It was abandoned on May 22, 1867.

(Paul I. Wellman, *Death on Horseback*, 1947; C. M. Oehler, *The Great Sioux Uprising*, 1959; Robert W. Frazer, *Forts of the West*, 1965.)

Riggs, Stephen R. Reverend Stephen R. Riggs, a missionary for the American Board of Commissioners for Foreign Missions, was a native of Ohio. He and his wife, Mary, arrived in Minnesota in 1837 to work among the Sioux. He served them at Lac qui Parle and Traverse des Sioux before establishing a mission at Hazelwood, near the Yellow Medicine Agency.

During the Sioux uprising of 1862, Riggs and his family fled for their lives. When they arrived at Fort Ridgely they found it surrounded by the Sioux, went around it during the night, and reached safety at St. Paul. During the remainder of the outbreak he served as chaplain for General Sibley's army. After the defeat of the Sioux he interrogated the prisoners and interviewed survivors.

> The clergyman's long acquaintance with the Indians, his knowledge of the character and habits of most of them, and his familiarity with their language eminently qualified him. . . . He could tell, almost with certainty who had been implicated. —C. M. Oehler

When 38 warriors were condemned to death for murder, Riggs stayed in jail with them, seeking their conversions. He accompanied the warriors on their walk to the gallows at Mankato on December 26.

Riggs remained forty years with the Sioux. He compiled a *Dakota Grammar and Dictionary* and wrote several books and articles about missionary work among the Sioux. His seven children became missionaries, most of them to the Indians.

(S. R. Riggs, *Mary and I*, 1971; C. M. Oehler, *The Great Sioux Uprising*, 1959.)

Riley, Bennett C. Bennett C. Riley was born in Virginia in 1787. He joined the army as an engineer and was breveted major in 1828. In 1829, he commanded the first military escort of a caravan on the Santa Fe Trail. He and his Sixth Infantry battalion conducted the traders to the boundary of New Mexico and bivouacked to wait for their return from Santa Fe. One day later a trader dashed into camp seeking assistance, as the wagons were under attack by Kiowas and Comanches. Riley led his men into Mexican territory and drove the war party away.

Riley returned to his camp and skirmished with Indians who sniped at his sentries. When the caravan returned, the soldiers and teamsters repulsed an assault by Kiowas and Comanches. (See Round Grove Fight.)

Riley was promoted to brigadier general during the Mexican War. In 1848, he served as territorial governor of California. He died in 1853. Fort Riley, Kansas, is named for him.

(Fairfax Downey, *Indian Wars of the U. S. Army,* 1963; Josiah Gregg, *Commerce of the Prairies,* 1968; Richard H. Dillon, *North American Indian Wars,* 1983; David Lavender, *Bent's Fort,* 1954; R. L. Duffus, *The Santa Fe Trail,* 1975.)

Riley, Fort, Kansas. Fort Riley was established on the north bank of the Kansas River near the present city of Manhattan, Kansas, on May 17, 1853. It served as a base for several military campaigns against the Plains Indians during the mid-nineteenth century. The post remains a major military installation.

(Robert W. Frazer, *Forts of the West,* 1965.)

Roark, Elijah. Elijah Roark, a native of North Carolina, settled in Texas as a member of Stephen F. Austin's colony in 1824. On December 24, 1829, while driving a wagon to San Antonio to sell vegetables, he and an employee were murdered by Indians. His son, Leo, escaped into the woods and made his way safely to San Antonio.

(James T. De Shields, *Border Wars of Texas,* 1976.)

Robinson, Fort, Nebraska. Fort Robinson was founded on March 8, 1874, in the northwestern corner of Nebraska in order to control the Sioux on the Red Cloud and Pine Ridge Agencies. In 1876, soldiers from Fort Robinson played an important part in the campaign against the hostiles in the Powder River region. Almost 5,000 Indians surrendered by early 1877.

In October 1878, the Northern Cheyennes led by Dull Knife, fleeing from a reservation in Oklahoma, surrendered near Fort Robinson and were imprisoned there. When informed that they must return to the reservation in the south, they retorted that they would prefer to die. Half-starved and freezing, they broke out of the guard house on January 9, 1879, and scattered in the snow-covered valley of the White River. Most of them, especially the women and children, were easily overtaken and killed or recaptured. Sixty-four Cheyennes died in the outbreak, some escaped to the mountains, and others were sent to the Pine Ridge Reservation.

Fort Robinson remained an active post until 1948.

(George Bird Grinnell, *The Fighting Cheyennes,* 1956; Dee Brown, *Bury My Heart at Wounded Knee,* 1971; Paul I. Wellman, *Death on Horseback,* 1947.)

Robison, John G. John G. Robison (Robertson, Robinson) moved to Texas from Florida in 1831 and settled in Fayette County. In 1836, he was a member of the first Congress of the Republic of Texas. In February 1837, he and his youthful brother, Walter, were attacked by a Comanche war party while delivering groceries to a neighbor, and both lost their lives.

(James T. De Shields, *Border Wars of Texas,* 1976.)

Rock Creek Fight. On April 16, 1871, 12 Texas cowboys were attacked by about 50 Indians on Rock Creek, near Fort Belknap, Texas. They took refuge in a shallow ravine and defended themselves with six-shooters, while the Indians were armed with rifles. Five cowboys were killed before the Indians withdrew, driving off the horses and cattle.

(J. W. Wilbarger, *Indian Depredations in Texas,* 1985.)

Roman Nose, Cheyenne Warrior. Roman Nose (Woquini), a famous Cheyenne warrior, was born about 1830. He was not a chief, but because of his courage and skill in battle he developed a large following among the Southern Cheyennes. He believed himself invulnerable because of his sacred war bonnet, and he survived so many daring exploits that many warriors shared his opinion.

Roman Nose developed a deep hatred of white people as a result of the Sand Creek massacre. As an ally of Red Cloud he became the scourge of the Plains, attacking bands of soldiers or teamsters and engaging white men in hand-to-hand combat. (See Platte Bridge, Battle of.) In 1867 particularly, he led sanguinary attacks on wagon trains and railroad construction crews.

Roman Nose was killed in 1868 while leading a charge against a force of Indian fighters during the Battle of Beecher's Island. At first he declined to participate in the battle because he had inadvertently violated a taboo and believed that his war bonnet would not protect him. But urged on by his followers, finally he led 500 warriors in an attempt to ride right over the defenders. A rifle bullet struck him in the spine, and he died a few hours later. (See Beecher's Island, Battle of.)

(Frederick J. Dockstader, *Great North American Indians,* 1977; Paul I. Wellman, *Death on Horseback,* 1947; George Bird Grinnell, *The Fighting Cheyennes,* 1956; Richard H. Dillon, *North American Indian Wars,* 1983.)

Rose, Edward. Edward Rose was the son of a white trader and a mother of mixed Cherokee and African ancestry. He grew into a powerful and dangerous man known as Cut-Nose because he had lost its tip during a brawl in his youth. It was suspected that he had been a Mississippi River pirate before becoming a trapper for the Missouri Fur Company in 1807. He had lived among the Crow Indians at least two years when W. P. Hunt hired him as a guide to Astoria in 1811. Hunt suspected that he was leading the expedition into a trap and left him at a Crow village.

Rose lived among the Crows for eight years, becoming a chief before moving to the Arikara villages on the Missouri about 1820. In 1823, he served as interpreter for Ashley's brigade. He warned Ashley that the Arikaras planned a surprise attack, and he fought bravely in the ensuing battle. During Leavenworth's retaliatory campaign, Rose was the only man courageous enough to parley with the Arikaras inside their village, and he brought back their promise to surrender.

In 1825, Rose accompanied General Atkinson's army up the Missouri. While interpreting for Atkinson in a Crow village, he discovered that the Indians planned to attack the officers. He swung about him so fiercely with his rifle barrel that the warriors fled from the tipi. His life came to an end in a battle with the Arikaras on the Missouri River in 1833. According to legend he blew himself up with a keg of powder in order to prevent torture by his enemies.

(Hiram Martin Chittenden, *The American Fur Trade of the Far West*, 1954; J. Norman Heard, *The Black Frontiersmen*, 1969.)

Rosebud, Battle of the. In June 1876, General George Crook took the field with 1,200 men in search of Crazy Horse's hostile Sioux. On June 17, they halted to rest at a bend of the Rosebud River. Suddenly a mass of Sioux warriors, led by Crazy Horse himself, swept out of canyons and charged the unsuspecting troops. They were met by Crook's Crow and Shoshoni scouts who engaged them so fiercely that the soldiers gained the time needed to prepare for the battle, and Captain Anson Mills' battalion charged a heavy enemy concentration on a bluff and compelled the Sioux to retreat. But after two hours of fierce fighting, Crazy Horse attacked with such fury that his warriors rode right into the troops and hand-to-hand fighting ensued. Finally Mills' troop circled behind the hostiles and attacked from the rear, compelling them to abandon the field. Crook had 31 casualties. Sioux losses are unknown.

Crook claimed victory, but most historians believe that Crazy Horse won the Battle of Rosebud. "Actually," Richard H. Dillon asserted, "Crook was humbled by Crazy Horse. The neutralizing of Crook . . . guaranteed Custer's utter defeat at Little Bighorn."

(Richard H. Dillon, *North American Indian Wars*, 1983; Paul I. Wellman, *Death on Horseback*, 1947; George Bird Grinnell, *The Fighting Cheyennes*, 1956; Joe De Barthe, *Life and Adventures of Frank Grouard*, 1958; Oliver Knight, *Following the Indian Wars*, 1960.)

Ross, Lawrence Sullivan. Lawrence Sullivan (Sul) Ross, was born in Iowa on September 27, 1838. His father, Shapley P. Ross, brought the family to Texas in 1839 and became an Indian agent in 1855. Young Sul grew up among Indians, learned their languages, and fought against the hostile Comanches at the Battle of Rush Springs and on the Staked Plains. He redeemed Lizzie Ross and Cynthia Ann Parker from Comanche captivity while serving as a frontier Ranger captain from 1858 to 1861.

Ross was a brigadier general in the Confederate Army. Afterward he served as a sheriff, a state senator, and governor of Texas. He died on January 3, 1898.

(J. W. Wilbarger, *Indian Depredations in Texas*, 1985; Hugh D. Corwin, *Comanche & Kiowa Captives in Oklahoma and Texas*, 1959; *Handbook of Texas II*, 1952.)

Ross, Lizzie. Lizzie Ross was captured by Comanche Indians as an infant and never knew her real name. She was rescued by Lawrence (Sul) Ross during the Battle of Rush Springs on October 1, 1858. Ross named her Lizzie after his fiancee, and she was raised in the Ross family. She married a wealthy California merchant in 1889.

(Hugh D. Corwin, *Comanche & Kiowa Captives in Oklahoma and Texas*, 1959; J. Norman Heard, *White Into Red*, 1973.)

Ross, Shapley Prince. Shapley Prince Ross was born in Kentucky on January 11, 1811, and moved to Nashville, Texas, in 1839. He became a Texas Ranger, serving under Jack Hays. In 1842, he fought a famous hand-to-hand battle with Comanche chief Big Foot, killing him with a knife thrust to the heart. In 1846, he acted as captain of a company of volunteer Indian fighters, leading them in several campaigns against the Comanches and other tribes.

In 1855, Ross was appointed Indian agent for the Brazos River Reservation. He led his Indians to assist the Texas Rangers in a campaign against the Comanches in 1858. Soon afterward the Brazos River Reservation was closed, the Indians were removed to Oklahoma, and Ross retired to his farm at Waco. There he raised a son of Comanche chief Iron Jacket as a member of his own family. He died on September 17, 1889.

(James T. De Shields, *Border Wars of Texas*, 1976; John Salmon Ford, *Rip Ford's Texas*, 1963; *Handbook of Texas, II*, 1952.)

Ross, Sul. See Ross, Lawrence Sullivan

Rotten Belly, Crow Chief. See Arapoosh, Crow Chief

Round Grove Fight. The Round Grove fight, the first army skirmish with the Kiowa and Comanche Indians, occurred on June 11, 1829, at a place on the Santa Fe Trail called Round Grove. Major Bennett Riley and a battalion of the Sixth Infantry were escorting a wagon train when a hundred Indians attempted to steal a herd of cattle belonging to the traders. Riley fired cannon at them and the warriors fled.

(Richard H. Dillon, *North American Indian Wars*, 1983.)

Rush Springs, Battle of. The Battle of Rush Springs was fought in southwestern Oklahoma on October 1, 1858. Captain Earl Van Dorn and a column of four Second Cavalry companies from Fort Belknap attacked Bull Hump's Comanche band of 500 people, burned 120 lodges, and captured more than 300 horses. He was unaware that Bull Hump was leading his people north to seek peace at the time. The battle lasted almost two hours and resulted in the deaths of 58 Indians and 5 soldiers. Van Dorn was severely wounded but survived to fight Indians on many subsequent occasions.

(Richard H. Dillon, *North American Indian Wars*, 1983; W. S. Nye, *Carbine & Lance*, 1969.)

Sacred Heart Creek, Minnesota, Massacre. During the Minnesota Sioux uprising of 1862, some of the worst atrocities occurred on Sacred Heart Creek in Renville County. (See Krieger, Justina; Schwandt, John, Family of.) Men were slain in the fields, their wives raped, and their children burned to death in flaming cabins. In some instances infants were nailed to doors and left to die in agony. Sioux bands led by Shakopee and Red Middle Voice murdered more than a hundred settlers in the Sacred Heart area.

(C. M. Oehler, *The Great Sioux Uprising,* 1959.)

Saint Louis Missouri Fur Company. The Saint Louis Missouri Fur Company was established on March 7, 1809, in order to develop the Indian trade on the Missouri River and its tributaries. Manuel Lisa and Benjamin Wilkinson were the leading traders among ten partners, and William Clark served as company agent in St. Louis.

The company's first expedition up the Missouri left St. Louis in June 1809, with more than 150 men in nine barges transporting trade goods valued at more than $4,000. Posts were established among the Sioux, Arikaras, Mandans, Hidatsas, and Crows. An attempt was made to establish a fort among the Blackfeet on the Three Forks of the Missouri, but it was destroyed by the tribe with great loss to the company. This disaster was more than offset, however, by profits from other posts.

The company was reorganized in 1812 with William Clark as president. It was dissolved in 1814 and succeeded by the Missouri Fur Company, headed by Manuel Lisa, who led annual expeditions up the river. After Lisa's death in 1820, Joshua Pilcher became president. The Missouri Fur Company went bankrupt in 1825. (See Lisa, Manuel; Pilcher, Joshua.)

(Hiram Martin Chittenden, *The American Fur Trade of the Far West,* 1954; W. J. Ghent, *The Early Far West,* 1936; Dale Van Every, *The Final Challenge,* 1964; Le Roy R. Hafen, ed., *Mountain Men and Fur traders of the Far West,* 1982.)

St. Vrain, Fort. Fort St. Vrain was built by the Bent family in 1837 on the South Platte River north of Denver. A large adobe fort, it was intended to give the Bents a better opportunity to trade with the Indians of the northern Plains. It was abandoned about 1845 and temporarily reoccupied about 1850.

(David Lavender, *Bent's Fort,* 1954; George Bird Grinnell, *Beyond the Old Frontier,* 1976.)

Saline River, Kansas, Raid. During the spring of 1868, Indian agents issued arms and ammunition to Cheyenne Indians who claimed to need them for hunting. As a result, a war party of 200 Cheyennes, accompanied by a few Sioux and Arapahoes, attacked the settlers along the Saline about thirty miles north of Fort Harker in a raid described by General Phil Sheridan as "murder and rapine, which for acts of devilish cruelty, has no parallel in savage warfare." They scattered among the farm houses, killing or capturing the men and sexually assaulting the women. Two young women captives eventually were recovered in Black Kettle's village.

(P. H. Sheridan, *Personal Memoirs*, 1888; J. P. Dunn, Jr., *Massacres of the Mountains*, 1958.)

Salt Creek Massacre. See Warren Wagon Train Raid

Sand Creek Massacre. During the autumn of 1864, Cheyenne chief Black Kettle was rebuffed by Governor John Evans of Colorado when he tried to negotiate peace terms. Still seeking peace, the chief conferred with Major E. W. Wynkoop at Fort Lyon and was informed that if he and his followers would camp at Sand Creek, they would be protected until peace could be arranged. Unfortunately, Wynkoop was reassigned and Major Scott Anthony, a more belligerent officer, assumed command of the post. Meanwhile, Colonel J. M. Chivington of the Colorado Militia, with the governor's approval, set out with 700 men and four howitzers in search of hostiles. Joined on the trail to Sand Creek by Anthony, the troops surrounded the unsuspecting village on the morning of November 29. When some of Anthony's junior officers protested that the Indians believed themselves to be under Army protection, Chivington retorted that he had "come to kill Indians, and believe it is right and honorable to use any means under God's heaven to kill Indians."

Astounded to see the troops deploy for action, Black Kettle reassured the Cheyennes that he could correct whatever misunderstanding had occurred. He ran up both an American flag and a white flag over his tipi and, accompanied by an aged peace chief named White Antelope, advanced to meet the soldiers while the Cheyennes milled about the village in confusion. Suddenly, as Chivington ordered his men to kill them all ("nits make lice"), the troops opened fire. Black Kettle, realizing that it would be suicide to remain in front of the village pleading for peace, fled and escaped, but White Antelope stood his ground, singing his death song, until shot to death.

While men, women, and children were slaughtered, a few warriors attempted to provide covering fire for survivors to flee into the sand hills. They set up a line of defense in a creek bed and battled desperately until killed or dislodged by howitzer fire. Slowly retreating, then halting to make a brief stand, they delayed the attack long enough to permit most of the noncombatants to escape. At nightfall, having killed and scalped more than a hundred Indians with the loss of only nine men, the soldiers broke off the attack.

While Chivington was acclaimed a hero in Denver when he displayed the scalps, public opinion behind the frontier line turned to his condemnation and, throughout the Great Plains, the infuriated Indians went on the warpath.

> The Sand Creek Massacre, probably more than any other Indian conflict, set the stage for the years of bloody battle with the Plains tribes after the Civil War. In the years to follow, it would remain with the Indian as the most potent symbol of white-man treachery.— Stan Hoig

(Stan Hoig, *The Sand Creek Massacre*, 1961; Dee Brown, *Bury My Heart At Wounded Knee*, 1971; Paul I. Wellman, *Death on Horseback*, 1947; George Bird Grinnell, *The Fighting Cheyennes*, 1956.)

Sans Arc Sioux Indians. The Sans Arcs, a small division of the Teton Sioux, had a population of about 1,500. Although they signed the peace treaties of Fort Sully in 1865 and Fort Laramie in 1868, it was estimated that 1,000 of them remained hostile in 1869. They were assigned to the Cheyenne River Agency after the wars.

(F. W. Hodge, ed., *Handbook of American Indians, II*, 1912; Doane Robinson, *A History of the Dakota or Sioux Indians*, 1974; Stanley Vestal, *Sitting Bull*, 1957.)

Santa Fe Trail. The Santa Fe Trail, extending from Franklin, Missouri, to Santa Fe, New Mexico, some 780 miles, was blazed by William Becknell, a trader, in 1821. Most of the distance was on the Great Plains before the trail turned southward into the New Mexico mountains. Indian attacks occasionally were made on wagon trains and stage coaches along the trail, but Josiah Gregg reported that the tribes "are anxious to encourage the whites to come among them (and) instead of committing depredations upon those with whom they trade they are generally ready to defend them against every enemy."

(Josiah Gregg, *The Commerce of the Prairies*, 1968; R. L. Duffus, *The Santa Fe Trail*, 1975; David Lavender, *Bent's Fort*, 1954; Frank McNitt, *The Indian Traders*, 1962; Robert Glass Cleland, *This Reckless Breed of Men*, 1963.)

Santee Sioux Indians. The Santee Indians, an eastern Sioux division, included the Mdewakantons and Wahpekutes and are sometimes said to have included the Sissetons and Wahpetons. They sold 100,000 acres in Minnesota to the United States government in 1805 (see Pike, Zebulon M.), but fought on the side of the British in the War of 1812. In 1862, they massacred hundreds of settlers (see Minnesota Sioux Uprising) and afterward were moved first to Crow Creek in Dakota Territory and then placed on a reservation in northern Nebraska.

(Doane Robinson, *A History of the Dakota or Sioux Indians,* 1974; C. M. Oehler, *The Great Sioux Uprising,* 1959.)

Sappa Creek, Kansas, Fights. On April 23, 1875, in retaliation for the theft of horses, a band of buffalo hunters, joined by some soldiers, attacked Chief Bull Hump's Cheyenne village on Sappa Creek in northwestern Kansas. Led by Hank Campbell, the whites killed Bull Hump and 21 of his people.

In September 1878, when the northern Cheyennes were fleeing toward their homeland after leaving the reservation in Oklahoma, they sent warriors to attack the Sappa Creek settlers in revenge for Campbell's assault. They murdered 18 people on Sappa Creek, few of them residents of the area three years earlier, and extended their raid to the settlements on the Saline and Solomon rivers.

(Paul I. Wellman, *Death on Horseback,* 1947: Homer W. Wheeler, *Buffalo Days,* 1925.)

Satana, Kiowa Chief. See Setangya, Kiowa Chief

Satanta, Kiowa Chief. Satanta (White Bear), known as "the orator of the plains," was born about 1830. He grew up hating and scorning the whites, and after he became a war chief he led several daring raids against army posts and Texas settlements. In 1864, he ran off the Fort Larned horse herd, then sent word to the commanding officer that the mounts were of inferior quality and the army should demand better ones. In 1866, he attacked the James Box family in Texas, killed Box and his youngest child, and kidnapped and tortured his wife and three daughters.

Satanta signed the Medicine Lodge Treaty of 1867, promising to live on a reservation and to become a peaceful farmer, but his real intention was to acquire arms and ammunition. In 1868, Generals Sheridan and Custer located his winter camp, arrested him, and held him (still protesting his peaceful intentions) at Fort Sill until his band returned to the reservation. After his release in 1869, he ran off the stock at Fort Dodge while wearing a major general's uniform that had been given to him by General W. S. Hancock.

After a particularly stirring sun dance in 1870, most of the young Kiowas turned their backs on the peaceful principal chief, Kicking Bird, to follow Satanta and the celebrated medicine man, Mamanti, in waging war on the Texas settlers and buffalo hunters. In 1871, Satanta, Satank, Big Tree, and Mamanti attacked a wagon train, killed 12 teamsters, and stole 41 mules. (See Warren Wagon Train Raid.) Returning to Fort Sill,

Satanta boasted of his role in the raid. General Sherman ordered him arrested, and he was convicted of murder and imprisoned at Huntsville, Texas. (See Big Tree; Setangya.) In 1873, he was paroled upon promising good behavior, but when raids resumed in 1874 he was returned to prison. Unable to adjust to confinement, he committed suicide on October 11, 1878, by jumping out an upper-floor window in the prison hospital.

(Clarence Wharton, *Satanta*, 1935; Frederick J. Dockstader, *Great North American Indians*, 1977; Paul I. Wellman, *Death on Horseback*, 1947; Mildred P. Mayhall, *The Kiowas*, 1962; Benjamin Capps, *The Warren Wagontrain Raid*, 1974; W. S. Nye, *Carbine & Lance*, 1969.)

Schwandt, John, Family of. The John Schwandt family lived on Sacred Heart Creek at the time of the Minnesota Sioux uprising of August 1862. Schwandt, unaware of the hostilities, was shot to death by a Sioux war party while repairing his roof. Then the Indians murdered his wife, Christina, his pregnant daughter and her husband, Caroline and John Waltz; and his sons, Christian and Frederick. His son August, aged 12, was tomahawked and left for dead but managed to crawl and stagger to Fort Ridgely.

Mary Schwandt, aged 14, was a government school employee at the Lower Sioux Agency and not at home during the attack. At the onset of the outbreak, she and two other young women, Mary Anderson and Mattie Williams, fled from the agency in a wagon driven by Francis Patoile. They were overtaken near New Ulm by 50 warriors who killed Patoile and captured the women. Mary was raped repeatedly, but she survived and was redeemed by General H. H. Sibley on September 26. When the Sioux surrendered, she testified against several warriors, who were convicted of murdering Mary Anderson and Francis Patoile. (See Anderson, Mary.)

(C. M. Oehler, *The Great Sioux Uprising*, 1959; Charles S. Bryant, *A History of the Great Massacre by the Sioux Indians in Minnesota*, 1868.)

Scott, Fort, Kansas. Fort Scott was established on the Marmoton River in eastern Kansas on May 30, 1842. It was intended to protect travelers on the way from Fort Leavenworth to Fort Gibson. In 1853, the post was shut down, but it was returned to service at the beginning of the Civil War. The garrison played an important part in the Plains Indian wars of 1864. Fort Scott was abandoned in 1873.

(Robert W. Frazer, *Forts of the West*, 1965.)

Sedgwick, Fort, Colorado. Fort Sedgwick was established near Julesburg, Colorado, on May 17, 1864. It was called Camp Rankin when attacked by the Cheyennes and Arapahoes in 1865. Failing to capture the fort, the hostiles sacked Julesburg two times while the undermanned garrison was unable to assist the citizens of the town. Fort Sedgwick was abandoned on May 31, 1871.

(Robert W. Frazer, *Forts of the West*, 1965; Paul I. Wellman, *Death on Horseback*, 1947.)

Seger, John Hamer. John H. Seger was born in Ohio on February 23, 1846. After service in the Civil War he settled in Kansas until he was hired as a carpenter at the Darlington Reservation in Oklahoma. Well liked by the Cheyennes and Arapahoes, he spent the remainder of his long life serving them as an agricultural instructor and school superintendent. After a few years at Darlington, he founded an Indian school on Cobb Creek (Colony, Oklahoma) and brought his family to live there, the only whites within fifty miles. He died there on February 6, 1928, after fifty years of service to the tribes.

"Probably there was no white man living in his day who had been in such constant and immediate contact with Plains Indians as he."—Stanley Vestal

(John H. Seger, *Early Days Among the Cheyenne and Arapaho Indians*, 1956; Flora Warren Seymour, *Indian Agents of the Old Frontier*, 1975.)

Setangya, Kiowa Chief. Setangya (Satank, Sitting Bear) was born in the Black Hills about 1810. A fierce enemy of white intruders on lands claimed by the Kiowas, he was a principal war chief for almost fifty years and leader of the formidable Crazy Dog society.

In 1870, Setangya's eldest son was killed in a Texas raid. He recovered his son's bones, carried them with him, and redoubled his determination to bring death and destruction to the hated Texans.

In 1871, he was arrested at Fort Sill for murdering teamsters (see Warren Wagon Train Raid), tried for murder, and sentenced to prison at the Texas State Penitentiary. He refused to get into the army wagon for transport to Texas until four soldiers picked him up and threw him in. Then, preferring to join his son in the spirit land, he began to sing his death song. He told fellow prisoners Satanta and Big Tree that he would not live to pass a nearby tree. As the wagon approached the tree, he managed to slip out of his handcuffs, drew a concealed knife, and attacked one of the guards. Corporal John B. Carleton mortally wounded the chief, and the train halted until he died. The soldiers buried him in a ditch beside the trail.

(Frederick J. Dockstader, *Great North American Indians*, 1977; Richard H. Dillon, *North American Indian Wars*, 1983; Benjamin Capps, *The Warren Wagontrain Raid*, 1974; Mildred P. Mayhall, *The Kiowas*, 1962; W. S. Nye, *Carbine & Lance*, 1969.)

Shahaka, Mandan Chief. See Big White, Mandan Chief

Shakehand, Yankton Sioux Chief. Shakehand (Weucha) was principal chief of the Yankton Sioux when the Lewis and Clark Expedition encountered them at the mouth of the James River in South Dakota on August 28, 1804. A council was held in which Shakehand announced that he had received peace medals from the Spanish and English. Lewis then gave him a medal and an officer's uniform and persuaded him to try to make peace with the Pawnees.

(Doane Robinson, *A History of the Dakota or Sioux Indians,* 1974.)

Shakopee, Mdewakanton Sioux Chiefs. Shakopee was the name of a succession of nineteenth-century Sioux chiefs who lived on the Minnesota River near the present city of Shakopee, Minnesota. The first Shakopee known to history conferred with Major Stephen H. Long in 1817. His son and successor, known as Eaglehead Shakopee, was friendly to Americans. Eaglehead's son, known as Little Six Shakopee, was a leading hostile chief during the Minnesota Sioux uprising of 1862.

After the Acton murders on August 17, Little Six and his uncle, Red Middle Voice, demanded a war to the death with the whites. They avoided battle with soldiers but scoured the countryside for unarmed settlers to slay. After the war, Little Six fled to Canada, but he was arrested by the British and sent to St. Paul for trial. He was convicted of murder and hanged in November, 1865.

"Little Six . . . was the most incendiary of the tribe."—Doane Robinson

(Doane Robinson, *A History of the Dakota or Sioux Indians,* 1974; C. M. Oehler, *The Great Sioux Uprising,* 1959.)

Sharitarish, Pawnee Chief. Sharitarish (White Wolf, Angry Chief), chief of the Grand Pawnees, wore medals bestowed upon him by both the United States and Spanish governments. He was principal chief as early as 1806 and held that status until his death in 1812.

(George E. Hyde, *The Pawnee Indians,* 1974.)

Shaw, Jim, Delaware Scout. Jim Shaw, a highly regarded Delaware Indian scout, interpreter, and Indian diplomat, was active in Texas by 1841. Texas President Sam Houston employed him to contact the Plains Indians in the interest of peace. Speaking several Indian languages as well as the sign language, he was of tremendous help to Houston as a message carrier.

In 1843, Shaw was a guide for J. C. Eldridge, Commissioner for Indian Affairs, when he negotiated peace with a Comanche band. He interpreted at numerous conferences and guided John O. Meusebach in search of a site for his German colony. In 1849, he guided Major R. S. Neighbors in exploring the country around El Paso. He died in 1858.

(*Handbook of Texas, II,* 1952; John Salmon Ford, *Rip Ford's Texas,* 1963.)

Sheehan, Timothy J. Lieutenant Timothy Sheehan commanded Fort Ridgely during the Minnesota Sioux outbreak of 1862. Only 25 years old, he exhibited great military skill in defending the fort during an attack by a large Sioux war party. (See Ridgely, Fort.)

(Charles E. Flandrau, *The History of Minnesota,* 1900.)

Sheridan, Philip H., Plains Indian Campaigns. General Philip H. Sheridan was born in Albany, New York, on March 6, 1831, and grew up in Ohio. He graduated from West Point in 1853 and served as a lieutenant against the hostile Indians of the Pacific Northwest before attaining a distinguished record in the Civil War in the armies of the Potomac and the Shenandoah. He was promoted to major general in 1864 and sent to fight the Plains Indians after the war.

In 1868, Sheridan organized a major winter campaign, sending columns from Forts Bascom, Lyon, and Larned to converge on the hostiles in their winter camps. Led by Colonel George Armstrong Custer, Major A. W. Evans, and Major E. A. Carr, severe defeats were inflicted upon the Indians in the battles of the Washita, Soldier Spring, and Summit Springs. Most of the Indians were rounded up and returned to the reservations.

In 1874, Sheridan planned the invasion of the southern Plains Indians called the Red River War. Columns from forts in New Mexico, Texas, and the Indian Territory fought fourteen major engagements on the Staked Plains, and the relentless pursuit broke the spirit of the hostiles, sending them back to their reservations.

In 1876, Sheridan planned a similar invasion of the Indian strongholds on the northern plains. This time the three-pronged campaign was less successful, leading to Crook's defeat at the Rosebud and Custer's annihilation at the Little Bighorn. Later, however, victories at Warbonnet Creek, Slim Buttes, and Powder River forced most of the hostiles to surrender or flee to Canada.

In 1883, Sheridan succeeded Sherman as General-in-Chief of the United States Army. He died on August 5, 1888. "Dead Indians, to Sheridan, were good Indians."—Frederic F. Van de Water

(P. H. Sheridan, *Personal Memoirs,* 1888; De B. Randolph Keim, *Sheridan's Troopers on the Border,* 1870; W. S. Nye, *Carbine & Lance,* 1969; Frederic F. Van de Water, *Glory Hunter,* 1963; U. S. National Park Service, *Soldier and Brave,* 1963.)

Sherman, William T., Indian Affairs. General William Tecumseh Sherman, General-in-Chief of the United States Army, was in favor of a strict policy of Indian control. A member of President Grant's Peace Commission in 1867, he signed the recommendation favoring civilian control of Indian affairs, but stated later that he was outvoted. In 1868, he established two military districts, one for the Sioux and the other for the southern Plains tribes.

In 1871, Sherman visited Texas to ascertain the truth of reports of frequent forays by Indians from the reservations. He narrowly missed Satanta's attack on a wagon train (see Warren Wagon Train Raid) and he was present at Fort Sill when the Kiowa chief boasted of the deed. Sherman ordered his arrest and, again, he narrowly escaped death when the Kiowas resisted. Afterward Sherman advocated a more active role by the cavalry in controlling the Indians on and off the reservations.

(Francis Paul Prucha, *American Indian Policy in Crisis,* 1976; W. S. Nye, *Carbine & Lance,* 1969; Robert G. Athearn, *William Tecumseh Sherman and the Settlement of the West,* 1956.)

Shetak, Lake, Minnesota, Massacre. A dozen families settled on the shores of Lake Shetak during the late 1850s. Their presence annoyed the neighboring Sioux chiefs, Lean Bear and White Lodge. At the onset of the Sioux outbreak of 1862, these chiefs attacked the Lake Shetak settlers, killing one man and causing the families to flee in wagons. Overtaken along the way, the settlers abandoned the wagons and hid among tall reeds in a slough, but to no avail. After all of the men were shot to death, the women and children surrendered. In the massacre that followed, all of the whites were slain except three women and five children. The captives were held three months and finally rescued 300 miles away in South Dakota by 11 young Teton Sioux warriors.

(C. M. Oehler, *The Great Sioux Uprising,* 1959; Doane Robinson, *A History of the Dakota or Sioux Indians,* 1974.)

Short Bull, Brulé Sioux Chief. Born about 1845, Short Bull was a leader of the Ghost Dance religion. He visited the medicine man Wovoka in Nevada and returned to the Sioux country convinced that the Ghost Dance would drive away the whites and bring back the buffalo herds. About a thousand Sioux followed his instructions, but they lost faith in him when an Indian Christ failed to appear.

After the Ghost Dance failed, Short Bull became a Christian and a performer in Buffalo Bill's Wild West Show. He died on the reservation about 1915.

(Frederick J. Dockstader, *Great North American Indians,* 1977; Robert M. Utley, *The Last Days of the Sioux Nation,* 1963.)

Sibley, F. W., Scout. In 1876, a young lieutenant named F. W. Sibley was ordered by General Crook to lead 25 troopers on a scout for hostile Indians. With him was Frank Grouard, one of the best scouts on the Great Plains. A Sioux war party discovered their trail and followed them to a wooded area, and a battle ensued that lasted four hours. Then, abandoning their horses, the soldiers retreated over a steep mountain trail. They walked for two days and nights without rations and finally arrived at Crook's camp without losing a man.

(Joe De Barthe, *Life and Adventures of Frank Grouard*, 1958; John F. Finerty, *War-Path and Bivouac*, 1961.)

Sibley, Henry Hastings. Henry Hastings Sibley was born at Detroit on February 20, 1811. He was employed by the American Fur Company in 1829, working five years at Mackinac as a clerk. In 1834, he moved to Mendota, Minnesota, and quickly amassed a fortune in the fur trade by living with the Sioux and marrying an Indian woman. He served in Congress in 1849 and as governor of Minnesota in 1858-1859.

At the onset of the Minnesota Sioux uprising of 1862, Sibley was appointed to lead the state troops against the hostiles who were besieging Fort Ridgely. His performance in the campaign was criticized at the time, and even today, because it required eight days for his four companies to reach the beleaguered fort from St. Paul. "It was hard to believe that anyone could spend eight days getting to Ridgely. And, since hundreds of women and children at New Ulm and Ridgely had been in deadly peril every moment of the eight days, it was hard to forgive."—C. M. Oehler

His supporters, however, have been equally strong in their praise. "Sibley . . . tried to save the lives of hostages by avoiding precipitate attack and the lives of his own men by wooing defections among his opponents."—Roger G. Kennedy

"His caution, which was condemned, was one of his greatest virtues . . . and undoubtedly saved his forces from disaster and the lives of the helpless captives from sacrifice."—Doane Robinson

Sibley defeated the Sioux and drove many of them from Minnesota on September 23, 1862. (See Wood Lake, Battle of.) Those who surrendered were tried for murder, Sibley hoping to hang them, but President Lincoln spared the lives of all except 38.

In 1863 and 1864, Sibley led expeditions against the Sioux in the Dakotas and defeated them three times. (See Big Mound; Buffalo Lake; Stony Lake.)

In 1865, he served on a commission that negotiated peace treaties with several Sioux tribes. Afterward he lived at St. Paul until his death on February 18, 1891.

(Roger G. Kennedy, *Men on the Moving Frontier,* 1969; Doane Robinson, *A History of the Dakota or Sioux Indians,* 1974; C. M. Oehler, *The Great Sioux Uprising,* 1959; Paul I. Wellman, *Death on Horseback,* 1947.)

Sihasapa Sioux Indians. The Sihasapa Indians, known also as the Blackfoot Sioux, constituted a small division of the Teton Sioux. They were frequent companions of the Hunkpapas and joined them in several battles in the Platte River region. (See Kelly, Fanny, Captivity of.) After they were placed on the Cheyenne River Reservation, they made significant advances along the white man's road, and they took little part in the Ghost Dance unrest.

(F. W. Hodge, ed., *Handbook of American Indians, II,* 1912; Robert M. Utley, *The Last Days of the Sioux Nation,* 1963.)

Siksika Indians. See Blackfoot Indians

Sill, Fort, Oklahoma. Fort Sill was established on January 7, 1869, near the present city of Lawton, Oklahoma. Intended to oversee the Comanches and Kiowas on the nearby reservation after Custer's victory over the Cheyennes at the Washita, it was established by General Phil Sheridan at the junction of the Cache and Medicine Bow creeks. Many of the Indians left the reservation to raid the Texas settlements and returned immediately afterward to draw rations. (See Tatum, Lawrie; Sherman, William T.; Satanta.) The fort served as a base for campaigns against the Plains Indians and the site for peace negotiations. It remains an active artillery installation today.

(W. S. Nye, *Carbine & Lance,* 1969; Robert W. Frazer, *Forts of the West,* 1965; Richard H. Dillon, *North American Indian Wars,* 1983.)

Simpson, Thomas, Captivity of. During the summer of 1842, a Comanche war party raided Austin, Texas, and captured Thomas Simpson, age 12, and his sister, Emma, about 14. Emma was so terrified that she screamed and fought the Indians constantly, despite her brother's warning to calm herself or she would surely be killed. The Indians camped about five miles north of Austin at a place called Spicewood Springs, and two warriors dragged the girl over a hill, returning a few minutes later waving her scalp. Thomas was a Comanche captive for two years before he was ransomed by traders at Taos, New Mexico.

(J. W. Wilbarger, *Indian Depradations in Texas,* 1985; John Holland Jenkins, *Recollections of Early Texas,* 1958; James T. De Shields, *Border Wars of Texas,* 1976.)

Sioux Indians. The Sioux (Dakota, Nadouessioux) Indians, a numerous and powerful nation, were located in Iowa, Minnesota, and Wisconsin when first encountered by French traders and missionaries about 1640. They were pushed westward by the Chippewas, who possessed firearms, until many of them left the forests to live on the Great Plains. There they found vast buffalo herds, acquired horses before 1800, and raided over an enormous area from Hudson's Bay to the Gulf of Mexico.

In 1862 the Santee Sioux, led by Little Crow, murdered some 800 settlers in Minnesota (see Minnesota Sioux Uprising) and were driven out of the forests to join their kinsmen in Dakota. As a result, warfare spread to the plains and many of the bloodiest battles in frontier history were fought against the armies of Sibley, Sully, Custer, Miles, Carr, Carrington, and other prominent officers and Indian fighters. (See Sitting Bull; Crazy Horse; Red Cloud; Rain-in-the-Face; Gall.)

The Sioux lived on reservations after 1878, and many of them adopted ways of the white men. In 1890, however, they joined in the Ghost Dance unrest, resulting in a bloody encounter at Wounded Knee Creek. Afterward the Sioux were allotted lands in severalty in the Dakotas and Nebraska. (See Mdewkanton; Wahpeton; Wahpekute; Sisseton; Yankton; Yanktonai; Teton; Brulé; Hunkpapa; Miniconjou; Oglala; Sans Arc; Sihasapa Sioux Indians.)

(Doane Robinson, *A History of the Dakota or Sioux Indians*, 1974; Robert M. Utley, *The Last Days of the Sioux Nation*, 1963; John R. Swanton, *Indian Tribes of North America*, 1952.)

Sisseton Sioux Indians. The Sisseton Indians, an eastern division of the Sioux nation, were first encountered by French explorers and traders in the Mille Lacs region of Minnesota before 1650. By 1804, they were located by Lewis and Clark on the headwaters of the Minnesota River. In 1820, they murdered two employees of the Missouri Fur Company. During the Minnesota Sioux uprising of 1862, they participated in the attack on the government warehouse at Yellow Medicine. Two of their chiefs, White Lodge and Lean Bear, were among the leading hostiles during the outbreak, but Standing Buffalo was able to keep most of them out of the war. Afterward, fearful of the punishment administered to other bands, they fled to Devil's Lake. Subsequently they were gathered on a reservation.

(F. W. Hodge, ed., *Handbook of American Indians, II*, 1912; Doane Robinson, *A History of the Dakota or Sioux Indians*, 1974.)

Sitting Bull, Hunkpapa Sioux Chief. Sitting Bull (Tatanka Iyotanka) was born near the site of the present city of Bullhead, South Dakota, on March 31, 1834. He became a famous warrior during his youth, joining his first war party at the age of 14. Limping throughout his adult life as a result of a wound sustained in a battle with the Crow Indians, he was chosen leader of the Strong Heart warrior society, men who wore a sash to be pinned to the ground during battle as testimony that they would never retreat. A natural leader, he recruited many warriors who shared his hatred of white people during the Indian wars of the 1860s. Cheyennes and Arapahoes as well as Sioux flocked to his standard.

While Sitting Bull exhibited bravery and skill as a war leader, his reputation as the foremost Indian patriot on the western plains was earned as a medicine man and diplomat. Uncompromising in his determination to preserve the Indian way of life, he had the political skills (rare among Indians) to keep his followers together and prepared to fight on an instant's notice. By 1875 he was recognized as head of the war council in spite of the fact that he was not a hereditary chief.

Sitting Bull's most amazing feat as a medicine man occurred in June 1876, during a sun dance. In a vision he saw hundreds of soldiers falling from the sky into an enormous Indian camp. The vision foretold the fate of Custer's army at the Little Bighorn. During that battle, Stanley Vestal surmised, he played the role of a general rather than a warrior:

Such skill in forecasting the enemy's movements, such canny sizing up of a situation, were what made Sitting Bull peerless as a leader. . . . Brave men were plenty in their camps: but a man who combined intelligence and skill and courage as Sitting Bull did was hardly to be found.

After the victory over Custer, Sitting Bull led his followers to Canada. He returned to the United States five years later and surrendered at Fort Buford, Montana, on July 19, 1881. He was imprisoned two years, then permitted to settle on the Standing Rock Reservation. In 1885, he toured the United States and Canada with Buffalo Bill's Wild West Show, but he declined to accompany the show on its European tour.

Sitting Bull had a difficult time adjusting to reservation life, and Agent James McLaughlin considered him to be a dangerous trouble-maker. When the Ghost Dance began at Standing Rock, Sitting Bull participated, although he was not convinced that the prophecy of Wovoka could be believed. McLaughlin, who had been seeking the right opportunity to arrest Sitting Bull, seized upon the Ghost Dance as pretext. He sent the Indian Police on that mission, Sitting Bull resisted arrest, and Sergeant Red Tomahawk shot him to death on December 15, 1890.

"His intransigence, in the face of white aggression, his courage in defending his people, and his refusal to step aside in an impossible struggle, have made him into an almost mythical figure in American history."—Frederick J. Dockstader

(Stanley Vestal, *Sitting Bull*, 1957; Frederick J. Dockstader, *Great North American Indians*, 1977; Paul I. Wellman, *Death on Horseback*, 1947; Doane Robinson, *A History of the Dakota or Sioux Indians*, 1974; Robert M. Utley, *The Last Days of the Sioux Nation*, 1963; Joe De Barthe, *Life and Adventures of Frank Grouard*, 1958.)

Skitok, Osage Chief. See Mad Buffalo, Osage Chief

Sleeping Wolf, Kiowa Chief. There was a succession of at least five Kiowa chiefs bearing the name Sleeping Wolf (Guikati, Wolf-Lying Down). The first negotiated peace with the Comanches in 1790 and forged an alliance that resulted in sanguinary raids into Mexico and Texas for almost a century. One of the Sleeping Wolf chiefs was killed by Mexicans during a horse-stealing raid across the Rio Grande about 1858. The last of the five, second chief of the nation, visited Washington in 1872. He was a leader of the hostiles during the Indian war of 1874 and was killed by another Indian in 1877.

(F. W. Hodge, ed., *Handbook of American Indians, II*, 1912; Mildred P. Mayhall, *The Kiowas*, 1962.)

Sleepy Eyes, Sisseton Sioux Chief. Sleepy Eyes, a controversial Sisseton Sioux chief, was born near Mankato, Minnesota. He became a chief of his band about 1825. Generally friendly to whites, especially to Reverend S. R. Riggs, he signed the treaties of Prairie du Chien in 1825 and 1830, St. Peters in 1836, and Traverse des Sioux in 1851, removing many of his people to reservations.

Contemporaries have charged that Sleepy Eyes or members of his band participated in attacks on settlers during the Spirit Lake Massacre of 1857 and the Minnesota Sioux uprising of 1862. At the conclusion of the latter conflict, he fled to the Dakotas, and his name appears on the list of fugitives that General H. H. Sibley sought to hang. If guilty, however, it seems unlikely that the white citizens of Sleepy Eye, Minnesota, would have erected a monument over his grave.

(F. W. Hodge, ed., *Handbook of American Indians, II*, 1912; Doane Robinson, *A History of the Dakota or Sioux Indians*, 1974; C. M. Oehler, *The Great Sioux Uprising*, 1959.)

Slim Buttes, Battle of. The Battle of Slim Buttes was fought near the present site of Reva, South Dakota, on September 9, 1876. General George Crook, attempting to punish hostile Sioux bands that had participated in the Battle of the Little Bighorn, sent a detachment under Captain Anson Mills ahead of the main column to scout for Crazy Horse's camps. Mills discovered a Sioux village of 37 lodges—American Horse's band—and sent a message to Crook to hurry. He waited until morning, then ordered an attack that took the Indians completely by surprise. Most of the Sioux fled to the hills, but American Horse and a few warriors halted in a box canyon and resisted stoutly. Crook's main army arrived during the final phase of the battle, and the mortally wounded chief surrendered. (See American Horse.)

The Battle of Slim Buttes reversed the trend of recent army defeats and raised the morale of the soldiers. Casualties on both sides were surprisingly light.

(Joe De Barthe, *Life and Adventures of Frank Grouard*, 1958; Richard H. Dillon, *North American Indian Wars*, 1983; Paul I. Wellman, *Death on Horseback*, 1947.)

Slim Face, Cheyenne Chief. Slim Face (Viponah), a peaceably inclined Cheyenne chief, went to St. Louis in 1844 to plead with government officials to prevent the sale of liquor to his people. In 1867, he signed the Treaty of Medicine Lodge. Two years later he received General Custer in a friendly manner, but the officer arrested him and two other chiefs to serve as hostages until the tribe released two white women held in captivity. The women were brought in, but Custer refused to release the chiefs. Taken to Fort Hays, a fracas erupted, and the eighty-year-old Slim Face was bayoneted by the guards.

(Stan Hoig, *The Peace Chiefs of the Cheyennes*, 1980; George Bird Grinnell, *The Fighting Cheyennes*, 1956.)

Smith, Bill, Massacre. In March, 1870, Bill Smith led 275 Wyoming miners to punish a band of Arapahoes that had raided their camps, killing eight people. Unable to locate the hostiles, Smith and his followers fell upon the village of the friendly chief, Black Bear. The chief and 17 of his people were killed, and 9 women and children were captured.

(Virginia Cole Trenholm, *The Arapahoes, Our People*, 1970.)

Smith, Blackfoot. See Smith, John Simpson

Smith, C. F., Fort, Montana. Fort C. F. Smith was established August 12, 1866, on the Bighorn River to protect the Bozeman Trail from the Sioux Indians. For two years it was besieged most of the time by the Sioux. (See Hayfield Fight.) As a result of the Treaty of Fort Laramie, it was abandoned on July 29, 1868, and destroyed soon afterward by Red Cloud's warriors.

(Robert W. Frazer, *Forts of the West*, 1965.)

Smith, Clinton, Captivity of. Clinton Smith was captured at the age of 11 near Dripping Springs, Texas, on March 3, 1869. During his four years of captivity, he became thoroughly assimilated. As an apprentice warrior he was wounded during one of his many raids on the Texas settlements. When the Comanches were compelled to release their captives at Fort Sill, he was so determined to rejoin them that it was necessary to lock him in the guardhouse. While on the way to San Antonio under military escort, he tried to steal a horse to escape. Restored to his relatives, he experienced great difficulty readjusting, but he eventually married and became a successful rancher.

(Clinton Smith, *The Boy Captives*, 1927; J. Norman Heard, *White Into Red*, 1973.)

Smith, James, Family of. Judge James Smith settled in Austin, Texas, when the capital was a raw frontier village. In January 1841, he and his small son were riding double near the outskirts of town when a Comanche war party pursued them. Finally their terrified horse ran under a tree and both riders were knocked off by a low limb. The Indians killed the judge and captured the child. A year later he was ransomed for $60.

(John Holland Jenkins, *Recollections of Early Texas*, 1958; James T. De Shields, *Border Wars of Texas*, 1976; J. W. Wilbarger, *Indian Depradations in Texas*, 1985.)

Smith, John Simpson, (Blackfoot). John S. (Blackfoot) Smith was born at Frankfort, Kentucky, in 1810. In 1826, he fled to the Great Plains to escape from life as a St. Louis tailor's apprentice. He lived with the Blackfeet, then the Sioux, and finally married a Cheyenne girl and settled with her tribe in 1846.

Smith trapped in the Rocky Mountains until William Bent employed him as a trader. On one occasion he and his Cheyenne friends robbed a band of New Mexico traders and, as a result, the governor placed a $500 price on his head. In 1847, he became an interpreter for the Cheyenne agency on the upper Arkansas and, four years later, he accompanied a delegation of chiefs to Washington. In 1858, Smith had a trading establishment on Cherry Creek, Colorado, and at that time he became one of the founders of Denver.

In 1864, Smith accompanied the Cheyenne chief Black Kettle in an unsuccessful attempt to make peace with Colorado Governor John Evans. He was present in Black Kettle's village in November, 1864 (see Sand Creek Massacre), and his half-Cheyenne son was killed by J. M. Chivington's Colorado Volunteers. He accompanied the Cheyennes when they were removed to a reservation in Oklahoma, and he remained with them as interpreter and trader until his death on June 29, 1871.

(Lewis H. Garrard, *Wah-To-Yah and the Taos Trail*, 1955; George Frederick Ruxton, *Life in the Far West*, 1951; Walter O'Meara, *Daughters of the Country*, 1968; David Lavender, *Bent's Fort*, 1954; Frank McNitt, *The Indian Traders*, 1962.)

Smithwick, Noah. Noah Smithwick, a native of North Carolina, settled in Texas in 1827. He fought both Mexicans and Indians as a soldier and Texas Ranger, and he rescued a child from captivity in 1836. In 1837, he was appointed to negotiate peace with the Comanche Indians. He remained with the tribe for some time, gained the confidence of the chiefs, and restored an uneasy peace.

(Walter Prescott Webb, *The Texas Rangers,* 1965.)

Snelling, Fort, Minnesota. Fort Snelling was established on August 24, 1819, at the juncture of the Mississippi and Minnesota rivers on land purchased from the Sioux by Lieutenant Zebulon M. Pike. It was intended as protection against hostile Indians and to encourage settlement of the region. For many years it was the nation's most northerly government post. Both Sioux and Chippewas drew rations at the St. Peters Agency nearby, and the garrison was called upon more often to prevent battles between tribes than to protect settlers from the Indians. The fort was abandoned in 1857 and regarrisoned in time to play an important part in the Minnesota Sioux uprising of 1862. It remained an active post until 1946.

(Charles E. Flandrau, *The History of Minnesota,* 1900, Robert W. Frazer, *Forts of the West,* 1965; Doane Robinson, *A History of the Dakota or Sioux Indians,* 1974.)

Soldier Spring, Battle of. The Battle of Soldier Spring was fought on December 25, 1868, between troops from Fort Bascom, New Mexico, led by Major A. W. Evans, and Arrow Point's band of Comanche Indians. Evans had departed from Bascom on November 17 with six cavalry companies, one infantry company, and a battery of mountain howitzers. His mission was to punish Indians who had murdered settlers in the Spanish Fort, Texas, area.

On Christmas morning, Evans located Arrow Point's village of 60 lodges on the north fork of the Red River near the mouth of Devil's Canyon. He attacked the camp with howitzers, killing Arrow Point and scattering the Comanches. Resistance stiffened for a short time near Soldier Spring, and when the Indians retreated, Evans did not pursue. He destroyed the village and deprived the disheartened Comanche band of its winter food supply.

(W. S. Nye, *Carbine & Lance,* 1969.)

Solomon River, Battle of the. In July 1857, the Southern Cheyennes were assured by their medicine men, Ice and Dark, that white men's bullets could not harm them. After some depredations along the Solomon River in western Kansas by both Indians and whites, Colonel Edwin V. Sumner led six cavalry troops from Fort Leavenworth to restore order. On July 29 he found 300 Cheyenne warriors, confident that they could not be killed, on the Solomon River waiting in a line to offer battle. Sumner ordered his cavalry to charge with drawn sabers, a tactic rarely employed on the plains, and the startled Indians fled for their lives. Mounted on swift horses, most of them escaped, but 9 warriors were slain. Sumner had 11 men wounded, including J. E. B. Stuart of Confederate Cavalry fame. The troopers destroyed the Cheyenne village.

(George Bird Grinnell, *The Fighting Cheyennes*, 1956; Richard H. Dillon, *North American Indian Wars*, 1983.)

Spanish Fort, Texas, Raid. On September 1, 1868, 13 Comanche and Wichita warriors raided Spanish Fort just south of the Red River. They rushed inside a house, ravished and murdered a woman, and killed three of her children.

(W. S. Nye, *Carbine & Lance*, 1969.)

Spirit Lake Massacre. A small settlement on Spirit Lake, Iowa, just below the Minnesota boundary, was attacked by Inkpaduta's outlaw Sioux band during the second week of March 1857. For four days the Indians continued their attacks, killing 32 settlers and capturing 4 women. (See Gardner, Rowland, Family of.) The massacre was instigated by a dispute that arose when an Indian killed a settler's dog that had bitten him. The settler assaulted the warrior, and Inkpaduta retaliated by raiding the settlements all the way to Springfield, Minnesota. The death toll rose to 42 before the Indians fled to the Pipestone Quarry to escape pursuit by troops from Fort Ridgely.

(Charles E. Flandrau, *The History of Minnesota*, 1900; Doane Robinson, *A History of the Dakota or Sioux Indians*, 1974; Abbie Gardner-Sharp, *History of the Spirit Lake Massacre*, 1918.)

Spirit Walker, Wahpeton Sioux Chief. Spirit Walker was born about 1795 at Lac qui Parle, Minnesota. He was friendly to white settlers and missionaries, but he rejected conversion to Christianity. He refused to participate in the Minnesota Sioux uprising of 1862. After the outbreak was quelled, he fled to Dakota, fearing that the army would take out its wrath on Indian friends as well as foes.

(F. W. Hodge, ed., *Handbook of American Indians, II*, 1912; Doane Robinson, *A History of the Dakota or Sioux Indians*, 1974.)

Spotted Elk, Sioux Chief. See Big Foot, Miniconjou Sioux Chief

Spotted Tail, Brulé Sioux Chief. Spotted Tail (Sinta Gleska) was born in South Dakota about 1823. Not a hereditary chief, he rose to prominence as a result of his leadership abilities and skill as a warrior. During his youth he was friendly with the soldiers at Fort Laramie, but he led several raids against the whites in 1863. He was imprisoned at Fort Laramie for murder and, while serving a brief sentence, he learned to read and write.

Spotted Tail signed the Treaty of Fort Laramie in 1868, an act that aroused the enmity of some Indian leaders. One of his enemies, Big Mouth, attacked him in 1869 and was slain in the fight. This fray divided the Brulés into factions, and Spotted Tail's position was weakened by a government policy of destroying the power of the chiefs. In 1881, he was killed by Chief Crow Dog in a dispute over a woman.

"Spotted Tail was a handsome, smiling Indian who loved fine feasts and compliant women. He enjoyed his way of life and the land he lived upon, but was willing to compromise to avoid war."—Dee Brown

(Dee Brown, *Bury My Heart at Wounded Knee*, 1971; Doane Robinson, *A History of the Dakota or Sioux Indians*, 1974; George E. Hyde, *Spotted Tail's Folk*, 1961; Ernest L. Shusky, *The Forgotten Sioux*, 1975; Frederick J. Dockstader, *Great North American Indians*, 1977; Robert M. Utley, *The Last Days of the Sioux Nation*, 1963.)

Spy Knob Raid. Comanche Indians left the reservation at Fort Sill in the spring of 1875 and crossed the Red River to steal horses in Jack County, Texas. They were pursued by Texas Rangers led by Lieutenant Ira Long and overtaken at Spy Knob. All of the Indians, including one woman, were slain.

(W. S. Nye, *Carbine & Lance*, 1969.)

Standing Bear, Ponca Chief. Standing Bear (Mochunozhin) was born about 1829. He became one of the most famous Indian patriots as a result of his campaign to preserve Ponca tribal lands for his people. In 1868, the government determined to include Ponca lands within the Sioux reservation. Warriors raided Ponca villages and, ignoring Standing Bear's protests, the government did nothing to stop them. Finally heeding the voices of white humanitarians, officials agreed in 1876 to protect the Poncas, but instead of restoring their lands to them, they determined to remove the tribe to the Indian Territory.

When Standing Bear refused to leave his homeland on the Niobara River, he was imprisoned until his people, threatened by military action, agreed to go. In January 1879, his son died in Oklahoma and the chief brought his body back to the Niobara for burial. General George Crook, ordered to arrest Standing Bear and his followers, imprisoned them at Fort Omaha. Crook interviewed the chief in the guardhouse and was so impressed by his account of the plight of the Poncas that he consented to act as defendant in a test case. Judge Elmer S. Dundy ruled that "in time of peace no authority, civil or military, existed for transporting Indians from one section of the country to another without the consent of the

Indians or to confine them to any particular reservation against their will."
As a result, Standing Bear was released, but Secretary of the Interior Carl
Schurz prevented the Poncas in Oklahoma from rejoining Standing Bear
and his followers in Nebraska.

In 1880, Standing Bear and Thomas H. Tibbles, a newspaper editor
married to an Omaha Indian (Bright Eyes), made a lecture tour of eastern
cities to describe the mistreatment of Indian tribes. (See La Flesche,
Susette; Tibbles, Thomas H.)

Standing Bear died in 1908 on land allotted to him on the Niobara.
In spite of his eloquent pleas, most of his people remained in Oklahoma.

(Thomas H. Tibbles, *Buckskin and Blanket Days*, 1958; Frederick J. Dockstader,
Great North American Indians, 1977; Flora Warren Seymour, *Indian Agents of the
Old Frontier*, 1975; Muriel H. Wright, *A Guide to the Indian Tribes of Oklahoma*,
1951; Dee Brown, *Bury My Heart at Wounded Knee*, 1971; Francis Paul Prucha,
American Indian Policy in Crisis, 1976.)

Standing Buffalo, Sisseton Sioux Chief. Standing Buffalo was the
principal Sisseton chief during the Minnesota Sioux uprising of 1862.
Although he tried to avoid white settlers by establishing his village at the
northwestern edge of the reservation, he refused to take part in the
massacre that occurred in August, 1862. Many of his men took to the
warpath in spite of his protests, and he promised to try to prevent the
hostiles from fleeing across his territory at the end of the outbreak.

(Doane Robinson, *A History of the Dakota or Sioux Indians*, 1974; C. M. Oehler,
The Great Sioux Uprising, 1959.)

Starving Bear, Cheyenne Chief. See Lean Bear, Cheyenne Chief

Stem, Jesse. Jesse Stem, a native of Ohio, was appointed Special Indian
Agent for Texas by the United States Government in 1850. From his
headquarters at Fort Belknap he served both the woodland and Plains
Indians. As a result of frequent visits to their villages, he gained the respect
of the eastern Indians and some of the Comanches. He resigned in 1853
in order to sell vegetables from his farm to the military at Fort Belknap.
On February 12, 1854, he was murdered and robbed by two Kickapoo
Indians.

> This remarkable man had served as father confessor, peace-
> maker, and reprover . . . often he scolded the warriors for stealing
> horses and sought to persuade them, without too much success,
> to return them to their rightful owners.—Carl Coke Rister

(Carl Coke Rister, *Fort Griffin on the Texas Frontier,* 1956; Mildred P. Mayhall, *Indian Wars of Texas,* 1965.)

Stony Lake, Battle of. On July 28, 1863, General H. H. Sibley defeated the Sioux Indians in a battle at Stony Lake, near the Missouri River in North Dakota. The hostiles, some 1,600 warriors, charged in a long line, trying to envelop the soldiers, but Sibley's men fired with such accuracy that they abandoned the attempt and withdrew to the Missouri.

(Doane Robinson, *A History of the Dakota or Sioux Indians,* 1974; U. S. National Park Service, *Soldier and Brave,* 1963.

Strike the Ree, Yankton Sioux Chief. See Struck-by-the-Ree, Yankton Sioux Chief

Struck-by-the-Ree, Yankton Sioux Chief. Struck-by-the-Ree was born at the present site of Yankton, South Dakota, on August 30, 1804, the day that the Lewis and Clark Expedition arrived at their village. Lewis wrapped the baby in a United States flag and proclaimed him to be an American citizen. He grew up to be a firm friend of white soldiers and settlers. He dissuaded the Yanktons from joining the hostiles during the Minnesota Sioux uprising of 1862 and protected the Dakota settlers from the marauders. He died at the Yankton Agency on July 29, 1888.

"He was an extraordinary man, possessing honesty and excellent judgment, and he adhered to the provisions of their treaty of 1858 with a fidelity which amounted to a religious zeal."—Doane Robinson

(Doane Robinson, *A History of the Dakota or Sioux Indians,* 1974.)

Stumbling Bear, Kiowa Chief. Stumbling Bear was born about 1832. In his youth he was a fierce warrior, fighting enemy Indians and whites. In 1865, he joined such famous raiders as Satanta, Satank, Big Tree, and Big Bow in terrorizing the Texas frontier.

The Treaty of Medicine Lodge of 1867 had little effect on most Kiowa raiders, but it transformed Stumbling Bear into an advocate of peace. In 1872, he visited Washington with a group of chiefs. Six years later the government built a home for him on the reservation. He died there in 1903.

(Frederick J. Dockstader, *Great North American Indians,* 1977; Mildred P. Mayhall, *The Kiowas,* 1962.)

Sullivan, D. C. (Doc). D. C. (Doc) Sullivan assisted John Salmon (Rip) Ford in blazing a trail from San Antonio to El Paso in 1849. The Comanches of western Texas were amused by his antics, decided that he was insane, and permitted him to pass freely among them.

Afterward, Sullivan served in Ford's Texas Ranger Company. On May 12, 1850, they encountered some of the same Comanches in an altercation on the Nueces River. One of the warriors mimicked Sullivan's earlier antics, and the Ranger responded by shooting him to death. Soon afterward Sullivan and a Ranger companion were killed by Comanches on Santa Gertrudis Creek.

(John Salmon Ford, *Rip Ford's Texas*, 1963.)

Sully, Alfred, Sioux Campaigns. After the Minnesota Sioux uprising of 1862, Brigadier General Alfred Sully was assigned to punish the hostiles in the Dakotas. At the head of an army of 2,200 Dakota, Iowa, and Nebraska citizen soldiers, he defeated Inkpaduta's Sioux war party on September 3, 1863, killing 300 braves and capturing 250 women and children. His losses were 22 killed and 50 wounded. (See Whitestone Hill, Battle of.)

Sully wintered near the present site of Pierre, South Dakota. On July 11, 1864, he established Fort Rice, then resumed his invasion of the Indian country. On July 28, he defeated 1,600 Santee and Teton Sioux in North Dakota, killing or wounding about a hundred warriors and burning their village at a cost of 5 dead and 10 wounded. (See Killdeer Mountain, Battle of.) Afterward he marched his men through the Dakota badlands, harrying the Sioux until they were ready to make peace.

(Richard H. Dillon, *North American Indian Wars*, 1983; Doane Robinson, *A History of the Dakota or Sioux Indians*, 1974.)

Sully, Fort, South Dakota. Fort Sully was established below the present site of Pierre, South Dakota, by General Alfred Sully on September 14, 1863. It was intended as a bastion in the Plains Indian wars, and it may have been targeted for a Sioux attack (see Kelly, Fanny), but its most significant role in frontier history was as the site of treaties with the Sioux in 1865. Between October 10 and 28, U. S. commissioners Edward B. Taylor, H. H. Sibley, S. R. Curtis, Henry W. Reed, and Orin Guernsey negotiated peace with the Miniconjou, Brulé, Two-Kettle, Blackfoot, Sans Arc, Hunkpapa, Yanktonai, and Oglala Sioux. An annuity was paid to each tribe. The fort was removed to a new location above Pierre in 1866 and abandoned in 1894.

(Robert W. Frazer, *Forts of the West*, 1965; Charles J. Kappler, ed., *Indian Affairs: Laws and Treaties, II*, 1972.)

Summit Springs, Battle of. During the spring of 1869, the Cheyenne Dog Soldiers, led by Tall Bull, attacked several settlements in western Kansas and eastern Colorado. In retaliation, Major E. A. Carr led five cavalry companies, accompanied by Frank North's Pawnee scouts, to their stronghold at Summit Springs, Colorado. The Cheyennes surrounded Carr's camp on the night of July 10 and made an unsuccessful attempt to drive off their horses.

On the following morning Carr's forces charged Tall Bull's village. In a brief battle they killed 52 Indians, including Tall Bull, and captured 117. Carr had none of his men killed and only one wounded.

(Paul I. Wellman, *Death on Horseback*, 1947; George Bird Grinnell, *The Fighting Cheyennes*, 1956; Ruby E. Wilson, *Frank J. North*, 1984.)

Surveyor's Fight. See Battle Creek Fight, Navarro County, Texas

Sutaio Indians. The Sutaio Indians, an Algonquian people closely related to the Cheyennes, were camped near the Missouri River when first encountered by Europeans. Eventually they were absorbed by the Cheyennes.

(John R. Swanton, *Indian Tribes of North America*, 1952.)

Swift Bird, Teton Sioux Chief. Swift Bird, son of a French trader named Chapelle and a Sioux woman, was born about 1842 in South Dakota. He was reared as an Indian and joined the Fool Soldier band. During the Minnesota Sioux uprising of 1862, he redeemed several white captives from Chief White Lodge's band. He remained a friend of white settlers until his death in 1905.

(F.W. Hodge, ed., *Handbook of American Indians, II*, 1912.)

Sword Bearer, Crow Medicine Man. Sword Bearer was born in 1863. A prominent Crow medicine man, he received his name by always carrying a cavalry sword into battle. His reputation was strengthened substantially when he advanced alone toward American troops who retreated when their cannon failed to fire. After a particularly impressive sun dance in 1887, he taunted troops at the Crow Agency, charged them with his sword, and was shot to death.

(Frederick J. Dockstader, *Great North American Indians*, 1977.)

Tabananica, Comanche Chief. Tabananica (Hears-the-Sunrise), a Yamparica Comanche Chief, was a prominent participant in the Texas Indian wars between 1860 and 1875. During the summer of 1860, Texas Rangers attacked his village, killing several men, women, and children. On May 28, 1870, he led a raid on the agency near Fort Sill, driving off 20 horses and mules and challenging the garrison to come out and fight. In 1872, during a Comanche conference with Captain Henry Alvord, he asserted that he would prefer to remain on the prairie and eat dung then to be penned up on a reservation. Nevertheless, Comanche defeats at Adobe Walls and Palo Duro Canyon in 1874 compelled him to accept life on the reservation. After settling near Fort Sill, he became a successful cattleman.

(W. S. Nye, *Carbine & Lance*, 1969; Mildred P. Mayhall, *Indian Wars of Texas*, 1965.)

Tabeau, Pierre-Antoine. Pierre-Antoine Tabeau, an employee of the prominent French trader, Régis Loisel, made his first trip up the Missouri in 1802. He was living among the Arikaras when visited by Lewis and Clark, and he provided much information to the explorers about the condition of neighboring tribes. Although he and the Arikaras held each other in the greatest contempt, he was protected by Chief Kakawita and therefore made substantial profits in the fur trade. He died in 1820.

(Bernard De Voto, ed., *The Journals of Lewis and Clark*, 1953; Mildred P. Mayhall, *The Kiowas*, 1962; Roy M. Meyer, *Village Indians of the Upper Missouri*, 1977.)

Table Creek, Nebraska, Treaty of. Table Creek, near the site of the present Nebraska City, provided the setting on September 24, 1857, for the government's acquisition of most of the land claimed by the Pawnee Indians. Commissioner J. W. Denver persuaded the Pawnees to part with all of their territory except for a reservation on the Loup Fork of the Platte River. In addition to a promise to protect them from the Sioux, the Pawnees received an annuity of $40,000 for the first five years and $30,000 thereafter. The United States agreed to build forts and to provide black-smiths, cattle, and agricultural implements.

(George E. Hyde, *The Pawnee Indians*, 1974, Ruby E. Wilson, *Frank J. North*, 1984; Charles J. Kappler, ed., *Indian Affairs: Laws and Treaties, II*, 1972.)

Tahan. See Tehan

Taliaferro, Lawrence. Lawrence Taliaferro, a prominent military officer and Indian agent, was born in Virginia on February 28, 1794. He fought in several battles during the War of 1812 and the Indian hostilities that followed. In 1819, he was sent to Fort Snelling by President Monroe to serve as agent to the Indians of Minnesota.

During twenty-one years of service, Taliaferro gained the respect of the Sioux and tried with some success to curtail warfare between that tribe and the Chippewas. Representatives of the American Fur Company and other traders tried to have him removed from office, but his friendship with presidents blocked the attempt. He married a Sioux, and they had a daughter.

In 1837, Taliaferro took a delegation of Santee chiefs to Washington, where they agreed to sell some of their land. He resigned in 1839 and died on January 22, 1871.

(Doane Robinson, *A History of the Dakota or Sioux Indians*, 1974; Flora Warren Seymour, *Indian Agents of the Old Frontier*, 1975.)

Tall Bull, Cheyenne Chief. Tall Bull, one of the more hostile Cheyenne chiefs, was born about 1830. An associate of Roman Nose in battle, he commanded the militant Dog Soldier organization that terrorized travelers along the Platte and Smoky Hill trails during the 1860s. On May 30, 1869, he attacked settlements along the Saline River in western Kansas, killing or wounding 13 people and capturing Mrs. Maria Weichell and Mrs. Susan Allerdice. On July 11, 1869, Major Eugene A. Carr's cavalry and Pawnee Scouts attacked his village, and at the onset Tall Bull murdered Mrs. Allerdice and wounded Mrs. Weichell. Tall Bull was killed by a scout, Frank J. North, or Buffalo Bill Cody, while firing at the troops from a ravine. (See Summit Springs, Battle of.)

(Frederick J. Dockstader, *Great North American Indians*, 1977; Richard H. Dillon, *North American Indian Wars*, 1983; Carl Coke Rister, *Border Captives*, 1940; George Bird Grinnell, *The Fighting Cheyennes*, 1956; Paul I. Wellman, *Death on Horseback*, 1947; Dee Brown, *Bury My Heart at Wounded Knee*, 1971.)

Tamaha, Mdewakanton Sioux Chief. Tamaha (Rising Moose, One-Eyed Sioux) was born at Winona, Minnesota, in 1775. In 1806 he met Zebulon M. Pike's expedition on the upper Mississippi, and he was one of the chiefs that sold the government the land on which Fort Snelling was built. At that time he became a firm friend of the Americans.

At the onset of the War of 1812, Tamaha was one of a few Sioux chiefs to support the United States. He served as a scout and messenger for William Clark, carrying dispatches in the area under British control. In 1814, he helped an American gunboat repel an attack by the British and their Indian allies. Captured by the British partisan Robert Dickson, he refused to divulge information about American troop movements even when threatened with execution. He was imprisoned at Prairie du Chien for a time, and after release he returned to his scouting activities.

In 1816, Tamaha was given a medal of honor, and, in 1819, Clark presented him with a captain's uniform. He died at Wapasha in 1860.

"It is noteworthy that his allegiance to the Americans did not in the least militate from his popularity with the majority of his tribe, who supported the English."—Doane Robinson

(Doane Robinson, *A History of the Dakota or Sioux Indians*, 1974; Hiram Martin Chittenden, *The American Fur Trade of the Far West*, 1954.)

Tatarrax, Pawnee Chief. Tatarrax, a legendary chief who is believed to have lived on the Kansas River, is reported to have met the Coronado Expedition at the head of 200 warriors in 1541. The Turk, their guide, told them that Tatarrax "said his prayers from a book and addressed them to a woman who was queen of heaven." The Spaniards who met him, however, asserted that he was an "old naked wretch with white hair and a copper bangle around his neck."

(Paul Horgan, *Great River, I*, 1954.)

Tatonka Sapa, Minneconjou Sioux Chief. See Black Buffalo, Minneconjou Sioux Chief

Tatum, Lawrie. Lawrie Tatum, one of the bravest and most dedicated United States Indian agents, was a devout member of the Society of Friends. A native of New Jersey, he moved to Ohio in 1844 when he was 22 years old. In 1869, he was appointed agent under Grant's peace policy and assigned to work among the Comanches and Kiowas as a replacement for General William B. Hazen.

Tatum arrived at the agency on July 1, 1869. With the intention of coaxing the Indians to become farmers, he constructed a school and mill near Fort Sill, but few of his charges were interested in abandoning the traditional Plains Indian way of life. True to his convictions, he attempted to administer the agency without military assistance, but in a short time he realized that the Indians scorned the peace policy as a sign of weakness. Afterward, by threatening the use of force and cutting off rations, he secured the release of some hundred captives from Texas and Mexico. (See Diaz, Martina.)

When Tatum's charges continued their raids into Texas, he refused at first to believe that they were guilty. After the raid on Warren's wagon train, he was compelled to change his view, however, for Satanta boasted openly of the deed. As a result he joined General W. T. Sherman in arresting Satanta and other prominent raiders in 1871. (See Satanta; Big

Tree; Warren Wagontrain Raid.) When the Governor of Texas released Satanta from prison, the disillusioned agent resigned in 1873.

(Lawrie Tatum, *Our Red Brothers,* 1970; Flora Warren Seymour, *Indian Agents of the Old Frontier,* 1975; Mildred P. Mayhall, *The Kiowas,* 1962; Benjamin Capps, *The Warren Wagontrain Raid,* 1974; W.S. Nye, *Carbine & Lance,* 1969; Carl Coke Rister, *Border Captives,* 1940.)

Tecumseh, Fort, South Dakota. Fort Tecumseh was established by the Columbia Fur Company in 1822 on the Missouri River near the site of the present city of Pierre, South Dakota. Five years later it was purchased by the American Fur Company. After Fort Union, it was for a decade the most important trading post on the Missouri. Undermined by the river, it was replaced by Fort Pierre in 1832.

(Hiram Martin Chittenden, *The American Fur Trade of the Far West,* 1954.)

Tehan, Captivity of. Tehan, a red-haired Texas boy, was captured by Kiowa Indians about 1856. He was so young that he could not recall his name. In 1873, he went on his first raid with the fearsome warrior, Big Bow. In September 1874, he was captured by Major Frank D. Baldwin's cavalry troop. The Kiowas made several unsuccessful attempts to recapture the youth that day, and during the night he escaped and rejoined them. Afterward he went on several raids with Zakoyea's Kiowa band. When that chief decided to surrender, he feared that Tehan would tell the soldiers about their depredations. It is frontier tradition that the chief silenced him by shooting him through the heart, but Zakoyea asserted that the white youth died of thirst and heat on the Staked Plains.

(Hugh D. Corwin, *Comanche & Kiowa Captives in Oklahoma and Texas,* 1959; W. S. Nye, *Carbine & Lance,* 1969.)

Ten Bears, Comanche Chief. Ten Bears (Par-roowah Sermehno), a Yamparica Comanche chief, was born about 1792. An eloquent speaker, he was more effective as a negotiator than a warrior. He represented the tribe at several peace conferences and visited Washington in 1863. During the Medicine Lodge Treaty negotiations of 1867, he characterized himself as a man of peace but conceded that he prized his memories of wars with the Texans:

> They made sorrow in our camps, and we went out like the buffalo bulls when the cows are attacked. When we found them we killed them, and their scalps hang in our lodges. The Comanches are not weak and blind. . . . They are strong and far-sighted, like grown horses. We took their road and we went on it. The white women cried and our women laughed.

Ten Bears agreed to camp on the reservation, but he hated that kind of life. He died at Fort Sill in 1873.

(Frederick J. Dockstader, *Great North American Indians*, 1977; T. R. Fehrenbach, *Comanches*, 1983; Ernest Wallace and E. Adamson Hoebel, *The Comanches*, 1952.)

Teton Indian Tribes. The Teton Sioux, largest Dakota division, comprised the bands that ranged west of the Missouri before they were joined by the eastern Sioux in 1862. A very warlike people, they were encountered by French explorers by 1680. They were visited by Lewis and Clark in 1805, and they signed their first peace treaty with the United States in 1815.

Wars with the Tetons began in 1854. (See Grattan, John L.) In 1865, they negotiated peace treaties, and in 1868 they agreed to live on reservations, but Sitting Bull and Crazy Horse aroused them to desperate resistance in 1876. (See Little Bighorn; Powder River; Slim Buttes). In the final conflict their spirits were crushed by the massacre at Wounded Knee in 1890.

"The highest values of the Tetons centered on war."—Robert M. Utley (see Oglala; Brulé; Miniconjou; Hunkpapa; Oohenopa; Sihasapa Sioux).

(Doane Robinson, *A History of the Dakota or Sioux Indians*, 1974; Robert M. Utley, *The Last Days of the Sioux Nation*, 1963.)

Teton River, Treaties of, 1825. On July 5 and 6, 1825, Henry Atkinson and Benjamin O'Fallon negotiated treaties with the Teton Sioux and Cheyenne Indians at the mouth of the Teton River. Government protection was promised to the Indians, licensed traders were offered, and the tribes agreed to refuse to trade with citizens of other nations.

(Charles J. Kappler, ed., *Indian Affairs: Laws and Treaties, II*, 1972.)

Texas Rangers. Although there were forces called rangers in Texas as early as 1823, the designation did not achieve legal status until 1835, when a corps was established to guard the Indian frontier. During the period of the Republic, under the leadership of John Coffee Hays, the Rangers played crucial roles in conflicts with the Comanches, particularly at the Battle of Plum Creek in 1840. During the Civil War, the Rangers represented the best hope of survival for citizens in northwestern Texas. In 1874, during the Red River War, the Frontier Battalion (six Ranger companies) guarded the frontier against Comanche and Kiowa raids. The Indian wars ended soon afterward.

(Walter Prescott Webb, *The Texas Rangers,* 1965; John Salmon Ford, *Rip Ford's Texas,* 1963; D. E. Kilgore, *A Ranger Legacy,* 1973; T. R. Fehrenbach, *Comanches,* 1983.)

Tibbles, Thomas Henry. Thomas Henry Tibbles, a newspaper reporter and freelance writer, was born in Ohio on May 22, 1840. In 1856, he lived with the Omaha Indians and fought beside them in battles with the Sioux. He was a Union soldier during the Civil War and a circuit-riding preacher from 1871 until 1877. In 1879, at the suggestion of General George Crook, he used his newspaper column to champion the rights of the Ponca Indians in their land disputes with the government and the Sioux. (See Standing Bear, Ponca Chief.) In 1882, he married Susette La Flesche (Bright Eyes) of the Omaha tribe and they toured the eastern United States and England, lecturing on Indian rights. He served as newspaper correspondent during the Ghost Dance excitement, and he witnessed the Wounded Knee Massacre in 1890. He died on May 14, 1928.

(Thomas Henry Tibbles, *Buckskin and Blanket Days,* 1958; Francis Paul Prucha, *American Indian Policy in Crisis,* 1976.)

Tohaha Indians. The Tohaha Indians, a Tonkawan tribe or band, lived along the Colorado River in Texas. They were visited by Spanish and French explorers as early as 1683, but they disappeared from notice about 1721.

(F. W. Hodge, ed., *Handbook of American Indians, II,* 1912.)

Tomassa, Captivity of. Tomassa was born in Mexico about 1841 and captured by Comanche Indians at an early age. Adopted by an Indian family, she was well treated and content until ransomed by the Mexican government and given as a servant to a wealthy family. Longing for her Indian adoptive parents, she recruited a small boy (also a redeemed captive) to run away from the hacienda. They appropriated a horse and rode toward the Rio Grande, finally killing and eating him to avoid starvation.

Tomassa and her companion found their Comanche families north of the Red River and joyfully resumed their lives as Indians. When she grew to womanhood, she married a white trader, Joseph Chandler, and they had four children. After Chandler's death she married George Conover and bore him three children. She adopted the ways of the whites and warned them frequently of impending raids. On one occasion she saved two captives by hiding them under the floor of her house. She died on December 6, 1900.

(Lawrie Tatum, *Our Red Brothers*, 1899; Thomas C. Battey, *The Life and Adventures of a Quaker Among the Indians*, 1875; J. Norman Heard, *White Into Red*, 1973.)

Tomlinson, John James. See Tumlinson, John James

Tongue River, Battle of, 1865. During the Powder River Expedition of 1865, General Patrick E. Connor's Pawnee scouts located Black Bear's Arapaho and Cheyenne camp on the Tongue River. On August 29, Connor launched a surprise attack with 400 men and 2 cannon. After their initial fright, the Arapahoes rallied in nearby timber, but in the face of cannon they were forced to withdraw. The soldiers destroyed the village (more than 200 lodges), and the Pawnee Scouts captured the horse herd.

(George Bird Grinnell, *The Fighting Cheyennes*, 1956; Virginia Cole Trenholm, *The Arapahoes, Our People*, 1970.).

Tonkawa Indians. Located in central Texas, the Tonkawan tribes constituted a distinct linguistic stock. Between 1746 and 1756, they lived near the Spanish missions on the San Gabriel River. In 1758, because of their hatred of the Apaches, they helped to destroy the San Sabá mission. After the Texas Revolution they provided scouts for military expeditions against the Comanches. In 1859, they were removed to Anadarko, Oklahoma. There, in 1862, most of them were massacred by Caddo, Delaware, and Shawnee Indians, who accused them of being cannibals and Confederate sympathizers. The survivors fled to Fort Griffin, Texas, for protection. In 1884, they received a new reservation in northern Oklahoma, where their descendants still live. (See Johnson, Big Nose.)

(*Handbook of Texas, II*, 1952; Mildred P. Mayhall, *Indian Wars of Texas*, 1965; T. R. Fehrenbach, *Comanches*, 1983; W. W. Newcomb, Jr., *The Indians of Texas*, 1961.).

Traverse des Sioux, Treaty of, 1851. The Treaty of Traverse des Sioux was negotiated by U. S. commissioners Luke Lea and Alexander Ramsey with the Sisseton and Wahpeton Sioux Indians on July 23, 1851. The Indians ceded a vast territory in Iowa and Minnesota, retaining only an area ten miles wide on each side of the Minnesota River. They received a promise of payment of $1,665,000 over a fifty-year period. Amendments were made in the Senate, and the agreement was finalized on February 24, 1854.

(Charles E. Flandrau, *The History of Minnesota*, 1900; Doane Robinson, *A History of the Dakota or Sioux Indians*, 1974.)

Truteau, Jean Baptiste. Jean Baptiste Truteau (Trudeau) was appointed by a Spanish company at St. Louis to develop the fur trade on the Missouri and to seek a pathway to the Pacific. He led ten men up the Missouri in 1794, but he was robbed by the Sioux and forced to spend the winter with the Poncas. He tried again to ascend the Missouri in 1795, with similar results, and finally he returned to St. Louis in 1796.

"Truteau . . . was a schoolmaster, and perhaps a good one; but he was totally unfitted to command an expedition to deal with Indians."—W. J. Ghent

(W. J. Ghent, *The Early Far West*, 1936.)

Tsatangya, Kiowa Chief. See Satanta, Kiowa Chief

Tumlinson, John James, Family of. John James Tumlinson (Tomlinson), a native of Tennessee, arrived in Texas in 1821 and he and his three sons became prominent fighters against Indians and Mexicans. He fought in the Battle of San Jacinto in 1836 and the Battle of Victoria in 1840. His father, John Tumlinson, Sr., and his brother Andrew were killed by Indians. His brother Joe was severely wounded by Lipans in 1848. His brother Peter killed four warriors in a fight with the Lipans in 1855.

(D. E. Kilgore, *A Ranger Legacy*, 1973.)

Turk, Pawnee Guide. Called the Turk by members of the Coronado Expedition of 1540-1542, this Indian, believed to have been a Pawnee, was a prisoner of the Pecos Pueblo Indians when he convinced the Spanish officers that he could lead them to the golden land of Quivira. He served as their guide, but they strangled him when Quivira contained no gold.

(Paul Horgan, *Great River, I*, 1954.)

Turkey Leg, Cheyenne Chief. In August 1867, Turkey Leg tore up the Union Pacific Railway tracks. A wreck resulted, and he and his warriors plundered the train. (See Union Pacific Railway Wreck.)

(George Bird Grinnell, *The Fighting Cheyennes*, 1956.)

Turner, Jeff, Family of. Jeff Turner, a native of Kentucky, brought his wife and three children to Texas before 1836, settling near the Guadalupe River. Indians murdered his family during his absence, and he devoted the rest of his life to revenge. He is said to have collected 46 Comanche scalps.

(John C. Duval, *The Adventures of Big Foot Wallace*, 1870.)

Two-Kettle Sioux. See Oohenonpa Sioux

Two Moon, Cheyenne Chiefs. There were two fierce Cheyenne chiefs named Two Moon, the elder being the uncle of the younger. Both were active in battles with the whites, and it is difficult in some instances to identify the participant. In 1866, the elder Two Moon led the Cheyenne contingent in attacks near Fort Kearny. His nephew, known to have played an important part in the Battle of the Little Bighorn in 1876, surrendered to General Nelson Miles soon afterward and became a scout for the United States Cavalry. Two Moon the younger visited Washington several times before his death in 1917.

(Frederick J. Dockstader, *Great North American Indians*, 1977; George Bird Grinnell, *The Fighting Cheyennes*, 1956.)

Two Strike, Brulé Sioux Chief. Two Strike (Nomkahpa) was born in Nebraska about 1832. He led several raids against the whites, and he was a leader of the Ghost Dancers. In December 1890, however, he decided to avoid war and led his band to the Pine Ridge Reservation before the Wounded Knee massacre. After the massacre they fled the reservation but returned to surrender on January 15, 1891. On one occasion he visited Washington to plead for better living conditions for his people. He died about 1915.

(Frederick J. Dockstader, *Great North American Indians*, 1977; Robert M. Utley, *The Last Days of the Sioux Nation*, 1963.)

Twostars, Solomon, Sisseton Sioux Chief. Solomon Twostars, hereditary chief of the Sisseton Sioux, was born at Lac qui Parle in 1827. He was converted to Christianity by S. R. Riggs and Thomas Williamson at an early age and remained friendly to the white settlers of Minnesota. He attempted to prevent his people from participating in the Minnesota Sioux uprising of 1862, serving during that conflict as an army scout. In 1865, while scouting for General Sully, he led an attack on the hostile Sioux, killing 15 warriors including his own son.

(Doane Robinson, *A History of the Dakota or Sioux Indians*, 1974; F. W. Hodge, ed., *Handbook of American Indians, II*, 1912.)

-U-

Union, Fort, North Dakota. Fort Union was established on the Missouri River three miles north of the Yellowstone by the American Fur Company in 1828. The best-built fort in the northwest, it reaped enormous profits from the fur trade with the tribes of North Dakota, Montana, and Wyoming. In 1837, however, smallpox was spread to the tribes when Indians ignored warnings to keep away from the fort. About 15,000 people died from the disease. In 1864, General Alfred Sully occupied the fort. It was abandoned in 1865.

(Hiram Martin Chittenden, *The American Fur Trade of the Far West*, 1954; Robert W. Frazer, *Forts of the West*, 1965; George Catlin, *Letters and Notes on the Manners, Customs and Conditions of the North American Indians*, 1973.)

Union Fur Company. The Union Fur Company was active in the Missouri River Indian trade from 1841 to 1845. It profited for a time, but went out of business largely because the owners could not control the actions of company traders, many of whom were outlaws who would go to any length to defeat the opposition.

(Hiram Martin Chittenden, *The American Fur Trade of the Far West*, 1954.)

Union Pacific Railway Wreck. During the summer of 1867 the Northern Cheyenne chief, Turkey Leg, learned how to derail a train by bending the rails. A freight train was wrecked and plundered and every man on board was killed.

(George Bird Grinnell, *The Fighting Cheyennes*, 1956; Paul I. Wellman, *Death on Horseback*, 1947.)

Vanderburgh, Henry. Henry Vanderburgh, a leader among fur traders, was born at Vincennes, Indiana, about 1798. He entered West Point in 1813 but decided to become a trader instead of a military officer. Joining the Missouri Fur Company, he served as a captain in Leavenworth's battle with the Arikara Indians in 1823. After leaving the company he joined its competitor, the American Fur Company, as director of the Rocky Mountain division. In 1832, he was killed by the Blackfoot Indians near the Three Forks of the Missouri.

(Hiram Martin Chittenden, *The American Fur Trade of the Far West*, 1954; David Lavender, *Bent's Fort*, 1954.)

Van Dorn, Earl. Born at Port Gibson, Mississippi, on September 17, 1820, Earl Van Dorn graduated from West Point in 1842. He served with distinction in the Mexican War and the Seminole hostilities. In 1855, appointed captain of the Second Cavalry, he fought Indians in Texas and Oklahoma until the Civil War. He defeated the Comanches at Rush Springs, Oklahoma, on October 1, 1858, but was severely wounded in the stomach by an arrow. Not expected to live, he recovered so quickly that he was back on duty in just over a month. On May 13, 1859, he attacked a Comanche war party at Crooked Creek, killing 49 warriors and capturing 32 women. (See Nescutunga, Battle of.)

Van Dorn resigned from the U. S. Army in 1861 and served as major general of Confederate forces. Leading an army of untrained whites and wild Indians, he was defeated at the Battle of Pea Ridge in March, 1862. On May 8, 1863, he was murdered by a personal enemy.

(Richard H. Dillon, *North American Indian Wars*, 1983; W. S. Nye, *Carbine & Lance*, 1969.)

Vaughan, Alfred J. Major Alfred J. Vaughan, married to an Indian woman, was agent to the Upper Missouri tribes for fifteen years before being appointed to a similar post among the Blackfeet in 1857. He established successful farms in 1860, but because he was from Virginia he was replaced at the onset of the Civil War.

"It was a long time before the Blackfoot Indians received another 'father' who was as sincere, able, and experienced as Major Vaughan." —John C. Ewers

(John C. Ewers. *The Blackfeet*, 1961.)

Villasur, Pedro de, Expedition. Spanish officials in New Mexico, disturbed by French advances on the Great Plains, sent an expedition led by

Lieutenant Colonel Pedro de Villasur to establish relations with the Pawnees. At the head of 40 Spanish soldiers and 70 Pueblo Indians, he left Santa Fe in June, 1720. He recruited Apache Indian guides, and they led him to the Skidi Pawnees on the Loup Fork of the Platte. On the morning of August 13, the Skidis, assisted by French agents, attacked Villasur's forces while they slept, slaying 36 soldiers and 10 Pueblos. Villasur was among the dead. The survivors fled back to New Mexico.

(George E. Hyde, *The Pawnee Indians*, 1974; *Indians of the High Plains*, 1959.)

Von Claren, Oscar. Oscar Von Claren, a naturalist, was born in Germany in 1812. He emigrated to New Braunfels, Texas, in 1845. He had been there only a few months when he was killed by Indians while collecting snakes and turtles to send to German museums.

(*Handbook of Texas, II*, 1952.)

Wabasha, Sioux Chief. See Wapasha, Sioux Chief

Wagon Box Fight. The Wagon Box Fight occurred on August 2, 1867, when the Sioux chief Red Cloud attacked a detachment of 26 infantrymen guarding a civilian woodcutting detail near Fort Phil Kearny. The soldiers, led by Captain James Powell, were armed with recently developed rapid-fire rifles, an innovation that was as yet unknown to the Indians. Four of the civilians joined in the fight while the others fled to the fort.

The woodcutters' wagons were sturdy enough to provide protection against arrows, and few of the warriors had rifles. Powell, at the first sign of Indians, assembled the wagon beds to form a corral. Four men were slain before reaching the improvised fortress, but the others took refuge inside, all expecting to die but determined to sell their lives as dearly as possible.

Swarming out of the timber, hundreds of warriors charged the wagon boxes in an attempt to overwhelm the little force when the soldiers paused to reload. But the initial attack was thrown back with heavy losses when the repeaters kept firing. Consternation reigned briefly among the Sioux, but Red Cloud was determined to drive the army from Wyoming and the warriors charged five more times, racing in a circle around the corral and studding the wagons with bullets and arrows. Their losses mounted dramatically with each charge, and finally they withdrew when a relief party with wagon guns came into view.

(Paul I. Wellman, *Death on Horseback*, 1947; J. P. Dunn, Jr., *Massacres of the Mountains*, 1958.)

Wahpekute Sioux Indians. The Wahpekute Indians were living near Mille Lacs, Minnesota, when visited by French explorers about 1678. By 1804, when seen by Lewis and Clark, they were located along the Minnesota River. About 1850 they formed two bands, one of them moving to the Vermillion River of South Dakota. A party of those who remained in the east were perpetrators of the Spirit Lake massacre of 1857. (See Inkpaduta.) The Wahpekutes now reside on the Santee Reservation in Nebraska.

(F.W. Hodge, ed., *Handbook of American Indians, II*, 1912.)

Wahpeton Sioux Indians. The Wahpeton Indians, a primary Dakota division, were located near Mille Lacs, Minnesota, in 1680. By 1804, when visited by Lewis and Clark, they were near the mouth of the Minnesota River. They gradually moved up the Minnesota and established a large village near Lac qui Parle. Christian missionaries were among them by 1835. After the Indian wars they were assigned to the Sisseton Reservation.

(F. W. Hodge, ed., *Handbook of American Indians, II*, 1912.)

Walker, Samuel Hamilton. Samuel H. Walker fought in the Indian wars in Georgia and Florida before coming to Texas in 1836. He served in the Texas Rangers under John Coffee Hays, becoming a famous fighting man during the period of the Republic of Texas. In 1839, while in New York purchasing arms from Samuel Colt, he suggested a pistol modification that proved so successful that the Rangers were able to fight Indians without dismounting. He was killed while leading a charge during the Mexican War.

(Walter Prescott Webb, *The Texas Rangers*, 1965.)

Wallace, Fort, Kansas. Fort Wallace was established in September 1865, on the south fork of the Smoky Hill River near the present town of Wallace, Kansas. In 1867, the fort was attacked by Roman Nose's Cheyenne band, but the Indians were repulsed with the loss of several warriors. Men from the fort pursued Roman Nose in September 1868, and killed him during the Battle of Beecher's Island. The fort was abandoned in 1882.

(Robert W. Frazer, *Forts of the West*, 1965; U. S. National Park Service, *Soldier and Brave*, 1963.)

Wallace, William A. A. (Bigfoot). William (Bigfoot) Wallace was born in Lexington, Virginia, on April 3, 1817, and moved to Texas in 1836. He joined the Texas Rangers and fought Indians and Mexicans for many years. As a captain he fought in the Mexican War, and he protected the frontier settlements during the Civil War. At one time he was captured by Comanches and was about to be burned at the stake when an old woman adopted him to replace her lost son. He escaped a few months later. On another occasion he killed a Comanche warrior in hand-to-hand combat.

"Though often attacked by Indians, he managed to live until 1899 and to die a natural death."—Walter Prescott Webb

(Walter Prescott Webb, *The Texas Rangers*, 1965; John C. Duval, *The Adventures of Big-Foot Wallace*, 1870.)

Wamdisapa's Band. Wamdisapa (Black Eagle) was chief of the Wahpekute Sioux from 1842 until 1851. A very warlike chief, he frequently fought with the Sacs and Foxes, and his band was regarded as a gang of outlaws by many Indians as well as whites. After his death his son, Inkpaduta, became chief. His band was responsible for the Spirit Lake massacre in 1857.

(Doane Robinson, *A History of the Dakota or Sioux Indians*, 1974.)

Wamditanka, Mdewakanton Sioux Chief. Wamditanka (Big Eagle) was born near the present town of Mendota, Minnesota, in 1827. A noted raider against enemy Indians, he became chief of his band at an early age. He was not friendly toward white settlers, but he believed it expedient to maintain peaceful relations with them.

At the onset of the Sioux uprising of 1862, Big Eagle advocated peace, but he agreed to lead his young braves who insisted upon war. He refrained from attacking unarmed settlers, but he fought soldiers at Fort Ridgely, New Ulm, and Birch Coulee. Afterward he urged seeking an end to hostilities.

Big Eagle was tried as a prisoner of war rather than a murderer, and he served three years in prison while warriors convicted of atrocities were executed. After his release he became a Christian, adopted the name Jerome, and lived forty years on a farm near Granite Falls, Minnesota.

(C. M. Oehler, *The Great Sioux Uprising*, 1959; F. W. Hodge, ed., *Handbook of American Indians, II*, 1912.)

Waneta, Yanktonai Sioux Chief. Waneta, generally considered to be the most powerful Sioux chief on the upper Missouri during the first half of the nineteenth century, was born about 1795 in South Dakota. In 1813, he joined the British in their war with the Americans and served with distinction in the attacks on Forts Meigs and Stephenson. "He killed seven men in battle and received nine wounds," Doane Robinson asserted. "His intrepidy won for him the admiration of whites and Indians alike, and he gained the reputation of being the most powerful Indian upon the continent."

After the War of 1812, Waneta was awarded the salary of a captain in the British Army. Such was his reputation for valor that he was escorted to England and received by the king. In 1820, he participated in a scheme to seize Fort Snelling. The plot failed and he was arrested. During his imprisonment he was impressed by evidence of American power, and thereafter he modified his hostile attitude. In 1825, he signed the treaties of Fort Pierre and Prairie du Chien that delineated the bounds of tribal territory. He died in 1848 at Standing Rock.

(Doane Robinson, *A History of the Dakota or Sioux Indians*, 1974; Frederick J. Dockstader, *Great North American Indians*, 1977.)

Wapasha, Mdewakanton Sioux Chiefs. Wapasha (Wabasha, Red Leaf) was the name of a hereditary line of Sioux chiefs for more than a century. The first Wapasha recorded in history was born about 1718 in Minnesota. Some forty years later he went to Quebec to offer his life in reparation for the murder of a trader by one of his people. This event made a powerful impression upon English authorities, and they treated him so well that he fought on their side during the American Revolution. He died in 1806.

The second Wapasha to leave his name on the written record was born about 1799. He was more important as a civil chief than a war leader, but he supported the British during the War of 1812. After that conflict he became a friend to American settlers. He died about 1836.

The third Wapasha was born about 1825 and became principal chief at an early age. He strongly opposed the Minnesota Sioux uprising of 1862, but he led his warriors in several battles when they insisted upon joining the hostiles. He protected the lives of white captives and turned them over to General Sibley at the first opportunity. After the defeat of the Sioux he was placed on the Niobara Reservation, where he died on April 23, 1876.

(Frederick J. Dockstader, *Great North American Indians,* 1977; Doane Robinson, *A History of the Dakota or Sioux Indians,* 1974; C. M. Oehler, *The Great Sioux Uprising,* 1959.)

War Bonnet Creek. See Warbonnet Creek

War Eagle, Santee Sioux Chief. War Eagle was born about 1785. He became a friend of the whites at an early age and served them as a scout on exploring and military expeditions. During the War of 1812 he fought on the American side and persuaded many of his people to follow his example. Afterward he served as a guide for the American Fur Company. In 1837, while visiting Washington he participated in the Sioux cession of lands located east of the Mississippi. He died in 1851.

(Frederick J. Dockstader, *Great North American Indians,* 1977.)

Warbonnet Creek Fight. The Warbonnet Creek fight occurred on July 17, 1876, when Colonel Wesley Merritt and a Fifth Cavalry detachment attacked 800 Cheyennes on Warbonnet Creek, Nebraska. The hostiles were on their way to join the Sioux who had defeated Custer, but Merritt trapped them by hiding most of his soldiers in wagons that appeared to be without escort. The warriors charged the wagons but fled back to their reservation when they discovered their mistake. One Indian was killed. (See Yellow Hand.)

(Richard H. Dillon, *North American Indian Wars,* 1983; John F. Finerty, *War-Path and Bivouac,* 1961.)

Warren Wagon Train Raid. The Warren Wagon train raid, one of the fiercest fights in western Texas history, occurred on May 18, 1871, when a hundred Kiowa and Comanche braves led by Satanta and Mamanti charged a train of ten wagons owned by the government contractor, Henry Warren. Hearing a blast of Satanta's bugle, wagonmaster Nathan S. Long saw a line of warriors emerging from the shadow of Cox Mountain. He circled the wagons with the mules in the center and resolved to fight to the death.

While attempting to erect a barricade of grain sacks, Long and four of his teamsters were slain. The others defended themselves from inside the wagons, and one of them, Samuel Elliott, shot away a portion of an Indian's jaw. Then, as the Indians drew back temporarily, seven teamsters fled toward the woods. Two of them were killed, but five survivors eventually reached safety at Fort Richardson. Elliott, too severely wounded to run, was pulled from his wagon, chained to its wheel, and set on fire. When he screamed in agony, Gun-Shot, the wounded warrior, cut out his tongue, and he strangled on his own blood.

General William T. Sherman, camped at Fort Richardson, sent Colonel Ranald Mackenzie in pursuit of the hostiles, but they escaped into a pounding rainstorm. Later, several of the leaders were arrested at Fort Sill. (See Sherman, William Tecumseh; Satanta; Setangya; Big Tree; Tatum, Lawrie.)

(Benjamin Capps, *The Warren Wagontrain Raid*, 1974; W. S. Nye, *Carbine & Lance*, 1969; Mildred P. Mayhall, *The Kiowas*, 1962; T. R. Fehrenbach, *Comanches*, 1983; J. W. Wilbarger, *Indian Depradations in Texas*, 1985.)

Washington D. C., Treaties of. More than a dozen treaties were negotiated at the nation's capital with Plains Indians between 1824 and 1867, most of them Siouan-speaking tribes. Chief negotiators were George W. Manypenny and Charles E. Mix.

(Charles J. Kappler, ed., *Indian Affairs: Laws and Treaties, II*, 1972; Doane Robinson, *A History of the Dakota or Sioux Indians*, 1974.)

Washita, Battle of the. The Battle of the Washita, George Armstrong Custer's most important victory over Plains Indians, was fought on November 27, 1868, near the present community of Cheyenne, Oklahoma. Custer led the Seventh Cavalry southward from Fort Larned to the Washita River, near the Oklahoma-Texas boundary, during a blizzard and located the camp of the Cheyenne chief Black Kettle (some 200 warriors). Apparently he was unaware of some 2,000 warriors—Arapahoes, Kiowas, and Comanches—camped nearby. His attack caught the Cheyennes completely by surprise, and he captured the village before the other tribes could come to their assistance.

Custer, in his official report, described the action as follows:

The men charged and reached the lodges before the Indians were aware of their presence. The moment the advance was ordered the band struck up "Garryowen" . . . The Indians were caught napping for once. The warriors rushed from their lodges and posted themselves behind trees and in deep ravines, from which they began a most determined resistance. Within ten minutes after the charge the lodges and all their contents were in our possession, but the real fighting, such as had been rarely, if ever, equalled in Indian warfare, began when attempting to drive out or kill the warriors posted in ravines or ambush. Charge after charge was made, and most gallantly too, but the Indians had resolved to sell their lives as deadly as possible. The conflict ended after some hours, the entire village—fifty-one lodges in all, under command of their principal chief, Black Kettle—were conquered.

While Custer gained a major victory, depriving the Cheyennes of their horses and winter rations and killing their leader, Black Kettle, his detractors have found much to condemn in his actions during the battle and especially in his decision to withdraw without making a more determined attempt to locate a missing platoon. (See Elliott, Joel H.) It has been charged that of the 103 dead Cheyennes found in the village, most were women and children.

Veterans of that campaign like to refer to "the glory of the Washita." Peering past that phrase one finds little glory there for any white man, even for George Armstrong Custer, whose fame as an Indian fighter grew from that blind and vengeful massacre so strangely stained with callousness or a cowardice stranger still.—Frederic F. Van de Water

But Richard H. Dillon has pointed out the skill with which Custer extricated his men when hundreds of warriors from nearby villages rushed to the scene. He lacked sufficient men and ammunition to fight such a force, and he brought his men safely out of a trap.

(Frederic F. Van de Water, *Glory Hunter,* 1963; Richard H. Dillon, *North American Indian Wars,* 1983; George Bird Grinnell, *The Fighting Cheyennes,* 1956; Stan Hoig, *The Battle of the Washita,* 1976; De B. Randolph Keim, *Sheridan's Troopers on the Borders,* 1985; Paul I. Wellman, *Death on Horseback,* 1947; Elizabeth B. Custer, *Following the Guidon,* 1966.)

Washita River, Council of the. In 1865, Jefferson Davis hoped to persuade the Plains Indians to cease their attacks on southern frontier communities. He sent Tukabatche Miko, a Creek chief, as an envoy to invite the tribes to a council on the Washita River. On May 1, approximately 20,000 Indians attended. The southern plains tribes and the Confederate government, unaware of Appomattox, agreed to establish peaceful relations.

(John Tebbel and Keith Jennison, *The American Indian Wars*, 1960.)

Watts, H. O., Family of. Major H. O. Watts was collector of customs at the port of Linnville, Texas, at the time of the Comanche raid of 1840. (See Linnville, Texas, Raid.) While most of the citizens escaped on boats into the bay, Watts remained at his post and was shot to death. His young bride was carried into captivity. When a force of Texans overtook the Comanches (see Plum Creek, Battle of), her captor attempted to kill her, leaving her for dead with an arrow firmly lodged in her breast. Two men cut around the shaft and extricated the arrowhead with great difficulty, and she survived the ordeal.

(A. J. Sowell, *Rangers and Pioneers of Texas*, 1964; James T. De Shields, *Border Wars of Texas*, 1976.)

Webster, James, Family of. James Webster, a Virginian, brought his family to Texas in 1839. With a twelve-man escort they set out across the prairie toward their home in the present Williamson County, but they were attacked by Comanche Indians on the San Gabriel River. Forming their wagons into a circle, the Texans fought the Indians until the last white man was killed. Mrs. Webster and her small daughter, Virginia, were captured and held for more than a year. They escaped in March 1840, when the Comanches camped near San Antonio.

(James T. De Shields, *Border Wars of Texas*, 1976.)

West Lake, Minnesota, Massacre. West Lake, Minnesota, a small community of Scandinavian settlers, was attacked by a Sioux war party on August 20, 1862. Twenty-two people were slain.

(C. M. Oehler, *The Great Sioux Uprising*, 1959.)

Whipple, Henry B. Henry B. Whipple was born at Adams, New York, on February 15, 1822. He became an Episcopal priest in 1850 and was appointed Bishop of Minnesota in 1859. From his headquarters at Faribault he visited Indian villages and developed strong friendships with several Sioux and Chippewa chiefs.

Whipple became convinced that government Indian policy was unjust and that agents among the Sioux were corrupt. Consequently, he wrote to congressmen, bureau administrators, and even to the president, urging reform. He predicted that the Sioux would attack agency employees unless conditions improved, and his warnings were remembered during the uprising of 1862 in which 800 white settlers were slain. (See Minnesota Sioux Uprising.)

After the defeat of the Sioux, 307 warriors were condemned to death for murder. Whipple appealed to President Lincoln to spare their lives, asserting that corruption at the agencies caused the uprising. After studying the trial transcripts, Lincoln spared all except 38. President Grant's peace policy with the Indians was based in large part upon Whipple's recommendations.

As the Sioux were removed from Minnesota, Whipple's last years were devoted to helping the Chippewas. He was still exposing government fraud among them in 1898 when the last Indian battle in American history was fought at Leech Lake. He died in 1901.

(H. B. Whipple, *Lights and Shadows of a Long Episcopate*, 1900; Francis Paul Prucha, *American Indian Policy in Crisis*, 1976.)

White Antelope, Cheyenne Chief. White Antelope, a fierce warrior against Indian enemies, was among the peace chiefs who consistently befriended the whites. In 1851, after signing the Treaty of Fort Laramie, he accompanied government negotiators to Washington. Afterward he did his best to promote peace, finally giving his life in the attempt during the Sand Creek massacre on November 29, 1864.

> He died, in fact, walking toward the soldiers of Colonel John M. Chivington's command without a weapon, bullets flying around him, to tell the troops that the Cheyenne camp was peaceful. Thus dying, when he could have been escaping to save his own life, White Antelope was a martyr to the cause of peace.—Stan Hoig

(Stan Hoig, *The Peace Chiefs of the Cheyennes*, 1980; David Lavender, *Bent's Fort*, 1954.)

White Eagle, Ponca Chief. White Eagle, one of the most important Ponca chiefs, was born on the tribe's Nebraska reservation in 1840. Enjoying the confidence of both Indians and whites, he successfully removed his tribe to the Indian Territory in 1877, and he attempted to lead his people to accept the best elements of the white man's civilization. He supported schools and opposed the liquor trade. He died in 1914.

(Charles Leroy Zimmerman, *White Eagle*, 1941.)

White Hair, Osage Chief. White Hair (Pawhuska) was one of the most important eighteenth-century Osage chiefs, rivaling Clermont for command of the large and powerful tribe. He was a friend of the wealthy Chouteau family and received many favors from their traders. Pierre Chouteau took him to Washington, where President Jefferson presented him with a United States flag, a general's uniform, and a stovepipe hat. Afterward he signed several land cession treaties. He died in 1825 at the approximate age of sixty-five.

(Frederick J. Dockstader, *Great North American Indians*, 1977; John Joseph Mathews, *The Osages*, 1961.)

White Horse, Kiowa Chief. White Horse was one of the most fearsome Kiowa raiders during the early 1870s. His forays in Texas, Kansas, Colorado, and New Mexico resulted in dozens of deaths and the capture of several white women and children. (See Lee, Abel, Family of; Koozer, Gottlieb, Family of.) On June 12, 1870, he stole 73 mules from Fort Sill. On April 20, 1872, he attacked a wagon train in Texas, killing 17 teamsters. (See Howard Wells Massacre.) In 1875, after the Kiowas surrendered, White Horse and 73 other infamous raiders were imprisoned in Florida.

(Mildred P. Mayhall, *The Kiowas*, 1962.)

White Lodge, Sisseton Sioux Chief. White Lodge was a leading war chief in the Minnesota Sioux uprising of 1862. With the assistance of Lean Bear and 40 warriors, he destroyed the settlement at Lake Shetak, killing men and capturing women and children. (See Shetak, Lake, Minnesota, Massacre.) After the defeat of the Sioux, he fled to Canada. He died there about 1870.

(F. W. Hodge, ed., *Handbook of American Indians, II*, 1912; C. M. Oehler, *The Great Sioux Uprising*, 1959; Doane Robinson, *A History of the Dakota or Sioux Indians*, 1974.)

White Man Runs Him, Crow Warrior. White Man Runs Him was chief of Custer's Indian scouts during the campaign that culminated in the Battle of the Little Bighorn. With other Indian scouts, he was sent to the rear before the battle began. He died in 1925 at the age of seventy.

(Frederick J. Dockstader, *Great North American Indians*, 1977.)

White Paint Creek, Treaty of. On June 9, 1825, U.S. commissioners Henry Atkinson and Benjamin O'Fallon negotiated a treaty with the Ponca Indians at the mouth of White Paint Creek. The Poncas were placed under government protection, promised licensed traders, and agreed not to trade with others.

(Charles J. Kappler, ed., *Indian Affairs: Laws and Treaties, II*, 1972.)

White Shield, Cheyenne Chief. See Wopohwats, Cheyenne Chief

Whiteshield, Harvey. See Hiskowits, Cheyenne Interpreter

Whitestone Hill, Battle of. The Battle of Whitestone Hill was fought between General Alfred Sully's army and Inkpaduta's Sioux on September 3, 1863. Near the location of the present community of Merricourt, North Dakota, Sully surrounded 4,000 Sioux, including some 1,000 warriors, in a ravine. A brief but bloody battle ensued in which the soldiers killed 300 Indians and captured 250 women and children. Sully's casualties were 22 killed and 50 wounded. The battle was a devastating blow to the Sioux.

(Doane Robinson, *A History of the Dakota or Sioux Indians,* 1974; Richard H. Dillon, *North American Indian Wars,* 1983.)

Whitney, Ann. On July 11, 1867, 11 Indians attacked a small log school on the Leon River in Hamilton County, Texas. Most of the children escaped through a window when they saw the warriors approaching, but the teacher, Ann Whitney, who weighed 230 pounds, was unable to do so. One child, Mary Jane Manning, clung to her skirts while the teacher begged for the lives of her pupils. The warriors shot arrows through the cracks of the building until Miss Whitney was killed. They spared the lives of the children, but carried John Kuykendall into captivity. He was ransomed soon afterward.

(J. W. Wilbarger, *Indian Depradations in Texas,* 1985.)

Wichita Indians. The Wichita Indians, a principal tribe of the Caddoan linguistic family, lived on the Canadian River near the headwaters of the Washita during prehistoric times. When seen by the Coronado Expedition in 1541, they were located near the great bend of the Arkansas River in central Kansas. A Franciscan missionary, Juan de Padilla, was slain by them about 1544.

During the eighteenth century the Wichitas moved to the Red River at Spanish Fort (present Ringgold, Texas). French traders from Louisiana who lived with them gave them the name Pawnee Picts, and the Spanish in New Mexico called them Jumanos. They formed a nucleus of Caddoan tribes, related to the Caddos in eastern Texas and Louisiana and the Arikaras on the Missouri, who gathered at Spanish Fort for protection against the Osages, Comanches, and Apaches.

The Wichitas were an agricultural people who lived in permanent villages of tall grass huts. In comparison to other Plains Indians, they were not fierce enemies of white people. In 1835, they signed the Camp Holmes Treaty with the United States. During the Civil War they moved to Kansas, hoping to avoid hostilities. Afterward they were assigned a reservation in Caddo County, Oklahoma, where their descendants live today.

(George E. Hyde, *The Pawnee Indians,* 1974; W. S. Nye, *Carbine & Lance,* 1969; W. W. Newcomb, Jr., *The Indians of Texas,* 1961; Muriel H. Wright, *Indian Tribes of Oklahoma,* 1951.)

Wilbarger, John. John Wilbarger, son of Josiah Wilbarger, was a Texas Ranger serving under Captain John S. Ford. In 1850, while scouting along the Nueces River, he and two companions were attacked by Comanche Indians. They killed several warriors before Wilbarger and one companion were slain. The remaining Ranger survived several severe wounds.

(John Salmon Ford, *Rip Ford's Texas,* 1963.)

Wilbarger, Josiah Pugh. Josiah Pugh Wilbarger was born in Bourbon County, Kentucky, on September 10, 1801, and moved with his wife and children to Texas in 1827. They settled near the frontier community of Bastrop, and Wilbarger and his sons became noted Indian fighters. In August 1833, he was with a party of surveyors near the future site of Austin when severely wounded and scalped by Comanche Indians. Left for dead, he was found still conscious by Reuben Hornsby the following day and nursed back to a semblance of health. He lived until 1844, expiring of a scalp wound infection.

(J. W. Wilbarger, *Indian Depradations in Texas,* 1985; James T. De Shields, *Border Wars of Texas,* 1976.)

Wild Hog, Cheyenne Chief. Wild Hog, a Northern Cheyenne chief, was born about 1840. In his youth he became a skilled raider and warrior. In 1873, he was among the Cheyenne chiefs selected to visit Washington, and four years later he served as an army scout in the campaign against Crazy Horse.

Removed with his people to Oklahoma, Wild Hog was one of the leaders in 1879 when the Northern Cheyennes fled from the reservation in a desperate attempt to return to their homeland. He tried to prevent the murders of Sappa Creek settlers while crossing western Kansas. When the tribe divided in Nebraska, he accompanied Dull Knife's party to surrender at Fort Robinson. While imprisoned there he acted as spokesman during appeals to remain in their northern homeland. To weaken the band's resistance, he was kept isolated from the other prisoners and therefore was not involved in the escape from the guardhouse that resulted in a large number of Cheyenne casualties. (See Dull Knife; Robinson, Fort.) He was acquitted of committing atrocities at Sappa Creek and permitted to remain on the northern plains.

(Peter John Powell, *People of the Sacred Mountain,* 1981.)

William, Fort, Colorado. See Bent's Fort, Colorado

Williams, Leonard H. Leonard H. Williams was a settler near Nacogdoches, Texas, by 1827. In 1842 he was appointed by President Sam Houston as a commissioner to negotiate treaties with Indian tribes. He conducted councils with several East Texas tribes in 1843 and with the Comanches in 1844, redeeming several children from captivity. Afterward he was a freighter from Houston to the Waco Indian villages. In 1846, he was killed by Comanche Indians.

(*Handbook of Texas, II,* 1952.)

Williamson, Thomas S. Dr. Thomas S. Williamson was born in South Carolina in 1800. Licensed as a medical doctor in 1824, he practiced in Ohio until he became a Presbyterian minister in 1834. In 1835, he established a mission among the Sioux Indians at Lac qui Parle, Minnesota, and remained with the tribe 44 years, offering medical assistance as well as religious instruction and gaining the respect of many Native Americans. In 1846, at the invitation of Little Crow, he established a mission in the village of that important chief.

Williamson and the members of his family were compelled to flee when Little Crow took the lead in the Minnesota Sioux uprising of 1862. They attempted to reach Fort Ridgely, but found it besieged by the Sioux and went around it at night, finally reaching a safe haven the following day. After the uprising was crushed, he served as a chaplain to warriors awaiting execution.

(Stephen R. Riggs, *Mary and I,* 1971; C. M. Oehler, *The Great Sioux Uprising,* 1959; Charles E. Flandrau, *The History of Minnesota,* 1900; Doane Robinson, *A History of the Dakota or Sioux Indians,* 1974.)

Wilson, Jane, Captivity of. Jane Wilson and her husband, James, were attacked by Comanche Indians near El Paso, Texas, in July, 1853. James was killed, but his 15-year-old bride and several other members of their wagon train escaped to El Paso. Soon afterward she joined another train that was leaving for eastern Texas, only to be captured in a Comanche attack near Fort Phantom Hill. She received such brutal treatment that she determined to escape or die, and she almost starved while hiding in a hollow tree. Finally she was found by Comancheros and taken to safety in Santa Fe, New Mexico.

(Carl Coke Rister, *Border Captives,* 1940.)

Wise, Fort, Colorado, Treaty of, 1861. The Treaty of Fort Wise was negotiated with the Arapaho and Cheyenne Indians by United States commissioners Albert G. Boone and F. B. Culver on February 18, 1861. The tribes ceded an enormous territory, convinced that white settlers would seize it in any event, and consented to live on a reservation. The government agreed to protect them, to pay an annuity of $30,000 for fifteen years, and to provide livestock, mills, farm machinery, and buildings. The Indians granted permission for roads to cross the reservation. Many warriors ignored the treaty, however, and warfare continued.

(Charles J. Kappler, ed., *Indian Affairs: Laws and Treaties, II*, 1972; George Bird Grinnell, *The Fighting Cheyennes*, 1956.)

Wizikute, Sioux Chief. Wizikute (Pine Shooter) was a principal Sioux chief who befriended Duluth and Hennepin in 1680. His village was located at the head of Rum River in Minnesota. With his assistance the explorers were enabled to return safely to Canada.

(F. W. Hodge, ed., *Handbook of American Indians, II*, 1912; Doane Robinson, *A History of the Dakota or Sioux Indians*, 1974.)

Wolf Mountain, Battle of. The Battle of Wolf Mountain was fought near the Tongue River in Rosebud County, Montana, on January 8, 1877. General Nelson A. Miles, in search of hostiles who had defeated Custer at the Little Bighorn, camped at the base of Wolf Mountain, his howitzers disguised as supply wagons. Crazy Horse led a force of Sioux and Cheyennes, estimated at 500 to 800 warriors, against the troops, but the attackers retreated when the artillery opened fire. Taking position on top of bluffs, they fought soldiers struggling up the snow-covered elevations until Major James S. Casey's company managed to reach the top. Then the Indians withdrew under cover of a snowstorm. Casualties were limited on both sides.

(Richard H. Dillon, *North American Indian Wars*, 1983; George Bird Grinnell, *The Fighting Cheyennes*, 1956; U. S. National Park Service, *Soldier and Brave*, 1963.)

Wood, John. John Wood, an Iowa law-enforcement officer, was appointed Indian agent to the Blackfeet in 1875. Finding the Indians demoralized by addiction to alcohol, he managed to convince most of them that the tribe would become extinct unless they overcame that weakness. He built a new agency and moved the Indians to better buffalo hunting grounds. Under his leadership the living conditions of the Blackfeet were improved considerably.

(John C. Ewers, *The Blackfeet*, 1961.)

Wood Lake, Minnesota, Battle of. The Battle of Wood Lake, the decisive victory over the Sioux in the Minnesota outbreak of 1862, was fought on September 23 near the present city of Granite Falls, Minnesota. Colonel Henry H. Sibley, leading 1,400 volunteer troops in search of hostiles near the Yellow Medicine River, camped at Wood Lake on September 22. Little

Crow's warriors planned to ambush them the following morning as they marched by a ravine, but the plan went awry when foragers stumbled upon concealed warriors and caused the battle to begin before the army broke camp.

Shots fired at the foragers alerted the troops, and the battle was over before most of the Sioux arrived within firing range. Sibley formed his men on a hill and brought his artillery to bear on the surrounding woods, beating back charge after charge until the Sioux abandoned the attempt and retreated from the field. Seven soldiers were killed, while Indian casualties were some 30 dead and a large number wounded. Afterward most of the hostiles became discouraged and fled to Canada or to the Dakota badlands.

(C. M. Oehler, *The Great Sioux Uprising,* 1959; Paul I. Wellman, *Death on Horseback,* 1947.)

Wooden Lance, Kiowa Chief. Wooden Lance was the last principal chief of the Kiowa nation. Born about 1860, he was a follower of the Ghost Dance religion until he visited its founder, Wovoka. Afterward he decided that the Indians would have to live under the domination of white people. He died in 1931.

(Frederick J. Dockstader, *Great North American Indians,* 1977.)

Wooden Leg, Cheyenne Chief. Wooden Leg, a Northern Cheyenne, was born in the Black Hills about 1858. He was attacked by soldiers on the Powder River in March, 1876, but escaped to join Sitting Bull in time for the Battle of the Little Bighorn. Afterward he was removed with the Northern Cheyennes to the Indian Territory, but he became an army scout and was permitted to return to his homeland. After the Indian wars he became a Christian and the judge of an Indian court. He died in 1940.

(Frederick J. Dockstader, *Great North American Indians,* 1977.)

Wopohwats, Cheyenne Chief. Wopohwats (Buffalo Beard) was born in Wyoming about 1830. A nephew of peace chief Black Kettle, he refused to take part in wars against the whites. In 1871, while visiting Washington, he was awarded a treaty medal. Until his death in 1883, he lived on the Cheyenne Reservation in Oklahoma, urging his people to send their children to school.

(F. W. Hodge, ed., *Handbook of American Indians, II,* 1912.)

Wounded Knee, Battle of. The Battle of Wounded Knee, one of the most terrible tragedies in American ethnohistory, occurred on December 29, 1890, on Wounded Knee Creek, near the Pine Ridge Agency in South

Dakota. The battle, or more properly the massacre, was the result of an attempt by the Seventh Cavalry to disarm Big Foot's band of Miniconjou Sioux for participating in the Ghost Dances.

After the death of Sitting Bull, some of his followers joined Big Foot's band, refusing to return to their reservation. Soldiers sent out to arrest the dancers located the band on December 28, and Big Foot (desperately ill with pneumonia) decided to surrender. The troopers marched the Miniconjous to Wounded Knee Creek and instructed the 250 men, women, and children to camp there before resuming their journey to the Pine Ridge Reservation.

On the morning of December 29, Colonel J. W. Forsyth, commanding the cavalry, surrounded the camp with 500 soldiers and trained four Hotchkiss guns at the tipis. When he ordered the warriors disarmed, a medicine man, Yellow Bird, began chanting and dancing, urging the warriors to resist and promising that their ghost shirts would protect them. One warrior refused to give up his rifle, a scuffle ensued, and a shot rang out. "It was what the 7th Cavalry was waiting for," Paul I. Wellman asserted.

> For fourteen years they had wanted to wipe out the Custer disaster in blood. This was too good a chance to miss. Right into the crowd of sitting and standing warriors . . . the soldiers discharged a shattering volley. Nearly half the warriors in Big Foot's band were killed or wounded by that first discharge.

The survivors, many of them unarmed, charged the soldiers, and the Hotchkiss guns opened up on the Sioux with devastating results. Men, women, and children died in heaps after every discharge, and those who escaped into a ravine were pursued and most of them slain. "This," Wellman charged, "was massacre in all its horror."

How many Miniconjous were killed at Wounded Knee will never be known. Almost 150 were buried on the battlefield, and others died elsewhere of their wounds. "Many innocent women and children died there. What is more, the Sioux nation died there."—Robert M. Utley

Seventh Cavalry casualties at Wounded Knee were 29 killed and 33 wounded. Obviously the Sioux did not die without a last courageous attempt to defend a way of life free of white intrusion that the Ghost Dances promised.

(Robert M. Utley, *The Last Days of the Sioux Nation*, 1963; Paul I. Wellman, *Death on Horseback*, 1947; Dee Brown, *Bury My Heart at Wounded Knee*, 1971; Doane Robinson, *A History of the Dakota or Sioux Indians*, 1974; Elaine Goodale Eastman, *Sister to the Sioux*, 1978; S. L. A. Marshall, *The Crimsoned Prairie*, 1972; Robert M. Utley and Wilcomb E. Washburn, *The American Heritage History of the Indian Wars*, 1977; Peter Farb, *Man's Rise to Civilization*, 1968.)

Wynkoop, Edward W. Major Edward W. Wynkoop played an important role in the Indian wars of the 1860s. As commanding officer of Fort Lyon, he led 130 men in search of hostile Cheyennes in August, 1864. Encountering more than 600 warriors prepared to do battle, he rode forward alone to meet the chiefs and persuaded them to release four white captives. Then he escorted Black Kettle to Denver to discuss peace terms with Governor John Evans, but that official insisted upon punishing them first. Wynkoop instructed friendly Cheyennes to camp at Sand Creek and promised to protect them until peace could be restored. Unfortunately, he was relieved of command soon afterward, and his successor participated in the massacre that followed. (See Sand Creek Massacre.)

In 1867, Wynkoop served as agent for the Cheyenne and Arapaho tribes. He understood Indians as did few military men of his time, and he succeeded in persuading many of the chiefs to cease hostile activities. This achievement was undone, however, by the Hancock Expedition, conducted over his objections, and warfare flamed once more on the central plains. When Hancock burned an Indian village, Wynkoop filed a written protest.

Wynkoop served as one of the peace commissioners during the negotiations of the Medicine Lodge Treaty of 1867. He resigned as agent after the Battle of the Washita in 1868, believing that the Indians felt he had betrayed them.

(George Bird Grinnell, *The Fighting Cheyennes*, 1956; Frederic F. Van de Water, *Glory Hunter*, 1963; David Lavender, *Bent's Fort*, 1954.)

Yankton Sioux Indians. The Yankton Indians, a primary Sioux division, were encountered by Father Louis Hennepin in the Leech Lake region of Minnesota in 1680. By 1700 they had moved to the Missouri near the present Sioux City, Iowa. History is silent about them thereafter until 1804, when Lewis and Clark found them in Minnesota near the pipestone quarry. Afterward traders met them along the Missouri and later on the Vermillion in South Dakota. They ceded their lands in 1858 except for a reservation on the north bank of the Missouri.

During the Minnesota Sioux uprising of 1862, the Yanktons warned the settlers of South Dakota to take refuge in forts, thereby saving them from the slaughter taking place just over the boundary. They have lived peacefully on the reservation since that time, and they received allotments in severalty after 1887.

(F. W. Hodge, ed., *Handbook of American Indians, II,* 1912; Doane Robinson, *A History of the Dakota or Sioux Indians,* 1974.)

Yanktonai Sioux Indians. The Yanktonai Indians, a major Sioux division, were encountered by French traders about 1700 in the area around the headwaters of the Sioux and James rivers. They hunted over an enormous territory on both sides of the Missouri.

The Yanktonais played a minor role in the Minnesota Sioux uprising of 1862. A few warriors murdered agency employees near Big Stone Lake, but most members of the tribe were hunting buffalo on the plains during the hostilities. Before 1865 they divided into two bands, and after the treaty negotiated that year the upper band was placed on the Standing Rock Reservation and the lower at Crow Creek and Fort Peck. They accepted the white man's way rather readily and avoided participation in the Ghost Dance unrest.

(F. W. Hodge, ed., *Handbook of American Indians, II,* 1912; C. M. Oehler, *The Great Sioux Uprising,* 1959; Robert M. Utley, *The Last Days of the Sioux Nation,* 1963.)

Yellow Bird, Sioux Medicine Man. Yellow Bird, a fiery Sioux medicine man, played an important part in touching off hostilities at Wounded Knee. He urged the Sioux to refuse to surrender their arms, and, clad in the costume of the Ghost Dance, he pranced around the sullen warriors, instigating them to attack Seventh Cavalry troopers. When the battle began, he hid in a tent and shot several soldiers before his den was discovered. Then the troops ignited the tent, which "burned to the ground, revealing the shattered, charred body of the man who bore the largest responsibility for the Wounded Knee tragedy."—Robert M. Utley

(Robert M. Utley, *The Last Days of the Sioux Nation*, 1963.)

Yellow Hand, Cheyenne Chief. Yellow Hand was born about 1850. He participated in the Battle of Warbonnet Creek on July 17, 1876, and was killed by Buffalo Bill Cody after challenging him to individual combat.

(Frederick J. Dockstader, *Great North American Indians*, 1977.)

Yellow Nose, Cheyenne Chief. Yellow Nose, a Ute captive raised by the Cheyennes, distinguished himself during the Battles of the Rosebud and the Little Bighorn. He lives in tribal legend as a hero of the battle of November 25, 1876, on Powder River with the forces of General Ranald S. Mackenzie. When the soldiers attacked the Cheyenne camp, Yellow Nose and a few warriors took position on a knoll commanding the field and fired continuously until after the chief was severely wounded. This action gave the women and children time to escape. After the surrender of Dull Knife's village, Yellow Nose lived on a reservation in Oklahoma well into the twentieth century.

(Paul I. Wellman, *Death on Horseback*, 1947; George Bird Grinnell, *The Fighting Cheyennes*, 1956.)

Yellow Wolf, Cheyenne Chief. Yellow Wolf (Ocunnowhurst), chief of the Hairy Rope band of Southern Cheyennes, was a prominent warrior against enemy tribes and a friend of white people. He welcomed the Bent brothers to the Arkansas about 1825 and promised to bring his people to trade if they established a post nearby. In 1838, he was awarded a medal by William Clark because of his efforts to preserve peace in the region. He was killed during the Sand Creek Massacre in 1864 at the approximate age of eighty.

(George Bird Grinnell, *The Fighting Cheyennes*, 1956; David Lavender, *Bent's Fort*, 1954; Stan Hoig, *Peace Chiefs of the Cheyennes*, 1980; Peter John Powell, *People of the Sacred Mountain*, 1981.)

Yellowstone, Battle of the. On August 4, 1873, a large Sioux war party attacked General George A. Custer's advance guard on the Yellowstone River, almost opposite the mouth of the Tongue. Custer, who was guarding surveyors employed by the Northern Pacific Railway, led his men into nearby woods, dismounted them, and opened fire on the 300 warriors racing their ponies past the edge of the timber. After three hours of fighting, Custer remounted his men and charged the Sioux, putting the warriors to flight. The cavalry pursued the war party three miles but could not overtake the well-mounted Indians. Two warriors were killed and one trooper wounded in the engagement.

(Frederic F. Van de Water, *Glory Hunter*, 1963.)

York, John. John York was born in Kentucky in 1800 and settled near San Felipe de Austin, Texas, in 1829, becoming a prominent Indian fighter. In October 1848, he recruited a company of volunteers to pursue 40 Indians who had killed several settlers in Gonzales County. They found the hostiles camped on Escondida Creek, fought with them for three hours, and finally compelled them to flee. During the fight, York and two of his men were killed, as well as several warriors.

(J. W. Wilbarger, *Indian Depradations in Texas*, 1985.)

Young Man Afraid of His Horses, Oglala Sioux Chief. Young Man Afraid of His Horses (Tasunka Kokipapi), hereditary Oglala chief, was born about 1830. His Indian name, properly translated, was Young Man so Feared that Even the Sight of His Horse Terrifies the Enemy. He was a leader, along with Red Cloud, in holding back expansion of white settlers onto the northern plains for many years. After moving to the Pine Ridge Reservation, however, he cooperated with agency authorities and made several trips to Washington as President of the Indian Council. He opposed the Ghost Dance religion and kept his followers at peace during the Wounded Knee hostilities. He died in 1900.

(Frederick J. Dockstader, *Great North American Indians*, 1977; Paul I. Wellman, *Death on Horseback*, 1947; Dee Brown, *Bury My Heart at Wounded Knee*, 1971.)

-Z-

Zarah, Fort, Kansas. Fort Zarah was established near the site of the present community of Great Bend, Kansas, on September 6, 1864. Troopers from the post served as escorts for wagon trains on the Santa Fe Trail. It was abandoned on December 4, 1869.

(Robert Frazer, *Forts of the West*, 1965.)

Zotom, Kiowa Warrior. Zotom was born about 1853 and became a fearless raider in Texas and Mexico at an early age. In 1875, he was captured, branded one of the most incorrigible Kiowas by Chief Kicking Bird, and imprisoned at Fort Marion, Florida. While incarcerated, he displayed remarkable artistic talent and, in 1878, he was sent to study at Hampton Institute. Afterward he became an Episcopal clergyman and, in 1881, he returned to Oklahoma to establish a mission to his people. Eventually, however, he joined the Native American Church. Until his death in 1913 he enjoyed a successful career as an artist.

(Frederick J. Dockstader, *Great North American Indians*, 1977.)

About the Author

J. NORMAN HEARD (M.J.; M.L.S., University of Texas at Austin; Ph. D., Louisiana State University at Baton Rouge) has been administrator, acquisitions librarian, and collection development specialist at eight university libraries in Texas and Louisiana. After retiring in 1982, he established and served as curator of the Mississippi Valley Missionary Museum at Lafayette, Louisiana, and presently he serves as a volunteer tour guide at the museum. Dr. Heard is the author of the following books: *Bookman's Guide to Americana* (Scarecrow, 1953-1986); *Hope Through Doing* (John Day, 1968); *The Black Frontiersmen* (John Day, 1969); *White Into Red* (Scarecrow, 1973); *Handbook of the American Frontier*, Vols. 1-2 (Scarecrow, 1987-1990); *The Rewards of Hope* (Christopher, 1992). The present work is Volume 3 of a projected 5-volume handbook.